The Political Economy *of* Indian Ocean Maritime Africa

The Political Economy *of* Indian Ocean Maritime Africa

Dennis Rumley
Curtin University, Perth, Western Australia

Foreword by

Ambassador K V Bhagirath
Secretary-General
Indian Ocean Rim Association

INDIAN OCEAN RIM ASSOCIATION

INDIAN OCEAN RESEARCH GROUP

PENTAGON PRESS

The Political Economy of Indian Ocean Maritime Africa
by Dennis Rumley

ISBN 978-81-8274-807-1

First Published in 2015

Published by
PENTAGON PRESS
206, Peacock Lane, Shahpur Jat,
New Delhi-110049
Phones: 011-64706243, 26491568
Telefax: 011-26490600
email: rajan@pentagonpress.in
website: www.pentagonpress.in

Branch
Flat No.213, Athena-2,
Clover Acropolis,
Viman Nagar,
Pune-411014.
Email: pentagonpresspune@gmail.com

Printed at Avantika Printers Private Limited.

For Hilary, a truly brave and beautiful lady

Contents

	Foreword	*ix*
	Acknowledgements	*xi*
	Contributors	*xii*
1.	Introduction *Dennis Rumley*	1
2.	The Indian Ocean Region: The evolving context and rising significance of Indian Ocean Maritime Africa *Christian Bouchard and William Crumplin*	17
3.	Infrastructure and Influence: China's Presence on the Coast of East Africa *Ross Anthony*	52
4.	Revisiting Alternative Futures in the Indian Ocean Nexus: CHIMEA vs Great Power Rivalry *Francis A. Kornegay, Jr.*	75
5.	Africa and Contested Constructions of the Indian Ocean Region *Timothy Doyle and Dennis Rumley*	91
6.	African Countries' Trade and Investment with Indian Ocean Rim States *Saman Kelegama and Dharshani Premaratne*	101
7.	Trade and Investment Relations in the IORA Area: The Case of India-Tanzania Trade and Investment Flows *Honest Prosper Ngowi*	150

8. The Geopolitics of Official Development Assistance in Indian Ocean Africa: An Australian Perspective 160
Dennis Rumley

9. The Indian Ocean Region and Opportunities for Global South-African Development 183
Siphamandla Zondi

10. Law of the Sea: Maritime Security Enforcement and Jurisdictional Issues for the Indian Ocean Rim Association (IORA) Member States 203
Bimal N. Patel

11. Myriad Maritime Threats and Multilateral Approaches: the Indian Ocean and East Africa 217
Vijay Sakhuja

12. Maritime Security and Its Impact on Trade in the IORA Region 231
Nancy Karigithu

13. Silences on Maritime Security in Existing Regional Security Architecture: the case of East African and Indian Ocean Waters 237
Paul Wambua

14. A Virtual Open University for the Real Transformation of Regional Cooperation and Trade: Lessons Learned from the Pan-African E-Network Project 266
K.S. Sukon

15. Africa's Economic Relations with the Indian Ocean Rim: A Systems of Innovation Approach 279
Mario Scerri

16. Conclusion: Towards an Agenda for Stronger Africa-Indian Ocean Linkages 302
Dennis Rumley

Index 306

Foreword

The Indian Ocean Rim Association (IORA) Conference on the 'Political Economy of Maritime Africa in the Indian Ocean Region' brought together scholars, researchers and officials from Member States and Dialogue Partner States to share experiences on three broad themes, namely, Africa's Perception of and Linkages with Indian Ocean States, Africa and the Indian Ocean Region, and the Future Potential for Regional Cooperation.

With Australia as the current Chair of the IORA and Indonesia and South Africa following as Chairs in 2015 and 2017, respectively, the potential for creating a renewed architecture of regional cooperation is enormous and the nature of the engagement amongst the Indian Ocean states will experience a paradigm shift. The emergence of Africa as an important player in the international arena and its increasing significance in the developmental discourse of states is evident from the high priority assigned by the global community to forging new linkages with this great continent and Africa becomes a crucial strategic partner in the developmental narrative in this region.

This Conference has shed light on the multi-faceted and multi-sectoral potential of Africa, demonstrating the progress in maritime research and has also analysed the prospects for enhancing a cooperative regional maritime environment. This outstanding collection of research papers focuses on these issues thereby supporting the critical role of effective maritime security and safety in the region. In addition, the perseverance of the Indian Ocean Research Group (IORG), an IORA Observer, in implementing the proposal is commendable and signals the beginning of a new chapter in our interaction.

I am confident that this Conference is a first step towards building a consensus for closer linkages with Africa resulting in regional cooperation and hope that this objective of IORA is fulfilled in the future.

Ambassador K V Bhagirath
Secretary-General
Indian Ocean Rim Association

Acknowledgements

The contents of this book are part of a broader Indian Ocean Research Group (IORG) 'Africa and the Indian Ocean' Project and were several years in the making. Thankfully, due to the generous assistance and determined perseverance of a number of governments, organisations and enlightened individuals, this first phase of the wider Project is now complete.

All who participated in the stimulating and highly successful Nairobi Conference owe an enormous debt to the generosity and assistance of the Kenyan Government.

Special thanks are due to Ambassador John Lanasunya, Kenyan Ambassador-designate to Algeria, who was present at the birth of the idea and encouraged its development at the IOR-ARC meeting in Bangalore in 2011.

The Indian Ocean Rim Association (IORA) Secretary-General, Ambassador K V Bhagirath, was instrumental in the success of this whole venture. He was supported extremely ably by the IORA Secretariat, especially Graham Anderson, as well as Shem Pillay and, of course, many others who work in Mauritius.

All of the local organisers in association with IORA were wonderfully efficient and supportive.

The Kenyan Maritime Authority gave us very helpful local sponsorship. Geoff Tooth, Australian High Commissioner, and his staff provided invaluable support to the local organisers and to IORA to ensure the success of the meeting.

We received very generous financial support from the IORA Special Fund and several IORA states, including Australia, India, Oman, and South Africa and Sri Lanka.

Curtin University and the University of Western Australia provided significant logistical and financial assistance.

Warmest thanks are due to all of my IORG close friends and colleagues—especially Christian Bouchard, Sanjay Chaturvedi, Timothy Doyle, P.V. Rao, Vijay Sakhuja and Clive Schofield—for their valuable comments and suggestions on the earliest proposal for the first stage of this project more than three years ago and for their participation and continued support and involvement thereafter.

Additional thanks go to Sanjay Chaturvedi for his kind efforts to set up this meeting on the ground in Nairobi, and for his brotherly support from the birth of IORG, which was finally and irrevocably "let out of the bag" in Chandigarh in November 2002, and throughout our breathtaking journey around the Region and elsewhere since then.

Thank you Vijay Sakhuja for helping to facilitate the publication of this book.

All of the authors of the chapters included in this book deserve special thanks for their excellent and timely contributions.

The participants at the Nairobi Conference in March 2014 from which this volume is drawn contributed greatly to the success of the meeting.

Timothy Doyle took the photograph on the cover page of this book during our visit to the unique Nairobi National Park in March 2014. Tim is also a dear brother, and, like Sanjay, has been a great rock of support, stimulation and good humour throughout.

Sincere thanks also to Graham Seal, Sue Summers and Black Swan Press of Curtin University for initiating a very effective book 'flyer' for distribution at the IORA Perth October 2014 Conference and for their ongoing local support at Curtin.

I would like to acknowledge the funding of the Australian Research Council Discovery Project DP120101166: "Building an Indian Ocean Region" for their generous assistance in the conduct and completion of this research.

Last, but not least, I owe an incredible debt to my very dear family—Hilary, Alison, Christopher, Tomoko, David, Nina and Ewan—for their love, humour and support.

Dennis Rumley

Contributors

Ross Anthony is Acting Head, Centre for Chinese Studies, Stellenbosch University, South Africa.

Christian Bouchard is Professor of Environmental Studies at Laurentian University, Sudbury, Canada.

William Crumplin is Associate Professor of Environmental Studies at Laurentian University, Sudbury, Canada.

Timothy Doyle is Chair/Co-Director, Indo-Pacific Governance Research Centre, University of Adelaide, South Australia;Distinguished Research Fellow, Australia-Asia-Pacific Institute, Curtin University, Western Australia;Chair, Politics and International Relations, Research Centre for Politics, International Relations and Environment, Keele University, Staffordshire, United Kingdom. He is currently Chair of the Academic Group of the Indian Ocean Rim Association (IORAG).

Nancy Karigithu is Director-General, Kenya Maritime Authority.

Saman Kelegama is Executive Director, Institute of Policy Studies of Sri Lanka, Colombo, Sri Lanka.

Francis Kornegay Jr is Senior Research Fellow, Institute for Global Dialogue associated with University of South Africa, Pretoria, South Africa.

Honest Prosper Ngowi is Senior Lecturer, researcher and consultant in Economics at Mzumbe University, Dar es Salaam, Tanzania.

Bimal N. Patel is Professor of Public International Law and Director, Gujarat National Law University, Gandhinagar (Gujarat), India.

Dharshani Premaratne is a researcher at the Institute of Policy Studies of Sri Lanka, Colombo, Sri Lanka.

Dennis Rumley is Professor of Indian Ocean Studies, Curtin University, Perth, Western Australia and is Chair of the Indian Ocean Research Group (IORG), an Observer to the Indian Ocean Rim Association (IORA).

Vijay Sakhuja is Director, National Maritime Foundation, New Delhi.

Mario Scerri is Professor of Economics, Institute for Economic Research on Innovation (IERI), and Centre of Excellence in Scientometrics and STI Policy, Faculty of Economics and Finance, Tshwane University of Technology, Pretoria, South Africa.

K.S. Sukon is Director-General, Open University of Mauritius, Réduit, Mauritius.

Paul Musili Wambua is Professor and Associate Dean, School of Law, University of Nairobi, Kenya.

Siphamandla Zondi is Director, Institute for Global Dialogue, Institute for Global Dialogue associated with University of South Africa, Honorary Professor of Development Studies & Politics at Unisa, Mentor at Thabo Mbeki African Leadership Institute (TMALI).

Chapter 1
Introduction

Dennis Rumley

This book has three principal aims. The first is to examine the states of maritime Africa in the Indian Ocean Region in terms of their changing geopolitical and geo-economic context. Among other things, this requires an analysis of the region's emerging economic and political significance, the development of new and developing geo-economic and geopolitical linkages, the regional process of competition for influence, and the contested nature of Africa's place in the Indian Ocean Region as a whole. The second aim is to discuss the changing pattern of the region's trade, investment and aid relationships with both extra-regional states and with countries that are members of the Indian Ocean Rim Association (IORA). It is argued in this volume that the latter intra-regional linkages are currently underdeveloped and that there is considerable scope for strengthening them over the next few decades. Furthermore, there is significant potential to enhance African cooperation within IORA on a variety of regional issues of common concern. This, in turn, will inevitably lead to improved social, economic and political development among African Indian Ocean states. The third principal aim of the volume is to analyse the extent of actual cooperation of regional states with other IORA members, especially in terms of two fundamentally important regional issues—maritime security and education and innovation. The main observations and conclusions on each of these aims will be described in turn below and the regional policy implications will be summarised in the final chapter of the book. The ultimate goal of this Project is the creation of an Agenda for Stronger African-Indian Ocean Linkages (ASAIL).

The Geopolitical and Geo-Economic Context

Christian Bouchard and William Crumplin discuss the evolving context and increasing significance of what they refer to as the "African Indian Ocean littoral and hinterland" in Chapter 2. Since the 19th Century, problems associated with colonialism, neo-colonialism and the Cold War have served to emasculate Indian Ocean Maritime Africa's relations with other Indian Ocean states. As a result, linkages with IORA member states have remained relatively weak. However, as Bouchard and Crumplin argue, this is now in the process of change. African Indian Ocean states are beginning to experience indications of relatively strong economic growth and associated human development.

This process of change has led to a re-evaluation of the African Indian Ocean geopolitical narrative. For example, in the immediate post Cold War period, the region was characterised as being a part of the "Quarter-Sphere of Marginality" that would:

> destabilize the world through local and regional conflicts, unless greater economic and political attention is accorded the region. It is especially imperative that the U.S. redirect its foreign aid to these needy lands, rather than continue to concentrate nearly all of its economic and military aid on a handful of military allies (Cohen 1991, page 555).

In addition, the region did:

> not benefit from the exchange that is so important to the developmental process. Much of Sub-Saharan Africa...lies outside the world economic system (Cohen 1991, page 566).

Even in the early 21st Century, some geopolitical commentators were portraying nearly all of Indian Ocean Maritime Africa (IOMA) as being 'unglobalised' and as part of a "non-integrating gap" comprising states that are "poor", and as places where life is "nasty", "short", "brutal" and "solitary". The only exception is South Africa that was seen as being a part of Barnett's so-called "Functioning Core" (Barnett 2004, pp. 161-166).

A decade later, terms such as "African Century" are now being used, and, as the OECD Secretary-General recently observed:

> With the right policies and strategic approach, the social and economic progress of recent years could be the prelude to long-lasting sustained prosperity in Africa (Gurria 2013)

Bouchard and Crumplin point out that the current wave of regional economic growth is propelled primarily by a resources boom—arable land, minerals, energy and ocean resources—and an associated considerable increase in foreign investment especially during the last decade. While the region is presently one of low socio-economic development and one which faces many challenges, the authors argue that substantial improvements are in progress associated with improving demographic processes, the growth in urbanisation and a broader, more stable economic performance. These changes in turn have implications for enhanced interactions with other IORA states, especially in terms of economic, political, environmental, military and maritime issues.

In Chapter 3, Ross Anthony critically evaluates the view that Chinese infrastructural support and development in IOMA is solely designed to enable its broader regional geostrategic goals. He suggests that Chinese involvement in the 21st century differs in a variety of ways from the 19th century European presence in the region. Anthony argues that there has been a tendency to over-exaggerate the negative nature of the Chinese regional presence and perhaps to over-inflate it as a geopolitical threat to the interests of 'competitors'. The author suggests that, in order to fully comprehend the processes involved, that Chinese regional aid and investment need to be situated in a context of post-colonial African sovereignty as well as part of a broader market context within which other states are operating. As a result, it would be incorrect to conclude that China would necessarily be able to fully mobilise its regional infrastructural activities to solely foster its own geopolitical interests.

Anthony refers to some of the "geostrategic anxieties" engendered among other non-African regional competitors for influence and the US and Indian concern over what some see as an explicit Chinese geopolitical strategy to construct an Indian Ocean 'string of pearls' (development locations designed to serve as nodes of Chinese regional influence). The author notes that some (invariably non-regional) analysts portray these activities within an "alarmist discourse" and that the Chinese presence will serve only its own interests at the expense of local communities. Chinese activity has thus been described as 'neo-colonial' and even as part of a 21st century 'great game'.

The author concludes that when commentators attempt to discuss the nature of Chinese regional influence in IOMA in these terms, their views must be carefully qualified and evaluated. In reality, Chinese companies operate primarily according to market interests and regional states employ a variety of actors to develop national infrastructure.

Francis Kornegay in Chapter 4 raises a fundamental question as to whether the IOMA will evolve as a peaceful region or whether it is destined to become another "theatre of tension". As the editors noted in a recent monograph:

> If we consider the IOR as an overall 'arena of competing influence', then it is instructive to locate a significant United States and Chinese presence and add to this the regional presence of India. We end up with an interesting geographical distribution of Chinese 'pearls', USA 'diamonds' and Indian 'nuggets', principally reflecting concerns over energy security and secure access to SLOCs. For the sake of the present discussion and putting aside the veracity of arguments in favour of a 'string of pearls' strategy, China has nonetheless some presence in four northern Indian Ocean rim locations—Chittagong in Bangladesh, Gwadar in Pakistan, Hambantota in Sri Lanka and Sittwe in Burma. Furthermore, according to the US Department of Defense Base Structure Report, the United States has some presence in 12 Indian Ocean locations—the centrally-located Diego Garcia, five in the Persian Gulf (Bahrain, Kuwait, Oman, Qatar and UAE), three in Africa (Egypt, Djibouti and Kenya) and a further three on the easternrim (Australia, Indonesia and Singapore). If we add to these India's presence in the Andaman Islands, Mauritius and Maldives, we are left with a number of what might be called 'contested spaces'—that is, they remain competitive arenas which have yet to be incorporated into the influence of powerful external states. These include the failed states of Somalia and Yemen and much of Oceanic Africa (Rumley 2013a, page 41).

Irrespective of alarmist discourse, it is clear that, from a geopolitical perspective, the IOMA qualifies as a 'contested region' within the context of Klare's "scramble for Africa" scenario (Klare 2008, pp. 147-176).

Kornegay is careful to point out that the competition for influence in IOMA may actually be more nuanced and play out as a process of low intense rivalry as extra-regional states jockey for position with regard to cooperative arrangements. However, as the author points out, geopoliticians have implicated IOMA in alternative narratives—from Walker's 'nexus' scenario of China-India-Middle East-Africa (CHIMEA) portrayal to Kaplan's *Monsoon* view of Sino-Indian rivalry.

In order to maximize the prospects of long-term regional stability and security IORA potentially has a very significant role to play in terms of strengthening the linkages of IOMA to the other member states. As the author indicates, there is considerable potential for enhancing community building through an increased emphasis on maritime security as well as via a range of aspects of ocean governance. Furthermore, Kornegay offers up the India-Brazil-South Africa (IBSA) trilateral model—an "Afrocentric global South paradigm" - as a "neutralizing balancing framework" to offset the Walker and Kaplan scenarios.

In Chapter 5, Timothy Doyle and Dennis Rumley discuss the contested place of Africa in the discourse of Indian Ocean regionalism. The authors argue that to date IOMA states have not been accorded due consideration with regard to the broader governance of the Indian Ocean community. Since the peoples of the region are undergoing a "Third race for Africa", it is suggested that by strengthening Indian Ocean regional ties, the outcomes of this 'race' will consequently prove to be more profitable for regional communities.

While Africa is clearly a force in the western Indian Ocean, its place in the dominant Indian Ocean constructs is hotly contested. On the one hand, the broadest definition of the Indian Ocean Region comprising more than 50 states includes IOMA as does the 20-member IORA. However, alternative regional constructions such as the East Indian Ocean (EIO) model would exclude IOMA states. A third major regional construction—Indo-Pacific (I-P)—may or may not include IOMA depending on the purpose and source of the definition. To some degree, therefore, EIO and I-P definitions tend to marginalize maritime Africa.

Ideological concerns and differences in emphasis over 'hard' (traditional) and 'soft' (non-traditional) security tend to separate Africa-inclusive from Africa-exclusive regional constructions. Doyle and Rumley argue for a more inclusive definition of Indo-Pacific, along the lines used by the University of Adelaide Indo-Pacific Governance Research Centre (IPGRC). Furthermore, in order to give due weight to the sub-regional concerns of IOMA states, they suggest that there is a place for a *Western Indian Ocean Dialogue* (WIOD) within the broad umbrella of IORA to supplement the current *Indian Ocean Dialogue* (IOD) hosted by India and the *Trilateral Dialogue on the Indian Ocean* (TDIO) comprising Australia, India and Indonesia.

Trade, Investment and Aid

Saman Kelegama and Dharshani Premeratne provide a comprehensive description and analysis of the changing pattern of IOMA state trade and investment with other Indian Ocean Rim countries in Chapter 6. One of the principal goals of the 8 African IORA member states—Comoros, Kenya, Madagascar, Mauritius, Mozambique, Seychelles, South Africa and Tanzania—is to gain preferential treatment for trading goods and services with other IORA members, leading, as a result, to greater regional economic integration. The authors evaluate whether IOMA states have as yet garnered the potential economic benefits of regionalism.

The authors identify a multiplicity of structural economic issues that militate against freer intra-regional trade for IOMA states. For example, many possess relatively weak institutions and poor state infrastructure and need to develop a more business-friendly environment. Nonetheless, while the "trade architecture" of the 8 IOMA states has not significantly changed, their volume of trade with other IORA members has shown signs of improvement over the past two decades. In addition, there has been a continued strong increase in Foreign Direct Investment (FDI) and a growth in particular sectors, such as tourism. India and South Africa continue to be important trading partners, but trade linkages with Australia still remain underdeveloped.

While tourism remains a key driver for regional economic growth and a source of considerable employment, it has also played a role in the preservation of cultural heritage and the natural environment. However, there are several issues which inhibit further growth in this important sector, including the nature of the investor environment, policy and governance issues, problems of risk management and weak and expensive air services.

Overall, the 'resource gap' in terms of investment in IOMA states, which has impeded development in the past, is being bridged by increases in FDI, including from India and Malaysia and from Australia in the mining sector. Kelegama and Premaratne point out that accumulated capital in the mining and energy sectors provide good prospects for further growth. Trade in consumer goods and the continued growth in FDI also show good prospects and there is potential to exploit spillovers from tourism. Nonetheless, the need to improve governance, to enhance further the investor environment and the fundamental requirement to improve regional educational programmes as well as road, maritime and air infrastructure will all act as inhibitors to more rapid economic development.

In Chapter 7, Honest Prosper Ngowi describes in depth one such intra-regional interactional case study—India-Tanzania trade and investment. Ngowi emphasises the need to understand the broader historical, cultural and political context in order to fully explain and understand the nature of economic interactions between states. In the case of Tanzania-India economic linkages, they are in part a product of a long period of trade and cultural contact. In addition, the nature of the ideological context goes some way to explain the relationship, particularly a commitment to anti-colonialism, anti-racism and socialism. Furthermore, both states wished to enhance the strength of South-South linkages. Over time, the structure of trade and investment has become more diversified, but a major early driving force was the arrival in Tanzania of the Indian Diaspora - now some 40,000 persons—shortly after the first world war. Even today, many of the main business establishments in Tanzania are owned by individuals of Indian origin.

Indian lines of credit have helped to finance the Tanzanian agricultural sector including the export of trucks, tractors and agricultural machinery. For Tanzania, India is the main export destination and its second most important import source. Trade has been growing although there has been some annual variability. However, the trade balance is strongly in favour of India—exports to Tanzania were almost eight times those of imports from Tanzania in 2011. The main reason why the balance of trade continues to be so strongly in favour of India relates to its composition. India's to Tanzania, for example, are primarily finished manufactured goods, while Tanzania's main exports to India are raw materials.

While the most important sources of FDI into India are from Europe, India remains an important non-Western economic partner and the largest source of FDI in Asia. Tanzania is a net recipient of FDI from India. Ngowi concludes that this is primarily because the private sector in Tanzania is still quite young, is still relatively 'unglobalised' and remains in the developmental stage.

Dennis Rumley argues in Chapter 8 that donor priorities over the spatial allocation of Official Development Assistance (ODA) have become increasingly guided by geopolitical and geo-economic imperatives rather than humanitarian concerns, especially since the end of the Cold War. This 'new paradigm' is bolstered to a considerable degree by the prospect of exploiting the natural resources and energy potential in those states. The neo-liberal ODA paradigm thus emphasises the efficacy of trade and foreign direct investment (FDI) rather than state-derived ODA as a more effective mechanism to facilitate economic development in the less developed states.

While most ODA since the end of the Cold War has been delivered by the 27 Development Assistance Committee states, in absolute terms aid allocations have been dominated by 5 states—USA, Germany, UK, France and Japan—each with their own IORA state priorities. Interestingly, only Germany is a non-Dialogue Partner of IORA. However, also since the end of the Cold War, ODA to sub-Saharan Africa has been in overall decline.

Rumley shows that ODA given to IORA states is not allocated on the basis of need (measured in terms of a poverty index) and that some recipient states appear to be "under-aided". There has also been a growth since the end of the Cold War in the number of so-called 'non-DAC' aid donors operating outside of pre-existing OECD guidelines. Differential goals have helped to initiate a competitive process into ODA allocations and donor states (DAC and non-DAC) have become increasingly interested in resource-rich African states.

It is noted that while Australia has been an 'average' DAC donor, this is likely to change as a result of significant recent reductions in the ODA budget. Furthermore, since the end of the Cold War, there has been no relationship between per capita aid allocations and development need. Rather, Australian aid has become increasingly (geo)politicised, as exemplified by the use of ODA as a vote-buying exercise in Africa and elsewhere to obtain a seat in the UN Security Council. Aid to sub-Saharan Africa and to IORA states is declining at the same time that there is an increasing regional focus on Southeast Asia and the South Pacific as part of Australia's 'new paradigm' of ODA.

In Chapter 9, Siphamandla Zondi argues from a South African perspective, that, in order to enhance development, regional integration and South-South cooperation, it is imperative to recognise the strategic significance not just of the Indian Ocean but of *both* oceans located either side of southern Africa. South Africa, like Australia is a "two-ocean state".

Zondi makes the point that development/international development is a contested area and that it is generally associated with development agencies of the North. He argues that the European capitalist economic system, while taken to be unproblematical, resulted in subjugation and colonisation, exploitation, underdevelopment and the homogenisation of colonised political economies. Furthermore, he suggests, it led to the imposition of Western moral, rational and individualistic concepts. Zondi argues that, in the post-colonial period, "development aid" was accepted as a major contribution of the developed states towards "building common humanity".

The author suggests that South-South cooperation and the "de-westernisation of modernity" has arisen out of the "imperiality of the international system" in order to achieve greater self-reliance, endogenous development and a collective concern for the pursuit of a better life for all. Zondi points out that the potential contribution of the maritime domain to African development began to emerge in the 1990s associated with the emergence of "regionness" in the Indian Ocean that would find expression in economic growth and development among regional states.

As the author stresses, there has been an increasing interest in the 21st century among African states in maritime issues since increasing insecurity in the Indian Ocean was negatively affecting state regional economic development. In order to overcome insecurity and associated underdevelopment, Zondi argues that IOMA states need to work to consolidate Indian Ocean "regionness" and to strive to redefine "global cosmopolitanism". The end result will be increased South-South cooperation in terms of trade and investment, development partnerships, cooperation in science and technology and human development.

Maritime Security

Birman Patel lays out an ambitious and compelling Policy Agenda in Chapter 10 for improving the legal framework in all IORA states for dealing with a wide range of maritime security issues—terrorism, WMD trafficking, drug trafficking, smuggling, people trafficking, illegal, unreported and unregulated (IUU) fishing, the marine environment and marine biodiversity. The author notes the relatively weak and fragmentary nature of the present legal and regulatory framework among IORA states for tackling regional maritime security. Patel raises a host of questions regarding the efficacy of the present regional legal system to deal with such important matters. Furthermore, since IORA states have generally regarded maritime security as primarily one of military security, little attention has been paid to other relevant and important non-military issues.

The author argues that there is a need to adopt a uniform legal framework among IORA states to deal more effectively with regional maritime security matters. Regular legal training is also required for this involved in administering relevant regulations. Patel also argues that it is important for IORA states to enact of amend existing legislation to appropriately meet maritime security challenges—in short, the regional legal and regulatory framework needs to be strengthened.

There is a need for the development of a regional cooperation legal framework for maritime security using the 2003 Caribbean Agreement as a model, Patel suggests. In addition, all IORA member states need to ratify all relevant international Conventions and agreements to deal with maritime security threats. Many of these threats are 'non-military'—for example, IUU fishing is a threat to maritime security given the importance of fishing as a source of protein in many IORA states (Rumley, Chaturvedi and Sakhuja 2009).

In order to strengthen the regional maritime security regulatory framework Patel calls for the creation of an IORA Legal Group of Experts (LEGOE) that, among other things, can act as a standing body that provides ongoing legal advice and operates regional legal training programmes.

In Chapter 11, Vijay Sakhuja once again reminds us of the geo-economic significance of the Indian Ocean as an avenue for trade and that the regional sea lanes and choke points are strategically important for the functioning of the global economy. The nature and range of maritime asymmetric threats and challenges potentially not only undermine the economic stability of the Indian Ocean Region. Sakhuja's fundamental point, therefore, is that the goal of Indian Ocean long-term regional economic prosperity needs to be underpinned by the maximisation of regional maritime security.

The author reviews the principal maritime security threats in IOMA and discusses the various policy initiatives taken by Indian Ocean states at various levels to deal with these. He highlights problems of poor governance and a paucity of resources to enhance security in the region that in turn provide a congenial environment for many types of non-state actors to deal in illegal activities—piracy, drug smuggling, gun running, WMD proliferation and human trafficking.

The piracy threat has attracted significant international regional and sub-regional responses in recent years, including the adoption of UN resolutions, the intervention of states and groups of states, the shipping organisations and the involvement of private security groups. Counter piracy intelligence sharing programmes have been devised and training assistance envisaged. Sakhuja points out that a small number of terrorist groups have used the Indian Ocean littorals to attack targets on shore—that is, "from the sea". However, attacks "at sea" and "under the sea" also require appropriate policy responses. The contraband trade in drugs and guns plays a role in undermining the stability of vulnerable regional states. Sakhuja notes that, while bulk contraband consignments are moved over the seas, only a few interceptions have been effected in the Indian Ocean.

Ethnic and religious conflict within regional states and the existence of human trafficking organisations have facilitated increasing "illegal" and "forced" human migration around the Indian Ocean. The latter creates a situation:

> in which people are commodified in various other ways through forced labour, sex trafficking, bonded labour, debt bondage among migrant workers, involuntary domestic servitude, forced child labour, child soldiers and child sex trafficking (Rumley 2013a, page 48).

These are issues that should actively and collectively engage all IOMA states. However, the current inability to effectively deal with the range of non-traditional maritime security threats in the Indian Ocean outlined by Sakhuja necessitates a coordinated regional maritime security strategy associated with an overall strengthening of regional state legal regimes associated with these issues as Patel argues in Chapter 10. As two critical pan-regional groupings, IORA and IONS possess a fundamental responsibility to collaborate and to develop such a strategy. At the Perth IONS meeting in March 2014, this issue was raised once again and it was felt by some commentators that perhaps IORA needs to approach IONS in order to initiate a closer dialogue.

Nancy Karigithu in Chapter 12 distils the financial impacts of maritime (in)security on regional trade, reinforcing Sakhuja's argument that maritime insecurity is bad for business. She argues for the development and implementation of an integrated regional maritime development framework since the prevailing legal framework for maritime security does not deal effectively with all relevant issues.

The author re-emphasises the geo-economic importance of the Indian Ocean as a routeway and as an economic region in its own right and argues that maritime insecurity will expose the global supply chain to unacceptable risk. She outlines the nature of maritime domain security concerns including the need to properly manage marine resources and to preserve the marine environment and reiterates some of the other maritime security concerns raised by Sakhuja. Many aspects of Indian Ocean environmental management need to be addressed, including dealing more effectively with the illegal dumping of toxic waste.

Karigithu details the considerable costs per vessel involved in paying ransoms from piracy, insurance premiums, risk surcharges, deterrence measures and the provision of security guards. In more extreme situations, the cost of re-routing ships due to maritime insecurity can be very great. In addition to the cost to the shipping companies, maritime insecurity can significantly impact negatively on employment and on regional economies. This is very important for the Indian Ocean Region,

Karigithu notes, since the total cost of piracy prosecutions in 2010, for example, was very significantly higher than in Europe or North America. In short, maritime insecurity places the Indian Ocean Region in a situation of considerable relative global economic disadvantage and even the perception of insecurity can be economically harmful.

Paul Wambua in Chapter 13 provides a wide-ranging and comprehensive critique of the "silences" that have been associated with the development of maritime security policies in the Indian Ocean in general and the IOMA in particular. The solution, he argues, is to generate "regional maritime security enlightenment".

The author argues that the current regional maritime security framework in the Indian Ocean is essentially *ad hoc*. He proposes a more structured conceptual framework which adopts a "widener" view of security (see Rumley 2013a, pp. 16-17) and calls for a more clearly-defined set of regional maritime security legal instruments. Wambua argues that IOMA states are dependent for their survival on the Indian Ocean and that, in general, they have tended to be more inward-looking regarding security concerns, partly as a result of domestic issues.

In addition, as the author argues, questions related to the lack of available resources to deal effectively with maritime security threats, the differential commitments by regional states to current arrangements, and contrasting state views regarding access to maritime resources all have reinforced " a lack of political enlightenment" and have thus militated against the emergence of a coherent regional strategy.

Wambua describes some of the regional impacts of four essential elements of maritime insecurity—environmental degradation, piracy, uncontrolled exploitation of marine resources and maritime terrorism—and proceeds to critically evaluate international and regional state responses to these threats.

The author argues that the present sub-regional organisation of IO maritime security has frustrated the potential for a more effective overall regional framework. He discusses the various IOMA cooperative responses to security threats and highlights the limitations and gaps in these approaches. These include the fact that arrangements tend to be codes of conduct rather than binding agreements or treaties; that most have been principally concerned with piracy at sea and with the prosecution of pirates; and that, not enough has been undertaken to understand and deal with the causes of maritime insecurity.

Wambua calls for the creation of a four-layered regional maritime security system that involves the enhancement of developmental infrastructure, the improvement of institutional capacity, the tightening of cooperative legal frameworks and the maximisation of community participation.

Education and Innovation

It is beyond question that education, when viewed as a human right and as an investment, rather than solely as an individual responsibility and as a cost to the state, can contribute fundamentally to long-term state development in the broadest sense of that word. As K S Sukon in Chapter 14 stresses, one of the most important constraints to state socio-economic transformation is a shortage of skills. Clearly, educational linkages around the Indian Ocean Region can contribute substantially to this process but, in addition, can facilitate regional integration and foster a sense of "regionness". This is one of the many reasons why the Indian Ocean Rim Academic Group (IORAG) is potentially of great regional significance and why initiatives such as the University Mobility in the Indian Ocean Region (UMIOR) are potentially of such regional importance to development. Unfortunately, the IORAG is in need of considerable reform (Rumley 2013b) and UMIOR is not supported by all IORA member states.

In addition, regional Open Universities can play an important role in furthering Indian Ocean educational linkages and enhancing regional skill levels, and the concept of an Indian Ocean University can act as a fundamental focus and catalyst for ongoing regional collaboration. Sukon discusses the concept of an Indian Ocean Rim Virtual Open University (IORVOU) in the context of his role as Director-General of the Open University of Mauritius. Such an IORVOU would be aimed at supporting states to transform regional cooperation and trade and thus will be beneficial to all.

The author critically describes and analyses all of the practical issues surrounding the setting up, operation and maintenance of such an important facility and how the lessons learned from this are essential to bear in mind for the creation of a broader Indian Ocean Regional facility. Sukon identifies all of the key elements for the setting up of a Virtual Open University based directly out of his concrete experience with the Pan-African e-Network (PAeN) Project, the biggest project in South-South cooperation, which has given added impetus to Africa-India relations. He proposes a model for the setting up of an IORVOU that sets out in detail all of the requirements needed to ensure its success.

In Chapter 15 Mario Scerri examines the linkages that Kenya, Mozambique, South Africa and Tanzania have with other IORA economies through the lens of a systems of innovation approach. He discusses the historical determinants of the viability of current national systems of innovation (NSI) in sub-Saharan Africa and concludes that their prospects have been relatively poor. For example, Scerri shows that the degree of aid dependency, a basic indicator of the viability of a NSI, is relatively high among IOMA states and that other indicators show a relatively low NSI—a relatively low human development index (HDI), a high poverty index, and a high level of income inequality and state instability.

Taking a broad conception of NSI, Scerri notes that knowledge and the human capabilities associated with it occupy the core of economic change. The generation of human capacities, appropriately directed education and science policy and the provision of basic human needs are major concerns of development policy. However, many IOMA states, due in part to their narrowly-based economies, lack the capacity to generate sufficient human capabilities.

The colonial creation of a fragmented African political and economic map has severely militated against sustainable development. Weak states are a major constraint to sustainable development. The author argues that this needs to be "meaningfully eroded" in order to ensure an effective programme of institutional and economic integration in sub-Saharan Africa. While there exist various obstacles to increased regional integration, including the lack of political will to cede any degree of state sovereignty, Scerri suggests that there is nonetheless some cause for optimism for greater regional integration. In addition, stronger links with IORA states provide the potential through which this might be facilitated. As a result, the author argues that IORA is an important institutional mechanism through which a developmental transformation of national systems of innovation might take place in IOMA.

The final Chapter of this book summarises all of the specific policy recommendations discussed in the various chapters in order to provide a basis for the creation of an Agenda for Stronger African-Indian Ocean Linkages (ASAIL).

REFERENCES

Barnett, T. P. M. (2004), *The Pentagon's New Map: War and Peace in the Twenty-First Century*, New York: Penguin.

Cohen S. (1991), 'Global geopolitical change in the post-Cold War era', *Annals*, Association of American Geographers, Vol. 81 (4), pp. 551-580.

Gurria, A. (2013), 'Realising Africa's potential', *OECD Observer*, No 296, Q3, page 3.

Kaplan, R. D. (2010), *Monsoon: The Indian Ocean and the Future of American Power*, New York: Random House.

Klare, M. (2008), *Rising Powers, Sinking Planet: The New Geopolitics of Energy*, New York: Metropolitan Books.

Rumley, D. ed. (2013a), *The Indian Ocean Region: Security, Stability and Sustainability in the 21st Century*, Melbourne: Australia India Institute. This is available on line at: http://www.aii.unimelb.edu.au/sites/default/files/IndianOceanSecurity Taskforce_0.pdf

Rumley, D. (2013b), 'Towards a reform agenda for the Indian Ocean Rim Academic Group (IORAG): a discussion paper', unpublished paper to IORA for dissemination and discussion, August.

Rumley, D., Chaturvedi, S. and Sakhuja, V., eds. (2009), *Fisheries Exploitation in the Indian Ocean: Threats and Opportunities*, Singapore: ISEAS.

Walker, M. (2008), 'Indian Ocean Nexus', *Wilson Quarterly*, Spring 2008.

Chapter 2

The Indian Ocean Region: The evolving context and rising significance of Indian Ocean Maritime Africa

Christian Bouchard and William Crumplin

ABSTRACT

The African littoral of the Indian Ocean is a significant part of the Indian Ocean Region. In the context of the Indian Ocean Rim Association (IORA), the focus here is on Indian Ocean Maritime Africa, which consists of 10 states plus three French island territories. However, an African Indian Ocean extended area of 24 states plus the French islands can be identified as part of the broader Indian Ocean Region, which we refer to as the African Indian Ocean littoral and hinterland. Overall, this is a region of low socio-economic development facing many challenges. Nonetheless, it is a region on the move, and some substantial changes and improvements can be expected during the entire 21st century. The potential, and perhaps even expected outcome of a much larger and healthier population, a better performing and more open economy, and an increase in and more efficient management of maritime activities will set the scene for the rising significance of Maritime Africa to both the Indian Ocean Region and the Indian Ocean Rim, thus also increasing its geopolitical and geostrategic significance.

Keywords: Africa, Indian Ocean, Maritime Africa, Indian Ocean Maritime Africa, Indian Ocean Region, Indian Ocean Rim, African Indian Ocean littoral and hinterland.

Introduction

Africa and the Indian Ocean Region share a long and fertile history that includes human migration, social relations and cultural exchanges, commercial relations, and maritime trade. However, centuries of colonialism followed by decades of neo-colonialism and Cold War divisions have profoundly altered and weakened the relations of the Indian Ocean African peoples with their counterparts of the Indian Ocean Region. It also left the recently independent African states facing very serious social, economic and political difficulties that greatly limited their abilities to develop and prosper as well as deterring their participation in and limiting the benefits from the world-wide economic globalisation process. As a consequence, the African littoral of the Indian Ocean largely remained poorly integrated into the reinvigorated Indian-oceanic regionalism process that has been emerging since the 1990s and building through many initiatives, including the Indian Ocean Rim Association (IORA, previously known as the IOR-ARC)[1] . But this is now changing as the African states develop an interest in and relations with the rest of the Indian Ocean and thus the African littoral becomes a land of promise for new economic opportunities.

This is particularly significant at this moment in time after many decades of post-independence frustration and difficulties. Africa is now showing signs of possible long-lasting strong economic growth and consequent human development. Specialists and commentators speak of "Africa's new start", "Africa's second chance", "rising Africa", "African miracle" and even "Africa renaissance" while the continent and especially Sub-Saharan Africa are revitalised by a resources boom and massive foreign investments, with the promise of a better future (Dörr*et al.* 2010; *The Economist* 2011; Shaw 2012; Bevarez 2013; Devarajan and Fengler 2013). For its natural resources, including available arable land, oil and minerals, its working force and its emerging markets, Africa is again a very coveted continent (Brunel, 2011; Fiorina 2013)—basically the coveted continent of the moment. This new context could impact quite significantly on relations between the Indian Ocean Maritime Africa states and the other states of the Indian Ocean Region, leading to a better integration of the African littoral with the rest of the Indian Ocean Rim.

It is on this premise of Africa's rising significance that we propose in this chapter a general overview of the African waters, littoral and hinterland in the specific contexts of the Indian Ocean Region and the Indian Ocean Rim. In so doing, we first discuss what can be considered as the *Indian Ocean Maritime Africa* and the *African Indian Ocean littoral and hinterland* and then discuss the maritime, human, economic and political dimensions of this part of the Indian Ocean Region.

The African Dimension of the Indian Ocean Region

Determining what part of Africa can be considered as being included in the Indian Ocean Region depends very much on the approach and concepts used. When looking at this by considering the states as basic units, at least three concepts can be considered to define a more or less inclusive Indian Ocean Region, namely the Indian Ocean Rim states, the Indian Ocean coastal states and the Indian Ocean land-locked states (Table 1). Promoted by the Indian Ocean Rim Association (IORA), the concept of the Indian Ocean Rim considers all the states that have a littoral on the main body of the Indian Ocean, which excludes the Red Sea and the Persian Gulf, but includes the Gulf of Aden, the Gulf of Oman, the Arabian Sea, the Bay of Bengal, the Andaman Sea, the Malacca Strait and Singapore Strait. Therefore, in addition to the obvious regional Indian Ocean littoral states of Africa and Asia, plus Australia, this should also include France for its island territories in the Southwest and Southern Indian Ocean[2] (Bouchard and Crumplin 2011) as well as the United Kingdom for the British Indian Ocean Territory[3]; even though France and UK are first and foremost European and foreign states and are considered as such by the other Indian Ocean Rim states.

Table 1. The African states and territories of the Indian Ocean Region

Indian Ocean Rim States and other island territories	*Other Indian Ocean coastal states (Red Sea coastal states)*	*Land-locked states linked to the Indian Ocean*
Comoros	Egypt	Botswana
Djibouti	Eritrea	Burundi
Kenya	Sudan	Ethiopia
Madagascar		Lesotho
Mauritius		Malawi
Mozambique		Rwanda
Seychelles		South Sudan
Somalia		Swaziland
South Africa		Uganda
Tanzania		Zambia
Mayotte (France)		Zimbabwe
Réunion (France)		
Scattered Islands (France)*		

*Official French Name: *îlesÉparses de l'océanIndien*, commonly simplified to *îlesÉparses*.

However, the area covered by the Indian Ocean Region can be expanded by considering the Red Sea and the Persian Gulf as Indian Ocean waters, which they are according to the revised definition for the Indian Ocean as proposed by the International Hydrographic Organization (IHO 2002), and by considering the land-locked states that rely upon transit to and from the sea mainly or solely focused on the Indian Ocean. This broader definition of the Indian Ocean Region is consistent with that of the Indian Ocean as a Zone of Peace (IOZP) as it was formulated in 1979 at the Meeting of the Littoral and Hinterland States of the Indian Ocean (United Nations 1979)[4] . Within these broad limits, the Indian Ocean Region includes a total of 38 coastal states and 14 land-locked states[5], of which 24 are African and 25 are Asian, plus Australia, France (for Crozet, Kerguelen, Mayotte, Réunion, Saint-Paul and Amsterdam, and the Scattered Islands) and the United Kingdom (for the British Indian Ocean Territory).

Thus, **Indian Ocean Maritime Africa** consists of ten Indian Ocean Rim states, plus France's three African island territories, while the case of the Chagos Archipelago (UK's BIOT) is more debatable and, as a result, is not considered as African land in this chapter[6] . But the African area included in the Indian Ocean Region can be expanded to as many as 24 African states when all Indian Ocean coastal states and land-locked states are accounted for, an area that we refer to as the **African Indian Ocean littoral and hinterland** (Figure 1). The differences between these two areas are very significant with a land territory of either 4.8 or 11.7 million sq km, a population of 196 or 513 million inhabitants, and a gross national income of 452 or 831 billion of dollars (Table 2).

Altogether, the island component, the land-locked states and the Red Sea coastal states very much increase the significance of the African littoral in the context of the Indian Ocean Region. However, if we look at global data for the entire Indian Ocean Region (52 states, including France and the UK for their island territories), we find that the African Indian Ocean littoral and hinterland (24 African states and three French island territories) accounts for some 35% of the regional land area, but only for about 19% of the population, 13% of the GDP and less than 10% of the international trade (exports plus imports). Thus, the demographic and economic weight of this area is actually low compared to the other sub-regions of the Indian Ocean Region (Persian Gulf, South

Figure 1: The African Indian Ocean littoral and hinterland

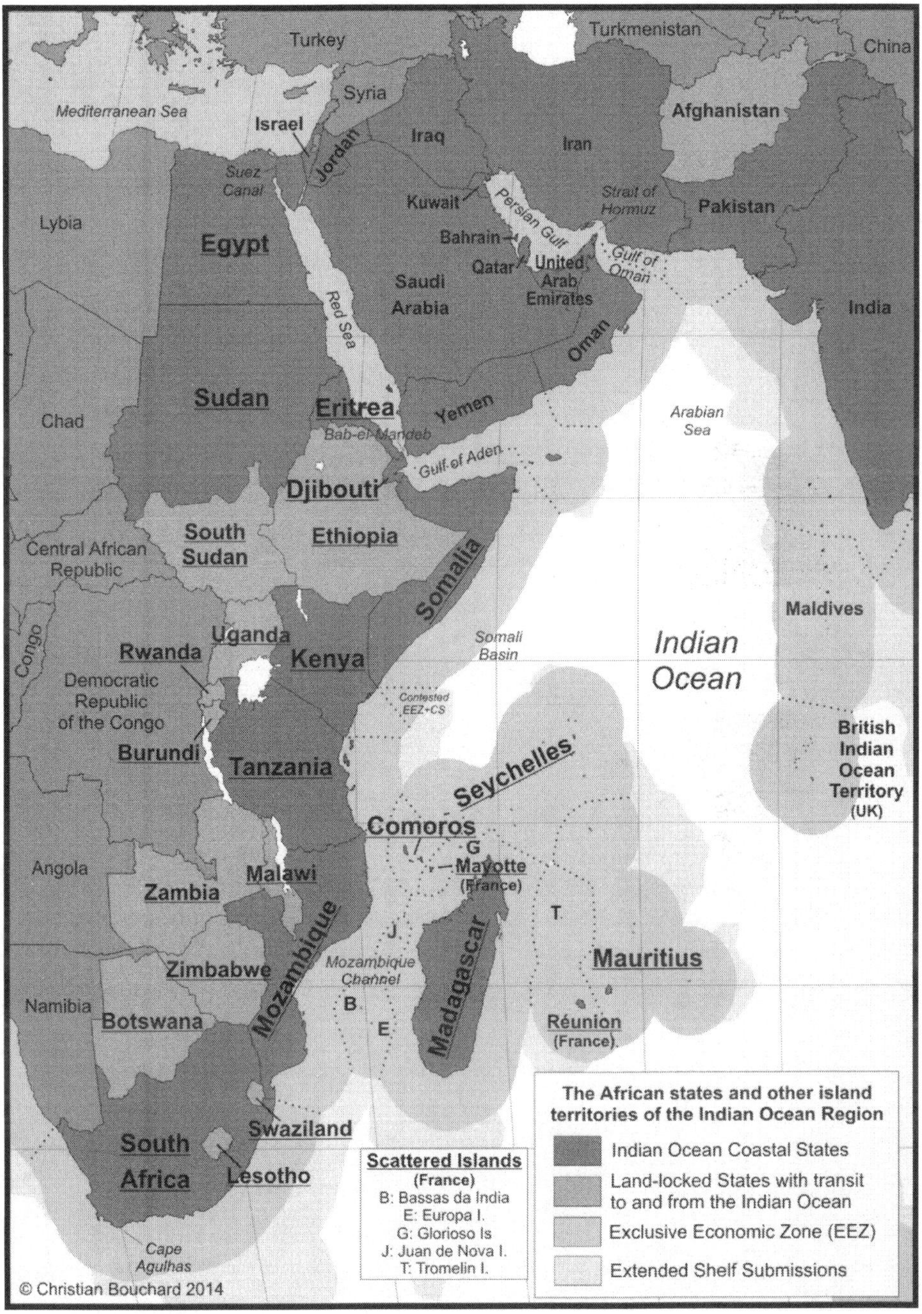

Table 2. Basic data for the African Indian Ocean littoral and hinterland

	Land Area (sq km)	*Population 2010 (Thousand)*	*Population Density (inh./sq km)*	*HDI 2012*	*GNI 2010 ($ millions)*	*IO TS+EEZ Area (sq km)*
Indian Ocean Rim	**4,801,690**	**195,905**	**40.8**	**0.505**	**452,249**	**7,931,770**
Comoros	2,235	683	305.6	0.429	539	164,691
Djibouti	23,200	834	35.9	0.445	1,120	6,947
Kenya	580,367	40,909	70.5	0.519	32,040	111,999
Madagascar	587,041	21,080	35.9	0.483	8,628	1,198,722
Mauritius	2,040	1,231	603.4	0.737	9,833	1,272,787
Mayotte (Fr)	374	204	545.5	(0.65)	(1,000)	63,078
Mozambique	799,380	23,967	30.0	0.327	9,127	571,955
Réunion (Fr)	2,512	845	336.4	(0.83)	(10,000)	315,058
Scattered Is (Fr)	39	–	–	–	–	622,572
Seychelles	455	91	200.0	0.806	896	1,332,031
Somalia	637,657	9,636	15.1	nd	nd	830,389
South Africa	1 219,090	51,452	42.2	0.629	356,294	(1,200,000)
Tanzania	947,300	44,973	47.5	0.476	22,772	241,541
Red Sea Costal States	**2,980,534**	**119,469**	**40.1**	**0.573**	**277,030**	**246,770**
Egypt	1,001,450	78,076	78.0	0.662	214,530	(80,000)
Eritrea	117,600	5,741	48.8	0.351	2,097	78,703
Sudan	1,861,484	35,652	19.2	0.414	60,403	88,067
Land-Locked States	**3,935,143**	**197,572**	**50.2**	**0.413**	**101,442**	–
Botswana	581,730	1,969	3.4	0.634	14,699	–
Burundi	27,830	9,233	331.8	0.355	2,033	–
Ethiopia	1,104,300	87,095	78.9	0.396	29,576	–
Lesotho	30,355	2,009	66.2	0.461	2,711	–
Malawi	118,484	15,014	126.7	0.418	4,928	–
Rwanda	26,338	10,837	411.5	0.434	5,580	–
Swaziland	17,364	1,193	68.7	0.536	3,472	–
South Sudan	644,329	9,941	15.4	nd	nd	–
Uganda	241,038	33,987	141.0	0.456	16,865	–
Zambia	752,618	13,217	17.6	0.448	14,300	–
Zimbabwe	390,757	13,077	33.5	0.397	7,278	–
Grand total	**11,717 367**	**512,946**	**43.8**	**0.485**	**830,721**	**8,178,540**

HDI: Human Development Index. GNI: Gross National Income (nominal, current prices).
TS+EEZ: Territorial Sea and Economic Exclusive Zone. nd: no data available.
Note: Data in parenthesis are rough estimations.
Sources: CIA 2013 (land area); United Nations 2013 (population); UNDP 2013 (HDI); World Bank 2013a (GNI), Sea Around Us 2013 (TS+EEZ area).

Asia and Southeast Asia) or even compared to the regional giant, India, which alone accounts for some 44% of the regional population, 30% of the GDP and more than 10% of the international trade. Unsurprisingly, we find only two African representatives on the list of 12 states with the highest Geo-Socio-Economic Index (GSEI), an index that roughly represents the relative geo-socio-economic importance of regional states in the context of the Indian Ocean Region—these two states being South Africa and Egypt, respectively in 9th and 11th position (Bouchard and Crumplin 2010, p. 37). Nevertheless, the demographic and economic weight of the African Indian Ocean littoral and hinterland is actually growing and should increase very significantly in the course of the 21st century, as most of the African countries have the potential to gain much in terms of geo-socio-economic importance.

Finally, the African Indian Ocean littoral and hinterland appears today as the least developed area of the Indian Ocean Region whether it is in terms of overall economic performance or in terms of human development. This is clearly evidenced by its low overall human development index of 0.485 in 2012 (Table 2). Only one country and one French territory, namely Seychelles (0.806, 46th rank) and Réunion (estimated at around 0.830), qualify as having a very high human development, while Mauritius (0.737, 80th rank) can be considered to have high human development. The only other countries in this region with HDIs over 0.600 include Egypt (0.662, 112th rank), Botswana (0.634, 119th rank), South Africa (0.629, 121th rank) and Mayotte (estimated at around 0.650), while the HDIs of Swaziland and Kenya are respectively of 0.536 (141th rank) and 0.519 (145th rank). This means that 17 countries have HDIs below 0.500, with 7 of them actually scoring less than 0.400 (including Somalia and South Sudan, estimations). This is a clear indication of the serious development challenges that the African Indian Ocean littoral and hinterland is facing today.

The Maritime Dimension

The Indian Ocean itself and associated maritime issues represent very central aspects of Africa's relation with and significance to the Indian Ocean Region. Taking into account the territorial sea and exclusive economic zone of the African coast from Djibouti to Cape Agulhas

(South Africa), as well as the territorial sea and exclusive economic zone surrounding the African islands states and French island territories, we find that the African coastal states of the Indian Ocean Rim exercise sovereignty (territorial sea) and exclusive rights (EEZ) on a maritime domain of some 7.9 million square kilometres (Table 2). This would be expanded even more if we were to add the extended continental shelf claims made by most of the coastal states in this area of the Indian Ocean (Figure 1)[7]. To put this more into perspective, the three largest Indian Ocean EEZs are those of Australia (close to 5 million sq km)[8], India (2.3 million sq km) and Indonesia (some 2 million sq km)[9]. These are followed by the EEZs of Seychelles (just over 1.3 million sq km), Mauritius (close to 1.3 million sq km), South Africa (around 1.2 million sq km) and Madagascar (1.2 million sq km), while the combined EZZ of France for its three African island territories comes next (1.0 million sq km).

Two particular issues are of great regional and international significance in what can be framed as the **African Indian Ocean waters**, which consist of the coastal states' territorial sea and exclusive economic zone as well as by their bordering high se as,an area covering much of the Western Indian Ocean (Figure 1). These issues are (a) shipping and maritime trade, and (b) the marine environment with its various marine resources. General awareness of the geostrategic value of these waters has been raised in the last decade following the development of the Somali-based maritime piracy and the international response to eradicate it (Potgieter and Schofield 2010; Hughes 2011; Winner *et al.* 2012; Lehr 2013; Luke 2013). Nonetheless, their importance is long recognized especially for the waters of the Gulf of Aden, the Bab-el-Mandeb, the Red Sea and the Gulf of Suez since the opening of the Suez Canal in 1869. This area represents the second most important maritime gateway between the Indian Ocean and the rest of the world, only after that of the Malacca and Singapore Straits. The closure of the Suez Canal in 1956-1957 and again from 1967 to 1975 highlighted the usefulness of the CapeRoute as the other Western Indian Ocean gateway that required that the Cape of Good Hope and Cape Agulhas at the southern tip of Africa be navigated. Today, the main sea lanes that use this passage originate either from the east (Australia), the northeast (Southeast Asia), or the north (Persian Gulf). In the latter case, the ships used to operate near the African continent coasts and pass through the Mozambique Channel, a practice that has been recently disturbed by the Somali maritime piracy problem.

Above all, these waters are of pivotal significance for the world economy as a large share of the international oil trade and of the maritime container traffic travels through the area. The intensification of the shipping sector and its supporting activities in the region dovetail with the development of maritime trade by the African states (boosted by increasing imports and exports). This is further supported through better connections between the African ports and global shipping networks. Therefore, maritime safety and maritime security are critical in this region as the long-haul maritime cargo needs to cross the area in a fluid and safe manner, as well as regional cargo and local port activities needing to operate in a secure and favourable environment.

While the national capacities for policing the sea of the African coastal states are developing[10], bilateral and multilateral cooperation and international naval operations help to cope with the security issues arising in the high seas, especially in regard to acts of piracy and armed robbery at sea off the Somali coast. As a result, there are two very significant ongoing multinational naval operations specifically created for this latter issue, namely the Combined Task Force (CTF) 151[11], which is one of three task forces operated by the Combined Maritime Forces (CMF), and Operation Atalanta, also known as European Union Naval Force Somalia (EU-NAVFOR-Somalia)[12]. However, as Potgieter and Schofield (2010, p. 106) remind us, "though piracy is the centre of much international attention, the maritime situation goes beyond that and also encompasses smuggling and human trafficking, maritime terrorism, unrestricted poaching and environmental crimes", and with the noticeable exception of maritime terrorism, these are also commonly experienced in the rest of the African Indian Ocean waters (Bouchard 2007). Some African coastal states also have special duties in terms of maritime safety and maritime search and rescue in the Western Indian Ocean. For instance, South Africa is responsible for navigation and weather warnings in the IHO/IMO/WMO NAVAREA VII, as well as Kenya, Madagascar, Mauritius, Mozambique, Seychelles, Somalia, South Africa, Tanzania and France (from Réunion) each being responsible for an IMO search and rescue area.

In terms of the marine environment and its intrinsic resources, the African waters are also identified as of great interest for their rich biodiversity[13] and for having some important fisheries, both local and foreign-led. However, all of the coastal states in this region have experienced pressure on and even the destruction of critical marine ecosystems including but not limited to coral reefs, mangroves, beaches and sea grass (UNEP 2004, UNEP/Nairobi Convention Secretariat 2009). In terms of the regional marine environment, the main features of the African Indian Ocean waters are the Somali Current large marine ecosystem (LME), extending from the Comoros Islands and the northern tip of Madagascar up to the Horn of Africa, the Agulhas Current large marine ecosystem, stretching from the northern end of the Mozambique Channel to Cape Agulhas, and the tropical marine ecosystems east of Madagascar and surrounding the small islands of the Seychelles and Mascarene Archipelagos (Mauritius, Réunion and Rodrigues). Most of these waters fall under the authority of the Nairobi Convention for the Protection, Management and Development of the Marine and Coastal Environment of the Eastern African Region[14]. The area is also subject to several important regional multinational research projects, such as the ASCLME Project that aims to develop Strategic Action Programmes (SAP) for the effective management and governance of these ecosystems, the South Western Indian Ocean Fisheries Project (SWIOFP) that focuses primarily on commercial offshore fisheries, the WIO-LaB project that addresses land-based sources of pollution in the Western Indian Ocean, as well as other research projects and collaborative programmes of the Indian Ocean Commission, which, in turn, focus on the coastal environments and waters surrounding the islands.

Two regional fisheries bodies have influence in the African Indian Ocean waters, namely the Southwest Indian Ocean Fisheries Commission (SWIOFC)[15], which consists mainly of the African continent coastal states from Somalia to South Africa and of the African island states, and the Indian Ocean Tuna Commission (IOTC)[16], which is responsible for the management of tuna and tuna-like species across the entire Indian Ocean. While the African Indian Ocean waters may not be a main catch area for the world's fisheries, they nevertheless support locally important coastal fisheries as well as quite intense foreign fleet activities in and outside the EEZs, such as French and Spanish trawlers and East Asian distant fishing vessels. In the SWIOFC countries, Ye (2011, p. 126) points out that the catches for most countries have increased steadily since the 1950s (when the total landing was only 30,000 tonnes), with the fastest growth occurring from the 1980s to the early 2000s. The total catch reached about 400,000 tonnes in 2005, but declined by about 10 percent in the following four years; with Madagascar and Seychelles accounting for more than half of the SWIOFC catches. But the region is also well recognized for illegal, unregulated and unreported (IUU) fishing activities which have been linked to the development of the Somali piracy (Hughes 2011), contribute to commercial fish stocks depletion and constitute a barrier to effective fisheries management. Samoilys *et al.* (2007) called for the identification and monitoring of illegal fishing trawlers in these waters and for improved licensing mechanisms and port inspections, all of which are now on the agenda for increased regional cooperation.

However, a new era in the exploitation of the African Indian Ocean marine resources now seems to be in preparation with ongoing littoral and offshore oil and gas exploration activities. Natural gas discoveries have recently been made off the coasts of Kenya, Tanzania and Mozambique (Mair 2012; Trueblood 2013), with oil offshore exploration licenses already allocated in Madagascar, Seychelles, and even Juan de Nova in the Mozambique Channel (one of the small islands part of the French Scattered Islands). In addition, the prospects for oil and gas developments are also excellent onshore, including potential in the Rift Valley Basin (Evans 2013), the Ogaden Basin, Mozambique and Madagascar. According to U.S.E.I.A. (2013), "among the countries with emerging oil and gas developments, Mozambique, Tanzania, Uganda and Madagascar have shown the most progress towards commercial development [...]. Uganda and Madagascar will most likely be the next oil producers on the continent". If this area becomes an important producer of oil and gas, this should provide new revenue for the coastal states, and thus could help them in their quest for better human development; but it will also raise concerns in regard to safety of the operations, security matters and environmental issues. No doubt, local exploitation of oil and gas could enhance the geostrategic significance of the entire area, especially if the production is large and mainly exported.

Thus, the African Indian Ocean waters are of great significance at both international and regional levels. As well, the African Indian Ocean coastal states are now developing their maritime domain awareness and getting deeply involved in the maritime affairs and activities of the Western Indian Ocean. In many ways, and it has been the case for much of the past, the Ocean provides opportunities to link the African littoral communities and states with those of the rest of the Indian Ocean Region. Formal regional cooperation on maritime affairs through international and regional organizations, bilateral and multilateral cooperation on maritime affairs between African coastal states and other Indian Ocean Rim states, commercial relations and shipping networks, multinational marine research programmes and marine resources/ environment management systems, as well as military (navy) and coast guard cooperation, all contribute and testify to the great significance of the African coastal states and African Indian Ocean waters to the Indian Ocean, the Indian Ocean Rim and the Indian Ocean Region.

The Human Dimension

The demographics of the African littoral of the Indian Ocean represent a major, and perhaps the most significant potential driver for the long-term rising importance of this region of the Indian Ocean. It is noted that Sub-Saharan Africa as a whole is the region of the world where most of the world's population growth will occur in the 21st century. This growth will result in a work force (adult age group) and middle class that should continue to expand at a fast pace for many decades to come and well beyond the middle of the century. As shown by the data compiled by the United Nations and using the medium variant of the latest demographic projections until 2100 (United Nations 2013), this region has already seen its population increase threefold between 1970 and 2010, from 282 to 831 million inhabitants, and is predicted to reach nearly 2.1 billion inhabitants by 2050 and some 3.5 billion inhabitants by the end of the century (Table 3)[17].

The total population of the Indian Ocean Rim was 2.27 billion people in 2010, of which only 196 million or 8.6 % were living in Indian Ocean Maritime Africa. But the population and share of this area will increase significantly during this century, and is predicted to reach 438 million (13.5 %) in 2050 and perhaps 723 million (20.9 %) by 2090. It

Table 3. Population growth and projections, 1970 to 2090

	Population 1970 (thousand)	*Population 2010 (thousand)*	*Population 2050 (thousand)*	*Population 2090 (thousand)*	*Variation 1970-2010 (%)*	*Variation 2010-2050 (%)*	*Variation 2050-2090 (%)*
Comoros	232	683	1 508	2 374	194.40	120.79	57.43
Djibouti	160	834	1 244	1 314	421.25	49.16	5.63
Kenya	11,252	40,909	97,173	152,000	263.57	137.53	56.42
Madagascar	6,576	21,080	55,498	96,789	220.56	163.27	74.40
Mauritius	826	1,231	1,231	1,024	49.03	0.00	-16.82
Mayotte (Fr)	37	204	466	640	451.35	128.43	37.34
Mozambique	9,453	23,967	59,929	104,053	153.54	150.05	73.63
Réunion (Fr)	462	845	1,125	1,161	82.90	33.14	3.20
Seychelles	52	91	100	89	75.00	9.89	-11.00
Somalia	3,445	9,636	27,076	49,539	179.71	180.99	82.96
South Africa	2,503	51,452	63,405	65,301	128.65	23.23	2.99
Tanzania	13,605	44,973	129,417	249,035	230.56	187.77	92.43
IO Maritime Africa	68,603	195,905	438,172	723,319	185.56	123.67	65.08
African LLS	64,818	197,572	487,556	777,680	204.81	146.77	59.51
Afr. Red Sea states	48,372	119,469	213,250	268,198	146.98	78.50	25.77
African IO littoral and hinterland	181,793	512,946	1,138,978	1,769,197	182.16	122.05	55.33
Other IO Rim states	933,576	2,075,301	2,812,934	2,733,794	122.30	35.54	-2.81
Without India	378,376	869,676	1,192,883	1,149,611	129.84	37.16	-3.63
India	555,200	1,205,625	1,620,051	1,584,183	117.15	34.37	-2.21
IO Rim (total)	1,002,179	2,271,206	3,251,106	3,457,113	126.63	43.14	6.34
IO Region (total)	1,159,534	2,727,685	4,192,161	4,780,968	135,24	53,69	14,05
World	3,691,173	6,916,183	9,550,945	10,717,401	87.37	38.10	12.21
Sub-Saharan Africa	282,158	831,464	2,074,446	3,536,438	194.68	149.49	70.48

Note: medium variant for the population projections.

Source: United Nations, 2013, *World Population Prospects: The 2012 Revision.*

is noteworthy that the total population of the African land-locked states and African Red Sea coastal states will also grow significantly, which means that the total population of the African Indian Ocean littoral and hinterland should increase from its present 513 million people to 1.14 billion in 2050 and 1.77 billion in 2090. The pace of growth in this region will be much stronger in the first half of the century, but it will still be significant in the second half, a period when the rest of the IOR will see its population peak and even experience a small population decline. This means that the African Indian Ocean littoral and hinterland will account for some 27 % of the total population of the broad Indian Ocean Region (52 states, including France for its island territories) in 2050, and 37% by 2090. Consequently, and according to the available population projections, there will be more people living in the African Indian Ocean littoral and hinterland than in India before the end of the 21st century[18].

Thus, in pure demographic terms, the African littoral of the Indian Ocean will gain substantial mass in the contexts of both the Indian Ocean Region and the Indian Ocean Rim, and it is the only area of the region projected to grow during the second half of the 21st century. But demographic growth alone is not a certitude that Indian Ocean Maritime Africa and/or the African Indian Ocean littoral and hinterland will proportionately gain as much political and economical significance in the context of the Indian Ocean Region as their population increases might warrant. For example, and when considered as a whole, the states of the African Indian Ocean littoral and hinterland experienced a larger relative population increase from 1970 to 2010 (+182%) than what is expected for either 2010-2050 (+122%) or 2050-2090 (+55%), yet this historic growth was not matched by the same gain in political and economic significance. This situation occurred in a general context of widespread poverty, high insecurity, weak or failed states, insufficient economic development, and much environmental degradation. However, and again considering this area as a whole, improvement is now occurring along socio-economic measures, and advances have also been noted in several demographic areas with reductions in birth rates, child mortality and the number of new HIV/AIDS cases. In the period of 1970-2010, the demographic challenges were first and foremost linked to the very high number of children and the HIV/AIDS crisis. In the coming decades the proportion of children will decrease significantly while the number of adults is projected to grow at a much faster pace than it did during the 1970-2010 era. This will lead to a larger and increasing adult age group that will face huge challenges in regard to finding employment and housing (increasing numbers of families, new standards of living, and so on).

The question is therefore "can Africa benefit from positive and ongoing socio-demographic evolution as much as Southeast Asia did in the last 40 years when it basically experienced the same changes?" If the answer were known to be yes, then this would be very promising for the African littoral of the Indian Ocean. However, if progress towards improved human development is slower and harder in the context of the African Indian Ocean littoral and hinterland than it has been in Southeast Asia, significant progress can still be expected towards the entire 21st century. In regard to social needs, the main issues to be dealt with are widespread poverty, human insecurity, education, health, access to basic life resources (food, water, energy, and a healthy environment), employment, housing, and rapid urbanization.

The very high level of poverty and the low life expectancy at birth both testify to the actual difficult conditions of life in the African Indian Ocean littoral and hinterland. As an example, overall life expectancy at birth for both sexes combined is only 54 years in Southern Africa and 57 years in Eastern Africa, with four countries, Lesotho, Swaziland, Zambia and Zimbabwe, having rates of merely 48 years (PRB 2012). As for poverty, the latest available UNDP data show that the percentage of population in multidimensional poverty is lowest in Egypt (6%), South Africa (13.4%) and more generally in Southern Africa (13.4-39.6%). On the other hand, it is generally over 60% in Eastern Africa where it varies from 47.8% in Kenya to 65.6% in Tanzania, 66.9% in Madagascar, 79.3% in Mozambique, 81.2% in Somalia and even 87.3% in Ethiopia (UNDP 2013, pp. 160-161). But the overall situation is improving in most of the area as both life expectancy at birth and poverty levels are actually improving and are expected to continue to do so in the coming decades (United Nations 2013; World Bank 2011; UNECA 2012 and 2013).

At the same time, the African Indian Ocean littoral and hinterland are also urbanizing at a fast pace as the percentage of urban population is expected to increase from 58.5% in 2010 to 74.0% in 2050 in Southern Africa and from 23.3% in 2010 to 44.7% in 2050 in Eastern Africa (United Nations 2011, File 2). In absolute numbers this amounts to a respective increase of urban population from 33.8 to 49.8 million and from 78.0 to 359 million over the 40-year period (United Nations 2011, File 3). As an example, the largest urban agglomerations of Indian Ocean Maritime Africa continue to grow at a high pace especially those of Eastern Africa such as Dar-es-Salaam which is expected to see its population increase from 3.4 million in 2010 to 7.3 million in 2025, and Nairobi, that is predicted to see its population increase from 3.2 million in 2010 to 6.1 million in 2025 (United Nations 2011, File 12). Consequently, urban development issues will continue to pose challenges in the entire African Indian Ocean littoral and hinterland while rural development issues will also remain very important and present challenges especially in Eastern Africa. In Eastern Africa, the rural population is expected to continue to increase from 2010 to 2050, growing from 285 to 443 million, while in Southern Africa it will actually decrease from 24.0 to 17.5 million during the same period (United Nations 2011, File 24). Given this projected demographic growth, it is critical that solutions to regional and local environmental issues be incorporated as intrinsic components of socio-economic development and planning policies and procedures.

Finally, we should also highlight the fact that the situation in regard to socio-demographic context and human development is quite different in the small island states and French territories of the Southwest Indian Ocean compared to the continental states and Madagascar, with the noticeable exception of Comoros which presents a general profile closer to that of the African continent. Thus, the overall situation for Mauritius, Seychelles, Réunion and even Mayotte is characterized by higher human development scores, longer life expectancies at birth, higher population densities and percentages of urban population, as well as lower poverty levels than what is found in the other Southern and Eastern African states. However, this relatively better situation is quite minor when we consider the entire African Indian Ocean littoral and hinterland as these four small islands only represent a combined population of some 2.4 million (0.46% of the total population of the area, or 1.21% of the Indian Ocean Maritime Africa). Nevertheless, these small islands represent relatively rich points in a very poorly developed region, and their regional political and economic significance is much higher than their demographic weight might suggest.

The Economic Dimension

Strong local, national and regional economic performances are pivotal for Sub-Saharan Africa and the Indian Ocean Maritime Africa in order for these areas, their countries and individual citizens to experience improved living conditions and advances in human development. Considering these regions as a whole during the final decades of the 20th century, such economic performance was indeed lacking. However, the overall situation has improved considerably in the first decade of the 21st century as shown by the increased annual average in GDP growth and GDP per capita growth (Table 4). These improvements can serve as a clear signal that the economies of many of these states are doing better and that the environment for continued human development is more positive than what is was towards the end of the 20th century.

Table 4. Annual average GDP and GDP per capita growths for the Indian Ocean Maritime Africa (1980-89, 1990-99, and 2010-2010)

	Annual average GDP growth (%)			*Annual average GDP per capita growth (%)*		
	1980-89	*1990-89*	*2000-10*	*1980-89*	*1990-99*	*2000-10*
Comoros	2.7	1.6	2.0	-0.2	-0.9	-0.7
Djibouti	Nd	-2.0	3.6	nd	-4.5	1.5
Kenya	4.2	2.2	3.8	0.4	-0.7	1.1
Madagascar	0.4	1.6	3.0	-2.3	-1.5	0.0
Mauritius	4.3	5.2	4.3	3.3	4.0	3.5
Mayotte (Fr)	+	+	++	nd	nd	nd
Mozambique	0.4	5.6	7.2	-0.6	2.6	4.5
Réunion (Fr)	+	+	+	nd	nd	nd
Seychelles	2.1	4.9	2.5	1.2	3.3	1.8
Somalia	Nd	nd	nd	0.9	-1.9	nd
South Africa	2.2	1.4	3.6	-0.3	-0.8	2.2
Tanzania	3.8	3.3	6.8	0.6	0.3	3.9
IO Maritime Africa (mean)	**2.5**	**2.6**	**4.1**	**0.3**	**0.0**	**2.0**
Sub-Saharan Africa	2.2	2.1	4.8	-0.7	-0.6	2.2

Source: World Bank 2013a, *African Development Indicators 2012/13* (Tables 2.3 and 2.5).

This trend of better economic performance has continued in 2011 and 2012 as respectively shown by the GDP annual growth of the African Indian Ocean Rim States (Table 5) which results in a overall mean annual increase of 4.5% and 4.2% over the two year period (World Bank 2013b). This allowed for an overall mean annual improvement in per capita GDP of 2.7% and 2.3% in 2011 and 2012, which is noticeably higher than the Sub-Saharan Africa numbers of 1.8% and 1.5%. However, Comoros and Madagascar are well behind in terms of GDP per capita growth, as well as Kenya and South Africa which are under the regional average, while Seychelles, Mozambique, Tanzania and Mauritius recorded the best increases over the two year period. It is noteworthy that the same overall positive trends in GDP and GDP per capita were seen in the hinterland's largest economies (Table 5:

Table 5. Annual average GDP and GDP per capita growths for the Indian Ocean Maritime Africa and the five largest land-locked national economies (2010, 2011 and 2012)

	Annual average GDP growth (%)			*Annual average GDP per capita growth (%)*		
	2010	*2011*	*2012*	*2010*	*2011*	*2012*
Comoros	2.1	2.2	3.0	-0.5	-0.3	0,5
Djibouti	3.5	4.5	4.8	2.0	2.9	3.2
Kenya	5.8	4.4	4.3	3.0	1.6	1.5
Madagascar	0.5	1.9	3.1	-2.3	-1.0	0.3
Mauritius	7.7	3.8	3.2	7.2	3.4	2.7
Mozambique	7.1	7.3	7.4	4.4	4.6	4.7
Seychelles	7.1	5.0	2.9	4.2	7.8	2.5
Somalia	Nd	nd	nd	nd	nd	nd
South Africa	3.1	3.5	2.5	1.7	2.2	1.3
Tanzania	7.0	6.4	6.9	3.9	3.3	3.7
IO Maritime Africa (mean)	**5.0**	**4.5**	**4.2**	**2.6**	**2.7**	**2.3**
Botswana	8.1	8.0	6.1	7.2	7.1	5.2
Ethiopia	9.9	7.3	8.5	7.1	4.5	5.7
Uganda	5.9	6.6	3.4	2.4	3.1	0.0
Zambia	7.6	6.8	7.3	4.4	3.6	4.0
Zimbabwe	9.6	9.4	5.0	8.0	7.1	2.2
Sub-Saharan Africa	**4.0**	**2.8**	**2.2**	**2.2**	**1.8**	**1.5**

Source: World Bank 2013b, *World Data Bank*.

Botswana, Ethiopia, Uganda, Zambia, and Zimbabwe). This overall trend is predicted to continue in the coming years as shown by the latest World Bank forecast for Sub-Saharan Africa's GDP growth of 4.9% for 2013, 5.3% for 2014, and 5.5% for 2015 (World Bank, 2013, p. 10).

Thus, the overall economic performance has been quite positive since the turn of the new century for most of the African Indian Ocean littoral and hinterland. This is seen as evidence of a profound structural change that should allow the African economies of the area to maintain this growth trend for the foreseeable future. As stated by Dörr*et al.* (2010) for the continent as a whole, "government reforms, greater political stability, improved macroeconomics, and a healthier business environment are now taking hold in a region long dismissed as hopeless". Consequently, foreign investments are flowing into the region to develop and access more natural resources (essentially minerals and fossil fuels), to access arable land and expand agriculture, to develop services and some manufacturing, as well as to penetrate the emerging markets of the region. As mentioned in *The Economist* (2011), "The commodities boom is partly responsible... But the growth also had a lot to do with the manufacturing and service economies that African countries are beginning to develop". This coincides with an increasing working force, a burgeoning middle class[19], as well as continued high rates of urbanization and desires of these populations to participate in the modern economy. These four ground level factors will likely have positive effects on the general economic performance of the states in this region for many decades to come, if not the entire 21st century.

In addition to peace, security, and stability, three other important issues, central to the successful development of African economies in the coming decades, are the development of urban economies, improvements in transportation infrastructure and increased economic regional integration. These three issues are at the heart of the analysis in the *World Development Report 2009* which advocates that "Africa can reduce the limitations of its poor economic geography" as better urban agglomerations can deliver scale efficiencies, transport links can help domestic markets grow, and regional and global integration can promote trade (World Bank 2009, p. 285). Noting that "cities have traditionally functioned as 'engines' of economic growth and crucibles for social and cultural progress", Turok (2010, p. 12), however, remarks that "one of the puzzles about Africa's rapid urbanization is that this had not been accompanied by greater economic dynamism". Nonetheless, Turok agrees with the World Bank's assertion that regional economic integration would very much change this situation and help the urban economies to develop significantly. For the World Bank (2009, p. 285), "contrary to some thinking, urbanization, done right, can help development *more* in Africa than elsewhere. Despite five decades of low-quality urbanization, living standards in Africa's cities are much higher than in the countryside. If urbanization can be managed better, [...,] significant gains can be expected in productivity and poverty reduction".

Regional economic integration is far from a new idea in Africa, yet it has not developed to a sufficient and efficient level. As pointed out by Shaw (2012, p. 845), "because of overlapping memberships and mandates and insufficient resources, macro- to micro-regionalisms have typically lacked capacity and commitment". This is largely recognized by the Southern and Eastern African states that are now actively involved in several renewed regional integration processes at different geographical scales from local (examples of some bi-lateral cross-border initiatives as multinational development corridors), sub-regional (such as COMESA, EAC, IGAD and IOC), to continental (examples of the New Partnership for Africa's Development and of the African Economic Community). In what we have identified as the African Indian Ocean littoral and hinterland, regional economic integration has been the focal area of the ACP-EU's Regional Strategy Paper (RSP) and Regional Indicative Programme (RIP) for the Region of Eastern and Southern Africa and the Indian Ocean (ESA/IO)[20]. One of the main recent initiatives of such integration is the Tripartite Free Trade Area (T-FTA) negotiated since 2008 between the COMESA, the EAC, SADC and all of their respective member states[21].

Regional economic integration in the African Indian Ocean littoral and hinterland is a high priority and progress is expected in the short to medium timeframe as new cross-border initiatives, free-trade areas, customs unions, single markets and even currency unions are in preparation. This is happening at the same time that transportation infrastructures are being developed; as well international trade and foreign investment are increasing, which together stimulate urban and national economies. Better linkages between the hinterland and the littoral, and especially between the land-locked states and the main ports are required to get products (primary or secondary) to world market as well as to import goods and equipment more easily and at a better price. In this regard, completion of the corridor development initiatives linking ports (such as Maputo, Mombasa, Dar-es-Salaam, Beira, Lamu and others) with the hinterland is crucial. Thus, if the region can continue to make advances in terms of creating a more secure, stable, and better business environment, very favourable conditions would be in place for a long-lasting strong economic performance in the area, which, if properly managed, should allow considerable gains in terms of living conditions for many and improvements in overall human development.

As a consequence, the prospects look excellent for an increasing economically significant Indian Ocean Maritime Africa. Considerable foreign investment is flowing into the area and this should continue for a long time as the world economic powers are competing for the continent's resources, products, markets and opportunities, especially China and the United States, followed by Europe and India (Fiorina, 2013). As highlighted by Shaw (2012, p. 846), "the continent's pattern of inter-regional relationships is in the flux, from classic, inherited North-South dependencies towards a novel South-East axis around China and India but also Japan and Korea", to which we can add at least Singapore and Malaysia on the one hand, and the United Arab Emirates and Saudi Arabia on the other hand, thus placing the African littoral at the interface of these relations between Africa and Asia. This places emphasis on the role that South Africa intends to play as the 'gateway into the continent' (Scholvin and Draper 2012), as well as being itself a major investor in the rest of Africa since the early 1990s (Southall and Melber 2009)[22]. South Africa is by far the economic powerhouse of Southern and Eastern Africa with its GDI accounting in 2010 for 79 % of the total GDI of Indian Ocean Maritime Africa. Its accession as the fifth member of the BRICS[23] in 2011 is a recognition of its economic power and leadership role in linking Africa to the other BRICS[24].

However, several questions and uncertainties remain pertaining as to how much and at what pace Sub-Saharan Africa will develop in the coming decades. This region still has to cope with chronic hunger, widespread poverty, huge social inequities, common insecurity issues, limited access to basic life resources such as energy and clean water, and various environmental challenges. Social tensions between the poor and rich, rural areas and cities and autochthones and foreigners can become very tense if the fruits of economic growth are not fairly redistributed (Brunel, 2011). This supposes moving from failed or weak states to states with better capacities to simultaneously develop, direct and support their economic progress and their human development. Accordingly, UNECA (2011, p. 111) argues that "the urgent need for economic transformation and take-off by African countries underscores the importance of building developmental states on the continent. Developmental states, barring external shocks and adverse global conditions, can stimulate rapid economic growth and diversification, technological innovation, industrial development and social welfare in Africa".

The Political Dimension

Last to be considered in this chapter, but not of least importance, is the political dimension. Overall, states of both Indian Ocean Maritime Africa and its hinterland are facing political difficulties that lessen their capacities to provide a better social situation for their populations and a more favourable context for economic development. The two main issues are (1) the high level of insecurity and violence, and (2) the generalized weakness of the states. As noted by Rumley (2013, p. 51) in *The Indian Ocean Region: Security, Stability and Sustainability in the 21st Century*, "the relationship between economic insecurity and political conflict is evident both among and within states...

Within states it has been noted that economic insecurity has become part of a process of deepening social divisions and increasing political instability. Under conditions of increasing fragility it has been suggested therefore that the state faces the threat of losing control not only of its capacity to provide basic services but also of its monopoly over law and order and its political legitimacy[25]". This is a serious concern in the entire African Indian Ocean littoral and hinterland where the recent degradation of the Failed States Index provides some evidence of increasing fragility.

In regard to insecurity and violence, the data provided by the Heidelberg Institute for International Conflict Research's *Conflict*

Barometer 2013 (HIIK 2014) and by the International Maritime Bureau *Piracy and Armed Robbery Maps* (IMB 2013 and 2014a) give a first glance at the situation encountered both on land and at sea. More specifically, in the entire African Indian Ocean littoral and hinterland, 7 wars, 3 limited wars, and 25 violent crises were recorded by the HIIK in 2013 (Table 6), for a total of 35 violent conflicts, while another 21 non-violent conflicts were also recorded (disputes and non-violent crises).

In Indian Ocean Maritime Africa, Somalia (1 war and 1 violent crisis), Kenya (1 limited war and 3 violent crises), Tanzania (4 violent crises), South Africa (2 violent crises) and Mozambique (1 violent crisis) were afflicted by violent conflicts in 2013. Overall, there has recently been a degradation of the situation as only 9 violent conflicts were recorded in 2008 (HIIK, 2008), including one war in Somalia, two severe crises (equivalent of limited wars) and two crises (equivalent of violent crisis) in Kenya, and one crisis in each of Comoros, South Africa and Tanzania. While the crisis in Comoros was downscaled to latent conflict in 2009 (and is not anymore considered as a dispute in 2013), new violent crises erupted in Mozambique in 2012 (RENAMO), South Africa in 2011 (KwaZulu - Natal), and Tanzania in 2010 (Uamsho / Zanzibar), 2011 (Chadema) and 2012 (Christian groups vs Muslim groups). In the rest of the African Indian Ocean littoral and hinterland, the situation in 2013 was the most concerning in Sudan (3 wars and 1 violent crisis), South Sudan (2 wars and 3 violent crises) and Egypt (1 war, 1 limited war and 1 violent crisis).

At sea, 2013 has been the best year for maritime safety and security since the Somali piracy crisis erupted in 2007. While these waters remain very dangerous and still require heavy naval and coast guard resources, they are now at the heart of vibrant regional and international cooperation. Only 15 incidents of piracy or armed robbery against ships were reported to the International Maritime Bureau for the waters off Somalia and the Gulf of Aden, including eight vessels fired upon and two hijackings (IMB 2014b, p. 20). This is comparable with the data compiled by Oceans Beyond Piracy which reports that 23 ships and 486 seafarers were attacked by Somali pirates in 2013, and tracked a total of 145 suspicious approaches (OBP, 2014, p. 3). According to *The State of Maritime Piracy 2013*, the total cost of Somali piracy was down by

Table 6. Violent Conflicts in the African Indian Ocean littoral and hinterland (2013)

Wars	*Conflict parties*	*Conflict items*	*Start*	*+/-*
Egypt (opposition groups)	opposition vs. government	System/ideology, national power	1954	++
Somalia (Islamist groups)	al-Shabaab vs. ENA, government, KDF	System/ideology, national power	2006	=
South Sudan (inter-ethnic violence)	Murle vs. Dinka vs. Lou Nuer vs. variousethnic groups vs. ethnicsub-clans	Subnationalpredominance, resources	2011	=
South Sudan (SPLA defectors)	defected SPLA troops vs. government	System/ideology, subnational predominance	2013	New
Sudan (Darfur)	LJM, SRF vs. pro-gvt militias vs. reserve forces vs. government	Subnationalpredominance, resources, other	2003	=
Sudan (inter-ethnic violence)	Al-RezeigatAbballa, gvt vs. Beni Hussein vs. Misseriya vs. Salamat vs. Al-Gimir vs. BaniHalba vs. Maaliya	Subnationalpredominance, resources	2011	=
Sudan (SPLM/A-North / Southern Kordofan, Blue Nile)	SPLM/A-North, SRF vs. government	Autonomy	2011	=
Limited Wars	**Conflict parties**	**Conflict items**	**Start**	**+/-**
Egypt (Islamist groups / SinaiPeninsula)	Islamist groups vs. government	Secession, system/ideology	1992	+
Kenya (inter-ethnic violence)	Borana vs. Rendille and Gabra and Burji, Garre vs. Degodia, Orma vs. Pokomo, Turkana vs. Merille, Turkana vs. Pokot	Subnationalpredominance, resources	1991	=
Uganda (ADF-NALU)	ADF-NALU vs. government	National power, resources	1987	+
Violent crisis	**Conflict parties**	**Conflict items**	**Start**	**+/-**
Burundi (FNL)	FNL vs. government	National power	2005	=
Burundi (opposition groups)	ADC, MSD vs. gvt, Imbonerakure	National power	2006	=
Egypt (Muslims - Christians)	Muslims vs. Christians	Subnationalpredominance	1952	=
Ethiopia (OLF / Oromiya)	OLF vs. government	Secession	1973	=
Ethiopia (ONLF / Ogaden)	ONLF vs. government	Secession, resources	1984	=

Table 6 (Contd.)

Wars	*Conflict parties*	*Conflict items*	*Start*	*+/-*
Ethiopia (opposition)	BPLM, EUFF, Ginbot 7 et al., Semayawi, UDJ vs. government	National power	2005	=
Kenya (MRC / Coast)	MRC vs. government	Secession	2008	=
Kenya (Mungiki)	Mungiki vs. government	System/ideology, subnationalpredominance	1997	=
Kenya (TNA - ODM)	TNA vs. ODM	National power	1999	+
Mozambique (RENAMO)	RENAMO vs. government	National power	2012	=
Rwanda (FDLR)	FDLR vs. government	National power	1990	=
Somalia (Somaliland - Khatumo State)	Somaliland vs. Khatumo State	Subnationalpredominance	2009	-
South Africa (KwaZulu - Natal)	ANC vs. IFP vs. NFP	Subnationalpredominance	1990	=
South Africa (xenophobes - immigrants)	xenophobes vs. immigrants	Subnationalpredominance	1994	=
South Sudan (LRA)	LRA vs. government	Subnationalpredominance	2011	++
South Sudan (variousmilitias)	Militias David YauYau, SSDF, SSDM/A, SSLA vs. government	System/ideology, resources	2011	=
Sudan - South Sudan	Sudan vs. South Sudan	Territory, resources, other	2011	—
Swaziland (opposition)	COSATU, PUDEMO, SFTU, SNUS, SWACOPA, TUCOSWA vs. gvt	System/ideology, national power	1998	=
Tanzania (Chadema)	Chadema vs. government	National power	2011	=
Tanzania (Christians - Muslims)	Christian groups vs. Muslim groups	Subnationalpredominance	2012	=
Tanzania (CUF / Zanzibar)	Chadema, CUF vs. CCM)	Autonomy	1993	=
Tanzania (Uamsho / Zanzibar)	Uamsho vs. government	Secession, system/ideology	2010	=
Uganda (LRA)	LRA vs. government	Subnationalpredominance	1987	=
Uganda (opposition)	opposition vs. government	National power	2001	=
Zimbabwe (MDC-T, MDC-M - ZANU-PF)	MDC-M, MDC-T vs. government	National power	2003	=

Last column (+/-): Change in conflict intensity in 2013. Source: HIIK, *Conflict Barometer 2013.*

almost 50% from 2012 to 2013, yet cost estimates for 2013 are in the area of $3.0-3.2 billion, but the report "also underscores the fact that such a decline may be temporary unless systems to support stability and a healthy economy ashore take root. The international community interested in countering piracy needs to emphasize lasting solutions" (OBP, 2014, p. ii and p. 7).

In terms of state performance, many indicators show that there is an overall lack of institutional capacity, but there is a strong commitment by national governments to improve the situation when feasible. However, the majority of regional states are ranked quite high on the Failed States Index 2013 compiled by The Fund for Peace (FFP, 2013)[26], a composite index in which the higher the score or rank, the worse is the situation. In fact, 17 out of the 24 states of the African Indian Ocean littoral and hinterland appear in the first third of the world ranking (established for 178 countries), with the worst situations found in Somalia (1st), Sudan (3rd) and South Sudan (4th), but many more are not too far behind, such as Zimbabwe (10th), Kenya (17th), Ethiopia (19th), Burundi (20th), Uganda (22nd) and Eritrea (25th).

With the noteable exceptions of Somalia and Kenya, the states of Indian Ocean Maritime Africa are globally ranked much better on the Failed States Index 2013 than the land-locked and Red Sea coastal states (Table 7). However, the situation is not static and some states have made significant progress over the last five-year period between 2008-2013 such as Zimbabwe (-7.3 points), Seychelles (-5.5 points), and Malawi (-3.7 points). Unfortunately, the overall trend has not been positive at the extended region (littoral and hinterland) level with 16 states seeing some degradation of their index score from 2008 to 2013, with the strongest negative changes being registered by Eritrea (+7.6 points), Kenya (+6.2 points), Mozambique, Madagascar (+6.0 points), Swaziland (+5.6 points), Djibouti (+5.5 points), Zambia (+5.0), and even South Africa (+4.9 points). When aggregating these data for Indian Ocean Maritime Africa (10 states), the Red Sea coastal states (3 states) and the land-locked states (10 states), we find that the degradation has been highest for Maritime Africa with a state average index increase of +3.1 points and a progression upward of 11 ranks. This clearly highlights the fact that building state capacities, increasing human and economic security, as well as peaceful conflict resolution processes remain three critical challenges in Indian Ocean Maritime Africa.

Table 7. Failed States Index 2013 for the African Indian Ocean littoral and hinterland

State	*Rank 2013*	*Rank 2008*	*Rank difference*	*Score 2013*	*Score 2008*	*Score difference*
Somalia	1	1	0	113.9	114.2	0.3
Sudan	3	2	1	111.0	113.0	2.0
South Sudan	4	—	—	110.6	—	—
Zimbabwe	10	3	7	105.2	112.5	7.3
Kenya	17	26	-9	99.6	93.4	-6.2
Ethiopia	19	16	3	98.9	96.1	-2.8
Burundi	20	24	-4	97.6	94.1	-3.5
Uganda	22	16	6	96.6	96.1	-0.5
Eritrea	25	44	-19	95.0	87.4	-7.6
Egypt	34	40	-6	90.6	88.7	-1.9
Rwanda	38	42	-4	89.3	88.0	-1.3
Malawi	40	29	11	89.2	92.9	3.7
Zambia	45	63	-18	86.6	81.6	-5.0
Swaziland	49	71	-22	85.6	80.0	-5.6
Dijbouti	50	71	-21	85.5	80.0	-5.5
Comoros	56	74	-18	84.0	79.6	-4.4
Mozambique	59	85	-26	82.8	76.8	-6.0
Madagascar	61	86	-25	82.7	76.7	-6.0
Tanzania	65	75	-10	81.1	79.1	-2.0
Lesotho	71	61	10	79.4	81.7	2.3
South Africa	113	125	-12	67.6	62.7	-4.9
Seychelles	121	114	7	64.0	69.5	5.5
Botswana	121	120	1	64.0	65.9	1.9
Mauritius	148	148	0	44.5	42.4	-2.1
Average	49.7	58.1	-6.4	87.7	84.9	-1.8

In grey: States of the Indian Ocean Maritime Africa. Source: FFP, *Failed States Index 2013*.

There is no doubt that economic growth, human development and environmental sustainability are greatly impeded by this situation; and thus high insecurity, political instability and weak state capacities seems today to be the weakest part of the equation for much more successful development in Indian Ocean Maritime Africa.

Conclusion

The African littoral of the Indian Ocean is a significant part of the Indian Ocean Region. Although in the context of the IORA, focus is given to the IO Rim states and thus to Indian Ocean Maritime Africa, which consists of 10 states plus three French island territories, an African Indian Ocean extended area can be identified as part of the broader Indian Ocean Region. In addition to the IO Rim states, this area that we refer to as the African Indian Ocean littoral and hinterland includes three African Indian Ocean coastal states of the Red Sea as well as eleven land-locked states that rely upon transit to and from the sea mainly or solely focused on the Indian Ocean (Figure 1, Tables 1 and 2). This extended area is home to a total population of just over half a billion people with some 200 million living in Indian Ocean Maritime Africa.

Our survey of the overall context of the African Indian Ocean littoral and hinterland shows that it is a region of low socio-economic development facing many challenges. However, it is a region on the move, and some substantial improvements can be expected during the entire 21st century if the present positive trends and regional, national and multinational driven processes identified can continue along the path established during the first decade or so of this century. Some of the key factors contributing in this evolving context include ongoing and improving demographic processes, growth in urbanization, and a more stable, broader and stronger economic performance.

This changing landscape has implications in regard to the African littoral's significance in the Indian Ocean Region and Indian Ocean Rim. As seen in this chapter, Indian Ocean Maritime Africa as well as the African Indian Ocean littoral and hinterland, will, during the entire 21st century, experience very substantial demographic growth that could well be matched with a similar or even larger economic development. In addition, intensification of maritime activities in the area and increasing maritime domain awareness by regional and international agents with commensurate implications in maritime affairs from the African coastal states and other international maritime powers will enhance the significance of the African waters in the general context of the Indian Ocean and, more specifically, in the context of the Western Indian Ocean.

Even if it is not possible to assess it precisely, the potential, and perhaps even expected, outcome of a much larger and healthier population, a better performing and more open economy, and an increase in and more efficient management of maritime activities will set the scene for the rising significance of the African littoral to both the Indian Ocean Region and the Indian Ocean Rim; thus also increasing its geopolitical and geostrategic significance. On the one hand, this raises the issue of developing specific and effective national and regional strategies for the Indian Ocean by African countries and sub-regional organizations. This should be done while taking into account the transit needs of the land-locked states due to the significance of this vast hinterland. On the other hand, emerging issues such as social transformations, economic development, maritime security, oil and gas developments, human security, environmental challenges (including climate change, biodiversity conservation, pollution, etc.), as well as a renewed foreign interest for and involvement in the African Indian Ocean littoral and hinterland and the Western Indian Ocean will be central in the coming decades. Taking this into account, there is a definitive need to better acknowledge and analyse the relation between Africa and the Indian Ocean in general, and between Indian Ocean Maritime Africa and the rest of the Indian Ocean Rim in particular, especially in terms of economic, political, environmental, military and maritime matters.

In conclusion, Indian Ocean Maritime Africa now seems ready to better assume its Indian Ocean identity and connections. This can be successfully achieved by getting fully involved in the maritime affairs and activities of the Western Indian Ocean (marine resources exploitation and management, maritime safety and security, etc.), by capitalizing on being the oceanic doorway to a vast hinterland of 11 land-locked states (with an actual population of some 200 million, predicted to reach 800 million by the end of the 21st century), as well as by strengthening its economic, political and cultural relations with the other Indian Ocean states.

NOTES

1. Following the Indian Ocean Rim Initiative established in Mauritius on March 1995, the Indian Ocean Rim Association (IORA) was formally launched in March

1997 as the Indian Ocean Rim Association for Regional Cooperation (IOR-ARC). Its name was changed to IORA at the Association's 13th Meeting of the Council of Ministers that was held in Perth on November 1st, 2013.

2. These include the two inhabited islands of Mayotte and Réunion, as well as the uninhabited French Southern and Antarctic Lands' districts of Crozet, Kerguelen, Saint-Paul & Amsterdam and the Scattered Islands (Bassas da India atoll, Glorioso Islands, Juan de Nova Island, Europa Island, and Tromelin Island).
3. Which consist of the Chagos Archipelago and includes the atoll of Diego Garcia, well known for its American military base (U.S. Navy Support Facility Diego Garcia).
4. "In the context of the Declaration contained in General Assembly resolution 2832 (XXVI) of 16 December 1971, the Indian Ocean as a zone of peace should cover the Indian Ocean itself, its natural extensions, the islands thereon, the ocean floor subjacent thereto, the littoral and hinterland States and the air space above." (United Nations, 1979, Article 14)
5. Adaptation from Bouchard and Crumplin (2010) to include the land-locked state of South Sudan, which became independent from Sudan on July 9th, 2011.
6. The sovereignty of the Chagos Archipelago is being disputed between the UK and Mauritius. The archipelago was split from the Outer islands of Mauritius prior to Mauritian independence in 1965.
7. A list of all the submissions made to the Commission on the Limits of the Continental Shelf (CLCS), as well as the pertinent documentation for each case are available on the commission website at http://www.un.org/depts/los/clcs_new/clcs_home.htm.
8. Considering only the EEZ part of the Indian Ocean. The total area of EEZ claimed by Australia is 8.2 million square kilometres off Australia and its remote offshore territories, and 2 million square kilometres off the Australian Antarctic Territory (Geoscience Australia 2010).
9. Considering only the EEZ part of the Indian Ocean. The total area of EEZ claimed by Indonesia is 6.1 million square kilometres off the Indonesian archipelagic baselines (Sea Around Us Project 2013).
10. The lack of coastal states monitoring, control and surveillance capacities at sea are a main issue in the African Indian Ocean waters. However, coastal states have received some substantial aid from foreign powers to develop their capacities at sea. There are also important bilateral cooperations with other states on this matter, such as between Mauritius and India as well as Mauritius and France.
11. CTF-151's mission is to disrupt piracy and armed robbery at sea and to engage with regional and other partners to build capacity and improve relevant capabilities in order to protect global maritime commerce and secure freedom of navigation. It was established in January 2009 with a specific piracy mission-based mandate under the authority of UNSCRs 1816, 1838, 1846, 1851 and 1897. (source: http://combinedmaritimeforces.com/ctf-151-counter-piracy/)
12. Under the EU Council Joint Action, which is based on various UN resolutions, EU NAVFOR's mandate is to conduct: 1) the protection of World Food Programme (WFP) vessels delivering aid to displaced persons in Somalia, and the protection of African Union Mission in Somalia (AMISOM) shipping; 2) the deterrence,

prevention and repression of acts of piracy and armed robbery at sea off the Somali coast; 3) the protection of vulnerable shipping off the Somali coast on a case by case basis; and 4) some help in the monitoring of fishing activities off the coast of Somalia. On 23 March 2012 the Council of the EU extended the Mandate of Operation Atalanta until December 2014. At the same time, the Council also extended the Area of Operation to include Somali coastal territory and internal waters. (source: http://eunavfor.eu/)

13. As an example, a coral biodiversity hotspot has recently been identified and documented for the northern Mozambique Channel. See: Obura D (2012) "The diversity and biogeography of Western Indian Ocean reef-building corals", *PLoS ONE* 7(9); and Obura (2012) "Evolutionary mechanisms and diversity in a western Indian Ocean center of diversity", *Proceedings of the 12th International Coral Reef Symposium*, Cairns, Australia, 9-13 July 2012. According to Conservation International, the waters surrounding Madagascar and the Indian Ocean Islands represent one of world marine biodiversity hotspots (http://www.conservation.org).
14. The Nairobi Convention for the Protection, Management and Development of the Marine and Coastal Environment of the Eastern African Region was signed in 1985 and came into force in 1996, making it one of 17 regional seas conventions and action plans. The Convention was amended and adopted in April, 2010. (source: http://www.unep.org/nairobiconvention/)
15. The main objective of the Commission is to promote the sustainable utilization of the living marine resources of the South West Indian Ocean region, by the proper management and development of the living marine resources, without prejudice to the sovereign rights of coastal States and to address common problems of fisheries management and development faced by the Members of the Commission. (http://www.fao.org/fishery/rfb/swiofc/en)
16. The Indian Ocean Tuna Commission (IOTC) is an intergovernmental organization mandated to manage tuna and tuna-like species in the Indian Ocean and adjacent seas. Its objective is to promote cooperation among its Members with a view to ensuring, through appropriate management, the conservation and optimum utilisation of stocks and encouraging sustainable development of fisheries based on such stocks. (source: http://www.iotc.org/)
17. This means that while Sub-Saharan Africa only represented 7.6 % of the world's population in 1970, it is presently home to 12.0 % and it will likely expand throughout the coming century, reaching around 21.7 % in 2050 and, perhaps, 33.0 % in 2090.
18. According to the medium variant of the latest UN population projections (United Nations 2013), India's population is projected to be of 1 584 183 inhabitants in 2090 (United Nations 2013).
19. According to Shaw (2012, p. 839), "its burgeoning middle classes, both intra-continental and diasporic, have begun to attract appropriate attention: rising from 100 to 300 million over three decades. Baverez (2013) also speaks about the formation of a middle class of 300 million people, and adds that it will increase twofold by 2050 to 600 million peoples. Dörr*et al.* (2010) report that "the number of households with discretionary income is projected to grow 50 percent over the next 10 years to 128 millions. Already, Africa's household spending tops

$860 billion a year, more than that of India or Russia".

20. This is a region made up of four regional organizations, namely the Common Market for Eastern and Southern Africa (COMESA), East African Community (EAC), Intergovernmental Authority on Development (IGAD), and the Indian Ocean Commission (IOC).
21. According to Erasmus (2013), the Tripartite Free Trade Area (T-FTA) seems today to have deviated from its original intention and to be facing some new difficulties. SADC: Southern African Development Community.
22. Cited by Turok (2010, p.21).
23. Association formed by Brasil, Russia, India, China and South Africa.
24. South Africa's President Jacob Zuma hosted the Fifth BRICS Summit on 27 March 2013 in Durban under the theme "BRICS and Africa: Partnership for Development, Integration and Industrialisation". (source: http://www.brics5.co.za/)
25. Referring to UN DESA, 2008, *Overcoming Economic Insecurity: World Economic and Social Survey 2008*, p. xvi.
26. The Failed States Index is an annual ranking of 178 nations based on their levels of stability and the pressures they face. It is a composite measure built from 12 indicators of state vulnerability: demographic pressures, refugees and internally displaced persons (IDPs), group grievance, brain drain and human flight, uneven economic development, poverty and economic decline, state legitimacy, public services, human rights and rule of law, security apparatus, factionalised elites, and external intervention. The Failed States Index scores should be interpreted with the understanding that the lower the score, the better (FFP, 2013).

REFERENCES

Bevarez, N., 2013, "L'Afrique est bien partie", *Le Monde*, 3 April 2013, http://www.lemonde.fr/economie/article/2013/04/02/l-afrique-est-bien-partie_3151910_3234.html (July 2013).

Bouchard, C., 2007, "Maritime affairs in the Mozambique Channel" in Rumley, D., Chaturvedi, S. and M.T. Yasin, *The security of sea lanes of communication in the Indian Ocean Region*. Kuala Lumpur (Malaysia): Maritime Institute of Malaysia, chapter 5, pp. 73-92.

Bouchard, C. and W. Crumplin, 2010, "Neglected no longer: the Indian Ocean at the forefront of world geopolitics and global geostrategy", *Journal of the Indian Ocean Region*, Vol. 6, No. 1, pp. 26-51.

Bouchard, C. and W. Crumplin, 2011, "Two faces of France: France of the Indian Ocean/France in the Indian Ocean", *Journal of the Indian Ocean Region*, Vol. 7, No. 2, pp. 161-182.

Brunel, S., 2011, "L'Afrique est-elle bien partie?", *Sciences humaines*, Mensuel No. 225 (avril 2011), Rubrique "Comprendre", http://www.scienceshumaines.com/l-afrique-est-elle-bien-partie-sylvie-brunel_fr_26981.html (July 2013).

CIA, 2013, *The World Factbook*. Washington DC (United States): The Central Intelligence Agency, https://www.cia.gov/library/publications/the-world-factbook/index.html (July 2013).

Devarajan, S. and W. Fengler, 2013, "Africa's Economic Boom", *Foreign Affairs*,

Vol. 92, Issue 3 (May/Jun2013), pp. 68-81.

Dörr, N., Lund S. & C. Roxburgh, 2010, "The African miracle", *Foreign Policy*, December 2010, pp. 80-81.

Erasmus, G., 2013, *Redirecting the Tripartite Free Trade Agreement negotiations*, Stellenbosch (South Africa): Trade Law Centre (Tralac), Trade Brief No. S13TB02/2013, 11 p.

Evans, P., 2013, "Tullow's East Africa Rift Basin Campaign in Uganda and Kenya". London (UK): The Geological Society and Finding Petroleum, Finding big oil fields in East Africa Forum, 9 April 2013, 30 slides ,http://www.findingpetroleum.com/event/Finding_big_oil_fields_in_East_Africa/678b0.aspx (July 2013).

FFP, 2013, *Failed States Index 2013*. Washington (D.C.): The Fund for Peace, 39 p.

Fiorina, J.-F., 2013, *L'Afrique convoitée: Entre coopération et prédation, un continent "sous influence"*. Grenoble (France): ESC Grenoble, École de Management, *CLES-Comprendre Les Enjeux Stratégiques*, Note hebdomadaire n°102, 28 mars 2013, 3 p.

Geoscience Australia, 2010, "Oceans and Seas". Canberra (Australia): Geoscience Australia, http://www.ga.gov.au/education/geoscience-basics/dimensions/oceans-and-seas.html (July 2013).

HIIK, 2008, *Conflict Barometer 2008*. Heidelberg (Germany): Heidelberg Institute for International Conflict Research, 80 p.

HIIK, 2014, *Conflict Barometer 2013*. Heidelberg (Germany): Heidelberg Institute for International Conflict Research, 149 p.

Hughes, J., 2011, *The Piracy-Illegal Fishing Nexus in the Western Indian Ocean*, Nedlands (Australia): Future Directions International, Strategic Analysis Paper, 6 p. http://www.futuredirections.org.au/ (July 2013).

IHO, 2002, *Names and Limits of Oceans and Seas*, Final Draft Fourth Edition. Monaco: International Hydrographic Bureau, 10 chapters + appendixes.

IMB, 2013, "Piracy and Armed Robbery Map 2013". Kuala Lumpur (Malaysia): International Maritime Bureau Piracy Reporting Centre,http://www.icc-ccs.org/piracy-reporting-centre/live-piracy-map/piracy-map-2013 (May 2014).

IMB, 2014a, "Piracy and Armed Robbery Map 2014". Kuala Lumpur (Malaysia): International Maritime Bureau Piracy Reporting Centre, http://www.icc-ccs.org/piracy-reporting-centre/live-piracy-map (May 2014).

IMB, 2014b, *ICC IMB Piracy and Armed Robbery Against Ships – 2013 Annual Report*. London (UK): ICC International Maritime Bureau,75 p.

Lehr, P., 2013, "Piracy and maritime governance in the Indian Ocean", *Journal of the Indian Ocean Region*, Vol. 9, No. 1, pp. 104-119.

Luke, L. G., 2013, "EU, Australia, New Zealand Continue Anti-Piracy Efforts as Number of Incidents Falls". Nedlands (Australia): Future Directions International, 29 May 2013, http://www.futuredirections.org.au/ (July 2013).

Mair, P., 2012, "A New Frontier-Oil and Gas in East Africa', London (UK): Control Risks Group Limited, 16 p. http://www.controlrisks.com/Oversized%20assets/east_africa_whitepaper_LR_web.pdf (July 2013).

OPB, 2014, *The State of Maritime Piracy 2013*. Broomfield (Colorado): One Earth Future Foundation, Oceans Beyond Piracy, 115 p. [inc. Preface and Appendixes]

Potgieter, T. and C. Schofield, 2010, "Poverty, poaching and pirates: geopolitical instability and maritime insecurity off the Horn of Africa", *Journal of the Indian Ocean Region*, Vol. 6, No. 1, pp. 86-112.

PRB, 2012, *2012 World Population Data Sheet*. Washington (USA): Population Reference Bureau, 20 p.

Rumley, Dennis (Ed.), 2013, *The Indian Ocean Region: Security, Stability and Sustainability in the 21st Century*. Melbourne (Australia): The Australia India Institute, Task Force on Indian Ocean Security, 128 p.

Samoilys, M., Dominque, G., Kariuki, J., Payet, R., Hersi, A. and A. Mohammed, 2007, *Application of the PROFISH Global List of irresponsible fishing vessels as a tool to combat Illegal Unregulated and Unreported Fishing in Eastern Africa*. Nairboi (Kenya): The World Conservation Union (IUCN), 25p.

Scholvin S. and P. Draper, 2012, "The gateway to Africa: Geography and South Africa's role as an economic hinge joint between Africa and the world". *South African Journal of International Affairs*, Vol. 19, No. 3, pp. 381-400.

Sea Around Us Project, 2013, "Exclusive Economic Zone (EEZ)". Vancouver (Canada): Fisheries Centre, Aquatic Ecosystems Research Laboratory, University of British Columbia, http://www.seaaroundus.org/eez/ (July 2013).

Shaw, Timothy M., 2012, "Africa's Quest for Developmental States: 'renaissance' for whom?", *Third World Quarterly*, Vol. 33, No. 5, pp. 837-851.

Southall R.J. and H. Melber (eds.), 2009, *A new scramble for Africa: Imperialism, Investment and Development*. Scottsville (South Africa): University of KwaZulu-Natal Press, 440 p.

The Economist, 2011, "The hopeful continent: Africa rising", *The Economist*, 3 December 2011 (From the print edition), http://www.economist.com/node/21541015 (July 2013).

Trueblood, S., 2013, "Inhassoro: the southernmost oil field in the East African rift system" London (UK): The Geological Society and Finding Petroleum, Finding big oil fields in East Africa Forum, 9 April 2013, 14 slides, http://www.findingpetroleum.com/event/Finding_big_oil_fields_in_East_Africa/678b0.aspx (July 2013).

Turok, I., 2010, "The prospects for African urban economies", *Urban Research & Practice*, Vol. 3, No. 1, pp. 12-24.

UNEP, 2004, *Regional Profile: Eastern Africa Region*, New York (USA): United Nations Environment Programme, Regional Seas Programme, http://www.unep.org/regionalseas/programmes/unpro/easternafrica/instruments/r_profile_eaf.pdf (May 2014).

UNEP/Nairobi Convention Secretariat, CSIR and WIOMSA, 2009, *Regional Synthesis Report on the Status of Pollution in the Western Indian Ocean Region*. Nairobi (Kenya): United Nations Environment Programme, Nairobi Convention Secretariat, 116 p.

UNDP, 2013, *Human Development Report 2013, the Rise of the South: Human Progress in a Diverse World*. New York (United States): United Nations Development Programme, 203 p.

UNECA, 2011, *Economic Report on Africa 2011: Governing development in Africa - the role of the state in economic transformation*. Addis Abeba (Ethiopia): United

Nations Economic Commission for Africa, 130 p.

UNECA, 2012, *The MDG Report 2013: Assessing progress in Africa toward the Millennium Development Goals*. New York (USA): United Nations Economic Commission for Africa, 124 p.

UNECA, 2013, *The MDG Report 2013: Assessing progress in Africa toward the Millennium Development Goals*. New York (USA): United Nations Economic Commission for Africa, 124 p.

United Nations, 1979, *Report of the Meeting of the Littoral and Hinterland States of the Indian Ocean*. New York (USA): United Nations, General Assembly, Supplement No. 45 (A/34/45), 18 p.

United Nations, 2012, *World Urbanization Prospects, the 2011 Revision*. New York (USA): Population Division of the Department of Economic and Social Affairs of the United Nations Secretariat, http://esa.un.org/unup/ (July 2013).

United Nations, 2013, *World Population Prospects: The 2012 Revision*. New York (United States): Population Division of the Department of Economic and Social Affairs of the United Nations Secretariat, http://esa.un.org/unpd/wpp/index.htm (July 2013).

U.S.E.I.A., 2013, *Emerging East Africa Energy*. Washington (USA): U.S. Energy Information Administration, http://www.eia.gov/countries/regions-topics.cfm?fips=EEAE(July 2013).

Winner, A.C., Schneider, P. And A.T. Weldemichael (eds.), 2012, "Maritime terrorism and piracy in the Indian Ocean Region", *Journal of the Indian Ocean Region*, Special issue on Maritime terrorism and piracy in the Indian Ocean Region, Vol. 8, No. 2, pp. 109-218.

World Bank, 2009, *World Development Report 2009, Reshaping Economic Geography*. Washington (USA): The World Bank, 383 p.

World Bank, 2011, *Africa's Future and the World Bank's Support to It*. Washington (USA): The World Bank, 37 p.

World Bank, 2013a, Africa Development Indicators 2012/13. Washington (USA): The World Bank, 198 p.

World Bank, 2013b, *World DataBank*. Washington (USA): The World Bank, http://databank.worldbank.org/data/home.aspx (July 2013).

World Bank, 2013c, *Africa's Pulse: An analysis of issues shaping Africa's economic future*. Washington (USA): The World Bank, Vol. 8 (October 2013), 36 p.

Ye, Y., 2011, "Western Indian Ocean - FAO Statistical Area 51". In FAO, *Review of the state of world marine fishery resources*. Rome (Italy): Food and Agriculture Organization of the United Nations, FAO Fisheries and Aquaculture Department, chapter B8, pp. 121-132.

Chapter 3

Infrastructure and Influence: China's Presence on the Coast of East Africa

Ross Anthony

ABSTRACT

This chapter interrogates the notion that China's proposed development of ports and supporting hinterland infrastructure on the east coast of Africa serves greater geostrategic interests within Africa and the Indian Ocean Region. It cautions against a trend which renders Chinese commercial infrastructural and resource development as symmetrical with an almost colonial-like political influence. Through a comparison with 19th Century German and British colonialism in the Region, the chapter argues that, while there are certain affinities, the Chinese presence today is significantly different. Central to the argument is that Chinese port and hinterland developments are supplemented by a host of other actors, including host states, multinational corporations and regional development funds. These differences can be situated not only within the context of a post-colonial African sovereignty but also within a broader market economic system in which African states, China and other actors operate. This hybrid infrastructural development has implications for future regional security. The Chinese presence has been over-articulated at the expense of other actors and thus in any future conflict, it cannot be assumed that China will be able to mobilize its infrastructural activities in its interests. This has implications for the broader analysis of China's growing presence in the Indian Ocean.

Key words: China, East Africa, ports, infrastructure, colonialism, market economy, geopolitics

The Setting

Over the past decade, trade between China and Africa has been stratospheric, rising from $6.5 (US) billion in 2004 to an estimated $200 (US) billion in 2013 (*Xinhua* 2013). The lion's share of this trade entails the extraction of natural resources to China and machinery, textiles, chemicals and electronic goods into Africa. Chinese mineral extraction, which adds little value to African economies, is off-set with massive infrastructure projects carried out primarily by Chinese State Owned Enterprises (SOE). These include the construction of schools, hospitals and stadiums but also roads, railways, ports and pipelines, which, while enabling African states to increase their communication and trade capacities, also increase Chinese companies' ability to transport resources from the hinterland to the Ocean. A major reason for a recent surge in Chinese interest in East Africa is that the region has become a hot-spot for natural resource extraction with significant finds of oil, gas and coal. While it has been known for several decades that oil and gas are located in the region (Clarke 2008, p. 322), up until the early 2000s, exploration in "frontier" regions such as East Africa proved economically unviable, due to its geological complexity and political instability.

This has dramatically changed in recent years. The rise in global oil prices has offered increasingly lucrative rewards to companies willing to invest in the region, with substantial oil and gas discoveries in Ethiopia, Tanzania, Kenya, Mozambique, Uganda and Somalia.[1] Chinese companies are involved in a number of different projects, either in the production of oil and gas or in its supporting infrastructure. In Uganda, the Chinese National Offshore Corporation (CNOOC) is involved in oil extraction in Albertine Basin on the border of Uganda and the DRC; on the borders of South Sudan, the China National Petroleum Corporation (CNPC) has numerous operations. They are also involved in gas exploration in the Ogaden region of Ethiopia. Sichuan Hongda, a large Chinese conglomerate, signed a $3 billion (US) deal with Tanzania in 2011 for a project involving the construction of Mchuchuma coal mine, a 600-metawatt thermal power station and the Liganga iron ore mine in southern Tanzania (*Africa-Asia Confidential* 2013, p. 7).

The parallel rise of a Chinese infrastructural presence on the east coast of Africa is striking. In Kenya, the China Communications Construction Company (CCCC) has recently won a bid to develop the first three births at Lamu, where a new port is being constructed (which plans to be expanded to 32 berths). In 2012, CCCC also signed a $2.66 (US) billion deal to update Kenya's railways, announcing plans to construct a standard-gauged 479 km line between Mombasa and Nairobi (Jorgic 2013). In 2011, a $66.7 (US) million dollar deal was brokered to expand a number of berths at Mombasa, East Africa's largest port (Ibid.). In Tanzania, Chinese President Xi Jinping's visit to the country in March 2013 signalled the go-ahead for the Chinese financing of a $10 (US) billion port at Bagamoyo, due for completion in 2017. The port will be able to handle twenty times more cargo than the current port at Dear es Salaam (20 million containers per year as opposed to Dar es Salaam's 800 000) (Balile 2013).

Such ports do not only have the potential to serve Chinese security interests within the Indian Ocean but also to serve as, "a knot where ocean and inland transport lines meet and intertwine" (Weigend 1958 in Notteboom 2000). Ports serve as part of a much vaster network, ranging from roads, rail and pipelines in the host country to shipping and Sea Lines of Communication (SLOC) of the Indian Ocean to, ultimately, in our present context, to the refineries of China itself. From this holistic perspective, every link in the chain is as crucial as the next in terms of the movement of commodities from China to Africa. With regard to the East African context, Chinese firms are engaged in the construction of various land linkages to the ports they are constructing. In Lamu, the same company responsible for the port construction, China Road and Bridge Company (CRBC), a subsidiary of CCCC, is engaged in a $1.147 (US) billion dollar project to construct a Mombasa-Nairobi Railway. Tanzania has also been granted a soft loan of $39.9 (US) million by China to upgrade the Tanzania and Zambia Railways Authority (TAZARA) line which was originally constructed by China in the 1970s. There are also a number of other plans under consideration, including a $1.5 billion project to build a road which will connect northern Ethiopia with the port of Tadjurah Djibouti. In Tanzania, the state-owned giant CNPC is involved in the construction of a 500 km 1.2 billion (US) dollar pipeline which will transport Tanzania's gas from Mtwara to Dar-es-Salam.

Geostrategic Anxieties

From a geostrategic point of view, these East African port developments can be situated within the context of the greater Indian Ocean, in which they ports are but two of a much vaster array of Chinese infrastructural activity stretching from Africa to Myanmar. Christopher Peherson (and many others) has referred to this phenomenon as a 'string of pearls', in which each pearl functions as 'a nexus of Chinese geopolitical influence or military presence' (2006, p.3). This influence manifests itself in the form of various infrastructure projects in littoral regions stretching from the South China Sea to the African coast. Writing in 2006, Peherson includes as pearls military facilities on Hainan Island (a part of mainland China, some 20km south of Guangdong province), an upgraded airstrip on Woody Island in the Parcel archipelago, the construction of a deep water port at Sittwe, Myanmar, a shipping container facility in Chittagong, Bangladesh and the construction of a port in Gwadar. Pakistan (Ibid.).

Since this 2006 article, an array of potentially new 'pearls' have been added to the list. Sri Lanka's Hambantota Port is under construction by two Chinese SOEs, China Harbour Engineering Company and Sinoydro Corporation, costing over $400 (US) million dollars. A second phase of construction, costing $750 (US) million, is set to be completed by 2014 (*Portworld News* 2010). Additionally, the same two companies will be responsible for the expansion of Colombo South Harbour (*Sri Lankan Ports Authority* 2012). Further west, Chinese companies have been recently awarded an 879 million dollar contract to carry out work on the New Doha Port project in Quatar, including the construction of an 8km quay wall (Broomhall 2011). Port Sudan has undergone a $79 (US) million dollar upgrade, including a deepening of ports by the Chinese Engineering Works company, in order to better facilitate the shipment of oil from the Sudanese interior (*Sudan Tribune* 2006). In the vein of Peherson's argument, the ports in Tanzania and Kenya serve as a further extension of Chinese influence across the Indian Ocean.

This nexus of infrastructure and resource extraction has raised concerns among other Indian Ocean Powers (Hyung 2002; French and Chambers 2010). At a geo-strategic level, it has been anticipated that such influence will increasingly threaten the United States and its international partners (including India, Australia, Singapore, Japan

France and Canada) who have traditionally enjoyed command over the region (Berlin 2010, p. 52). One of the main drivers for maintaining the *status quo* has to do with resources, particularly in the Middle East region, where the United States possesses unfettered access to oil reserves. China, which, since 1993, has been a net importer of oil, increasingly requires access to foreign energy supplies in order to sustain its own rapid development. More imminently, it has been argued that India, who, due to its geographical positioning, has long held significant influence in the Indian Ocean, will increasingly face the risk of conflict with China (Kaplan 2010; Kumar 2009). Thus, it is anticipated that China will seek greater influence in the Indian Ocean while the United States and her allies will resist this rise.

The increased presence of the Chinese in the Indian Ocean Region and in Africa has generated elements of an alarmist discourse within the Euro-American sphere, permeating media, think-tanks and policy making circles. A common critique of Chinese infrastructure projects in Africa asserts that benefits for local communities are merely secondary to the swift removal of natural resources and the opening up of hinterland African markets to Chinese capital (Carmody and Owusu 2007, p. 507). There is frequently a tendency to associate this presence with the label of 'colonialism' or 'neo-colonialism'. To take an extreme example, the UK's *Daily Mail* in 2008 published an article entitled: "How China's taking over Africa and why the West should be VERY worried"; the article alleges that China plans to send 300 million Chinese to Africa to ease its domestic population (Malone 2008). On US Secretary of State Hillary Clinton's visit to Africa in 2012, in a comment widely believed to be pointed at China, she stated: "The days of having outsiders come and extract the wealth of Africa for themselves, leaving nothing or very little behind, should be over in the 21st Century" (Polgreen 2012). This logic of China's rise in Africa has extended into debates regarding Chinese influence in the Indian Ocean itself. David Scott refers to the economic and political rivalry between India and China as the 21st Century equivalent of the 'great game' whose contending sphere of influence includes the littoral states of the Eastern Indian Ocean (2008, p. 2).

Actually Existing Colonialism

As with the Chinese presence today, colonial impact upon coastal regions transformed not only the foreland but also the hinterland, while port forelands were influenced by maritime transport technology and maritime trading networks (Airriess 1995, p. 66). In the early colonial period, in fifteenth century West Africa, there was little attempt by Europeans to penetrate inland, with only the Senegal and Gambia Rivers offering limited movement into the interior (1969, p. 367). Penetration into the hinterland, however, was only properly realized in the later, more systematic, period of colonial control. A key element in the construction of ports and hinterland infrastructure within the colonial period was the fact that these powers were competing against each other in terms of geopolitical influence. Thus, the 'scramble for Africa' entailed various European states vying for a broader influence on the African continent. The penetration of the hinterland through road and rail was crucial to this enterprise. In West Africain the 19th Century for instance, the British hastily initiated an 1898 railway into the interior of Sierra Leone so as to combat the French, who had already made significant in-ways into the interior (Hilling 1969, p. 369).

Economic reasons for such infrastructure were also crucial. In response to accusations of colonial-like activity, it is instructive to compare China's current East African activities with those of the German and British annexation of East Africa in the 19th and early 20th centuries. By the late 19th century, improved transportation into the hinterland facilitated an equal improvement in commercial activity (Ibid.). This contributed to both Britain and Germany acquiring vast swathes of East Africa. Britain acquired the East Asian Protectorate (also referred to as British East Africa) which became the colony of Kenya in 1920. The inception of German East Africa, comprising of Burundi, Rwanda and Tanganyika (the mainland of present-day Tanzania), began in 1885 when the German government announced it had given an imperial charter to the German East Africa Company to establish a protectorate. The tropical belt allowed the cultivation of coffee, rubber, sisal, cotton and copra. The interior highlands were to be opened to sheep farming, cattle ranching and ostrich farming, which would employ native labour and be carried out by colonial settlers; there was also the anticipation of gold and mica mining (Brode 1911, p. 146).

As in various other colonial enterprises of the period, economic exploitation of the two regions was orchestrated by means of chartered companies—the German East Africa Company (Deutsch-Ostafrikanische Gesellschaft) and the Imperial British East Africa Company (IBEAC) respectively. While chartered companies comprised of a number of investors and shareholders, they were effectively economic arms of the state, bestowed with extraordinary powers. The IBEAC, for instance, granted immunity to British subjects and had the power to raise taxes, impose custom duties and act as a government within a colonized area. The governments offered financial assistance to these companies when ventures ran into trouble or re-assigned the work to companies closely aligned with the state.

Key to the flow of resources was the development of sound infrastructure which could get goods from the hinterland to Europe. Thus, an extensive infrastructure of ports, roads and railways was implemented in both territories. The British used the historical port of Mombasa as the terminus for the Uganda Railway, completed in 1896 and stretching over 1000 kilometres to Kisumu on the East shore of Lake Victoria. The German authorities selected three ports—Tanga, Dar es Salaam and Kilwa as key ports. The three ports were to serve as rail terminals which would connect with the hinterlands of Kilimanjaro, Lake Tanganyika and Lake Malawi respectively (Hoyle and Charlier 1995, p. 92). In 1893, the Eisenbahn-Gesellschaft für Deutsch-Ostafrika (Railway Company for German East Africa) began construction of the Usambara Railway, beginning in Tanga, the most northerly port in Tanzania, with the eventual intention of reaching Lake Victoria (although it only ever reached the Kenyan border town of Moshi). The Dar es Salaam line which was the most prominent, reaching Kigoma at Lake Tanganyika, covered over 12000 Kilometres, and was completed in 1914, just prior to World War One. The third of these lines was in fact never built (although it was later actualized in the form of the Chinese development of the TANZARA railway). Both British and the German rail lines connected the ports with two of the largest of the Great Lakes of Central Africa, Lake Victoria and Lake Tanganyika respectively. These links allowed for the launching of vessels onto the lakes to further both the interests of commerce and expand spheres of influence of the two imperial powers deeper within the African continent.

Sovereignty and 'non interference'

The most prominent factor which divides colonial era port and hinterland developments from those of today has to do with a massive shift in international norms regarding questions of global sovereignty. From a 19th century jurisprudence perspective, European countries were sovereign states while "uninhabited" regions in Africa, South America and Asia were 'non-sovereign entities' thus lacking 'the legal personality to assert any opposition' (Anghie 1999, p. 3). This gave powerful European states free reign to enter these regions with military backing. Additionally, these regions then became, in effect, extensions of these nation-states, with the imposition of foreign political, legal and economic frameworks. This acknowledgement of African sovereignty is one of the key-stones of China's current foreign policy, embodied in the notion of 'non-interference'. Chinese officials often like to highlight the fact that, unlike European countries, China has never attempted to colonize Africa, with its officials often making claims such as 'China has never interfered in the internal affairs of African Countries' (Taylor 2006a, p 89; *Capital Eritrea* 2010). Rather, China has, since the 1950s, viewed itself as a champion of anti-hegemonic struggle in Africa—and its current presence on the continent is viewed by some as an extension of that (Taylor 2006).

This stance is reflected in China's current military presence in the region, which, while growing to some degree, is still relatively weak, and by no means echoes the imperial deployment of force, or even contemporary Euro-American force, for that matter. Despite former president Hu Jintao expressing his wish for China to become a 'blue water' power (Erickson 2008, p. 656) its presence in the Indian Ocean and African coast is still modest. This is particularly so when contrasting the Chinese presence to that of the United States, with military bases in Djibouti (Camp Lemonnier) and Diego Garcia, as well as its United States African Command (AFRICOM), responsible for military operations in 53 African countries. Chinese UN peacekeepers have since the 1990s been stationed in Liberia, Western Sahara, Sudan and the Democratic Republic of Congo and have, in 2013, committed combat troops to Mali. They have additionally been involved in international anti-piracy operations off the coast of Somalia (Shinn 2009) and in 2011, a Chinese naval frigate aided in the evacuation of 35,000 Chinese During the Libyan civil war. Since 2010, Chinese naval ships have been making frequent port calls in the Seychelles. The Seychelles government has announced that it will provide resupply facilities for Chinese naval ships operating in the Indian Ocean (Mohan 2012). Yet despite this presence, naval analysts have noted that China still lacks the equipment, trained personnel and experience to orchestrate ocean surveillance and the long-range Sea Lanes of Control (SLOC) defence missions necessary to safeguard its interests in the region (Erickson 2008, p. 670).

Certainly, China has responded resolutely to claims that its economic engagements serve grander purposes. For instance, Chinese Defence Spokesman, Yang Yujin has commented with regard to its construction of the Bagamoyo port in Tanzania:

> The port in the Tanzanian town of Bagamoyo is a Sino-Tanzanian joint business project and any attempt to hype up its military purpose is meaningless … The project serves the shared interests of both peoples and is conducive to regional prosperity and development. (*The Economic Times* 2013).

This has been reiterated in China's port presence in Bangladesh, where its Ambassador in Dhaka stated in 2012 that the development is based solely on a 'business reason' and 'not for military use' (*Financial Express* 2012). This is part of a broader official discourse which refutes accusations of colonial resource grabbing (*China Daily* 2012). Such denials are part and parcel of the official Chinese line that its global economic rise will be one of 'friendship', "co-operation", 'harmonious relations' and, particularly in Africa, a 'win-win' situation.

Colonial Economics?

In Eric Hobsbwam's *The age of empire* (1875-1914), he argues that "overseas economic expansion and the exploitation of the overseas world were crucial for capitalist countries" (1987, p. 61). One of the primary similarities when contrasting this historical episode with contemporary Chinese activities is the fact that resources play a key role. In both instances, the condensing of space through port infrastructure and its hinterland connections is key for the swift movement of commodities out of the region. More specifically, it is striking that in both instances there is the deployment of large, powerful corporations with very tight relations to the state, that carry out the infrastructure projects. Just the European chartered companies contributed to such developments so, today, do China's State Owned Enterprises (SOEs). Across Africa a vast array of Chinese SOEs are involved in Africa, including the National Oil Companies (NOCs)— CNOOC, CNPC and Sinopec—as well as Sino-Hydro, China Railway Engineering Corporation (CREC) and China Holdings Company COSCO, the shipping and logistics firm.

Western firms, with long held undisputed command over international financial resources and influence in Africa, are being increasingly challenged by China's SOEs. Like other countries' SOEs, such as South Africa's Eskom or France's Elf-Aquitaine, these corporations' financial interests frequently overlap with state interests (Davies and Alden 200, p. 84). Many of the construction projects in Africa are financed by state development banks such as China-Export-Import Bank (Exim Bank) and China Development Bank (CDB). The banks frequently finance their own companies directly to carry out projects, without the money going into the bank accounts of the host governments (Brautigam 2009, p. 142). In strategic industries such as oil, the Chinese government has overtly engaged in a 'charm offensive' with oil-rich African states. Using its NOCs as a vehicle for this policy, the intention is to help feed growing domestic demand in China and in the long-term, position China as a global player in the international oil market (Taylor 2006b). Amongst China's oil SOEs, CEOs are engaged in a revolving door policy, in which they move from government to industry positions and vice-versa (Downes and Meidan 2011, p. 15).[2]

Official Chinese views on Africa appear to support its SOE's drive to link Africanports and hinterlands. This is reflected in the promotion of regionalism in official documentation. During the 'Fifth Ministerial Conference of the Forum on China-Africa Co-operation' (FOCAC)— a tri-annual official forum between the PRC and African states— its 'Beijing Action Plan' claims that its $600 million (US) funding of the new African Union headquarters shows China's firm support for African integration and Africa's self-enhancement through unity. The document continues that:

> The Chinese government will continue to encourage capable Chinese enterprises and financial institutions to participate in transnational and trans-regional infrastructure construction in Africa and provide preferential loans to support infrastructure building in Africa (*FOCAC* 2012).

In an interview with Mr Wang Chaowen, general director of the government mouthpiece Xinhua News Agency African Bureau, he stated:

> More and more African countries are now aware that one's power is limited when acting alone, and their synergy and regional advantage should be leveraged. They come to know that regional integration through substantive mutually complementary cooperation is the way forward (*Xinhua* 2012).

Within the context of the East African coast, the state owned enterprises involved in the construction of the ports are equally engaged in infrastructure projects linking these ports to the hinterland. CCCC, the conglomerate responsible for the construction of Port Lamu in Kenya, is one example. Not only is it building the port but is also involved in the road and rail projects which will link the ports of Kenyan to its interior and beyond. China Road and Bridge Company (CRBC), a subsidiary of CCCC will be carrying out a $1.147 billion (US) rail connection between Mobassa and Nairobi as well as the $1.5 billion (US) project to build a road which will connect northern Ethiopia with the port of Tadjurah Djibouti. In 2008, almost half the country's $9.6 billion (US) overseas revenue came from projects in Africa (Xinhua 2009). In terms of a greater Indian Ocean presence, such companies are equally relevant. CCCC, is one of the contractors for the port development at Hambantota in Sri Lanka, while China Merchants Group, the SOE responsible for the construction of the Bagamoyo port, is involved in the $879 million (US) construction of the New Doha Port project in Qatar, the rehabilitation of Port Sudan, and the development of the Sri Lankan Port of Colombo.

Africa's Vision of Integration

The deployment of large state companies to enhance coastal-hinterland infrastructure in East Africa so as to increase the flow of resources back to Beijing, appears to have echoes of neo-colonialism—a situation in which a powerful country dominates another primarily through economic power. A central problem with this thesis, however, is the fact that African states and regional bodies, rather than being merely passive recipients of such activity, are equally active promoters of such a project. At the 21st African Union (AU) Summit in Addis Ababa in 2013, a 'Solemn Declaration' was declared to 'Speedily implement the Continental Free Trade Area; ensure free movement of goods, with focus on integrating local and regional markets' (*African Union* 2013). The president of the African Development Bank stated at the African Union Commission during the same event that, 'We have to ensure that in this process of economic integration there is greater solidarity' (Jobson 2013). In March of 2012, then Kenyan president Mwai Kibaki, Ethiopian Prime Minister Meles Zenawi and South Sudan's president, Salva Kiir, jointly launched LAPSETT (Lamu Port and Southern Sudan-Ethiopia Transport Corridor), a $25.5 billion (US) dollar project which seeks to link landlocked South Sudan and Ethiopia to the Indian Ocean (Tekle 2012).

The Kenya Vision 2030, which charters government plans for LAPSETT, states that the project aims for 'competitiveness in global maritime trade'; "promotion of international trade" and to 'link East and Central African region to the international markets' (*Kenya Vision* 2030 2012). In this regard, the Chinese developments of Lamu and surrounding road and rail are only part of a much vaster regional vision which anticipates some of the following: two pipelines connecting Ugandan and South Sudanese oilfields to Port Lamu (Bosire 2013); an oil refinery, producing 120 000 barrels per day (Kenya Vision 2030); an 800 km road connecting Port Lamu to Lokichoggio in Ethiopia (Tekle 2012); a 750 km railway linking Juba to Gulu and Tororo (Okoth 2010) and a 400 kilometre power transmission line, running from Rabai to Port Lamu (Liloba 2012).

Multiple Players

The geographer David Harvey has argued that in today's market economy, greater openness to global capital flows "put pressures on all states to look to the quality of their business climate as a crucial condition for their competitive success" (2005, p. 92). It is this context in which we must situate China's contemporary business engagements in Africa. Within this context, African states, traditional Western powers and China (as well as states such as India, Brazil, Malaysia and others), all contend for a share of growing African markets. These companies are primarily interested in making profits. China's SOEs not only have to engage with global competitors but also compete with *each other* for tenders. In some respects, China's economically-driven 'go global' initiative has been so successful that it has undermined Beijing's ability to keep tight control over its SOE's, not to mention private Chinese multi-nationals, such as ZTE, Huawei and Haixin (Taylor 2012, p. 34; Gu 2009). Contemporary SOEs in many respects function primarily as multi-national, profit-making machines. As Fu Yuning, CEO of China Merchants Group (CMG), the company constructing the Port Lamu harbour, as well those in Colombo and Sri Lanka, recently stated:

> We have demonstrated over the last 30 years that a state-owned [enterprise] can adopt market practices, can effectively compete in the commercial market by serving the market and bringing returns to the shareholders (*Forbes* 2013).

Silvester Kasuku, chief executive of LAPSSET, states in relation to the Chinese construction of the first three berths at Port Lamu:

> We are doing the seed investment by constructing the first three berths just to break the ground and put government commitment and investment and provide incentives for private sector investors to come on board (Jorgic 2013).

Former Kenyan president Mwi Kibaki has openly appealed for trade partners, on a global scale, to participate in the projects, including Korea (one of Kenya's major trading partners); a Japanese company—Japan Port Consultants—was awarded the tender to carry out a feasibility study on the port (Kimani 2010). The Dutch company, Van Oord Dredging and Marine Contractors, has carried out a $62 million (US) contract in Port Mombasa, which was slated to be complete by the end of 2012 (*Kenya Ports Authority* 2012). The road linking Lamu and Mombasa to Ethiopia is co-financed by the African Development Bank (ADB), the European Union (EU) and the governments of Kenya and Ethiopia (Ibid.). The Development Bank of Southern Africa (DBSA) has expressed interest in contributing as much as $1.5 billion (US) towards the LAPSSET project (Jorgic 2013) and the Canadian firm CPCS Transcom has made a comprehensive study of the revamping of Tanzania's Central Line (Sumila 2012).

This economic primacy, in which China is but one of many global players looking to expand into Africa, entails that Chinese infrastructure projects are increasingly hybrid in nature insofar as they are often done in conjunction with a host of non-Chinese actors. This is increasingly true for the East African extractive landscape as a whole. Infrastructural underdevelopment in the region is obliging Chinese companies to engage on the continent in new ways including the rise of joint Chinese-Euro-American ventures. China has to compete with over 50 other energy firms currently involved in East Africa including Norway's Statoil, British Gas and Cove Energy (UK); America's ExxonMobil; France's Total; Italy's ENI, India's GAIL and ONGC and Thailand's PTTEP . Rather than dominating the field, Chinese state firms are involved in disparate and complimentary ways. [3] For instance, while CNPC is involved in the construction of a pipeline which will transport Tanzania's gas from Mtwara to Dar es Salaam, the actual extraction and production of the gas is carried out by a public-private partnership involving Tanzania Electric Supply Company (Tanesco) and the US companies, Symbion Power and General Electric (Daily News 7 July 2013). Upstream gas extraction is dominated by multi-nationals such as Statoil (Norway) and ExxonMobil (US).

In Uganda's Lake Albert region, China is involved in a joint, multi-national venture in which CNOOC holds a one-third stake, along with Tullow and France's Total, in the development of oil blocks within the region where reserves are estimated to be at around 2.4 billion barrels. A pre-cursor in this regard is the construction of Sudan's 1600km Greater Nile Oil Pipeline (GNOP), which involved Indian, Malaysian and Chinese companies (the latter of which, China National Petroleum Corporation, owns a 40 per cent stake in the operation as well as managing the operating of the pipeline).

Chinese companies have shown economic practicality in their African infrastructural projects. For instance, while there was an initial expectation that China would construct an oil pipeline connecting South Sudan to Port Lamu, the Chinese have now declined to carry out the project. One of the reasons is because CNPC has already constructed—and operate—three pipelines within Sudan which carries the very same oil deposits to Port Sudan. Juba wants to construct the new pipeline so as to counter its reliance on its long-time adversary, Sudan. A Japanese company, Toyota Rshusho, has already supplied feasibility studies and is in talks with various Japanese Banks that are now interested in financing the project (Africa-Asia Confidential 2013, p. 6).

While critics of China argue that the lion's share of commodities extracted in Africa are sent back to China, there is evidence to the contrary. In the case of East Africa, we see an increasingly interconnected picture in which China's National Oil Companies (NOCs) compete with an array of other companies. Erica S. Downs points out that the Chinese presence in the African oil market expands, rather than contracts the amount of oil available on global markets. Rather than having a tightly coordinated national energy security strategy, Chinese National Oil Companies (NOCs) compete with other companies with the primary focus of a return on investments (2007, p. 43). There is relatively poor co-ordination between the various Chinese NOCs in Africa and a significant portion of oil extracted by Chinese NOCs in Africa is sold on the global market (Ibid. 47) rather than being shipped back to China.

Geostrategic Implications, Historical Precedents

When we think about grander questions of Chinese influence within the Indian Ocean and East Africa—as well as potential regional or global conflict which may emerge from such influence—we need to understand such engagements within the context of a globalized, market-orientated world. As discussed above, while China has a significant presence in the region, and is in a position to wield a certain degree of influence, such influence must counter a number of other actors, including African state regional bodies and other global corporations. This complexity is something which certain critics of China, as well as certain geo-strategists, tend to gloss over. There is a tendency to posit a Chinese commercial presence in Africa, the Indian Ocean and even beyond, as symmetrical with a geopolitical influence. Additionally, there is a tendency to overstate Chinese presence and understate other state's presence. Ian Taylor makes the point when he states:

> When Shell engages in unsavoury activities in Nigeria's Delta region, no one blames the British Prime Minister and no one makes a direct link between Shell and 10 Downing Street. Yet if a Chinese corporation

> acts in an unscrupulous fashion in Africa, 'the Chinese' are instantly castigated, and Hu Jintao is almost personally implicated (2012, p. 34).

Not only is this an out-dated understanding of contemporary power, but it also misinforms the construction of models and scenario building which seek to understand the nature of future conflict in such regions. A persistent discourse which permeates the analysis of China's rise is potential conflict with other large powers such as the United States (Bernstein and Munro 1998; Babbin 2006; Navarro 2008). If we were to entertain a hypothetical scenario in which China and the United states were to engage in skirmishes, or full-scale war in a region such as East Africa, how might such a situation play out? According to those analyses which conflate the Chinese presence in Africa with an almost colonial-like presence, China would be able to quickly mobilize their ports, roads, railway and production sites in the interests of their own defence. This is, in effect what occurred, on the eve of World War One (1914-1918), where Anglo-German rivalry quickly spread to the colonies of Tanzania and Kenya. The mobilization of the various infrastructure projects constructed by the two colonies—the ports, roads and railways—were crucial in the engagement of battle.[4] But the reason they could easily transport troops and equipment from the sea up to Lakes Victoria and Tanganyika, was not only because they constructed the ports and railways but because they had unfettered ownership of this infrastructure.

If a similar conflict broke out today, it would not look anything like a 19th century colonial conflict. One reason for this is because powerful nation-states do not (mostly) claim sovereign control over other regions in today's political order. But more importantly with regard to the present context, China would not be able to simply mobilize the ports, roads and railways it is building in these regions because the infrastructure is under the influence of multiple stake-holders, including the Japanese, the Korean, the Americans, the Europeans and African nation-states themselves. During the colonial era, European states would focus their infrastructural projects within the realms they controlled, while today the Chinese, along with various other countries, invest in a number of different countries (as do other global actors). It is within this fractured and fluid field of influence in which we need to situate questions regarding the future security of East Africa and the Indian Ocean.

Conclusion

Given the hybrid nature of Chinese influence, rendered so by the competitive forces of global capitalism advocated not only by Western powers but also by China and many African states, how might Chinese geo-strategy play out in the region? This chapter has not attempted to address this question but only to point out that when we speak of 'Chinese influence', it must be carefully qualified. While it is true that the development of port regions and their connection to the hinterland in order to extract resources resembles a colonial pattern—as does the use of government companies to conduct such an enterprise—it is equally true that these companies operate largely according to market interests. Additionally, host states equally eager to promote regional interconnectivity employ an array of other commercial actors to develop such infrastructure. In terms of constructing a greater security picture of the Indian Ocean, it is thus necessary to closely interrogate the various instances of growing Chinese littoral presence within the domestic territories in which they operate. In this sense, this research invites comparative analysis of port activities in countries such as Sri Lanka, Burma and Bangladesh. Such investigations will contribute toward a more empirical understanding of what we mean when we speak of the growing Chinese presence in the Indian Ocean.

NOTES

1. For the oil producing countries, Ethiopia has reserves which can produce 430 000 bpd; Uganda 1 Billion, while Kenya's output is still unknown . With regards to the gas producing countries, Tanzania possesses an estimated 6.5 billion cubic metres; Uganda 14 Billion' Ethiopia 113 Billion; Mozambique 127 Billion and Somalia 5.6 Billion (Anthony 2012:
2. In key geostrategic energy projects, the overlap between the state and SOEs is prominent. This can be seen, for instance, in the Chinese construction of a port in Myanmar, from which stems a CNPC-built pipeline to Yunnan province in China, is widely regarded as a geostrategic measure to ensure the flow of oil in the wake of a Malacca Straits blockade (Collins and Erickson 2010. P. 98). In a similar vein, it is anticipated that the Chinese built port in Gwadar, Pakistan will eventually be connected via pipeline to Xinjiang Uyghur Autonomous Region in Western China.
3. Certainly, this kind of engagement is not only true of Africa but more globally. For instance, as Shankleman has illustrated, NOCs such as Sinopec collaborate with Total in Yemen in Canada; CNOOC is a shareholder in the BP operated Tangguh liquefied natural gas project and oil and gas fields off-shore West Java, as well as owning shares in BHP Billiton-operated assets in Australia and Total-

operated assets in Nigeria (2009: 33). Sinochem is partnered with Sweden's Lundin in its Tunisian operations and with Repsol in Ecuador (Ibid.).

4. On the 5th of August 1914, the first assaults began, with the British attacking German River posts on Lake Victoria. The British drew up a two-pronged plan the firstly, to attack the German town of Longido near Kilimanjaro and seize the western terminus of the Usambara Railway; and secondly, to strike at the port of Tanga and then advance up the same railway in a pincer movement, whereupon they would sweep southwards and conquer the territory 'in a few weeks' (Gardner 1963, p. 18). Both attacks failed. At Kilimanjaro, strong German resistance, and the disruption of supply-routes, forced the British back down the mountain. At Tanga, the Germans, under Lieutenant Colonel Paul Emil von Lettow-Vorbeck, reinforced defences of the port by bringing in troops by rail from New Moshi further inland, leading to a successful ambush on the British. In October 1914, the Königsberg, the most powerful German ship in the Indian Ocean, sought refuge in the Rufijin River Delta inside Tanganyika. By November, British ships had become aware of the boats presence and blockaded the ship in the delta until July of the following year when, aided by two small-gunships brought in from the Red Sea, they were able to skink the vessel. Other battles took place on Lake Victoria and Tanganyika. In the latter, the Germans, by the beginning of the war, had two warships, later adding a third which was brought over in instalments via the Central Line railway and assembled in secret. In order to counter this presence, the British had ships transported to South Africa from Britain and from there, via railway, river and dragged through the African jungle, brought to the lake. The British finally won the war with the help of Belgian - Congolese troops and South African troops under C.J. Smuts, who commanded an army of 13 000 Boers British and Rhodesians as well as 7000 Africans and Indians

REFERENCES

Alden, Chris and Davies, Martyn. (2006), 'A profile of the operations of Chinese multinationals in Africa', *South African Journal of International Affairs*, Vol 13, no 1, pp. 83-96.

Africa-Asia Confidential. (2013), 'Pipeline Politics', Vol. 6, no.8, pp. 6

Africa-Asia Confidential. (2013), 'Pipelines and transparency protests', Vol 6, no 9, pp 7.

African Union. (2013), *50th Anniversary Solemn Declaration*, Available at http://summits.au.int/en/sites/default/files/50%20DECLARATION%20EN.pdf, accessed June 2013.

Airriess, Christopher. (1995), 'Port-centered transport development in colonial North Sumatra', *Indonesia*, No. 59, pp. 65-91.

Al Jazera News. (2013), 'China: a new colonial power', 30 March, Available at http://www.aljazeera.com/programmes/countingthecost/2013/03/2013330125149342593.html, accessed May 2010.

Amanpour, Christina. (2013), 'Is China Buyng up Africa?', *CNN*, 29 March. Available at http://amanpour.blogs.cnn.com/2013/03/29/is-china-buying-up-africa/, accessed June 2013

Anghie, Antony. (1999), 'Finding the peripheries: sovereignty and colonialism in nineteenth century international law', '*Harvard International Law Journal* , Vol 40, no 1, pp. 1-80.

Babbin, Jed. (2006), *Showdown: why China want war with the United States*, Washington D.C.: Regenery Publishing

Balile Deodatus. (2013), 'Tanzania and China sign port development package', *SABAHI*, 27 March 27, Available at: http://sabahionline.com/en_GB/articles/hoa/articles/features/2013/03/27/feature-01, accessed May 2013.

Berlin, Don. (2010, 'Sea power, land power and the Indian Ocean', *Journal of the Indian Ocean Region*, Vol 6, no. 1, pp. 52-66.

Bernstein, Richard and Muro, Ross H. (1998). *The coming conflict with China*; New York: Vintage Books.

Bosire, Boniface, (2013), Kenya-Uganda-Rwanda oil pipeline aims to strengthen regional economy , *SABAHI*, 27 June 27, Available at http://sabahionline.com/en_GB/articles/hoa/articles/features/2013/06/27/feature-02, accessed July 2013.

Brautigam, Deborah. (2009), *The dragon's gift: the real story of China in Africa*, New York: Oxford University Press

Brode, H. (1911), *British and German East Africa: their economic and commercial relations*, London: Edward Arnold

Broomhall Elizabeth, (2011) 'China Harbour and Engineering wins Doha port deal', *Construction Week Online*, Available at http://www.constructionweekonline.com/article-11395-china-harbour-and-engineering-wins-doha-port-deal/#.Uc7GoTv7By0, accessed June 2013

Capital Eritrea, (2010), 'China says it will never interfere with internal politics of African countries', 16 March, Available at http://www.capitaleritrea.com/china-says-it-will-never-interfere-with-internal-politics-of-african-countries/, accessed June 2013

Carmody, Pádraig R and Owusu, Francis Y. (2007), Competing hegemons: Chinese versus American geo-economic strategies in Africa', *Political Geography*, Vol 26, no 5, pp. 504-524.

Clarke, Duncan. (2008), *Crude continent: the struggle for Africa's oil prize*, London: Profile Books

Daily News, (2013). 'Tanzania: construction on Mtwara gas plant project starts', 7 July, Available at http://www.dailynews.co.tz/index.php/local-news/19592-construction-on-mtwara-gas-plant-project-starts, accessed July 2013.

Damian Gramaticas. (2012), 'Chinese Colonialism' *BBC*, 19 July, Available at http://www.bbc.co.uk/news/world-asia-18901656, accessed May 2013.

DIFID. (2011), 'Regional integration and trade in Sub-Saharan Africa', *Trade and Investment Analytical Papers*, Topic 7 of 18, Available at https://www.gov.uk/government/uploads/system/uploads/attachment_data/file/32466/11-978-regional-integration-and-trade-africa.pdf, accessed July 2013

Downes, Erica S. (2007) 'The fact and fiction of Sino-African energy relations', *China Security*, Summer, pp. 42-68.

Embassy of the People's Republic of China in the Republic of Zimbabwe. (2004), 'Sino Africa relations' 16 September, Available at http://www.chinaembassy.org.zw/eng/zt/zflt/t150398.htm, accessed June 2013.

East African Trade Review. (2013). Kenya's taxpayers to pay dearly for the proposed Lamu port project as interest from neighbouring Ethiopia reduce', Available at http://www.eatradereview.net/index.php?option=com_content&view=article&id=273:kenyas-taxpayers-to-pay-dearly-for-the-proposed-lamu-port-project-as-interest-from-neighbouring-ethiopia-reduce&catid=48:investment&Itemid=170, accessed July 2013

Erickson, Andrew S. (2008). 'The growth of China's navy: Implications for Indian Ocean security', *Strategic Analysis*, Vol. 32, no 4, pp. 655-676.

Erickson, Andrew S. and Collins, Gabriel B. (2010), China's oil security pipe dream: the reality and strategic consequences of seaborne imports', *Naval War College Review*, Vol. 63, No. 2, pp. 88-111.

FOCAC. (2012), 'The fifth ministerial conference of the forum on China-Africa cooperation in Beijing: action plan', Available at http://www.focac.org/eng/zxxx/t954620.htm, accessed July 2013.

Financial Express. (2012), 'China placates worries over Bangladesh sea port', 23 December, Available at http://www.thefinancialexpress bd.com/index.php?ref=MjBfMTJfMjNfMTJfMV8yXzE1NDAyNA, accessed June 2013.

French, Paula and Chambers, Sam (2011), *Oil on water: tankers, pirates and the rise of China*, London and New York: Zed Books.

Gardner, Brian. (1963). *German East: The story of the First World War in East Africa*, London: Cassell.

Garver, John W. (1992). 'China's push through the South China Sea: the interaction of bureaucratic and national interests', *The China Quarterly*, Vol. 132, pp. 999-1028.

Gu, Jing. (2009), 'China's Private enterprises in Africa and the implications for African development' *European Journal of Development Research*, Vol. 21, pp. 570-587.

Harvey, David. (2005), *A brief history of neo-liberalism*, New York: Oxford University Press

Hilling, David. (1969), 'The evolution of the major ports of West Africa', *The Geographical Journal*, Vol 235, no 3. pp. 365-378.

Hobsbawm, Eric. (1987), *Age of Empire : 1875-1914*, New York: Vintage Books.

Hoyle, Brian and Charlier, Jacques. (1995). 'Inter-port competition in developing countries: an East Africa case study', *Journal of Transport Geography*, Vol. 2, no 2, pp. 87-103

Hyung, Lee Jae. 2002 'China's expanding maritime ambitions in the western pacific and the Indian Ocean' *Contemporary South East Asia*, Volume 24, no. 3, pp. 549-568.

Jobson, Elissa. (2013), 'Economic integration could shape 'different Africa' in next 50 years', *The Guardian*, 4 February , Available at http://www.guardian.co.uk/global-development/2013/feb/04/economic-integration-different-africa, accessed June 2013.

Johnson, Corey and Derrick, Matthew. (2012), 'A splintered heartland: Russia, Europe, and the geopolitics of networked energy Infrastructure', *Geopolitics*, Vol 17, pp. 482–501.

Jorgic, Drazen. (2013). 'Kenya says Chinese firm wins first tender for Lamu port project', Reuters, 11 April, Available at http://www.reuters.com/article/2013/04/11/kenya-port-lamu-idUSL5N0CX38D20130411, accessed June 2013.

Kalagho, Kenan. (2013). 'What Xi Jinping's visit means to Tanzania', *All Africa*, 3 April, Available at http://allafrica.com/stories/201304090395.html, accessed July 2013

Kaplan, Robert D. (2011), *Monsoon: The Indian Ocean and the Future of American Power*, New York: Random House

Kenya Ports Authority. (2012), *Handbook2012-13*, Colchester: Land and Marine

Kenya Vision 2030. (2012), 'Lamu Port and new transport corridor development to Southern Sudan and Ethiopia', Available at http://www.kenfreightgroup.com/Lamu%20Port%20and%20New%20Transport%20Corridor%20Development%20to%20Southern%20Sudan%20and%20Ethiopia%20(LAPSSET)..pdf, accessed July 2013.

Kimani, Mwaura. (2010), 'China joins contest to fund second port at Lamu', *Business Daily*, 4 May, Available at http://www.businessdailyafrica.com/Company%20Industry/China%20joins%20contest%20to%20fund%20second%20 port%20in%20 Lamu/-/539550/911498/-/item/0/-/u2jb9m/-/index.html, accessed July 2013

Liloba, Humphrey. (2012), 'Kenya: Lamu port completion on schedule', *East Africa Business Week*, 27 November, Available at http://www.busiweek.com/news/kenya/4072-lamu-port-completion-on-schedule, accessed July 2013.

Madeley, John. (1999), *Big business poor peoples: the impact of transnational corporations on the world's poor*, Zed books: London.

Maden, Michal, Downs, Erica S. (2012). 'Business and Politics in China: The oil executive reshuffle of 2011', *Brookings Institute*, February 8, Available at http://www.brookings.edu/research/articles/2012/02/08-oil-politics-downs, accessed June 2013.

Malone, Andrew. (2008). "How China's taking over Africa, and why the West should be very worried" *Daily Mail*, 18 July, Available at http://www.dailymail.co.uk/news/article-1036105/How-Chinas-taking-Africa-West-VERY-worried.html, accessed January 2013.

Mohan, Giles. (2013), 'The Chinese just come and do it: China in Africa and the prospects for development planning', *International Development Planning Review*, Volume 35, no 3, pp. v-xii.

Mohan, C. Raja. (2012), 'Military diplomacy: China woos Seychelles', *The Indian Times*, July 16, Available at http://www.indianexpress.com/news/military-diplomacy-china-woos-seychelles/975070/#sthash.5ED4mR7I.dpuf, accessed July 2013.

Montlake, Simon. (2013). 'Port In A Storm: An Interview With China Merchants Group' *Forbes Asia*, 9 January, Available at http://www.forbes.com/sites/simonmontlake/2013/01/09/port-in-a-storm-an-interview-with-china-merchants-group/, accessed March 2013.

Navarro, Peter. (2008), *The coming China wars: where they will be fought and how they can be won*, Upper Saddle River: F.T. Press

Notteboom, Theo E. (2000), 'ECMT Round Tables Land Access to Sea Ports', *OECD*, Public Affairs and Communication Directorate: Paris

Okoth, Jackson. (2010), 'Juba Abandons Plan for Raillink to Kenya', *Standard Digital*,

13 April 13, Available at http://www.standardmedia.co.ke/?articleID=2000007531&pageNo=1, accessed July 2013.

Polgreen, Lydia. (2012), 'U.S., too, wants to bolster investment in a continent's economic promise', *New York Times*, 8 August, Available at http://www.nytimes.com/2012/08/09/world/africa/us-seeks-to-step-up-africa-investment.html?pagewanted=all&_r=0, accessed July 2013.

Portworld News. (2010), 'Hambantota project 'five months ahead of schedule', 8 March, Available at http://www.portworld.com/news/noaccess?r=%2Fnews%2Fi92232%2FHambantota_project_five_months_ahead_of_schedule, accessed July 2013.

Scott, David. (2008), 'The great power 'grate game' between India and China', *Geopolitics*, Vol. 13, no. 1, pp. 1-26.

Shankleman, Jill. (2009), 'Going global: Chinese oil and mining companies and the governance of resource wealth', *Woodrow Wilson Centre*: Washington.

Shinn, David. (2009), 'China's Involvement in African Conflict Zones', *The Jamestown Foundation*, 20 May, Available at https://sites.google.com/site/davidhshinn/china-s-involvement-in-african-conflict-zones, accessed July 2013.

Sri Lankan Ports Authority. (2012), 'Colombo Port Expansion Project', Available at http://www.slpa.lk/colombo_south_harbour.asp?chk=4, accessed June 2013

Sudan Tribune. (2006), 'China, Sudan sign $79 mln contract to deepen Port Sudan harbour', 10 June, Available at http://www.sudantribune.com/China-Sudan-sign-79-mln-contract,16118, accessed June 2013.

Sumila, Veneranda. (2012), 'Over Sh3.8 trillion needed to revamp Central Line', *The Citizen*, 17 October, Available at http://www.thecitizen.co.tz/News/-/1840392/1828620/-/eyqkmbz/-/index.html, accessed May 2013.

Taylor, Ian. (2006 a.). *China and Africa: engagement and compromise*, Abingdon: Routledge.

Taylor, Ian, (2006 b.). 'China's oil diplomacy in Africa', *International Affairs*, Vol. 82, no. 5, pp. 937–959.

Taylor, Ian. (2012). 'From Santa Claus to serious business: Where should FOCAC go next?', *African East Asian Affairs/China Monitor*, June, pp. 31-39.

Tekele, Tesfa-Alem. (2012), 'African Development Bank finances Lamu road corridor project' *Sudan Tribune*, 8 May, Available at http://www.sudantribune.com/African-Development-Bank-finances,42520, accessed May 2013.

The Economic Times. (2013). 'Not using Tanzania port for military purposes: China', 28 March, Available at http://articles.economictimes.indiatimes.com/2013-03-28/news/38099460_1_china-today-defence-spokesman-yang-yujun-xinhua, accessed July 2013.

Weigend, G.G., 1958. Some elements in the study of port geography. *Geographical Review*, Vol. 48, pp. 185-200.

Xinhua News. (2009), 'Africa No 1. Target for CCCC as $4 bln projects mount up', 16 June, Available at http://news.xinhuanet.com/english/2009-06/16/content_11549529.htm, accessed June 2013.

Xinhua News. (2012), ''New colonialism' accusation against China unfair', August 23, Available at http://www.chinadaily.com.cn/world/2012-08/23/content_15701403.htm, accessed July 2013.

Xinhua News. (2013), Backgrounder: Facts about China-Africa economic, trade cooperation', 24 March, Available at http://news.xinhuanet.com/english/africa/2013-03/24/c_124496942.htm, accessed June 2013

Watkins, Kevin and Fowler, Penny. (2002) *Rigged rules and double standards: trade, globalization and the fight against poverty'*, Oxford: Oxfam

Chapter 4

Revisiting Alternative Futures in the Indian Ocean Nexus: CHIMEA vs Great Power Rivalry

Francis A. Kornegay, Jr.

ABSTRACT

Africa's Indian Ocean maritime future depends greatly on whether or not this central oceanic corridor evolves as a 'zone of peace' facilitating interregional integration or is destined to become yet another theatre of tension as is the case of the 'seas around China.' To be sure a more nuanced pattern may combine low intensity rivalry and jockeying for 'position' with more cooperative engagements. Yet the interplay between threat perceptions of conflict and prospects of accommodation tend to find variations of reflection in alternative narratives as the Indian Ocean has risen in the awareness of academic, political and policy practitioners in strategic affairs. Thus, Woodrow Wilson fellow at large, Martin Walker, penned an article in the Spring 2008 *Wilson Quarterly* envisioning a geopolitical economy linking China-India-Middle East-Africa which he dubbed 'CHIMEA.' Robert Kaplan, authoring *Monsoon: The Indian Ocean and the Future of American Power* (2012) is better known for emphasizing the potential for Sino-Indian rivalry requiring an 'umperial' role in the Indian Ocean for the world's sole superpower.

Keywords: CHIMEA, Indian Ocean Nexus, great power rivalry.

This chapter attempts to navigate these alternative patterns of unfolding Indian Ocean geopolitical, economic and security dynamics in sketching out the broader geostrategic landscape of this Afro-Asian interregional corridor. This involves identifying and examining the inter and intra-regional dimensions of intercourse characterizing Indian Ocean subsystems spanning its western and eastern perimeters and how these may relate to alternative futures implicit in the Walker and Kaplan narratives. There is already an increasing amount of economic, commercial and energy-related activities in play throughout the Indian Ocean Rim involving regional states and external powers.

The potential for interregional community-building emphasizing the maritime security and functional cooperation dimensions of oceans governance is considerable. Yet there are also threat perceptions in need of problematizing in examining how likely they are to shape the Indian Ocean future and how Africa might influence (and be influenced by) such scenarios. Here, the IBSA trilateralism of India, Brazil and South Africa will be offered up as a neutral balancing framework for consideration in 'calming the waters' of Walker's nexus and Kaplan's Monsoon.

Background: Revisiting CHIMEA Amid Threat Perceptions

There is something about major bodies of water that conjure up visions of great power rivalry, not that such visions are without foundation given the role sea power has played in the rise and decline of European powers over centuries of global expansion beyond continental Europe. In the proverbial 'rim land'-'heartland' narrative framing classical geopolitical analysis, this dynamic reached its apogee in the onetime sun that never set on the British Empire. Given the global air-sea presence and basing infrastructure of postwar American expansion, one cannot summarily discard the oceanic paradigm of sea power projection as totally irrelevant in the 'flat world' of the 21st century.

Here, the Indian Ocean has emerged as a particularly compelling arena of envisioned rivalries. These stem from the Cold War days of threat perceptions of Soviet-American rivalry where South Africa's Cape Sea Route inspired notions of a 'South Atlantic Treaty Organization,' pre-emptively begetting the anti-apartheid inspired Zone of Peace and Cooperation in the South Atlantic (ZPCSA) to today's preoccupation with Sino-Indian dynamics—the so-called 'string of pearls' theory of Indian strategic encirclement by a peacefully rising China. While this great power rivalry mantra geostrategically implicates the western Indian Ocean, only recently since the emergence of the Somali piracy threat in the Gulf of Aden, has the African dimension of stakes in this body of water begun to attract overdo attention.

This increasing attention has highlighted the growing external power extractive and logistical interests in Africa's mineral, energy and agricultural resources implicating less geopolitical than geoeconomic motivations behind the Indian Ocean looming ever larger in the agendas of China, India and other external actors—Asian and Australasian economic powers in particular: Japan, South Korea, Australia most notably in addition to the traditional presence of the US, France and the UK. As such, it is not for nothing that the Indian Ocean Rim Association (IORA) has made room for Dialogue Partners including China, the US, UK, France, Japan and Egypt.

There is no need to recite the data that have become almost obligatory in documenting how important the Indian Ocean has become given the global geoeconomic gravity shift from the economies of the transatlantic to those of the trans-Pacific; this is the new conventional wisdom of the west-to-east power shift. However, the reconceptualization of the Indian Ocean as a nexus between the economies of Africa as well as those of the Middle East, South and East Asia has only recently gained momentum since Martin Walker, affiliated with The Wilson Centre penned his *Wilson Quarterly* feature article titled "Indian Ocean Nexus." The sub-textual lead-in noted at the time that: "The Atlantic and Pacific now dominate the world's politics and trade, but the Indian Ocean is emerging as a new locus of power that increasingly unites China, India, the Middle East, and Africa."[1]

With a decidedly economic emphasis on trade, Walker differentiates between "potent and even somber historical memories " of a trade along its shores ranging "from the Arab slave trade down the East African coast to Zanzibar and beyond, to the celebrated 15th century oceanic explorations of the Chinese admiral Zhang He during the Ming dynasty" to today's trade flourishing across the Indian Ocean which is altogether different; it is different in scale and in range of products, and in its economic and strategic implications: "It is different above all in the flows of money and investment that are now binding the Indian Ocean states and China into a potential new hub of the global economy. *We might call it CHIMEA, for China, India, the Middle East and Africa*."[2]

In outlining the economic threads of mutual need knitting together this nexus, "China and India need energy supplies from the Persian Gulf states and oil and raw materials from Africa, and Africa needs the financial resources that the Gulf states are accumulating in unprecedented quantities. And now that India has become a net food importer once again, China, India and the Middle East all have an interest in developing African agriculture as perhaps the last great untapped food resource of a world whose population looks set to grow from today's 6.5 billion to 9.1 billion by 2050" while more than "half of the world's population now lives in the CHIMEA countries..."[3]

Africa, at 1 billion today, close in population to either India or China, is set to surpass both (individually) by 2050 reaching 2 billion with much of the current demographic explosion centred in and along the Indian Ocean's African Littoral. What this means is a future global centre of gravity reflecting a veritable Afro-South Asian demographic axis making all the more compelling the impetus in momentum needed to forge interregional integration among the African, South and Southeast Asian subsystems uniting the western and eastern expanses of the Indian Ocean.

Indeed this is happening on both sides of the ocean: 2015 being the target date for the Association of South East Asian Nations (ASEAN) becoming the ASEAN Economic Community along with the launching of the tripartite 'Cape to Cairo' mega-free trade area (FTA) between the Common Market of Eastern and Southern Africa (COMESA), the Southern African Development Community (SADC) and the East African Community (EAC). Herein lies the beginning of an interregional economic cooperation infrastructure fleshing out the CHIMEA nexus into a potential Indian Ocean community.

The African Littoral dimension of CHIMEA, as a zone of rapid economic growth, promises an economically integrated market of between 600-800 million people—and growing. This potential is motivating the companion North-South Corridor Infrastructure Initiative which is attracting diverse investments aimed at fleshing out the east, central and southern African logistical and port berthing capacity to handle increasing Afro-Asian trade and commercial traffic. Discoveries of on and off-shore oil and gas reserves add yet another dimension capped off by revelations in 2013 of South Africa having major shale oil potential which is currently under investigation for determining environmental sustainability for exploitation.

The South Africa potential, in this regard, does not end there. At the end of 2013 it was reported that the country's "long-awaited claim to vast tracts of territory, due to be heard...by a UN commission, means South Africa will could soon be the largest country on the continent."[4] Likely UN endorsement will "extend South Africa's marine territory way beyond the wide, gently slopping area called the continental shelf" resulting in a new 'new South Africa' that will be mostly underwater.[5] It will be accompanied by "rights to extract natural resources from the sea bed, including minerals, gas and oil deposits."[6]

This updated eastern and southern African dimension puts further flesh on a survey of trade and investment patterns by Walker which explored the substantial Arab investment dimensions interacting with Chinese, Indian and African interests, culminating in his assertion that "what is building around the Indian Ocean is far larger than simply Africa's future, and larger than Asian-African trade. The flowering of a commercial system is underway, a new form of that infamous triangular trade that helped finance Britian's 18th century industrial revolution, with cheap British beads and mirrors being sold in West Africa for slaves, who were shipped to the Americas, and the proceeds used to ship tobacco and sugar back to Britain."[7]

Walker continues: "The new triangular trade of the Indian Ocean sees the Middle Eastern countries export oil to Asia, then use the proceeds to export capital to Asia and Africa. Asia sends cash, consumer goods, and remittance workers to the Middle East, and investment capital, skills, and aid to Africa, which in turn sells oil and agricultural products to Asia, investing some of the proceeds in new industries, from mobile phones to Nollywood films."[8] However, at this point, as he concludes, Walker ventures into the territory of those who disseminate a more insecure narrative as he hotes that "the rivalry for resources is intense" as "the Indian Ocean is witnessing the beginnings of an arms race, with China building ports that can also serve as naval bases at Gwadar, Pakistan, which is near the mouth of the Persian Gulf, and at Sittwe in Myanmar, on the Bay of Bengal."[9]

Alarmed by China's ambitions, "India has been boosting its own forces with a new fleet of French-built Scorpene stealth submarines, a program of building three aircraft carriers" and so forth.[10] Thus, Walker closes on a note of caution in as much as "the economic promise of

CHIMEA is dazzling, but the geopolitical and strategic implications are sobering"—and so this may be the case.[11] But there is beginning to be some push-back in countering the Sino-Indian rivalry narrative with its assumptions of guaranteed Chinese Indian Ocean hegemony reinforcing its ascendancy in Africa's economic sweepstakes known popularly as 'the new scramble for Africa.'

Problematizing Sino-Indian IOR Rivalry

An exemplar of this debate were the point/counterpoints that emerged during India's National Maritime Foundation (NMF) annual maritime power conference at the Institute for Defence Studies and Analysis (IDSA). Devoted to the theme "Evolving Dynamics of the Indian Ocean: Prospects and the way Forward," the starting premise was the opening up of an alleged power vacuum in the Indian Ocean accompanying US military disengagement from Afghanistan and its 'pivot' to the Asian-Pacific. The underlying implication: the vacuum would be filled by China at India's expense. But, a particularly contrarian view regarding such threat perceptions was offered by David Brewster, visiting fellow at the Strategic and Defence Studies Centre, Australian National University.

In problematizing the "standard narrative about China in the IOR," Brewster argued that while Beijing's "overwhelming strategic imperative in the Indian Ocean is the protection of its sea lines of communication (or SLOCS)," India is and remains far and away the dominant naval power in the Ocean even though "China's overall naval capabilities *theoretically* exceed India's and that margin is likely to grow in the coming years."[12] (italics added) Why this is so is due to the fact that "China's ability to project power into the Indian Ocean is highly constrained by the long distance from Chinese ports and air bases" compared to India's much shorter SLOCS, and border as it does directly on the Indian Ocean at the pivot point between the eastern and western oceans.[13]

The comparative length of China's SLOCS in the Indian Ocean is accompanied by "the lack of logistical support, and the need for Chinese naval vessels to deploy to the Indian Ocean through chokepoints."[14] While pointing out that none of these fundamental constraints are likely to change any time soon, the 'String of Pearls' threat perception of

Indian encirclement by China due to the infrastructural port construction being carried out by Chinese companies in Pakistan, Sri Lanka, Bangladesh and Myanmar are unlikely to overcome China's strategic vulnerabilities in the Indian Ocean.

First of all, China's navy would have to be given rights to use the ports. In the unlikely event that they were, "they would have little value as military bases without significant additional expenditure over many years and then many of them would be highly vulnerable themselves to attack."[15] Rather, PLAN is more concerned about "places not bases" to facilitate logistical support for PLAN vessels for limited purposes such as involving anti-piracy operations.[16]

Finally, "unlike other areas of strategic competition between India and China, such as the balance of conventional military forces, nuclear weapons or economic power, the Indian Ocean is the one area in which India holds a clear military advantage over China. The Indian Ocean represents 'exterior lines' for China and 'interior lines' for India."[17] What emerges when viewed in its full geostrategic context is a balance of power between Indian dominance in much of the Indian Ocean, especially in the western sector and Chinese dominance in the eastern ocean where Beijing would/is more realistically focusing its resources and which merges into its main arena of strategic concern involving the South and East China Seas.

Yet India is seen by Brewster as facing difficult choices as well wherein its real challenge may be "to determine how its overwhelming geographic advantage in the Indian Ocean *vis a vis* China should best be used."[18] One option suggested is to "choose to work with the United States and others to try to leverage China's strategic vulnerability."[19] However, there are signs that Sino-Indian relations may be on their way toward normalization.[20] Therefore, a much less contentious option and one that might better enhance stability for all concerned would be an integrated maritime security and functional cooperation engagement with African Littoral states, South Africa especially, as well as other stakeholder countries in the Indian Ocean. More CHIMA and less strategic competition might be the narrative closer to reality. This will elaborated on later in this chapter.

The Geopolitical-Economics of the African Littoral

Africa has to be regarded as marginal to the Indian Ocean rivalry debate. Where its relevance may surface is in Brewster's 'places, not bases' argument in which both China and India are seen as vying for influence in the island members of the African Union (AU) and SADC: Mauritius, Seychelles and Madagascar. Certainly it would run against the grain of both the AU and SADC for naval basing access to be afforded any external power for whatever reason. This would be highly controversial in the African political context beyond security cooperation already involving certain littoral states in operations against piracy and the jihadist terror threat emanating out from the ongoing Somali conflict and its spillover into Kenya. As it is, the US use of Diego Garcia remains controversial.

However, Martin Walker's CHIMEA paradigm is instructive in contextualizing the external 'scramble' for Africa's resources and access to its expanding market. As such, Africa has become what might be more appropriately interpreted as a 'sphere of interest' as opposed to a 'sphere of influence' for external powers with the possible exception in the case of the European Union's bid to consolidate its dominance of the continent through its contentious Economic Partnership Agreements (EPAs).

From a geopolitical perspective, the EU-EPA bid can be interpreted as an attempt not only to pre-empt such emerging powers as China and India and other Asian powers but also the United States. In addition is the process of navigating an extension of the African Growth and Opportunity Act (AGOA) while negotiating its Transatlantic Trade and Investment Partnership (TTIP) with the EU. What emerges is a complicated picture of geopolitical-economic competition among external actors interacting with Africa's own geopolitical dynamics. These are especially salient to defining the political, economic and security prospects of 'maritime Africa' along the Indian Ocean littoral.

These prospects impinge most tellingly on the geopolitical-economics of African integration which, over time, will shape the geoeconomic terrain of the western Indian Ocean and linkages interregionally into South Asia and the prospective ASEAN Community. In other words, Africa's maritime prospects in the Indian Ocean will evolve as a function of progress made toward economic, security and political integration along the expansive littoral of eastern and southern Africa extending to and beyond the Northeast African Horn and into the hotly-contested Nile River Basin.[21] The African challenge within this geography is multifaceted. It entails the following:

- Conflict resolution and stabilization along the Somali coast, within South Sudan as well as between South and North Sudan and in the Great Lakes;
- Combating and containing jihadism, interacting with the ebb and flow of a piracy threat that potentially extends from the Horn of Africa into the southern African Mozambique Channel;
- Progress toward achieving effective and stable governance arrangements within virtually all member states of the Comesa-SADC-EAC eastern and southern African Littoral which reverts back to coming to terms with conflict resolution and stabilization imperatives;
- At the northern extremity of the Comesa-SADC-EAC complex, the urgent need to find a mutual accommodation between Egypt and the upstream countries over the developmental future of the Nile River Basin;
- At the southern extremity of the Comesa-SADC-EAC complex, the urgent need for South Africa and fellow members of the Southern African Customs Union (SACU) to move toward a political integration resolution of the future of SACU, which, in turn, might catalyse the evolution of SADC into a companion customs union with that of the EAC within the grand tripartite FTA;
- The urgent need for the Comesa-SADC-EAC states to prioritize the functioning of the *New Asia-Africa Strategic Partnership* (NAASP) as an integrated mechanism within the AU interacting with NEPAD as a means of developing coordinated synergies among the different Asian initiatives of engagement on the continent generally and within the African Littoral of the Indian Ocean in particular.

This cursory outlining of geopolitical-economic challenges confronting the African side of the Indian Ocean is intended to convey the unavoidable reality of how the prospects of maritime Africa are a function of the integrated stabilization of its on-shore hinterland. This reality underlines the apex priority of the continent as a whole having to do with advancing its economic and political integration as a means of overcoming its colonially inherited fragmentation. What amounts to *the Africanization of colonialism* in the 1963 founding of the Organization of African Unity on the basis of the Berlin partitioning of the continent keeps Africa in a perpetual reactive mode to the external initiatives of non-African powers that which to engage Africa in their own national interests.

In a very real sense, where the wider prospects of the Indian Ocean are concerned, the integration of eastern and southern Africa is simultaneously pre-conditional to overcoming this colonial legacy and to the building of an interregional Indian Ocean community as an organized, institutional expression of CHIMEA. The unfolding of such a scenario should, in the process, further transform the great power rivalry narrative as the dominant discourse on the future of the Indian Ocean.

Africa and Community-Building in the Southern Oceans

If the continent is to overcome the 'Africanization of colonialism' in achieving its pan-African goal of an integrated Continental African Free Trade Area (CAFTA) enroute to the African Economic Community (AEC) while establishing its sovereign maritime identity, the epicentre of this dynamic along the Indian Ocean littoral seems to be emerging in the East African Community. However, an interplay between the Kenyan and South African poles of economic cooperation and integration within the EAC and SADC will animate this process within the context of the prospective Comesa-SADC-EAC tripartite Grand FTA. But in spite of South Africa's economic dominance on the continent as a whole, the integration process within the SADC regional zone of the tripartite GFTA is being overtaken by the EAC integrationist dynamic.

East African dynamism is best reflected in a recent issue of the South African *Financial Mail* publication featuring how the "Smart money is on East African growth" in which the author, Michael Power, argues that "the industrialisation of Africa will be led by East Africa, not by SA or Nigeria."[22] He points out that:

> "...Africa's new economy is taking root in Eastern Africa, with Kenya and Ethiopia at the forefront and Tanzania and Uganda reinforcing this emerging regional cluster of more than 300m people. Revising the

> trends of the post-independence, post-1960 era, it is Africa inside the tropics—Middle Africa—much more than the north or south that is now recording the highest levels of GDP growth.
>
> For those not hidebound by the narrative of recent history, this should not be so surprising. After all, *East Africa is closest to Asia, and not just geographically. The Indian Ocean has connected the continents' littoral regions for over 2000 years: the earliest inhabitants of Madagascar made their way there from Borneo some 400 years before the birth of Christ.* (italics added)
>
> Eastern Africa's lingua franca, Swahili, draws heavily on the longstanding trade links it has with the Arabian Peninsula: swahel means 'coastal' in Arabic. Its coastal strip is also overwhelmingly Muslim, practicing (except perhaps in the failed state of Somalia) a far more approachable, less militant Islam."[23]

This observation amounts to a succinct description of the Indian Ocean geocultural connectivity of CHIMEA from the perspective of the African Littoral. As such, it points to the potential for interregional community-building between the Afro-western and Asiatic-eastern sides of the ocean pointing to a veritable 'pax-Afroasiatica.' This is where a revisiting of converging integrationist trends in eastern and southern Africa and Southeast Asia is instructive. This starts with prospects for a preferential trade agreement between Kenya and South Africa, where it was noted that this possibility, mooted under Most Favoured Nation conditions, "could come by default under a proposed tripartite agreement between the Common Market for Eastern & Southern Africa (Comesa), the East African Community (EAC), and the Southern African Development Community (SADC), to establish a free-trade area by 2015."[24]

ASEAN, meanwhile, which is set to re-launch itself as a proto-EU style economic community in the same year, has emerged at the epicentre of Greater East Asian economic integration given its Plus Three arrangement with China, Japan and South Korea on the one hand, and India (given its 'Look East' strategy) on the other. Reinforcing ASEAN's centrality in this regard is its certainty to form a major component of much larger trade regimes: the US-led Trans-Pacific Partnership and/or the Regional Comprehensive Economic Partnership (RCEP) involving China—and their possible convergence ultimately in an Asia-Pacific Economic Cooperation (APEC) free trade area.[25]

Given these geoeconomic trends on both sides of the Indian Ocean, it is hard not to perceive how these African and Asian initiatives might not converge into a greater transoceanic economic community at some point in the future. The one missing piece that could further cement these prospects, but would seem unlikely to be an impediment to its realization, is the stalled momentum on a South Asian Free Trade Area (Safta) once mooted by the South Asian Association for Regional Cooperation (SAARC). Until the Afghanistan-India-Pakistan trinity stabilizes into a sustainable regional accommodation there seems to be little likelihood that South Asian integration will figure as a major factor in the consolidation of the CHIMEA equation between eastern and southern Africa and Southeast Asia.

As far as the African Littoral dimension is concerned, however, although the Kenya-centred EAC is emerging as the driver of the tripartite GFTA, South Africa cannot be underestimated as a pivotal factor in driving the evolution of a greater southern hemispheric integration community. South Africa remains the geostrategic pivot at the sea lanes juncture between the Indian and South Atlantic oceans with a potential reinforced by its expansive marine domain extending beyond its continental shelf. But within the Indian Ocean context, for South Africa to realize this potential, much will hinge on how it calibrates its bilateral relations with India as well as more multilaterally with Australia and Indonesia within the IORA and the Indian Ocean Naval Symposium (IONS) and with Brazil in the southern Atlantic. This has to do with the trilateral potential of the India-Brazil-South Africa (IBSA) Trilateral Dialogue Forum as a neutralist anchor in Indian Ocean (as well as South Atlantic) community-building.

The South African-IBSA Nexus: Toward a 'Gondwanan Process'?

The 10th anniversary of IBSA came and went without a commemorative summit which was to have taken place in New Delhi. Having come under the shadow of the BRICS Forum to which the IBSA countries are members, questions have been raised about the future of this trilateral platform. It was launched in Brasilia in 2003 as a South-South cooperation initiative by India, Brazil and South Africa on the strength of their individual and collective potential as emerging democratic regional powers in their respective regions and continents. The comparative advantage of IBSA, compared to BRICS, is its trilateral geostrategic logic linking the southern cone of South America to the Indian subcontinent via South Africa sitting astride the southern sea lanes. The logic is Gondwanan in reference to the geological past of prehistory which had one united Africa, South America, the South Asian subcontinent, Australia and Antarctica into the southern supercontinent of Gondwanaland.

Among its many initiatives, IBSA is notable for its IBSAMAR naval exercises. These are tantalizingly suggestive of a larger potential that IBSA via IBSAMAR could develop as a cooperative point of convergence in evolving a coherent architecture of southern oceans hemispheric governance. Now that the IORA and IONS, under the chairmanship of Australia is set to find synergy through the development of an IORA-IONS working group on maritime safety and security, there is no reason why this linkage could and should not be extended to IBSA. IBSA, in turn, could serve as the lynchpin in expanding southern oceans governance and maritime cooperation to the South Atlantic which includes the Zone of Peace and Cooperation and the Gulf of Guinea Commission.

The main concern is political will on the part of the three countries to ensure that IBSA, after having developed a commendable track record of activities involving its several sectoral working groups over the past decade, does not fade into an oblivion of inactivity given the rise of BRICS. Given China's *de facto* dominance within BRICS, some see Beijing as seeking to make IBSA redundant by duplicating much of IBSA's agenda within BRICS. But there are limits to this, given the sensitivities of Sino-Indian geopolitical competitiveness. The prospect of making IBSAMAR redundant by launching a 'BRICSMAR' failed to materialize, no doubt, complicated by the lack of geostrategic coherence in BRICS which is primarily a revisionist platform for promoting global economic governance reform.

IBSAMAR would seem to have considerable potential for revitalizing IBSA with an expanded maritime security agenda along with naval exercises moving from South African waters to take place off the Brazilian Atlantic coast and in the waters around southern India. Such a prospect might be reinforced by IBSA launching a much discussed but indefinitely postponed outreach to bring other countries within its orbit. In this vein, IBSA could take a page out of the IORA's experience by recruiting other states as Observers or 'Dialogue Partners.' With regard to the Indian Ocean, IBSA-IBSAMAR Dialogue Partners could include Australia, Indonesia, SADC member Mauritius and Kenya, while, in the South Atlantic, Angola, Namibia, Argentina and Chile could be brought on board.

Taking a page out of the *Shangri-La Dialogues*, an IBSA/IBSAMAR-centred 'Gondwanan Process,' could involve the fashioning of a more multi-dimensional dialogue based on a government-think tanking NGO partnership (somewhere between track 1 and 2) and involving different working groups on the 'health of the oceans' and trade and investment and the 'blue economy' as well as on naval cooperation and maritime safety and security. Knowledge-sharing, reviewing lessons learned and facilitating targeted exchanges, including joint training and research in different fields related to oceans governance and security issues could inform such a dialogue agenda.

Indeed, the need for such a dialogue process was raised by South African President Jacob Zuma during his opening of the 5th IBSA summit in Durban in October 2011.[26] Now that South Africa has become more actively engaged in the IORA (though its chairing of IONS was reported to be decidedly lacklustre) and is in the line-up following the current troika of India, Australia and Indonesia to Chair it a few years down the line, it behoves the IBSA troika to give greater political attention and an exercising of political will to activate the appropriate outreach that can enable it to become an active player in southern oceans diplomacy.

From the Indian Ocean angle, reaching out to Australia, Indonesia, Mauritius and Kenya, would facilitate the type of cooperative inter-linkages between IBSA, the IORA and IONS that could lead ultimately to the shaping of the type of oceans governance and cooperative security environment which could pre-empt and prevent competitive pressures from escalating into the rivalries that some have envisioned as this region's future. As such, IBSA, as the point of departure for elaborating a more structured architecture of cooperation in the southern oceans, could serve as something of a neutral balancer with a positive focus on promoting a CHIMEA agenda.

Such an evolution in maritime relations should, it would seem, forestall temptations of a bandwagoning nature aimed at leveraging another power's strategic vulnerability on the assumption that geopolitical rivalry is an Indian Ocean given. The launching of a 'Gondwanan process' of open-ended and multifaceted ocean governance dialogue among the littoral states of the southern oceans, with a prominent role for maritime Africa, would seem a fitting starting point for elaborating an Afrocentric global South paradigm for Indian Ocean community-building.

NOTES

1. Martin Walker, "Indian Ocean Nexus," Wilson *Quarterly*, Spring 2008, p. 21.
2. Ibid., p. 21.
3. Ibid., p. 22.
4. "SA claims vast new territory," *Sunday Times*, December 1, 2013. "If successful, we would be the biggest country in Africa."
5. Ibid.
6. Ibid.
7. Walker, op.cit., p. 28.
8. Ibid., p. 28.
9. Ibid., p. 28.
10. Ibid., p. 28.
11. Ibid., p. 28.
12. David Brewster, "Beyond the String of Pearls: Sino-Indian Rivalry and the Indian Ocean," Draft-8 February 2014, p. 2.
13. Ibid., p. 2.
14. Ibid., p. 2.
15. Ibid., p. 3.
16. Ibid., p. 3.
17. Ibid., p. 3.
18. Ibid., p. 4.
19. Ibid., p. 5.
20. MK Bhadrakumar, "Substantial Inheritance," *Deccan Herald*, February 18, 2014. http://www.deccanherald.com/content/386944/substantial-inheritance.html. "To say that India-China relations are in much shape today than any time in the last half century will be stating the obvious. The facts speak for themselves—increasing trade and investment, sustained high-level exchanges, commencement of strategic dialogue and mil-to-mil interactions and, of course, the plain truth that not a drop of blood has been spilt on the disputed border despite all the verbal contestation and posturing."
21. "Row over Nile River dam could poison relations between Egypt and Ethiopia," *Sunday Independent*, 9 March 2014, p. 10.
22. Michael Power, "Smart money is on East African growth," *Financial Mail*, 6

February 2014.

23. Ibid.
24. Steve Mbogo, "SA business shows renewed interest in Kenya," *Financial Mail*, 6 February 2014.
25. Choi Byung-il& Lee Kyaunghee, "Future of Trade Architecture in Asia Pacific: TPP vs. ECEP," *KERI Brief* 23 February 2014: www.keri.org/...issue_2. Also: "Where does India stand amid changing Asia-Pacific trade dynamics," by SuviDogra & Jie Woo, *Financial Express*, 4 April 2013. Indian Ministry of External Affairs disseminated document.
26. See: Opening Remarks by President JG Zuma at the 5th IBSA Summit, Presidential Guest House, Pretoria, South African Government Information (GCIS), October 18, 2011.

Chapter 5

Africa and Contested Constructions of the Indian Ocean Region

Timothy Doyle and Dennis Rumley

ABSTRACT

This chapter seeks to address the place of Africa in contested and conflicting regional security constructions in the Indian Ocean Region. The content of the regional security debate and responses is primarily a reflection of three competing security constructions of the Indian Ocean Region: firstly, an all-embracing concept, which includes much of Southern and Eastern Africa, in an *Indian Ocean Region* comprising up to 51 states at its largest scale to 20 states at the scale of the Indian Ocean Rim (IORA); secondly, a scaled-down version of the first into the *East Indian Ocean*; and, thirdly, an *Indo-Pacific* concept which emphasises the pre-eminence of regional naval power and ensures that India (along with Indonesia, Japan and the United States, among others) potentially plays a central policing role not only within the Indian Ocean Region. The last two constructions exclude Africa, but for different purposes.

Keywords: Security; Indian Ocean; regional construction; Indo-Pacific.

For too long Africa has not been accorded its due respect in terms of the broader governance of the Indian Ocean community. This mighty continent abuts the Indian Ocean on its southern and eastern littoral zones, and many other countries without necessarily qualifying as littoral, increasingly look to the Indian Ocean in terms of trade, security, governance and culture. In many ways, the peoples of Africa are currently undergoing a 'Third Race for Africa', with many key traders (some national—some transnational) coming either *from* the region—such as India—or *through* the region, such as China or Japan. It is hoped that by forging strong regional ties, that this most recent 'race' for resources will prove more profitable for African peoples than the previous two historical occurrences, which largely saw Atlantic states expand their riches, largely to the detriment of local African peoples.

The current special volume was designed to publish some of the papers presented at the joint Indian Ocean Rim Association (IORA) and Indian Ocean Research Group (IORG), Symposium that took place in Nairobi during March of 2014. The Conference, entitled: *The Political Economy of Maritime Africa in the Indian Ocean Region*, examined reasons for Africa's recent lack of participation in the Indian Ocean Rim Association and considered strategies to 'bring maritime Africa back in' to the Indian Ocean regional community. Contributions from African and non-African presenters focused on the following three themes: Africa's perception of, and linkages with, Indian Ocean states; Indian Ocean state linkages with Africa; and future opportunities for stronger linkages.

The Symposium was part of an initial phase of a larger project on 'Constructing a sense of Indian Oceanness' initiated by Australia, India and Oman at the Indian Ocean Rim Academic Group (IORAG) reform sub-committee meeting held in Oman in February 2011. In turn, this phase is now supplemented by a large Discovery research project (DP120101166) funded by the Australian Research Council and administered by the University of Adelaide, on 'Building an Indian Ocean Region'.

As part of these processes, at a meeting of the Indian Ocean Rim Academic Group (IORAG) at the 12th Meeting of Ministers of the IORA in Gurgaon, India, the Indian Ocean Research Group (which has Observer status at IORAG), applied successfully for an additional grant from IORA to initiate this Symposium in Kenya.

The range of issues touched upon at the Nairobi conference—some of which are presented in this volume—will provide the basis of a long-term research agenda and research plan for both IORAG and the IORG, and will lead to a number of exciting projects specific to Africa and the Indian Ocean Region.

Scholars writing for this volume have considered the position of Africa in the context of the Indian Ocean from a range of angles. For example, Ross Anthony's chapter reviews the growing presence of

China in the Indian Ocean region. Anthony discusses China's proposed development of ports and infrastructure on the east coast of Africa, and the geostrategic interests involved. The piece compares Chinese commercial infrastructure and resource development in Africa with the earlier and aforementioned 'races for Africa' (19th Century German and British colonialism in the area), arguing that Chinese presence today is significantly different due to the developments being supplemented by other actors, including host states, multi-national corporations and regional development funds.

The collaborative chapter by Christian Bouchard and William Crumplin considers the rising significance of the African littoral in the Indian Ocean region. The authors outline how Africa's potential for growth, economic development and more efficient maritime activities bring high expectations for Africa's role in the region and increases its geopolitical and geostrategic significance.

Each of the chapters that feature in the current volume and which were presented at the Symposium highlight the presence of Africa as a force in the western Indian Ocean Region. It has been argued that superpowers, including China and the US, are already harnessing the western Indian Ocean for their own gain (Van Rooyen 2011). As Van Rooyen explains, Africa will benefit from exercising greater regional involvement:

> The Indian Ocean is also Africa's ocean, and the nations of Africa need to show pro-active ownership and management of its eastern seaboard, for only then will stability, development and co-operation ensure that the benefits flow towards the continent. (Van Rooyen 2011, p.24)

Pan-regional and sub-regional identity-building exercises are not zero-sum games. Pursuing a myriad of different forms of regionalisms can only lead to positive outcomes. One size does not fit all in policy response terms, whether it relates to trade, security, environmental or cultural exchange. These alternate visions of region challenge, on the one-hand, an overly homogenous view of globalization and, at the same time, privilege and celebrate relationships among countries and communities that share the same geographic space and place on our planet. The place of Africa in these dominant regional constructions is hotly contested.

Table 1. Alternative Indian Ocean Regional Constructions

Indian Ocean Region	*East Indian Ocean*	*Indo-Pacific Region*
Diplomacy	limited diplomacy	traditional security
US excluded re Iran/China Dialogue Partner China	Tripartite bloc	US-India centric/Excluding
Africa included; Pakistan excluded re India; China Dialogue Partner	Africa excluded Australia/India/Indonesia Japan also key player	Africa excluded Australia-China contested
Soft power Non-traditional security issues	Soft/hard power Traditional security	Hard power
Pan-regionalists	Sub-regionalists	Nationalists
Foreign affairs departments departments/consultants	Foreign affairs/defence Departments	Defence
Liberal commentators	Liberal/conservative Commentators	Conservative commentators

In recent years, the regional security debate and responses in have primarily reflected three competing security constructions of the Indian Ocean Region (Table 1). The first is an all-embracing concept of an *Indian Ocean Region* comprising up to 51 states at its largest scale to 20 states at the scale of the Indian Ocean Rim Association (IORA). The second is a scaled-down version of the first into the *East Indian Ocean.* The third and largest in area is an *Indo-Pacific* concept which emphasises the pre-eminence of regional naval power and ensures that India (along with Indonesia, Japan and the United States, among others) potentially plays a central policing role not only within the Indian Ocean Region. Both of the latter constructions marginalize maritime Africa, to a certain extent.

An *Africa-inclusive* narrative based on an Indian Ocean Regional security construction tends to be perpetuated by liberal practitioners and commentators concerned primarily with non-traditional security issues, with the cooperative use of diplomacy and smart power in a regional community context. On the other hand, the dominant narrative based on an *Africa-exclusive* Indo-Pacific Region security construction tends to be propagated by conservative practitioners and commentators concerned principally with the use of collective traditional security and hard power directed either overtly or covertly towards individual states, and more particularly, towards China. While there are subservient interpretations of the Indo-Pacific concept that are inclusive of China, these inclusive maps are not the dominant geopolitical construction currently espoused.

In this chapter, we argue that there is an overriding narrative at work that de-emphasises an Indian Ocean Regional security construction, while attempting to propagate a view in favour of a more US-centric/ China exclusive/Africa exclusive Indo-Pacific regional security construction. We argue for a more inclusive definition of the Indo-Pacific, one that includes China, Africa, and the United States.

The Indian Ocean Region

From a formal perspective, the Indian Ocean Region could be defined as comprising those states that border directly onto the Indian Ocean itself. From a functional point of view, we could define the Indian Ocean Region as comprising those 20 states that belong to the Indian Ocean Rim Association (IORA). The common formal and functional criterion is a border on, and an interest in, the Ocean itself. In the case of the latter criterion, we could include states associated with the tributary waters to the Indian Ocean as well as those land-locked states for which transit to and from the sea is primarily oriented towards the Indian Ocean. Using this broadest regional construction, we can identify a total of 51 states, 28 of which are Indian Ocean Rim states, plus a further 10 that are coastal states of the Red Sea and the Persian Gulf, together with an additional 13 Indian Ocean land-locked states (Bouchard and Crumplin 2010, pp. 34-5).

One view of a preferred regional security construction is that it be built around this Indian Ocean Region. This view argues that strategic reassessments of the Indian Ocean Region and associated security challenges are contributing to the development of a new collective Indian Ocean security paradigm built on maritime regionalism. This paradigm is primarily designed to facilitate confidence building and to deal effectively with a wide range of so-called 'non-traditional' security challenges. Significantly, however, the United States Unified Command Structure divides the Indian Ocean Region between USAFRICACOM and USPACOM, splitting the Indian Ocean in two, separating Africa from those countries to its east. This division has resulted in a "fragmented" security organisation structure as far as the US approach to the IOR is concerned (Hastings 2011). Often changes in overall strategic direction fail to transpire simply because bureaucratic and departmental structures are pre-existing and well-entrenched, rather than because there is an acceptance or rejection of a new institutional architecture that reflects power shifts and new regional constellations (Doyle 2011).

The East Indian Ocean

A second competing regional security construction centres on the East Indian Ocean (EIO). This construction has been largely championed by Australia, with successive Labor and Liberal Governments arguing that to engage with Africa is to embark upon foreign policies outside its budgetary and security visions. We have been reminded recently that: "Australia often forgets that it's a three-ocean country". While Australia has had a unified policy framework for the Pacific Ocean, such an approach is lacking for the Indian Ocean as a whole (Bateman and Bergin 2010, p. 33). A *full* Australian engagement in an Indian Ocean-wide set of security initiatives is subject to the constraint of "territorial overstretch": that is, the challenge of attempting to undertake too much engagement across too great a span of territory on too many issues (Rumley 2012, p. 103). Since Australia's "geographical reach is limited", a more limited regional security construction might be preferred to begin with. While not neglecting the rest of the Indian Ocean Region, Australia, it is argued, should focus on the geographically closer East Indian Ocean (EIO) sub-region to enable practical cooperation and constructive dialogue (Bateman and Bergin 2010, pp. 45-7). Importantly for this regional construction, the EIO is congruent with USAPACOM.

The Indo-Pacific Region

A third regional security construction is that of the Indo-Pacific region. Some commentators appear to take it for granted that we have now entered the "Indo-Pacific century" (Medcalf 2012, p. 13). Proponents exert us to believe that its emergence is both "irresistible" (Wesley 2011) and "inevitable" (Raja Mohan 2011). We are assured that the Asia-Pacific era died in 2011 and was replaced with the Indo-Pacific era. The conservative Australian journalist Greg Sheridan, for example, claims that the 60th anniversary AUSMIN meeting in San Francisco in September 2011 marked the "pivot point" at which both Australia and the United States began to "redefine their region not as the Asia-Pacific, but as the Indo-Pacific" (Sheridan 2011).

Significantly, the Indo-Pacific construction itself is contested. The University of Adelaide's *Indo-Pacific Governance Research Centre* defines the Indo-Pacific as the "region spanning the Western Pacific Ocean to the Western Indian Ocean along the eastern coast of Africa" (IPGRC 2011). The Indo-Pacific has also been defined as "the areas of the Indian Ocean and the West Pacific" (Curtis el al 2011, p. 1). Furthermore, it has been defined as "an emerging Asian strategic system that encompasses both the Pacific and Indian Oceans, defined in part by the geographically expanding interests and reach of China and India, and the continued strategic role and presence of the United States in both" (Medcalf, Heinrichs and Jones 2011, p. 56).

Furthermore, increasing economic and trade linkages—a process of *regionalisation*—necessitates the construction of an Indo-Pacific *regionalism*. It appears that one of the practical security aims of the re-introduction of this regional construction is to shift the centre of gravity of Indian and Australian security concerns towards the South China Sea as a part of a burden-sharing strategy with the United States. It is thus in part an attempt by the United States to engage India and Australia (and others), excluding others (such as maritime Africa) while simultaneously being a mechanism for facilitating its hegemonic transition.

It has been argued that the United States does not have a coherent geopolitical vision of the Indian Ocean Region and that the allocation of political and military resources makes it difficult for the US to make a credible commitment to the security of the Indian Ocean Region. To the extent that the US has an alliance structure in the Indian Ocean Region, it is composed of the residual relationships from other strategically important regions, thus decreasing its ability to be turned to the security of the Indian Ocean Region. While the US Department of Defense rhetorically recognises the geopolitical importance of the Indian Ocean Region, there is no single US military command structure dedicated to the Indian Ocean Region, as noted earlier. The military forces that are prepositioned in the region are not insignificant, but are ill-suited for making the necessary commitments to the region as a whole. This spatial distribution of resources has implications, consequently, for the United States' ability to claim that the Indian Ocean Region as a whole is at the core of its interests (Hastings 2011).

The new imperative of shifting from an Indian Ocean to an Indo-Pacific regional security construction is driven, in part, by concerns over possible Chinese naval expansionism and by a concern over the use of Chinese naval power both in the Indian Ocean *and* in the South China Sea. From an American perspective, effectively managing these concerns requires the cooperation not only of India, but also of Australia, Indonesia, Japan and other states that possess similar concerns. Australia gains, it is argued, because it will obtain a US presence in a remote region which is of national economic significance and which is thus a potential subject of future threat. From an overall regional geopolitical perspective, the coalition will affect a closer monitoring, and potential control over, the eastern exits and entrances of Indian Ocean access routes. The end result is clearly of *global* geopolitical significance.

The renewed interest in an Indo-Pacific construction on the part of the United States clearly has some basic implications for the long-term future of US-Australia security relations. The move away from an Indian Ocean and towards an Indo-Pacific security construction has reignited the basic trilateral geopolitical tension faced by Australia's external linkages: that, culturally, Australia identifies primarily with Europe; that, economically, Australia's strongest links are with Asia, and especially China; and that, militarily and politically, Australia is aligned with the United States (Rumley 2007, p. 137). Enhanced engagement has also been proposed by creating a formal trilateral dialogue among Australia, India and the United States that would be designed to face common security challenges in the Indo-Pacific Region (Curtis et al 2011).

Conclusion and Implications: Towards a More Inclusive Regional Security Construction

One of the more important dimensions of contested regionalism is whether the scale or the type of regionalism includes or excludes certain states, and whether the type of regionalism is in full accord with, or conflicts in some way with, state/non-state goals. This dimension of contested regionalism can be seen to operate in practice from, first, the viewpoint of the state wishing to be included, and, second, from the perspective of the state or states wishing to implement exclusion. In either case, inclusion in/membership of regional constructions/ organisations can be used as a mechanism for creating or reconstituting some form of regional identity (Rumley 2005). The depiction of the Indo-Pacific by most commentators and state actors in Australia, India and the United States, and the way it has been perceived in China, indicates that the current Indo-Pacific regional construction is *exclusive* and is thus directed towards China itself. The propagation of this concept in its present portrayal may well have unintended negative consequences which may lead to an increase in regional instability. As mentioned at the outset, we argue for model of regionalism that is inclusive of relationships with China, Africa and the United States.

The undoubted strength and influence of the Indo-Pacific regional security construction has some important implications for our other two Indian Ocean proposals—IORA and EIO. For example, as aforesaid, the prospects for EIO security cooperation along the lines discussed earlier in the chapter remain relatively bright, if only because the EIO is congruent with USAPACOM.

However, any potential security function—either traditional or maritime security cooperation-that IORA might consider undertaking will likely take place at other forums, though IORA will remain an extremely useful regional governance form for a whole array of other co-operative ventures. As a consequence, the current volume—a direct outcome of one such cooperative IORA/IORG venture—seeks to encourage a Western Indian Ocean dialogue, to supplement the Eastern Indian Ocean Dialogue recently-initiated Trilateral Dialogue between India, Australia and Indonesia. Despite a relatively quieter role in terms of participation in the IORA on behalf of Africa in recent years, the papers presented at the conference on maritime Africa prove the continent is host to key actors in the Indian Ocean Region.

Africa, with its rich natural beauty and resources; its diverse and vibrant cultures; and its resilient and inspired peoples will increasingly play a pivotal role in the future of the geopolitics of the Indian Ocean Region.

REFERENCES

Bateman, S. and Bergin, A. (2010), *Our Western Front: Australia and the Indian Ocean*, Barton, ACT: ASPI.

Curtis, L. et al (2011), *Shared Goals, Converging Interests: A Plan for US-Australia-India Cooperation in the Indo-Pacific*, Washington DC: Heritage Foundation, Department of Defense (2009).

Doyle, T. (2011), 'Building Indian Ocean regionalisms: an agenda for IORG research', in V. Sakhuja, ed., *Reinvigorating IORA*, New Delhi: Pentagon Press, pp. 1-17.

Hastings, J. (2011), 'The fractured geopolitics of the United States in the Indian Ocean Region', *Journal of the Indian Ocean Region*, Vol. 7 (2), pp. 183-199.

Medcalf, R., Heinrichs, R. and Jones, J. (2011), *Crisis and Confidence: Major Powers and Maritime Security in Indo-Pacific Asia*, Sydney: Lowy.

Medcalf, R. (2012), 'Unselfish giants: Understanding China and India as security providers', *Australian Journal of International Affairs*, Vol. 66 (1), pp. 1-13.

Raja Mohan, C. (2011), 'India and Australia: maritime partners in the Indo-Pacific', *The Asialink Essays*, Vol. 3 (7), November, pp. 1-4.

Rumley, D. (2005), 'The geopolitics of Asia-Pacific regionalism in the 21st century', *The Otemon Journal of Australian Studies*, Vol. 31 (1), pp. 3-25.

Rumley, D. (2007), 'Australia's regional security challenges: a geopolitical perspective', in D. Rumley and D. Gopal, eds., *Globalisation and Regional Security: India and Australia*, Delhi: Shipra, pp. 133-157.

Rumley, D. (2012), 'Refloating IORA: Australian perspectives', in V. Sakhuja, ed., *Reinvigorating IORA*, New Delhi: Pentagon Press, pp. 87-105.

Sheridan, G. (2011), 'New Australia-US push deals India in to Pacific', *The Australian* newspaper, 17 September and available at: http://www.theaustralian.com.au/news/opinion/new-australia-us-push-deals-india-in-to-pacific/story-e6frg76f-1226139302534

Tuathail, G. Ó (1992), 'The Bush Administration and the 'End' of the Cold War: A Critical Geopolitics of US Foreign Policy in 1989,' *Geoforum* 23: 437-452.

Van Rooyen, F 2011, 'Africa and the Geopolitics of the Indian Ocean', *South African Institute of International Affairs*, Occasion Paper no. 78, February 2011.

Wesley, M. (2011), 'Irresistible rise of the Indo-Pacific', *The Australian* newspaper, 4 May, accessible at:http://www.theaustralian.com.au/news/arts/irresistible-rise-of-the-indo-pacific/story-e6frg8nf-1226047014015.

Chapter 6

African Countries' Trade and Investment with Indian Ocean Rim States

Saman Kelegama and Dharshani Premaratne

ABSTRACT

The Indian Ocean Rim Association (IORA) was formed in 1997 not just to facilitate trade and investment within IORA members but also to strengthen their political linkages. Since its inception in 1997 and up until 2013 it has expanded its membership to a diversified range of 20 member countries from the Indian Ocean Rim, including six Dialogue Partners and two Observers. By 2013, IORA has accepted membership of eight African members, led by South Africa as the largest economy, followed by Comoros, Kenya, Madagascar, Mauritius, Mozambique, Seychelles and Tanzania. The focal interest of joining IORA by the small and less developed African states was to gain preferential treatment for trading goods and services and thereby looking forward to greater regional integration. IORA, like APEC, embraced the concept of open regionalism from the beginning, which does not discriminate between members and non-members in the provisions, and whether it has garnered the potential benefits of regionalism is extensively criticized in the literature (Kelegama, 2000).

Key words: Trade, investment, IORA, regional integration, regionalism.

Introduction

Today, the Indian Ocean Region stands at a critical juncture of growth and development. While some members of IORA such as Australia and India are driving world economic growth, emerging economies such as Indonesia, Malaysia, Singapore and Thailand are driving world trade, and petroleum giants like Iran and United Arab Emirates (UAE) are controlling the world's largest oil resources. Smaller and less developed members, for instance, Bangladesh, Comoros, Mozambique and Madagascar, on the other hand, are still struggling to find their feet in the world trade arena. Thus at present, the IORA faces multiple issues like, lack of preferential treatment for Least Developed Countries (LDCs) and small developing countries, free rider and reciprocity issues (all resulting from adoption of open regionalism), lack of efficient sectoral cooperation, issues of expansion before consolidation that has made housekeeping matters overriding economic matters, complexities of regional trade arrangements (RTAs) membership, weak role of the Secretariat, unclear vision, and nonexistence of the second track (Kelegama 2012, pp. 74-81). Most importantly, the weakening interest of most members who benefit more from preferential arrangements in other RTAs causes a great level of uncertainty that hampers long-term integration and growth prospects of the IORA.

The entrance of LDCs and small economies to IORA was to improve their trade and political links with the regional members and to what extent this has been achieved is thus far unclear. Although empirical evidence does not show a significant change in the trade architecture of the eight African members of the IORA their trade with the rest of IORA members has shown signs of improvement over the past two decades (UNCOMTRADE 2013). Both the traditional exports and imports remain unchanged with mining, plantations, gems, horticulture, textile and fisheries sectors leading the exports and petroleum, pharmaceuticals, palm oil and consumer goods such as sugar cane dominating the imports. However, net food importing countries, such as Mauritius, realize their entire domestic food requirement through imports from India and Thailand, namely rice, sugar and meat.

It could be noted that the African continent has recorded a high inflow of foreign direct investments (FDI) in the recent past owing to high returns on investments (UNCTAD 2013). Even during the global slowdown in FDI to developing countries in 2012, extractive industries, consumer-oriented manufacturing industries, and service industries in Africa have been able to attract FDI for their industrial expansions that marked a 5 per cent growth in FDI to the region in 2012 (UNCTAD 2013). Yet due to the weak institutions and poor state of the infrastructure, a business-friendly environment is still not full-fledged in Africa, except in South Africa. Tourism is yet another prospective avenue that has seen signs of growth amidst political and economic tensions in the African continent. Southern and Southeastern African states consider themselves as a doorway to the continent from the Indian Ocean. The shoreline cities of South Africa, Kenya, Tanzania, and Mozambique and island states, such as Seychelles, Mauritius, Madagascar and Comoros, have had multifaceted cultural and economic ties with the Indian Ocean Rim states. With today's liberalized global trade and investment flows these countries can position themselves to tap the potential of their strategic location. Hence the magnitude to which the existing channels of air and ocean connectivity with the counterparts of the Indian Ocean Rim have been able to garner the merits of the rewarding location and ways and means of improving the connectivity require greater attention.

Therefore, this chapter attempts to explore the rationale of having a regional arrangement as IORA for Indian Ocean Rim States merely due to the reason of sharing a common ocean. In doing so, the next section draws attention to a detailed analysis of the existing trade and investment patterns of African IORA members with non-African IORA members. The next section sheds light on the future prospects of IORA in terms of its capacity and viability to improve intra-IORA trade, investment and connectivity via sea and air.

Progress of IORA in African Member States

African Trade with Indian Ocean Rim States

The pattern of trade among the eight African members in IORA - namely Comoros, Kenya, Madagascar, Mauritius, Mozambique, Seychelles, South Africa and Tanzania - and non-African IORA members does not indicate a noticeable transformation from their respective traditional export and import baskets to a more diversified product range. Yet owing to the fast growing members like India, developed Australia and emerging economies such as Indonesia, Malaysia, Singapore and Thailand, African countries have been able to reap the spillover effects of those stronger economies to a certain extent. As shown in Figure 1, exports of African countries, especially South African exports, to non-African IORA members have escalated gradually since the 1990s until 2012. Nevertheless, most African members' (except South African and Kenyan) share of intra-IORA exports as a percentage of total world exports do not show a clear trend of any sort other than continuous fluctuations (Figure 2). Minerals, metals, precious and semi-precious stones, wood products, spices, edible nuts, dried and shelled vegetables, fish and crustaceans, fresh and dried fruits, oil for cosmetics and toiletries, and textile are main export products of Africa to the rest of IORA members.

Similarly, the imports of African countries, again led by South African imports, from non-African IORA members have significantly ascended improving their share of intra-IORA imports as a percentage of total world imports (Figures 3 and 4). Africa meets with its petroleum needs largely from UAE, India, Oman and Iran out of the IORA members, which accounts for nearly 50 per cent of their petroleum imports from the world. Africa's other major imports from non-African IORA countries include petroleum gases and hydrocarbons, palm oil, pharmaceutical products, cement, coniferous, wooden furniture, telecommunication equipment, rice, wheat and meslin flour, sunflower seeds and oil, sugar cane, dairy products, chemical compounds, computer parts and accessories, iron, printed manuscripts and typescripts, plastics and rubbers, transport vessels, and parts of machinery.

Kenya

Horticulture and tea are Kenya's major exports to the world and its largest export destinations for tea are United Kingdom, Egypt and Sudan that account for over 75 per cent of their total world exports of tea. Kenya's exports of tea to IORA members, chiefly to UAE, are only about 5 per cent of their total world exports. India and Sri Lanka hold the largest share, close to 75 per cent, of intra-IORA tea exports while Kenya has about 20 per cent share. However, demand for horticulture products from Australia has remarkably improved during the last decade and as at present Australia absorbs about 60 per cent of the horticulture exports of Kenya.

UAE and India are Kenya's largest export destinations in the Indian Ocean region that account for 70 per cent of Kenya's exports to non-African IORA members (Figure 5). Kenya's major exports to UAE and India consist of black tea (fermented) and other partly fermented tea (HS 90240), transmission apparatus incorporating reception apparatus (HS 852520), peas: seeds of a kind used for sowing split peas, green

Figure 1. Exports of African countries to non-African IORA member countries excluding South Africa

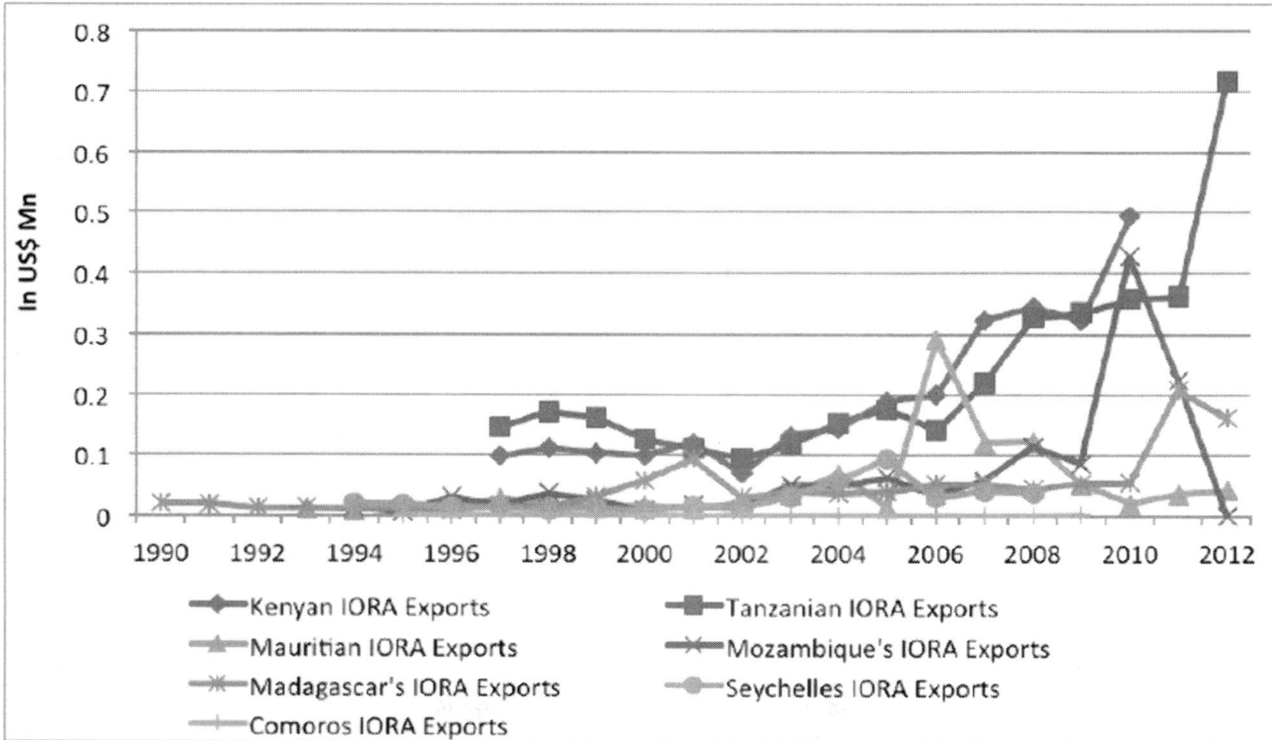

Source: Compiled using UNCOMTRADE data in WITS database.

Reason to exclude South Africa in this figure is to get a clear trend of other countries as the exceptionally high numbers in South Africa, compared to other trading partners, hides the trends of other countries.

Figure 2. Share of exports of African countries to non-African IORA members as a percentage of their total world exports

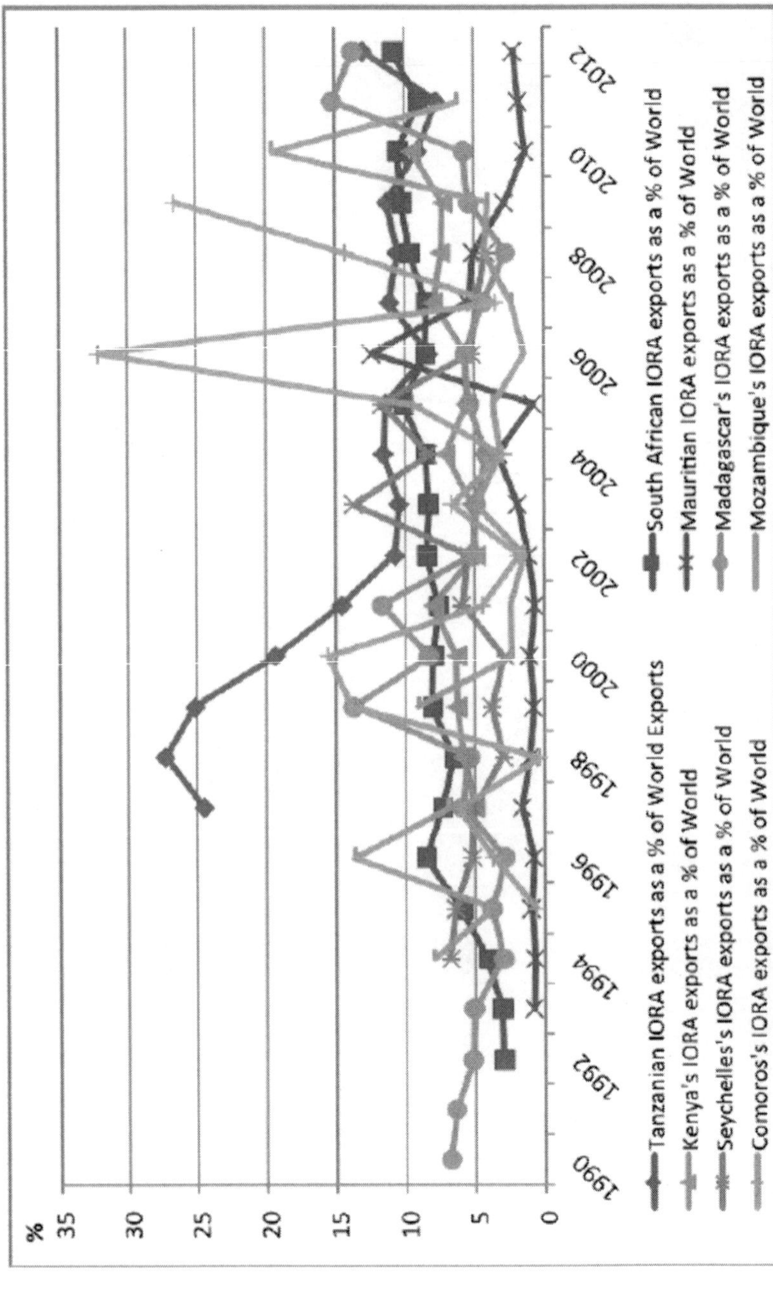

Source: Compiled using UNCOMTRADE data in WITS database.

Figure 3. Imports of African countries from non-African IORA member countries

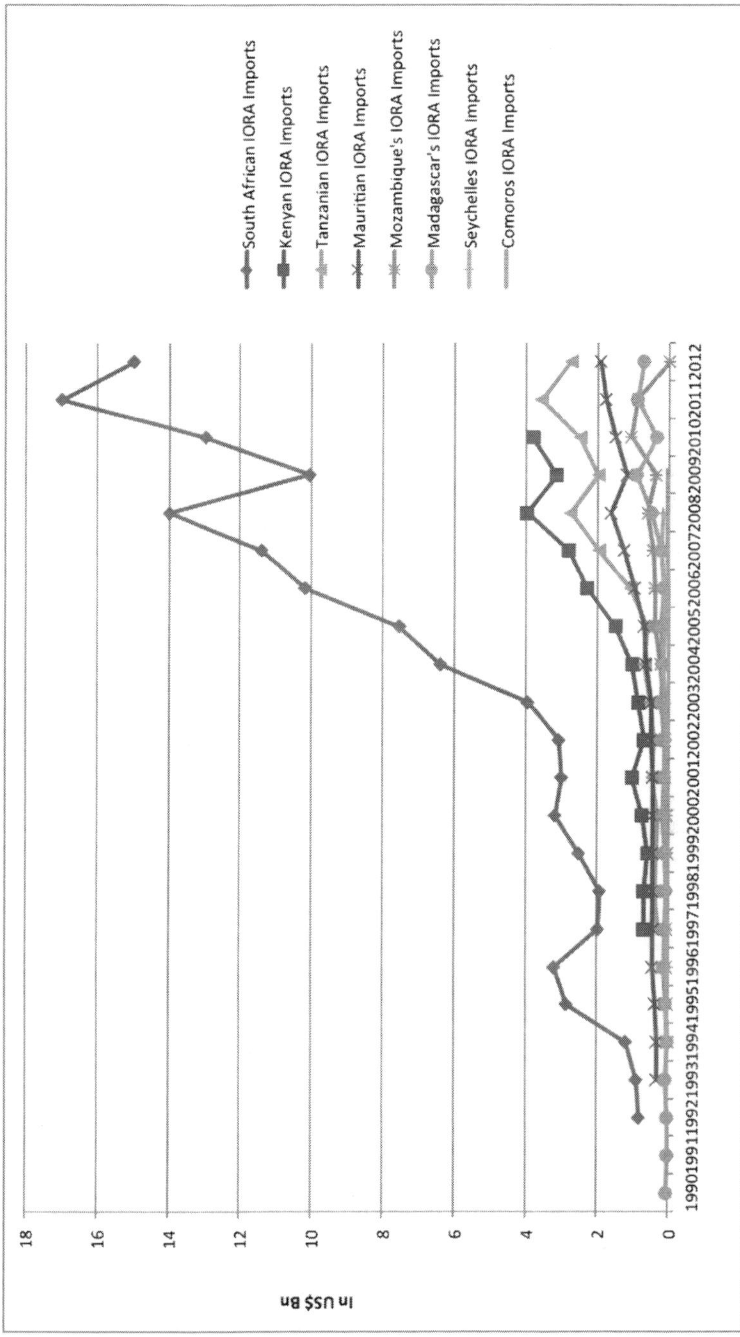

Figure 4. Share of imports of African countries from non-African IORA members as a percentage of their total world imports

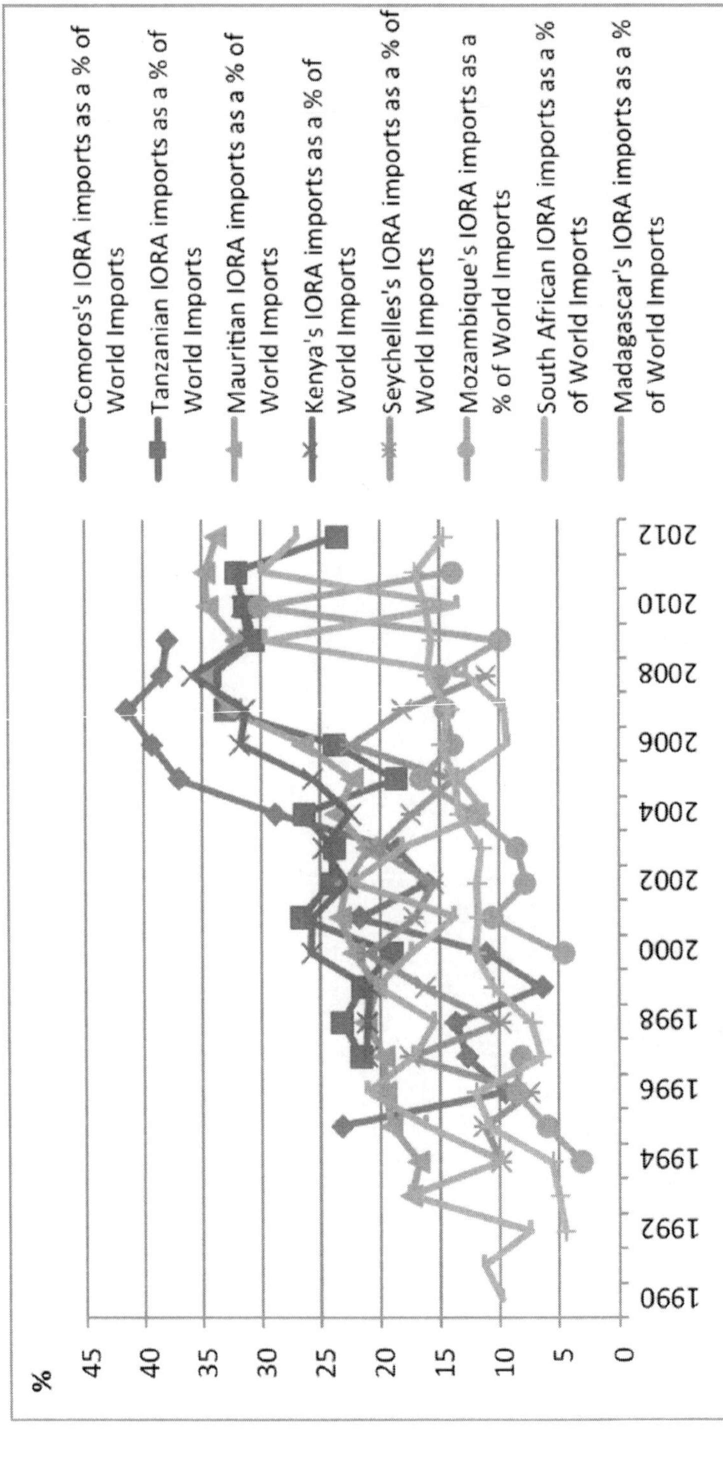

Source: Compiled using UNCOMTRADE data in WITS database

peas, yellow peas, Austrian winter peas (HS 71310), seeds of a kind used for sowing (HS 71390), carbonates, peroxocarbonates (Percarbonates) (HS 283699), fluorspar (containing more than 97% of Calcium Fluoride) (HS 252922), guavas, mangoes and mangosteens (HS 08450), and generating sets with compression-ignition engines, exceeding 375kva (HS 850213). Australia is the largest market for Kenyan fresh cut flowers and buds for bouquet etc., prepared (HS60310) and coffee (unroasted, not decaffeinated) (HS90111) among IORA members that accounts for nearly 60 and 65 per cent respectively of the intra-IOR-ARC exports of fresh cut flowers and coffee of Kenya. Moreover, UAE is the only IORA member country that sources Kenyan exports of gold in other semi-manufactured forms (HS 710813) that has multiplied in ten-fold from 1990s to 2012.

Kenyan imports from non-African IORA members are also dominated by India and UAE with petroleum oils, oils obtained from Bituminous mineral, preparations thereof (HS 271000) and Petroleum oils and oils obtained from Bituminous mineral (Crude) (HS 270900) imports accounting for nearly 70 per cent and 85 per cent respectively of Kenya's world imports of the said products. Kenya fulfills its entire domestic palm oil–crude oil (HS 151110) requirement solely from IORA members chiefly from Singapore, Indonesia and Malaysia. Further, India has secured nearly a 50 per cent share of Kenyan world imports of other medicaments (put up in packing for retail sale) (HS 300490) and transmission apparatus incorporating reception apparatus (HS 852520). Kenyan imports of cement clinkers (HS 252310) from IORA countries have fallen over time from a share of nearly 80 per cent in 2006 to 22 percent in 2010 as a percentage of its world imports of cement clinkers, while China, Japan and South Korea have taken over in catering to the Kenyan cement demand.

South Africa

A shift in South Africa's major export destinations from Thailand, Australia and Singapore, (since the 1990s), to India, Malaysia and UAE (from about 2008) can be identified. Today, South African exports to India, UAE and Malaysia account for over 60 per cent of South Africa's exports to non-African IORA members (Figure 7). Aluminum, not alloyed (HS 760110), chemical wood pulp, dissolving grades (HS

Figure 5. Kenya's exports to non-African IORA members

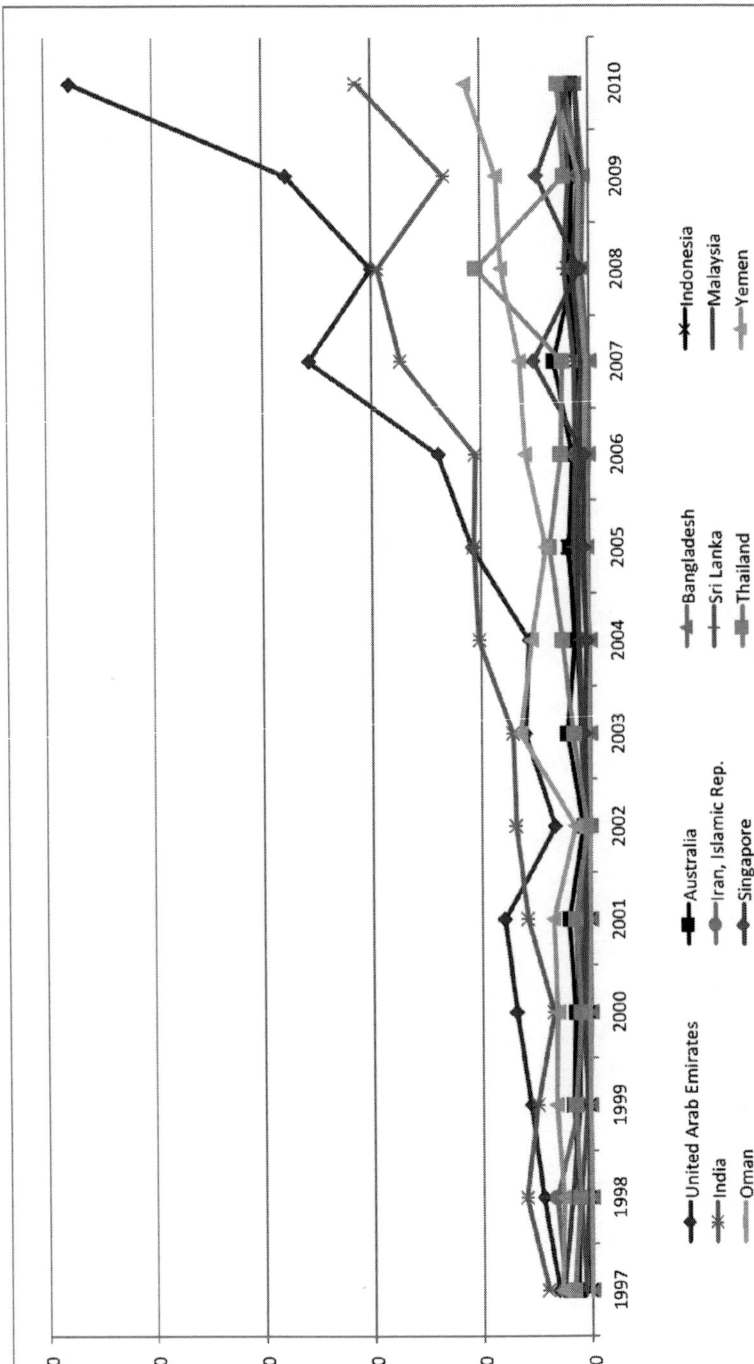

Figure 6. Kenya's imports from non-African IORA members

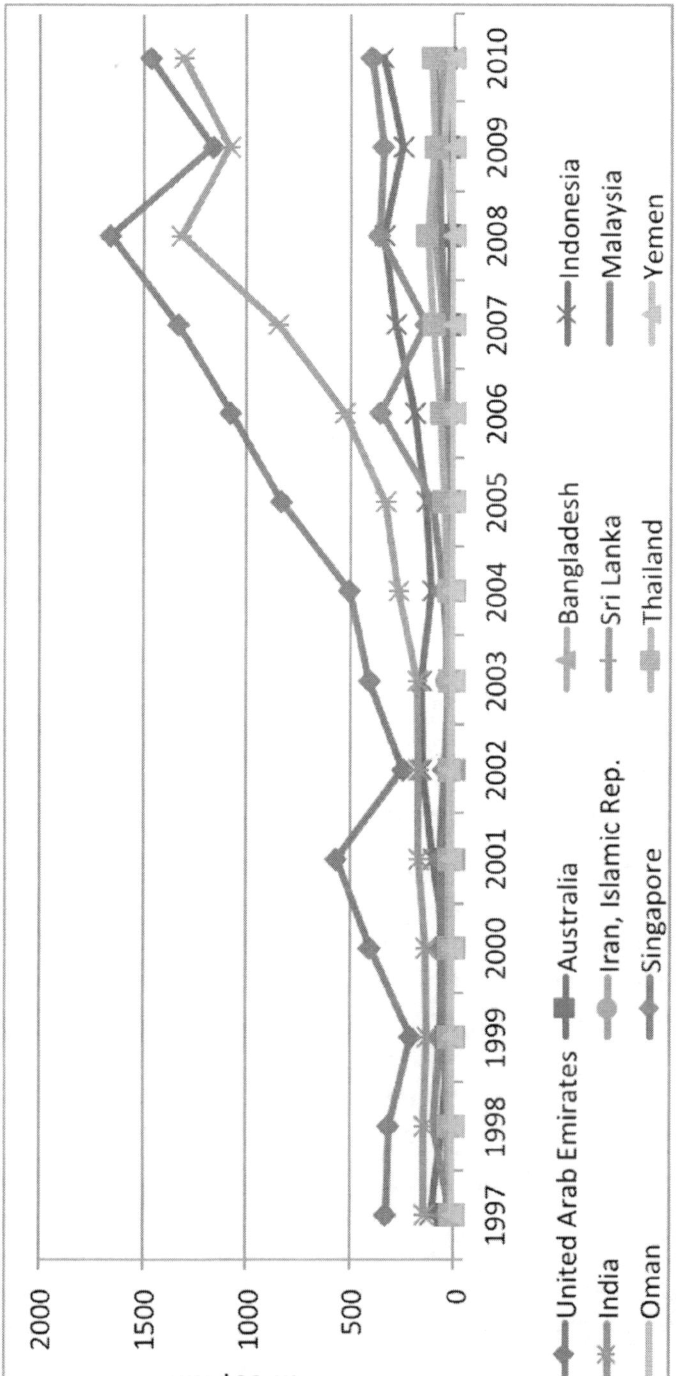

Source: Compiled using UNCOMTRADE data in WITS database

470200), waste and scrap of other ally steel (HS 720429), bituminous coal-coal, briquettes, ovoids etc., manufactured from coal (HS 270112), phosphoric acid and polyphosphoric acids (HS 280920), manganese ores and concentrates (HS 260200), copper ores and concentrates (HS 260300), diamonds unsorted (HS 710210), non-industrial diamonds, unworked or simply sawn, cleaved or bruted (HS 710231) and flat-rolled products of stainless steel (HS 721912) are South African main exports to IORA countries. Malaysia and UAE are the top export markets for fresh grapes (HS 80610) and oranges (HS 80510) of South Africa by 2012.

India absorbs the highest amount of mineral exports from South Africa namely, bituminous coal-coal, briquettes, ovoids etc., manufactured from coal (HS 270112), iron ores and concentrates (agglomerated) (HS 260112), unwrought or in powder form platinum content (HS 711011), iron ores and concentrates (non-agglomerated) (HS 260111), chromium ores and concentrates (HS 261000), manganese ores and concentrates (HS 260200), waste and scrap of other ally steel (HS 720429) and copper waste and scrap (HS 740400). Moreover, India has been the sole importer of South African gold in other semi-manufactured forms (HS 710813) up until the early 2000s yet since 2004 to date South African gold in other semi-manufactured forms exports have diverted to other destinations.

South African imports from non-African IORA members are dominated by Iran, India and Thailand with petroleum oils, oils obtained from bituminous mineral, preparations thereof (HS 271000), petroleum oils and oils obtained from bituminous mineral (crude) (HS 270900) and semi-milled or wholly milled rice (HS 100630) imports. Similar to Kenya, South Africa also fulfills its entire domestic palm oil-crude oil (HS 151110) requirement from IORA members, namely Singapore, Indonesia and Malaysia.

Other aluminum oxide (HS 281820) imports from Australia to South Africa are close to 95 per cent of South African total world imports of other aluminum oxide. Thailand and India caters to meet over 50 per cent of the domestic semi-milled or wholly milled rice demand and Malaysia holds a large market share in transmission apparatus incorporating reception apparatus (HS 852520), other telephonic apparatus (HS 851782), parts, of printing machinery, of machines for

Figure 7. South Africa's exports to non-African IORA members

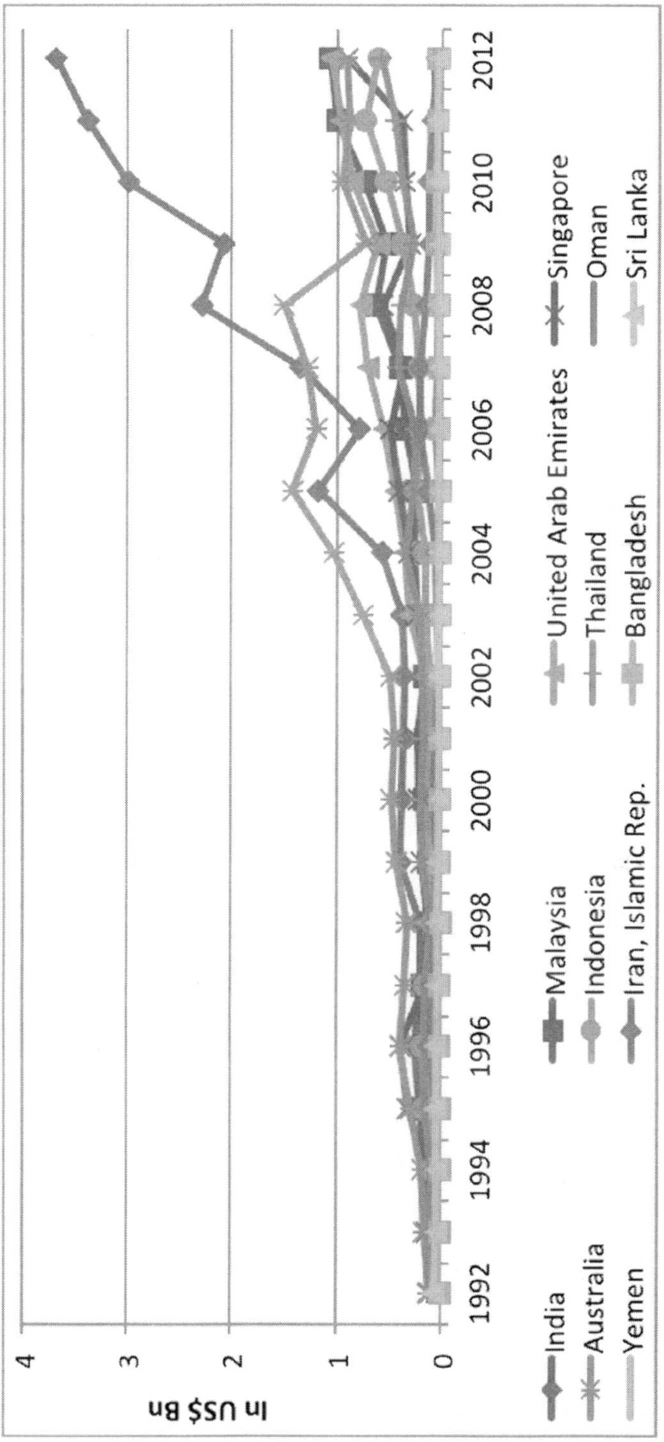

Source: Compiled using UNCOMTRADE data in WITS database.

uses ancillary to printing (HS 844390), input or output units - automatic data process machines, magnetic reader, etc. (HS 847592), parts and accessories of the automatic data processing machines (HS 847330), and storage units (HS 847193).

Tanzania

Tanzania's main export markets are UAE and India that accounts for 80 per cent of Tanzania's exports to non-African IOR-ARC members (Figure 9). The export basket to IOR-ARC countries consists largely of cashew nuts (HS 80130), cotton (not carded or combed) (HS 520100), cotton (carded or combed) (HS 520300), peas: seeds of a kind used for sowing split peas, green peas, yellow peas, Austrian winter peas (HS 71310), frozen fillets: cod halibut, fresh-water catfish, tilapia, Alaska pollock (HS 30420), oil-cake, solid residues resulting from extraction of sunflower seed oil (HS 230630), cloves (HS 90700), bran, sharps, other residues of wheat (HS 230230), antimony ores and concentrates (HS 261710), gold in other semimanufactured forms (HS 710813) and precious stones (other than diamonds) and semiprecious stones (HS 710310) by 2011. Moreover, IORA countries absorb almost 100 per cent of Tanzania's exports of cloves and peas.

India and UAE dominates Tanzanian imports from non-African IORA countries that draw 70 per cent of the share of Tanzania's total IORA imports. petroleum oils, oils obtained from bituminous mineral, preparations thereof (HS 271000), palm oil-crude oil (HS 151110), palm oil and its fractions (HS 151190), polypropylene-polymers of propylene or other olefins, prim forms (HS 390210), polyethylene having a specific gravity of 0.94 or more (HS 390120), worn clothing and other worn articles (HS 630900), motor vehicles for the transport of goods (HS 870423), digital automatic data processing machines (HS 847120), other cane or beet sugar, chemically pure sucrose (HS 170199), and other medicaments (put up in packing for retail sale) (HS 300490) are the main imports from IORA countries.

Tanzania sources its entire domestic palm oil-crude oil (HS 151110) requirement from IORA members chiefly from Indonesia and Malaysia. Further, India has secured nearly a 50 per cent share of Tanzanian world imports of pharmaceuticals that consists of vaccines for human medicine (HS 300220), other medicaments (put up in packing for retail sale) (HS

Figure 8. South Africa's imports from non-African IORA members

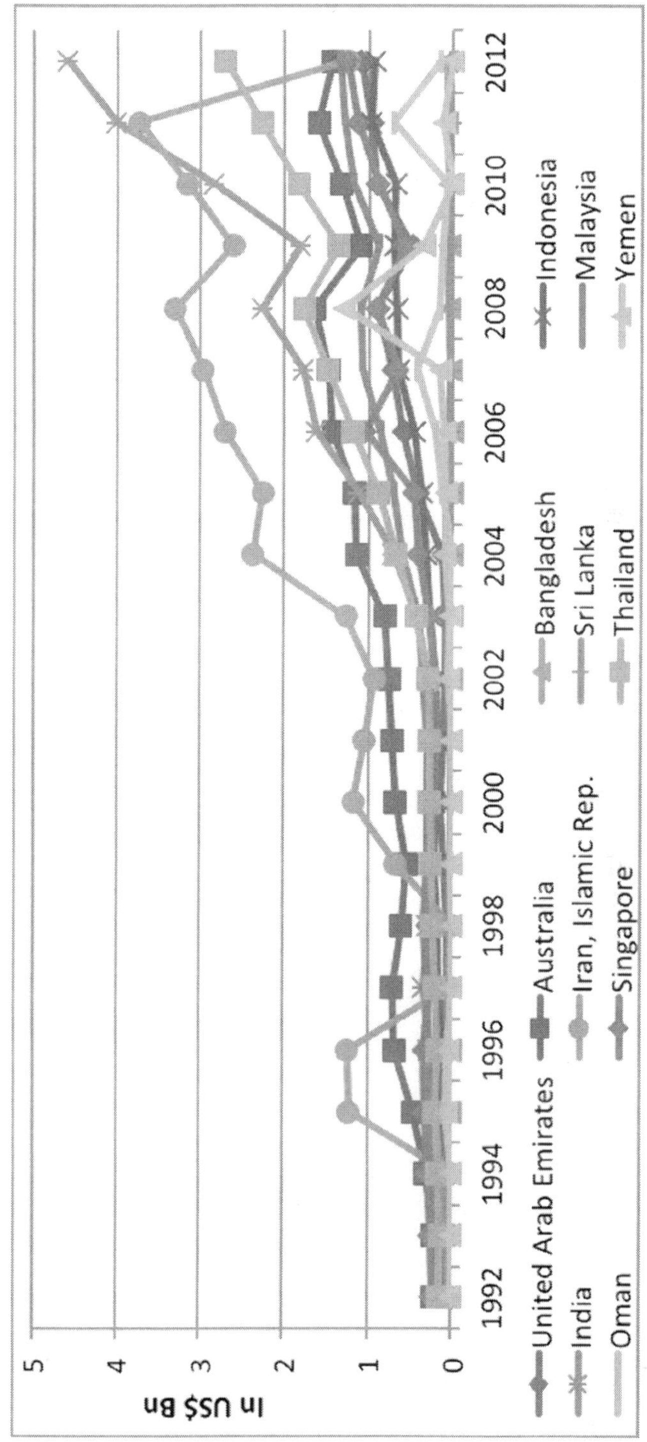

Source: Compiled using UNCOMTRADE data in WITS database.

Figure 9. Tanzania's exports to non-African IORA members

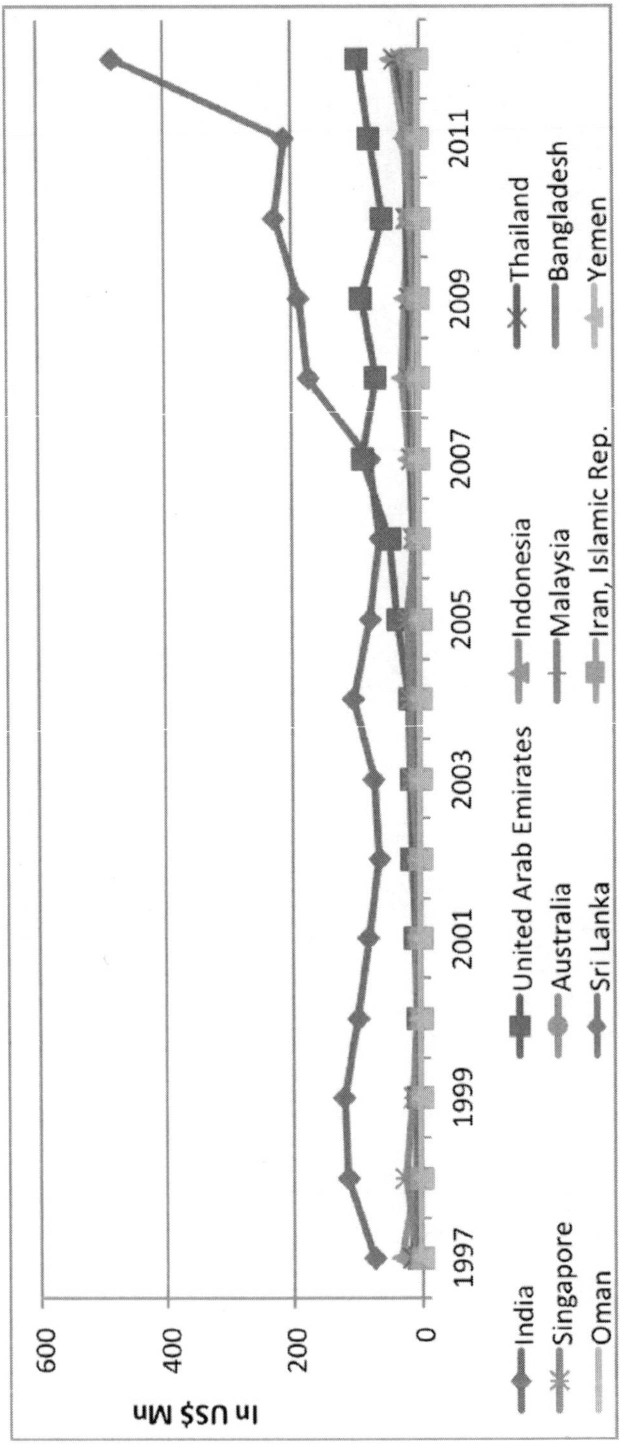

Source: Compiled using UNCOMTRADE data in WITS database.

300490), and other medicaments (HS 300390). Similar to Kenya, Tanzania's imports of portland cement (HS 252329) from IORA countries have dropped over time from a share of nearly 80 per cent in 2005 to 3 per cent in 2012 as a percentage of its world imports of portland cement, while China, Japan and South Korea have taken over in catering to the Tanzanian cement market.

Mozambique

India is the major export destination of Mozambique out of non-African IORA countries although since 2009 Iran and Malaysia have also attracted a significant amount of exports from Mozambique (Figure 11). Cotton (carded or combed) (HS 520300), cotton (not carded or combed) (HS 520100), zirconium ores and concentrates (HS 261510), bananas and plantains, fresh or dried (HS 80300), cashew nuts (HS 80130), waste and scrap of stainless steel (HS 720421) are the main exports of Mozambique to IORA regional members.

Although Mozambique had exported nearly 30 per cent of its total sugar cane (raw sugar not added flavour or colour (HS 170111) to India, Singapore and Indonesia in the early 2000s it has lost momentum since 2005. However, Mozambique had started exporting activated natural mineral products (HS 380290) to India and Singapore since 2012 that has a share of 60 per cent of its total world exports (HS 380290) and India imports a significant amount of titanium, zirconium and Stainless steel from Mozambique. Moreover, Mozambique's major export markets for textile, namely cotton products, are India and Bangladesh.

Mozambique's imports from non-African IORA members are dominated by India, UAE and Thailand with petroleum oils, oils obtained from bituminous mineral, preparations thereof (HS 271000) and semi-milled or wholly milled rice (HS 100630) imports having the largest share of total imports. India has a 55 per cent share of Mozambique's total world imports of other medicaments (put up in packings for retail sale) (HS 300490). Further, Mozambique sources 30 per cent of its world imports of worn clothing and other worn articles from Australia, India and UAE.

Figure 10. Tanzania's imports from non-African IORA members

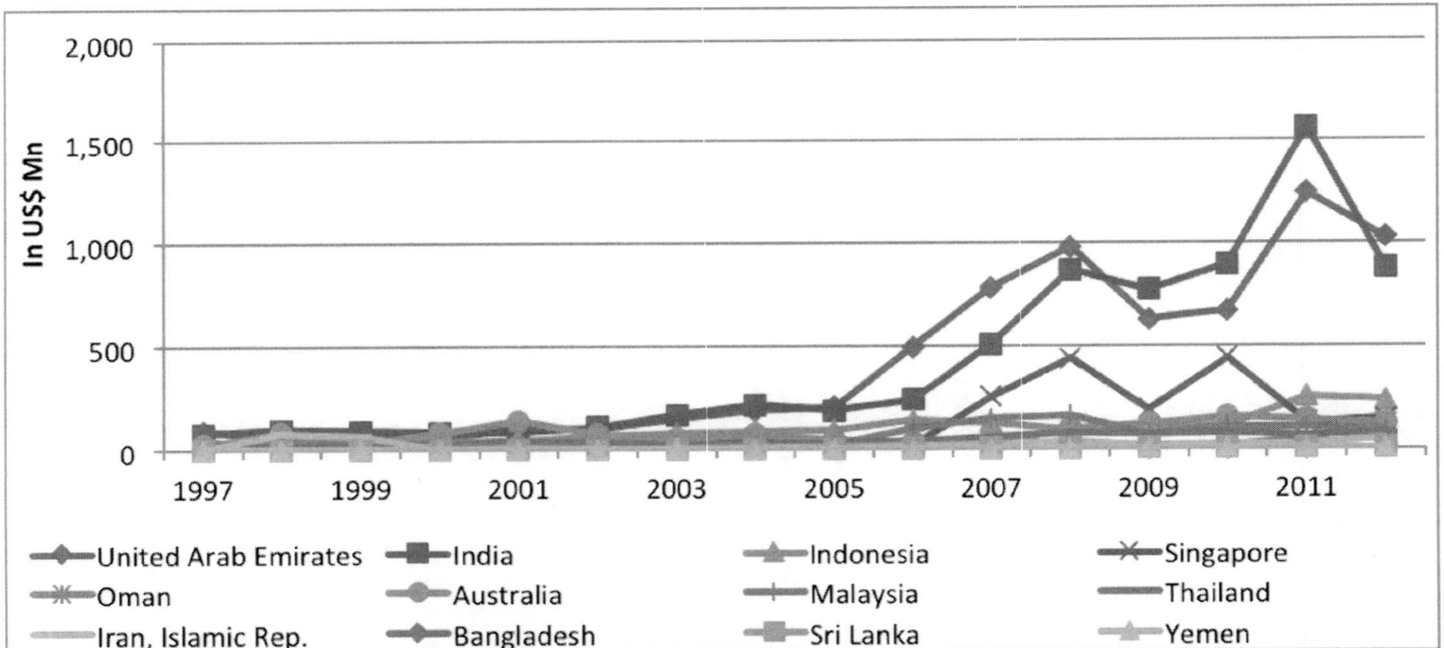

Source: Compiled using UNCOMTRADE data in WITS database.

Figure 11. Mozambique's exports to non-African IORA members

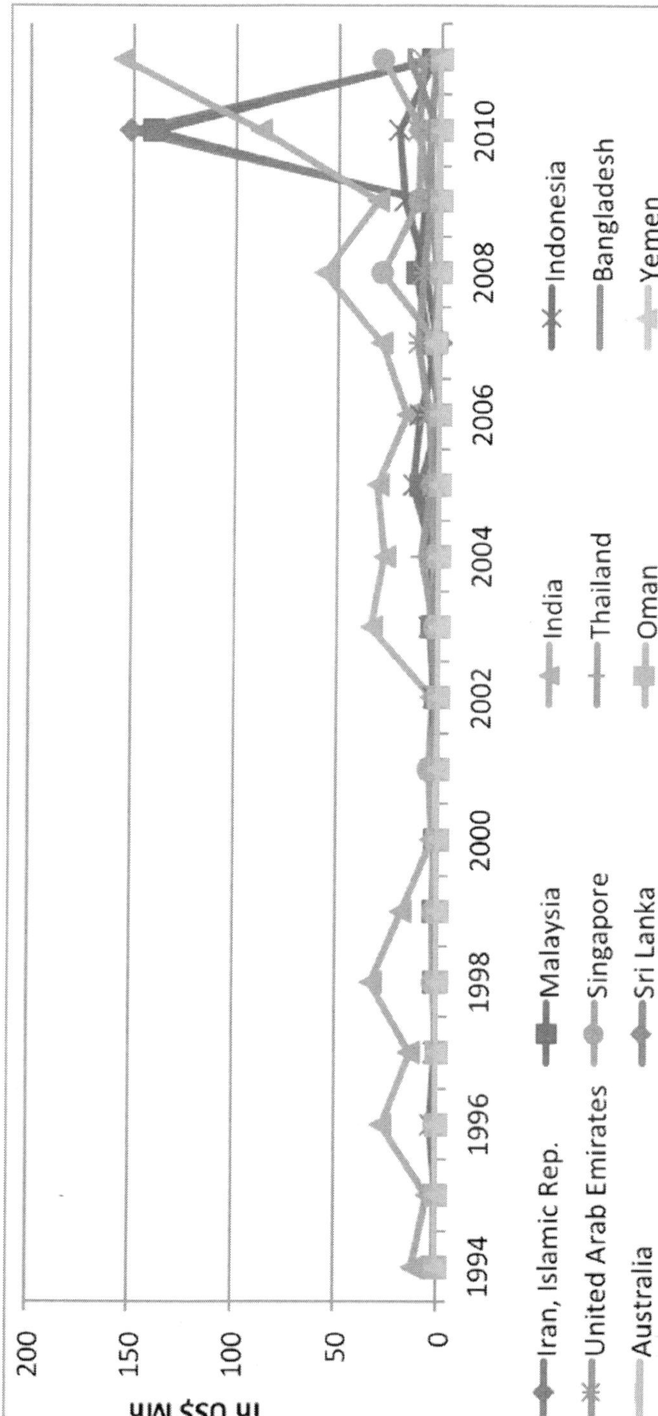

Source: Compiled using UNCOMTRADE data in WITS database.

Figure 12. Mozambique's imports from non-African IORA member

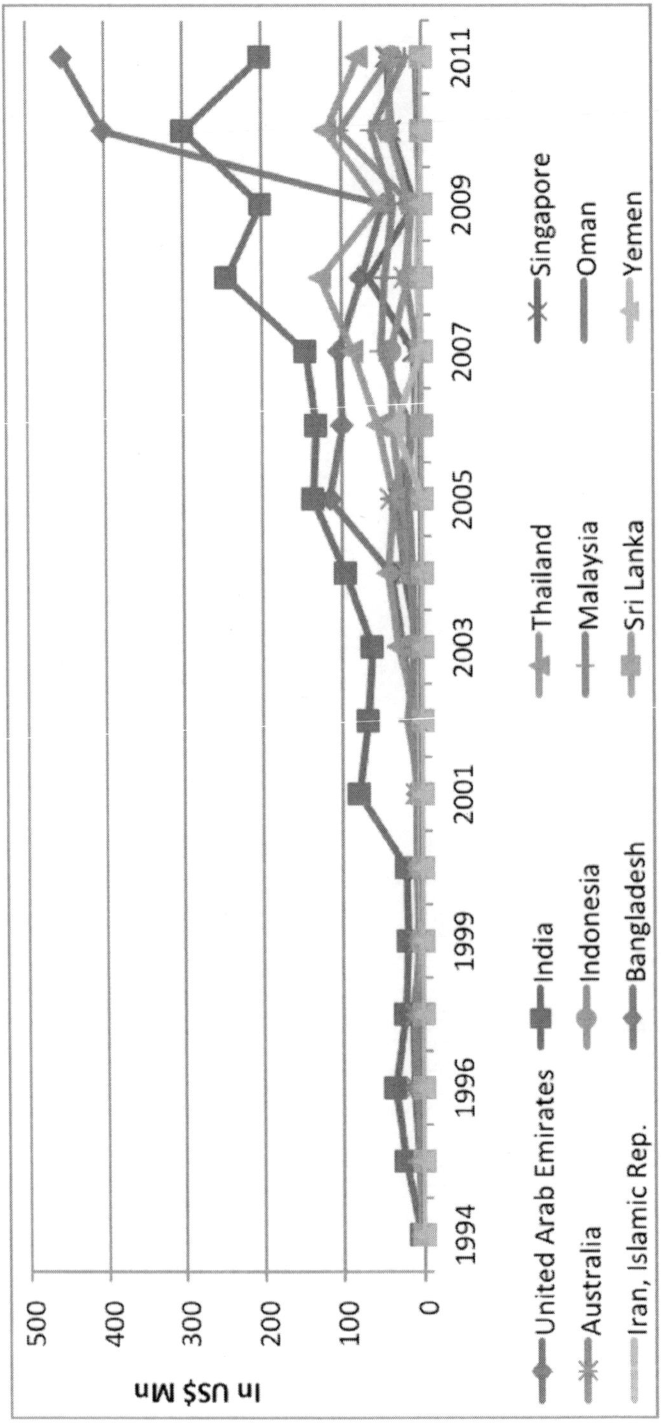

Source: Compiled using UNCOMTRADE data in WITS database.

Mauritius

Mauritius' main export markets are Australia and India that accounts for over 50 per cent of Mauritius's exports to non-African IORA members (Figure 13). The export basket to IORA countries consists largely of waste and scraps of cast iron (HS 720410), intimate wear or lingerie (HS 621410), waste and scrap of other ally steel (HS 720429), other pile fabrics of cotton, knitted or crocheted (HS 600191), copper waste and scrap (HS 740400), cotton yarn (HS 520522) and aluminum waste and scrap (HS 760200). Moreover, IORA countries absorb almost 100 per cent of Mauritius's total exports of waste and scraps of cast iron, intimate wear or lingerie and waste and scrap of ally steel.

India, Malaysia and Australia dominate Mauritius's imports from non-African IORA countries that draw over 80 per cent of the share of Mauritius's total IORA imports, while India secures an over 65 per cent share in total imports of Mauritius from IORA countries. While India possesses the total share of Mauritius imports of petroleum oils, oils obtained from bituminous mineral preparations thereof (HS 271000), it also has a larger share in products such as, other medicaments (put up in packing for retail sale) (HS 300490), semi-milled or wholly milled rice (HS 100630), broken rice (HS 100640), rice in the husk (paddy or rough) (HS 100610), frozen meat of bovine animals-processed and boneless (HS 020230) and cotton yarn (HS 520523).

Mauritius sources its entire domestic semi-milled or wholly milled rice, broken rice and rice in the husk (paddy or rough) requirement from IORA members chiefly from India and Thailand. Further, India has secured over 80 per cent share of Mauritian world imports of frozen meat of bovine animals-processed and boneless. Similar to other African countries, Mauritius's imports of portland cement (HS 252329) from IORA countries have melted down to 40 per cent in 2012 from a close to 100 per cent in 2000 as a percentage of its world imports of Portland cement.

Madagascar

India and Singapore are the two largest export destination of Madagascar out of IORA countries that attract about 70 per cent of the intra-IORA exports of Madagascar (Figure 15). Cloves (whole fruit, cloves and stems), nutmeg, mace and cardamoms (carded or combed) (HS 90700),

Figure 13. Mauritius's exports to non-African IORA member excluding UAE

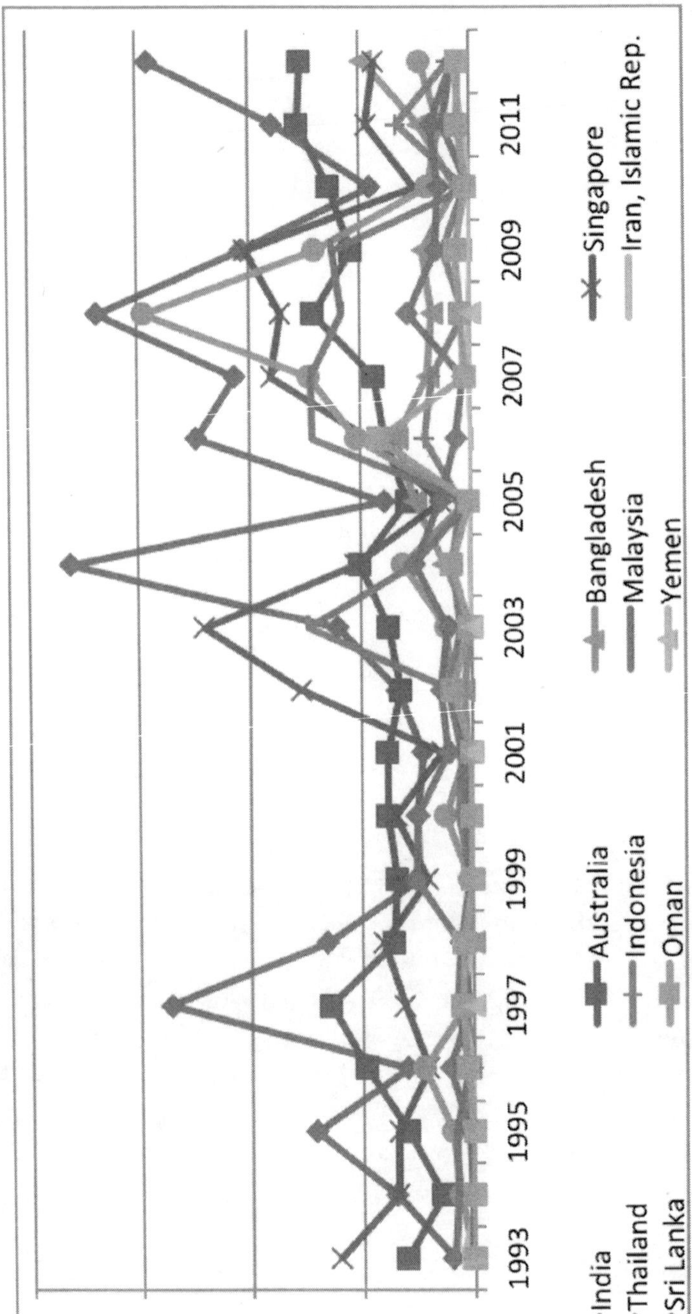

Source: Compiled using UNCOMTRADE data in WITS database.

Reason to exclude UAE in this figure is to get a clear trend of other countries as the numbers in UAE hides the patterns of other countries

Figure 14. Mauritius's imports from non-African IORA member excluding India

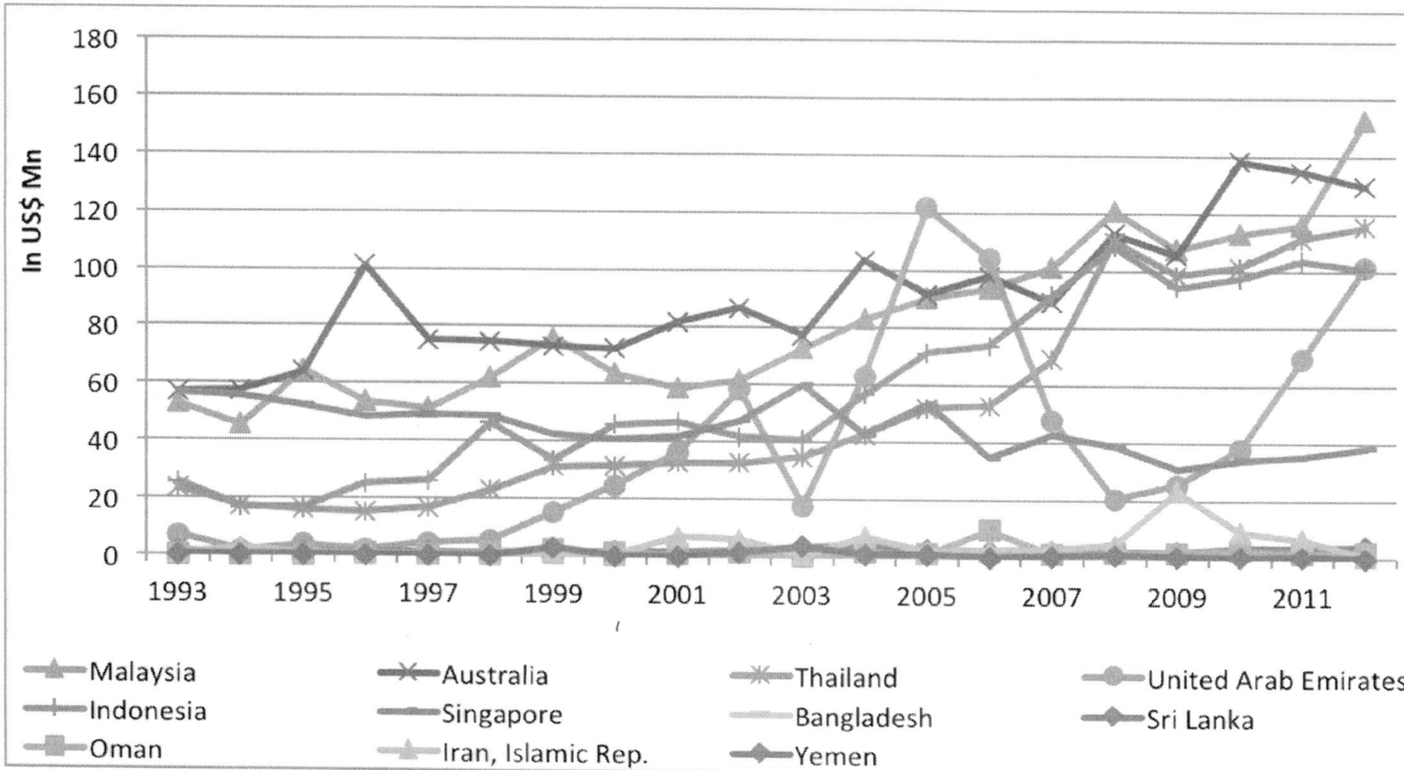

Note: Reason to exclude India in this figure is to get a clear trend of other countries as the numbers in India hides the patterns of other countries.
Source: Compiled using UNCOMTRADE data in WITS database.

Figure 15. Madagascar's exports to non-African IORA member

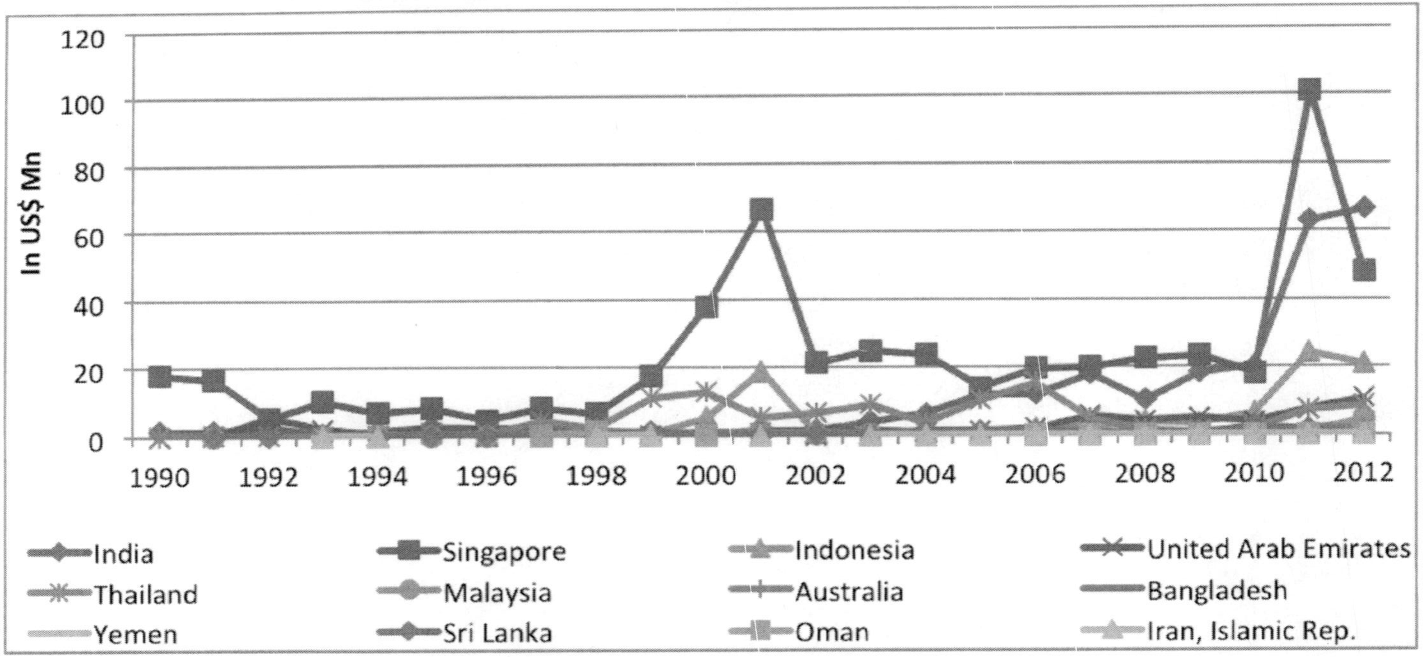

Source: Compiled using UNCOMTRADE data in WITS database.

precious stones (other than diamonds) and semiprecious stones (HS 710310), seeds of a kind used for sowing such as cowpeas, black beans etc. (HS 71339) and other ferrous waste and scrap (HS 720449) are the main exports of Madagascar to IORA members and these export products fall under Madagascar's top 20 world exports. Madagascar has not been able to diversify its traditional export basket over the past 15 years since its entrance to IORA.

Just as same as the exports, Madagascar's imports basket from non-African IORA members have not gone through an evident transformation from its traditional imports. Imports of Madagascar are dominated by UAE and India with petroleum oils, oils obtained from bituminous mineral, preparations thereof (HS 271000), other medicaments (put up in packings for retail sale) (HS 300490), other cane or beet sugar, chemically pure sucrose (HS 170199), vaccines for human medicine (HS 300220), sugar cane (raw sugar not added flavour or colour (HS 170111) imports having the largest share of total imports. Further, Madagascar sources 100 per cent of its world imports of palm oil–crude oil (HS 151110) from Indonesia, Malaysia and Singapore.

Seychelles

Seychelles has gained, withdrawn and regained membership in IORA since 1999 to date and its exports to IORA members do not indicate a significant trend rather it portrays apparent fluctuations. Nevertheless, Seychelles' imports have improved over time with UAE and Singapore having its highest share of intra-IORA imports. Sri Lanka is the major export market of Seychelles that attracts fish products such as other fish (salted or in brine) (HS 30569), flours, meals and pellets of fish, fit for human consumption (HS 30510), and flours, meals, pellets of fish, crustaceans, molluscs (non-edible) (HS 230120).

Seychelles' imports from non-African IORA countries consists primarily of petroleum oils, oils obtained from bituminous mineral, preparations thereof (HS 271000), coniferous (HS 440710), wooden furniture (HS 940360), portland cement (HS 252329), semi-milled or wholly milled rice (HS 100630), sunflower seed oil, safflower oil and their fractions (other than crude oil), wheat flour, meslin flour (HS 110100) and milk, cream (sweetened, fat content exceeding 1.5%) (HS 40229).

Figure 16. Madagascar's imports from non-African IORA member

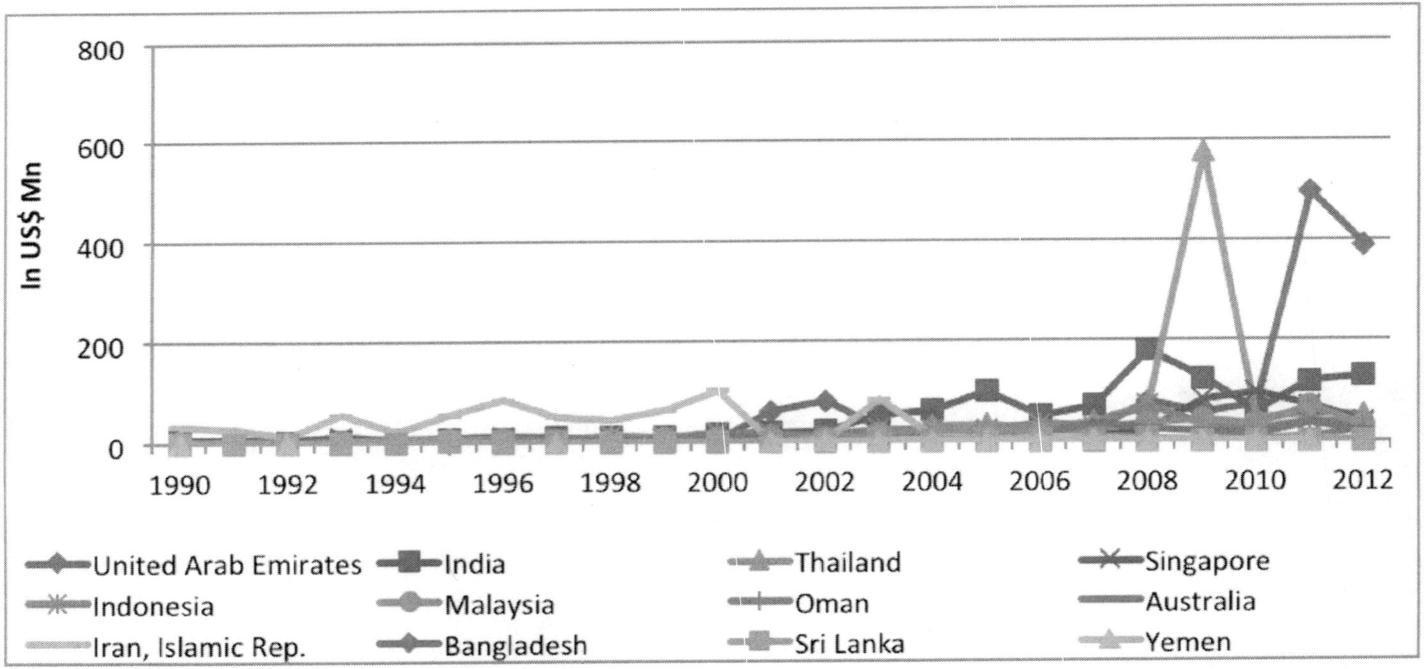

Source: Compiled using UNCOMTRADE data in WITS database.

Figure 17. Seychelles' exports to non-African IORA members

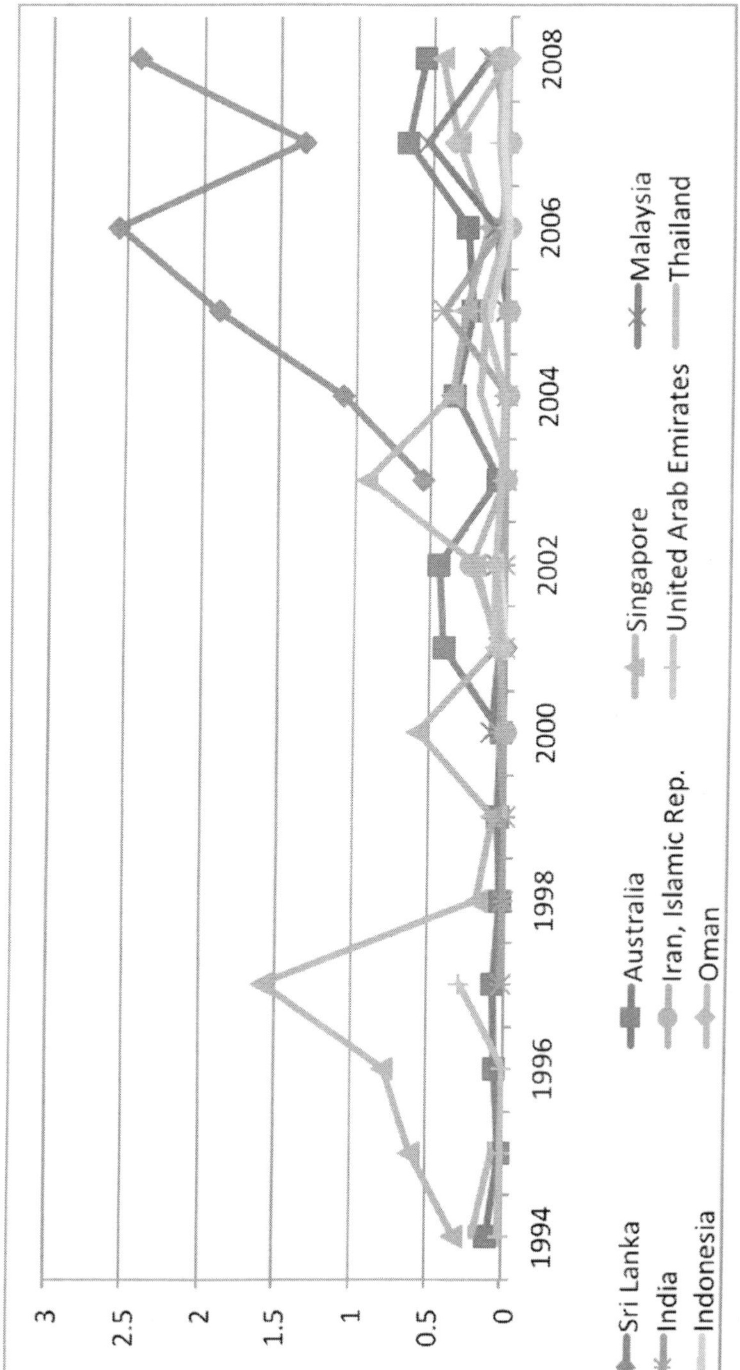

Source: Compiled using UNCOMTRADE data in WITS database

Figure 18. Seychelles' imports from non-African IORA member

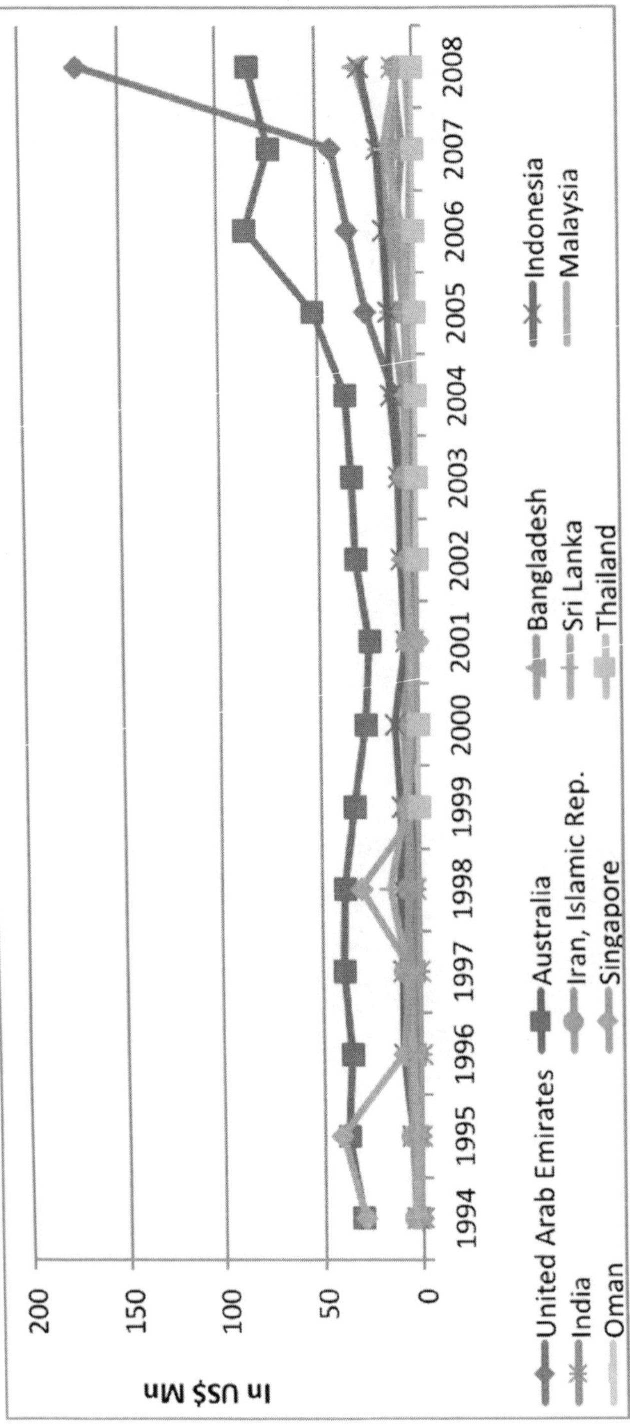

Source: Compiled using UNCOMTRADE data in WITS database

Comoros

Comoros as the latest member of IORA, who joined in November 2012, does not have data available since 2012 to analyze the impact of IORA on its trade pattern. However, even without being a member of IORA until 2012, Comoros has depicted signs of growth in imports from Indian Ocean regional members from 1995 to 2009.

The Status of Tourism Among African IORA Members

Tourism is one of the key industries that drives growth in African states that has not only contributed to improving the GDP but has also generated significant employment opportunities. One in twenty jobs is in the travel and tourism industry in the African continent and about 50 per cent of the hospitality industry is managed by women (UNWTO 2012). In an effort to attract tourists and facilitate tourism, the African continent has invested in infrastructure development in the recent years. South Africa, for instance, invested US$2.6 billion in upgrading the Johannesburg, Cape Town, and Durban airports in preparation for an influx of sports tourists for the 2010 FIFA World Cup (UNWTO 2012). However, the feeble state of the measures of risk management - economic and political, weak air services - inconvenient and expensive air routes, absence of an investor-friendly commitment to tourism, and policy and governance issues are major hindrances for tourism development in Southern and Southeast Africa (World Bank 2010; UNWTO 2012).

Importantly, tourism has led to some preservation of cultural heritage and the environment. Seychelles together with UNDP's Global Environment Facility (GEF) established a six-year biodiversity management project worth US$3.6 million in 2008 and the project is currently close to completion (World Bank 2013). Furthermore, owing to the successful achievement of high returns on investment, the tourism sector has encouraged and attracted Public-Private Partnerships (PPP) in infrastructure development, conservation and investments in most of the coastal countries in the African continent (World Bank 2013). For instance, Kenya's wildlife services, SANParks in South Africa and the National Parks initiative in Madagascar involve PPP (World Bank 2012).

Nevertheless, the state of the existing channels of sea and air connectivity is a major bottleneck that impedes the travel and tourism

Figure 19. Comoros's exports to non-African IORA members

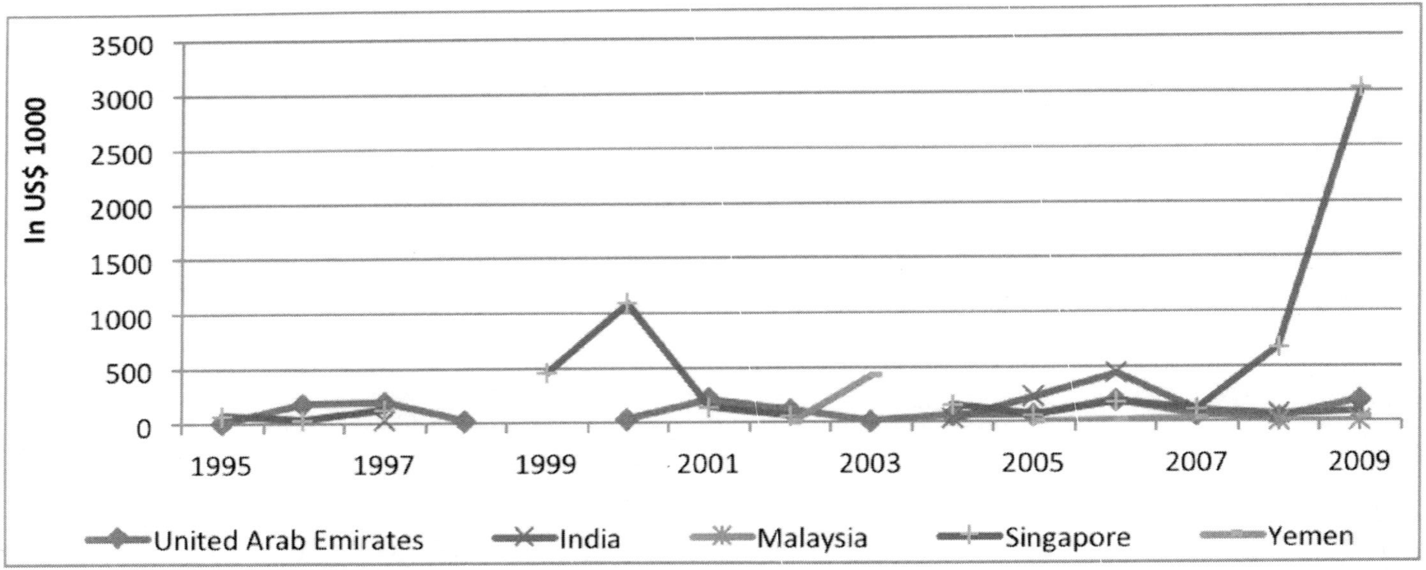

Source: Compiled using UNCOMTRADE data in WITS database

Figure 20. Comoros's imports from non-African IORA members

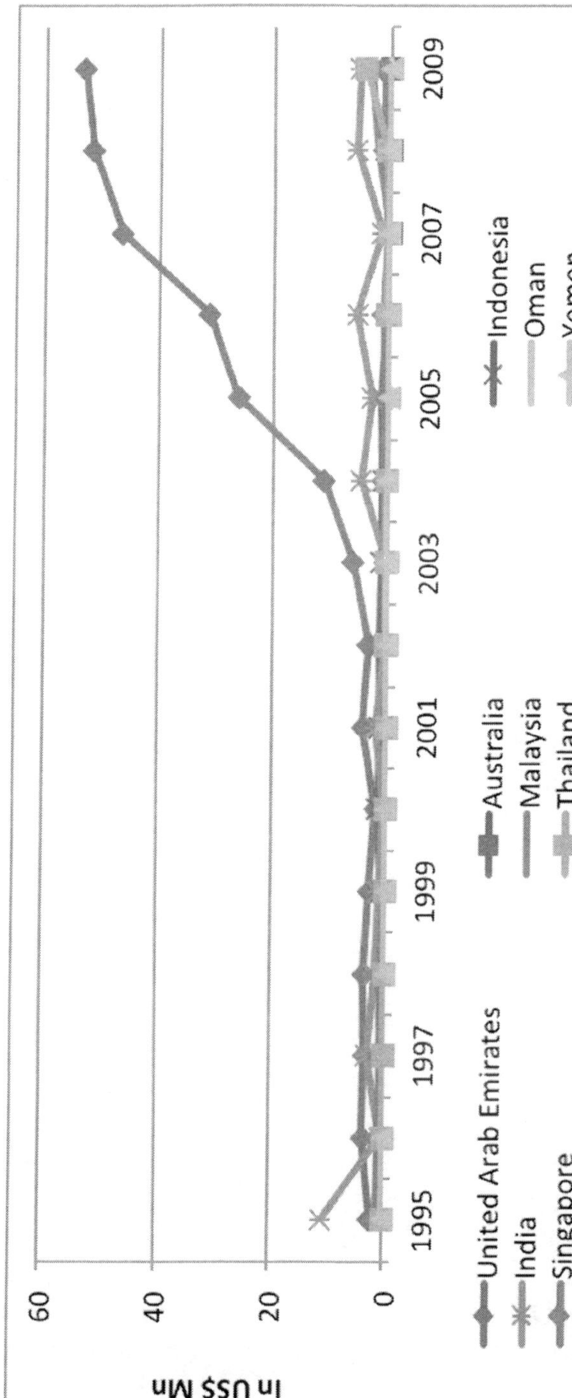

Source: Compiled using UNCOMTRADE data in WITS database.

sectors in Africa. Although the eight African members of IORA are located in a strategic maritime passage where a bulk of the maritime movement takes place, the appalling state of the port traffic, the poor state of port infrastructure, high costs due to rent-seeking and issues in administration, and security issues have held back the economies from reaping the benefits (IBRD & World Bank 2009). Similarly, the irregular and infrequent schedules with multi-stop itineraries, high airport taxes and charges, ineffective management of airlines and airports, and the power of monopolies and duopolies that set skyrocketing prices contribute to the existing weak air connectivity in Africa (World Bank 2012). Moreover, a study conducted by World Bank has found that the prices of charter tours in Africa are about 20-30 per cent higher than that of Latin America and the United States (2012). In addition, the fares of Safari tours are about 38 per cent higher than the fares of similar tours in India (World Bank 2012). The study has also shown that the airfare to the African continent is about 50 per cent higher than to Asian tourism destinations such as Indonesia, Thailand and Sri Lanka (2012). Consequently, elevated airfares and exorbitant accommodation costs have prompted an excessive jump in tour prices, making the tourism industry less competitive relative to their counterparts other parts of the Indian Ocean Rim.

African Investments with Indian Ocean Rim States

The resource gap, the outcome of low savings and investments, is what impedes growth and development in the African continent. FDI not only bridges the resource gap but also boosts the domestic capital stock. One of the main drivers of economic growth of LDCs and smaller developing economies in Africa has been public and private spending financed by FDI over the past decade. For instance, 50 per cent of the Gross Fixed Capital Formation (GFCF) in capitalscarce Madagascar and Mozambique was composed of FDI (RIS 2012). FDI inflows to Africa have recorded a 5 per cent increase up to US$50 billion despite the global slump in FDI in 2012 (UNCTAD 2013). A heavy influx of FDI from transnational companies (TNC) from emerging markets in Asia has driven the FDI inflow to Africa. At the same time, FDI outflows from Africa have tripled in 2012, recording US$14 billion from US$5 billion in 2011 as a result of large outflows from South Africa to the mining, wholesale and health care products sectors (UNCTAD 2013).

From the Indian Ocean Rim, India and Malaysia are the two largest investors in Africa. While the energy and mining sectors have attracted the bulk of Indian investments, Malaysian investments have been channeled to a diversified array of sectors: mining, hospitality, real estate, shipping broadcasting, banking, financial services, energy and telecommunications (UNCTAD 2013). Both the Malaysian and the Indian governments make provisions for their investors to engage in investment in Africa in order to promote South-South cooperation, and in trade and investment that generates mutual benefits such as ensure energy security, and to realize opportunities for growth and access to potential markets, and develop multinational enterprises.

Conversely, FDI inflows to Kenya have fallen over time from US$729 million in 2007 to US$ 259 million in 2012 mainly due to the various political and institutional challenges the country has encountered (UNCTAD 2013). The bulk of FDI in Kenya is concentrated in the manufacturing and services sectors where there had been a large domestic resource gap. Eventually, the market-oriented foreign investors have begun to be hostile towards investing in Kenya over time (Winkler 2013). The general perception among foreign investors that discourages FDI into Kenya is the apparent lack of commitment by the government to attract FDI and the governance issues that have been prevailing despite trade and investment liberalization since the 1990s (Winkler 2013; UNCTAD 2013). Recent political tensions in Kenya and its neighbours, and uncertainty caused by weak institutions and security issues are the main barriers that prevent a successful inflow of FDI to Kenya. For these reasons, recovering the investor-friendly climate through addressing the domestic political concerns is vital to replenish the FDI inflow to Kenya. Further, visa facilitation measures need high priority in the political agenda as they stimulate both FDI and tourism to the region.

The Future of IORA in Africa: Bridging Africa and the Indian Ocean Rim

The success of regional integration depends largely on geographic, political and institutional proximity, openness of economies to trade and investment, and the strength of connectivity measures. Although IORA shares a common Ocean, the rationale to have a regional agreement to

Figure 21. FDI inflow to African members of IORA from the world

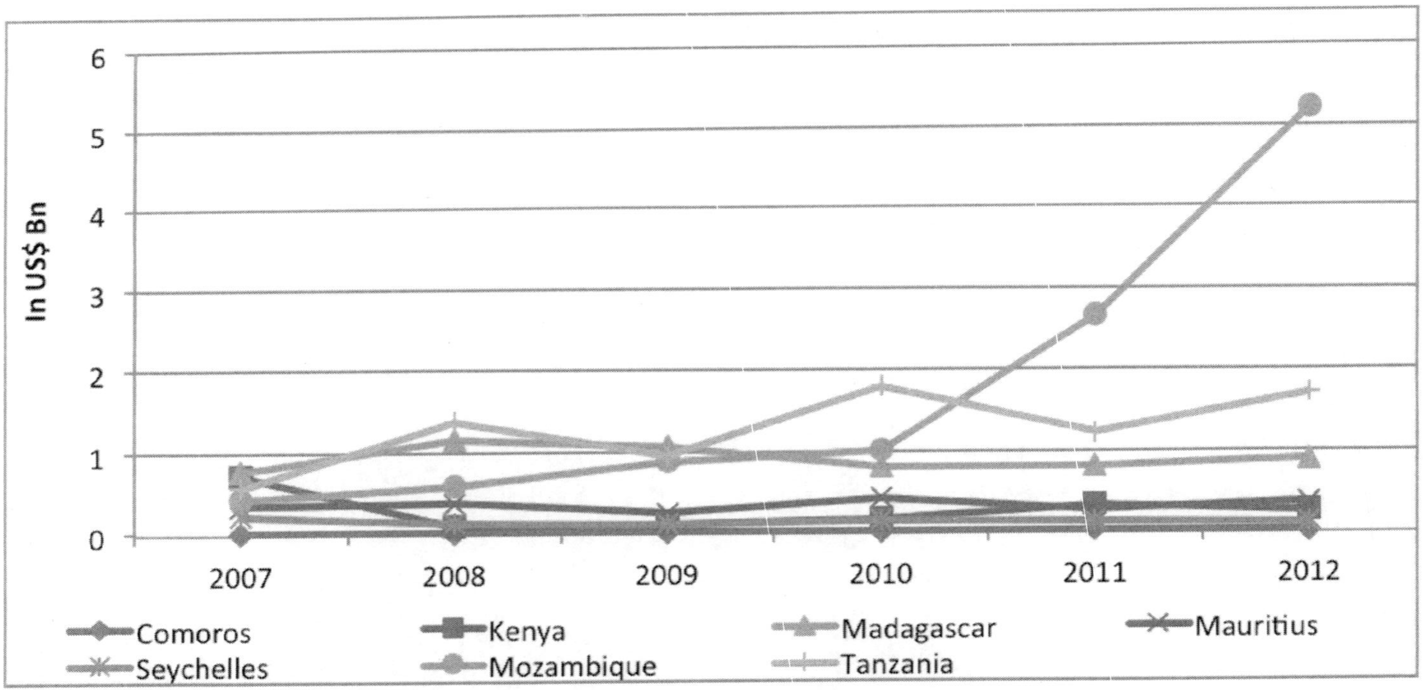

Source: World Investment Report 2013.

Reason to exclude South Africa in this figure is to get a clear trend of other countries as the numbers in South Africa hides the patterns of other countries.

reinforce trade, investment and political ties has been highly deliberated in both political and economic platforms ever since its inception in 1997 (Kelegama, 2012). With a view to promote deeper integration in the region the existing regional arrangement needs to be revised and reformed to attract participation of all member states. Lack of preferential treatment for member countries, at least for LDCs and smaller economies, has been seen as a major impediment that hinders regional integration in IORA. For instance, the reason to initiate a trilateral development arrangement among India, Brazil and South Africa (IBSA) is the slow pace of the open regionalism and is also due to the few tangible benefits that IORA generates. For this reason, to boost the spirit of IORA the existing constitutional aspects and trading mechanisms need to be revisited to accommodate the size and strengths of all the economies. The prospects for development and deeper integration in the Indian Ocean Rim are evident in different spheres. First, economic management of the accumulated capital in Africa, especially from the mining and energy sectors, is a key ingredient of continued growth. Second, trade in consumer goods between Africa and the Indian Ocean Rim together with FDI inflows has good prospects for growth. Third, developing and promoting tourism through improved channels of connectivity widens growth horizons as the hospitality industry in Africa has accommodated a labour force with different income groups. Thus, there are potential benefits of developing tourism infrastructure spillovers to households with low-income to high-income levels thereby reducing income and growth disparities. Yet in the short-run, increased spending on physical infrastructure and investment on natural resources may result in macroeconomic instability caused by a rise in inflation and a real exchange rate appreciation.

Although Australia is the largest market for Kenyan coffee among non-African IORA members, Australia's percentage share of coffee imports from Kenya is 1.5% of its world imports. Australia imports nearly 45 per cent of its coffee requirement from Brazil, Papua New Guinea, Vietnam and Indonesia. Furthermore, other African countries, such as Ethiopia, have a larger share in the Australian coffee market than Kenya. Kenya's coffee exports to Australia are about 1% of its total world exports while Germany, United States, Belgium and Sweden have an over 60 per cent market share for Kenyan coffee. Through Dubai's Multi-Commodities Center (DMCC) UAE has secured its position as the world's top tea re-exporter and the fifth largest coffee re-exporter with large storage facilities, mixing and packing equipment, tasting units, and several other value addition facilities. African tea and coffee traders have a greater chance in reaping the benefits of these new avenues in the world trade arena considering their strategic location from which they have easy port and air cargo access.

South Africa's diamond exports to non-African IORA countries have significantly escalated from 0.2 per cent in 2000 to 14 percent in 2012 as a share of its world exports of diamonds. UAE (10%) and India (3%) are at the forefront among IORA members who have the largest market share for diamonds from South Africa. Belgium, Israel and United Kingdom have more than a 65 per cent share of South Africa's diamond exports. India has become the chief exporter of cut and polished diamonds to UAE and imports rough uncut diamonds largely from Belgium, UAE and Hong Kong. As a result, India makes a domestic value addition of about 25 per cent and re-exports the cut and polished diamonds mainly to the 'Diamond Hub' in Dubai. Therefore, South Africa exporting rough uncut diamonds to India for value addition and re-exporting can make a more cost-effective and prospective means of trade than exporting to Europe and the Middle-East at a higher transport or delivery cost.

Next to Brazil, India and Thailand are among the top sugar cane producers in the world and Seychelles (33%) and Mauritius (77%) source a greater portion of their domestic sugar requirement from India and Thailand. While South Africa caters largely to the markets in Comoros, Kenya, Madagascar, Mozambique and Tanzania, the bulk of the sugar exports to the African continent are carried out by Brazil. Having realized the growing demand for sugar in the African region, Indian sugar producers have been encouraged to set up sugar mills in the arable land in Africa that may result in a win-win situation for both Africa and India.

India's pharmaceutical exports to African members of IORA are about 8 per cent of its total world exports. The eight African IORA members import pharmaceuticals from France, Germany, United Kingdom and United States and each share about 10 per cent of their total pharmaceutical imports, while India holds the largest share of 16 per cent of their total world imports of pharmaceuticals. There is greater scope to increase imports of pharmaceuticals from India at a much lower cost vis-à-vis importing from Western and European countries.

An improved physical infrastructure not only enhances efficiency in production and distribution but also facilitates travel and tourism industries. While the existing road, air and sea networks in African IORA members limit production and distribution capacities of their economies they also hamper labour mobility. Furthermore, Africa's dependence on a narrow export basket, dominated by minerals, plantation agriculture and gems, is owing to the lack of incentives for trade diversification; for instance, the poor state of port facilities, transport and telecommunications. A call for enhancing production capacities to encourage trade has thus arisen. However, the domestic negative impacts of increased spending on infrastructure development can be manifold[1].

The economic management of the capital gain to the natural resources sector and maintaining macroeconomic stability is crucial for growth and development in Africa while strengthening trade and investment ties with the Indian Ocean Rim states.

NOTE

1. While attracting FDI to natural resources-based industries strengthens domestic capital formation it can result in a resource curse led by a Dutch Disease overtime. Increased spending triggers macroeconomic instability and the rise in inflation is one of the causes. Excessive injection of money into the economy in the form of investment on infrastructure prompts an inevitable escalation in inflation that worsens the standard of living. Most resource-rich countries that increased public and private spending have suffered high inflation rates, for instance Norway and Botswana that invested heavily on infrastructure development experienced inflation rates at two digit levels (WDI various years). Nevertheless, they have managed to control the rising inflation in the subsequent years through effective fiscal management. As a consequence, a rise in domestic inflation rate will appreciate the exchange rate and thereby making its exports less competitive, which adversely affect the Balance of Payments.

REFERENCES

Christie, I, Fernandes, E, Messerli, H & Twining-Ward, L 2013, 'Tourism in Africa: Harnessing tourism for growth and improved livelihoods', International Bank for Reconstruction and Development—The World Bank, Washington DC.

Glaesser, D & Kester, J (2013), 'Visa facilitation: Stimulating economic growth and development through tourism', in J Blanke & T Chiesa (eds), *The Travel and*

Tourism Competitiveness Report 2013,

Kelegama, S (2012), 'IOR-ARC: Failures, successes and prospects', in V Sakhuja (ed), *Reinvigorating IOR-ARC*, Pentagon Press, Indian council of world affairs, New Delhi.

Kelegama, S (2000), 'Open Regionalism in the Indian Ocean: How Relevant is the APEC Model for IOR-ARC?', *Journal of the Asia Pacific Economy*, Vol.5, No. 3.

Mohanty, SK & Dash, P (2012), 'Trade and investment prospects of the IOR-ARC in the new millennium: New economic frontiers of the region', Research and Information System for developing countries (RIS), New Delhi.

Nyangito, H, Ikiara, M & Ronge, EE (2002), 'Performance of Kenya's wheat industry and prospects for regional trade in wheat products', Kenya Institute for Public Policy Research and Analysis (KIPPRA) *Discussion Paper* no. 17, Nairobi.

The World Bank Group (2007), 'Snapshot Africa-Kenya: Benchmarking FDI competitiveness', World Bank Group.

United Nations Conference on Trade and Development (UNCTAD) (2013), *World Investment Report 2013—Global value chains: Investment and trade for development*, United Nations Publications, Geneva.

United Nations World Tourism Organization (UNWTO) 2013, *Annual Report 2012*, Spain.

Vines, A & Oruitemeka, B (2008), 'India's engagement with the African Indian Ocean Rim States', *South African Journal of International Affairs* (SAJIA), vol. 14, no. 2. Winter/Spring 2007, pp111-124.

Winkler, D (2013), 'Potential and actual FDI spillovers in global value-chains: Role of foreign investor characteristics, absorptive capacity and transmission channels', The World Bank, *Policy Research Working Paper* 6424, WPS6424.

World Trade Organization (WTO) & Confederation of Indian Industry (CII) 2013, 'India-Africa: South-South – Trade and investment for development', WTO & CII.

Website

https://wits.worldbank.org/WITS/WITS/Restricted/Login.aspx

APPENDICES

Appendix 1. Exports of African countries to non-African IORA member countries ('000 US$)

Country	*1990*	*1992*	*1994*	*1996*	*1998*	*2000*	*2002*	*2004*	*2006*	*2008*	*2010*	*2012*
Kenya					112,197	99,735	69,588	145,586	198,841	345,682	494,348	
Tanzania					171,798	126,824	96,897	154,288	141,998	328,224	358,056	717,677
Mauritius			10,203	14,180	18,842	16,495	21,493	68,122	290,679	122,422	20,472	41,169
Mozambique			13,008	30,865	36,980	8,649	11,921	47,654	34,857	114,924	428,688	
Madagascar	19,787	14,058	9,866	8,565	12,698	57,937	30,953	37,561	53,260	44,090	54,919	162,050
Seychelles			19,787	14,058	9,866	8,565	12,698	57,937	30,953	37,561		
Comoros				228	14	1,117	177	238	832	771		
South Africa		626,904	1,019,230	1,983,207	1,269,547	2,092,442	1,947,128	3,428,663	4,471,955	7,098,883	7,479,397	9,368,510

Source: Compiled using UNCOMTRADE data in WITS database.

Appendix 2. Share of exports of African countries to non-African IORA members as a percentage of their total world exports (%)

Country	*1990*	*1992*	*1994*	*1996*	*1998*	*2000*	*2002*	*2004*	*2006*	*2008*	*2010*	*2012*
Tanzania					27.3	19.3	10.8	11.5	8.3	10.5	9.1	12.9
South Africa		3.0	4.1	8.5	6.5	8.0	8.4	8.5	8.5	9.6	10.5	10.8
Kenya					5.9	6.3	5.0	7.2	5.7	7.4	9.6	
Mauritius			0.8	0.8	1.1	1.1	1.2	3.4	12.5	5.1	1.4	2.2
Seychelles			6.8	5.2	3.0	2.9	5.4	8.3	5.2	4.2		
Madagascar	6.8	5.2	3.0	2.9	5.4	8.3	5.2	4.2	5.7	2.8	5.8	13.7
Comoros				3.7	0.4	15.6	1.9	3.0	32.1	14.3		
Mozambique			7.9	13.7		2.4	1.5	3.2	1.5	4.3	19.5	

Source: Compiled using UNCOMTRADE data in WITS database.

Appendix 3. Imports of African countries from non-African IORA member countries ('000 US$)

Country	*1990*	*1992*	*1994*	*1996*	*1998*	*2000*	*2002*	*2004*	*2006*	*2008*	*2010*	*2012*
South Africa		823,552	1,186,942	3,221,439	1,932,601	3,200,352	3,096,273	6,396,703	10,158,151	13,997,957	12,958,693	14,981,727
Kenya					696,518	746,841	700,895	1,027,563	2,301,002	3,990,011	3,820,107	
Tanzania					387,059	302,265	406,843	673,975	1,080,643	2,771,198	2,514,498	2,763,144
Mauritius			324,147	448,166	464,075	463,627	495,616	658,625	967,160	1,638,539	1,523,354	1,950,040
Mozambique			16,908	67,402	-	53,727	120,883	244,883	399,229	603,800	1,073,207	
Madagascar	56,275	29,226	43,302	126,957	86,827	173,641	135,216	185,066	165,581	496,112	345,528	719,080
Seychelles			56,275	29,226	43,302	126,957	86,827	173,641	135,216	185,066		
Comoros				5,412	6,435	4,066	5,957	18,717	39,869	62,642		

Source: Compiled using UNCOMTRADE data in WITS database.

Appendix 4. Share of imports of African countries from non-African IORA members as a percentage of their total world exports (%)

Country	*1990*	*1992*	*1994*	*1996*	*1998*	*2000*	*2002*	*2004*	*2006*	*2008*	*2010*	*2012*
Comoros				9.6	13.7	11.2	16.0	28.8	39.3	38.4		
Tanzania					23.2	19.1	24.1	26.4	23.9	34.3	31.4	23.6
Mauritius			16.8	19.7	21.3	22.3	22.9	23.7	26.5	35.1	34.6	33.8
Kenya					21.1	25.8	22.8	22.5	31.8	35.9	31.6	
Seychelles			9.9	7.5	10.0	21.1	15.6	17.5	22.5	11.2		
Mozambique			3.1	8.6		4.6	7.8	12.0	13.9	15.1	30.1	
South Africa		4.5	5.6	12.0	7.3	12.0	11.9	13.4	14.9	16.1	16.2	14.7
Madagascar	9.9	7.5	10.0	21.1	15.6	17.5	22.5	11.2	9.4	12.9	13.6	27.0

Source: Compiled using UNCOMTRADE data in WITS database.

Appendix 5. Kenya's exports to non-African IORA members ('000 US$)

Country	*1997*	*1998*	*1999*	*2000*	*2001*	*2002*	*2003*	*2004*	*2005*	*2006*	*2007*	*2008*	*2009*	*2010*
UAE	15,376	22,043	27,846	34,203	39,481	16,279	29,881	27,773	53,860	69,206	128,173	99,801	138,660	237,849
Australia	6,464	6,232	8,405	7,253	9,986	3,309	10,605	6,814	9,357	7,666	16,348	6,728	8,508	8,025
Bangladesh	310	271	585	260	320	170	376	214	1,489	425	402	3,308	2,626	6,171
Indonesia	1,066	1,330	1,707	1,373	904	917	3,388	6,028	10,156	4,414	6,239	9,731	7,330	12,477
India	20,272	30,251	24,956	17,358	29,108	34,503	35,635	50,818	53,108	52,218	86,725	96,955	66,479	106,933
Iran	12,703	16,646	6,480	4,836	5,266	132	999	1,586	4,639	6,493	3,651	7,297	4,906	10,830
Sri Lanka	3,035	5,080	2,030	2,632	2,440	960	3,904	4,682	7,466	6,425	7,067	11,520	9,193	11,163
Malaysia	3,420	1,674	1,139	4,816	3,137	2,375	4,598	5,467	5,998	4,677	4,159	8,208	4,187	6,140
Oman	160	284	918	736	41	253	705	756	1,004	1,923	1,598	5,177	4,402	15,449
Singapore	13,101	9,161	5,719	5,580	6,750	1,469	2,613	1,560	3,018	2,411	25,594	4,305	23,778	8,182
Thailand	8,316	5,842	7,556	4,916	7,043	1,828	7,824	12,919	18,571	13,393	12,514	52,127	11,394	14,125
Yemen	14,018	13,382	16,589	15,773	17,252	7,394	32,145	26,967	20,562	29,590	32,133	40,524	42,890	57,005

Source: Compiled using UNCOMTRADE data in WITS database.

Appendix 6. Kenya's imports from non-African IORA members ('000 US$)

Country	*1997*	*1998*	*1999*	*2000*	*2001*	*2002*	*2003*	*2004*	*2005*	*2006*	*2007*	*2008*	*2009*	*2010*
UAE	326,798	311,609	209,842	405,787	563,134	246,854	405,950	502,423	831,224	1,075,853	1,328,962	1,655,691	1,161,837	1,462,913
Australia	35,382	28,468	38,446	34,068	44,537	24,416	18,251	13,623	18,747	39,210	22,691	20,137	28,287	40,723
Bangladesh	520	392	1,168	719	2,343	1,484	1,883	2,051	2,082	2,580	3,560	2,613	2,616	5,019
Indonesia	108,603	50,621	23,549	34,918	101,378	150,728	154,151	105,622	131,341	190,909	278,798	335,699	243,148	339,791
India	141,082	142,970	127,623	132,305	170,349	166,580	175,360	262,623	326,044	524,285	844,550	1,309,547	1,078,089	1,301,586
Iran	11,881	9,172	19,208	4,914	10,331	2,684	32,672	26,230	8,542	7,965	49,911	95,098	83,763	39,578
Sri Lanka	5,427	4,362	963	2,919	1,193	1,854	1,363	3,083	3,812	3,657	3,349	4,464	2,384	10,436
Malaysia	17,653	99,834	71,301	40,370	26,074	14,318	15,267	18,115	23,340	36,457	40,803	67,286	75,892	93,341
Oman	359	336	615	472	517	6,195	695	1,180	2,499	2,399	6,707	7,042	59,317	19,033
Singapore	33,931	22,007	61,177	62,235	68,249	47,053	28,039	56,757	101,574	354,218	138,944	360,683	342,156	400,102
Thailand	12,579	23,604	19,114	21,051	23,621	18,344	24,108	30,359	46,896	63,157	99,309	131,376	91,610	107,338
Yemen	11	3,143	8,960	7,084	16,935	20,384	3,013	5,496	946	311	318	375	224	247

Source: Compiled using UNCOMTRADE data in WITS database.

Appendix 7. South Africa's exports to non-African IORA members ('000 US$)

Country	*1992*	*1994*	*1996*	*1998*	*2000*	*2002*	*2004*	*2006*	*2008*	*2010*	*2012*
India	6,995	135,778	245,848	191,305	371,741	351,546	567,192	783,553	2,279,522	2,980,649	3,674,818
Malaysia	3,084	86,282	165,579	53,934	157,269	166,026	267,015	350,698	624,707	737,874	1,063,034
UAE	24,009	70,803	104,158	131,749	146,257	152,313	344,088	556,461	769,902	850,653	1,045,877
Singapore	100,856	126,621	391,624	124,442	217,277	168,879	308,970	490,247	563,280	353,041	901,735
Australia	115,771	182,547	384,455	324,909	480,206	486,682	1,026,880	1,189,756	1,494,372	952,005	897,992
Indonesia	44,657	79,247	175,036	76,538	111,741	104,424	162,762	208,442	276,041	542,232	613,501
Thailand	118,384	95,055	141,854	100,196	200,385	188,643	353,041	266,353	395,254	384,797	585,904
Oman	2,206	8,887	3,531	3,214	4,970	5,640	25,730	49,683	45,780	28,186	87,644
Yemen	19	26	835	1,063	2,315	3,318	16,632	34,412	39,815	79,795	62,768
Iran	8,429	47,940	106,520	54,984	74,050	34,987	53,828	209,259	155,883	134,254	48,519
Bangladesh	1,242	365	4,362	2,414	4,471	4,902	7,442	24,684	18,098	49,936	38,798
Sri Lanka	64,040	41,380	45,497	40,622	26,866	24,668	25,303	22,519	34,119	40,637	26,578

Source: Compiled using UNCOMTRADE data in WITS database.

Appendix 8. South Africa's imports from non-African IORA members ('000 US$)

Country	*1992*	*1994*	*1996*	*1998*	*2000*	*2002*	*2004*	*2006*	*2008*	*2010*	*2012*
UAE	1,644	20,928	128,477	32,363	129,461	66,993	108,116	577,535	881,078	892,382	1,080,431
Australia	220,632	297,276	668,246	593,115	661,543	741,373	1,123,920	1,404,540	1,630,385	1,312,713	1,416,239
Bangladesh	8,047	7,520	7,265	4,344	2,705	3,301	5,657	11,563	43,136	45,050	73,103
Indonesia	46,481	74,282	113,389	159,739	204,500	184,550	308,642	441,643	650,062	671,353	919,749
India	38,341	114,147	259,332	279,186	253,412	280,582	706,174	1,613,235	2,261,935	2,839,394	4,597,525
Iran	5,754	13,763	1,229,396	10,841	1,163,781	921,114	2,366,674	2,697,758	3,290,393	3,147,956	1,233,427
Sri Lanka	11,814	11,830	13,439	11,233	10,953	10,555	11,786	15,319	18,140	22,776	31,023
Malaysia	125,040	210,345	251,827	320,082	297,277	345,954	590,941	851,955	1,084,622	1,165,965	1,330,249
Oman	10	48	7,375	233	332	1,750	3,739	202,488	150,574	63,254	138,302
Singapore	225,891	275,889	327,623	284,017	205,278	207,965	405,287	1,041,121	887,929	870,856	1,251,261
Thailand	135,600	156,666	167,717	232,392	264,556	283,149	663,438	1,174,012	1,756,054	1,829,898	2,700,853
Yemen	5	10	43,435	2	6	40,154	85,794	88,755	1,278,636	153	7

Source: Compiled using UNCOMTRADE data in WITS database.

Appendix 9. Tanzania's exports to non-African IORA members ('000 US$)

Country	*1997*	*1998*	*1999*	*2000*	*2001*	*2002*	*2003*	*2004*	*2005*	*2006*	*2007*	*2008*	*2009*	*2010*	*2011*	*2012*
UAE	4,962	7,114	6,442	6,196	9,483	14,555	15,506	17,821	35,401	47,049	89,266	68,066	91,442	57,231	77,854	95,979
Indonesia	31,355	9,158	5,975	4,374	2,879	4,142	7,339	5,909	7,018	8,284	15,854	25,772	21,499	14,666	22,361	40,881
Thailand	14,118	3,899	7,717	4,467	4,131	1,747	3,671	5,530	12,430	9,453	11,993	14,432	14,344	19,984	7,469	36,153
Singapore	7,196	25,006	12,044	6,423	5,913	3,992	13,388	15,606	20,114	5,480	4,194	11,962	6,546	13,970	11,656	25,497
Australia	2,121	3,998	2,364	1,181	2,339	3,033	1,789	2,111	2,659	3,956	7,800	6,341	7,321	12,550	16,255	14,831
Malaysia	5,682	2,192	5,003	3,072	2,937	2,965	1,191	2,315	16,254	1,423	1,745	12,970	3,068	4,899	8,921	9,929
Bangladesh	4,991	3,016	1,002	2,038	896	1,168	1,366	87	2,213	1,025	3,523	1,640	1,392	4,712	763	7,189
Oman	145	887	595	344	539	72	98	112	1,284	241	240	10,456	1,772	884	1,779	3,701
Sri Lanka	1,920	1,698	643	194	135	86	340	79	78	1,690	2,879	2,636	548	2,049	1,811	1,439
Iran		355	17	50	53	165	153	19	52	392	2,100	748	283	887	3,483	1,254
Yemen	77	52	75	97	96	34	38	62	150	195	105	235	300	40	88	188
India	73,627	114,424	119,366	98,389	81,634	64,940	73,147	104,638	78,088	62,812	78,656	172,967	187,834	226,186	210,175	480,638

Source: Compiled using UNCOMTRADE data in WITS database

Appendix 10. Tanzania's imports from non-African IORA members ('000 US$)

Country	*1997*	*1998*	*1999*	*2000*	*2001*	*2002*	*2004*	*2005*	*2006*	*2007*	*2008*	*2009*	*2010*	*2011*	*2012*
UAE	92,011	51,479	63,750	48,312	108,709	98,138	186,340	205,428	497,830	782,492	978,937	631,567	672,175	1,243,277	1,025,685
India	75,935	95,568	89,752	82,295	87,260	108,005	218,148	190,515	239,691	512,707	865,707	772,869	895,013	1,564,950	880,629
Indonesia	11,567	19,391	15,069	40,067	48,148	62,677	87,217	91,353	141,265	129,302	94,945	109,343	112,470	258,446	237,562
Singapore	38,890	9,851	12,868	5,288	8,966	5,829	44,809	9,319	13,496	254,289	441,861	192,042	444,418	128,528	147,851
Oman	2,572	2,170	2,729	2,455	4,195	4,408	6,178	8,821	6,803	21,492	8,037	11,929	15,349	49,882	125,856
Australia	23,332	82,281	28,722	78,635	140,969	73,283	75,863	47,222	33,482	26,842	102,831	125,735	161,023	145,018	124,164
Malaysia	17,030	24,242	35,222	13,666	18,170	12,689	19,661	21,114	94,944	147,975	162,968	67,808	106,911	105,703	88,369
Thailand	19,137	18,085	24,084	26,152	37,278	36,343	29,895	25,893	37,115	59,375	76,794	71,256	80,390	60,780	75,814
Iran	764	81,101	65,853	2,893	5,311	3,911	4,608	6,226	14,141	21,328	34,693	11,169	22,173	24,536	46,884
Bangladesh	551	2,651	1,238	1,097	1,028	214	397	557	28	109	434	87	127	336	5,250
Sri Lanka	291	227	87	1,393	188	402	820	1,169	1,657	3,040	2,714	2,445	2,498	3,589	3,481
Yemen	1	12	1,816	14	982	945	38	157	191	540	1,279	2,008	1,952	1,819	1,601

Source: Compiled using UNCOMTRADE data in WITS database.

Appendix 11.Mozambique's exports to non-African IORA members ('000 US$)

Country	*1994*	*1996*	*1997*	*1998*	*1999*	*2000*	*2001*	*2002*	*2003*	*2004*	*2005*	*2006*	*2007*	*2008*	*2009*	*2010*	*2011*
Iran			70	11	794	808	9	45				115			4,757	151,722	5,141
Malaysia	550	275		1,250	2,146	1,289	1,499	1,482	3,899	3,853	9,023	437	5,920	11,705	7,204	139,829	4,256
India	11,644	26,778	13,305	32,082	17,836	3,534	4,931	3,609	32,954	26,582	30,197	15,915	28,401	56,512	30,427	87,226	155,072
Indonesia		3,105	1,524		359	18	3,643	2,984	4,749	3,522	13,083	9,781	2,139	7,525	17,967	20,841	3,826
UAE	72		8		27	1,110	816	244	737	1,775	3,523	5,422	10,990	8,535	5,910	11,629	8,972
Singapore	553	414	169	2,032	2,401	1,173	4,780	501	2,191	2,447	3,494	1,292	1,886	28,377	10,986	9,616	28,270
Thailand	189		721	1,305	922	127	820	2,029	2,375	9,268	3,648	1,750	2,185	1,580	5,116	5,642	2,266
Bangladesh				203	114			958	3,889	131	584		0		401	1,616	15,364
Australia		3	11	99	50	590	658	24	37	45	12	145	387	657	2,554	263	100
Sri Lanka		290					17	46		4	29				275	157	
Oman										26			2,298	34		137	
Yemen					21				16				3,150			10	11

Source: Compiled using UNCOMTRADE data in WITS database.

Appendix 12. Mozambique's imports from non-African IORA member ('000 US$)

Country	*1994*	*1995*	*1996*	*1999*	*2000*	*2001*	*2002*	*2003*	*2004*	*2005*	*2006*	*2007*	*2008*	*2009*	*2010*	*2011*
UAE	2,161	5,234	11,376	2,688	3,810	6,997	10,575	24,406	37,885	114,184	99,541	103,572	75,618	47,618	401,084	454,065
India	5,599	23,703	35,799	20,372	22,049	79,301	68,041	63,716	96,724	136,842	131,816	144,361	244,684	201,562	300,521	200,919
Thailand	2,432	6,833	5,775	4,494	4,755	5,128	6,642	30,821	42,561	36,538	55,620	87,048	127,613	52,235	119,626	80,036
Singapore	565	4,830	2,760	1,494	4,052	3,361	5,583	6,227	23,422	29,306	7,445	10,201	67,225	7,869	37,056	43,525
Australia	3,486	1,697	10,271	6,239	8,530	9,117	5,833	2,697	16,812	39,393	7,990	4,604	20,815	13,150	104,075	39,697
Indonesia	2,068	1,107	926	4,167	5,341	3,536	4,683	11,084	13,779	25,538	36,308	38,937	16,036	14,504	41,095	35,804
Malaysia	296		268	3,828	4,194	5,045	18,322	10,017	11,714	17,809	15,573	52,097	46,274	34,910	63,367	18,806
Oman				16	19	22	9	15	90	638	1,715	2,446	1,950	669	5,660	7,725
Iran				979	739	684	728	742			7,876	461	2,618	761	452	991
Bangladesh	118	329	227	213	239	182	217	489	1,889	419	713	196	151	18	176	644
Sri Lanka	183			17		19	234			24	32	114	70	45	67	134
Yemen				354	0	16	18		7	2	34,600	310	747	49	28	28

Source: Compiled using UNCOMTRADE data in WITS database.

Appendix 13. Mauritius's exports to non-African IORA member ('000 US$)

Country	*1994*	*1996*	*1998*	*2000*	*2001*	*2002*	*2003*	*2004*	*2005*	*2006*	*2007*	*2008*	*2009*	*2010*	*2011*	*2012*
India	3,540	2,998	6,568	2,531	2,231	3,360	6,047	18,156	3,951	12,340	10,619	16,843	10,329	4,530	8,879	14,472
Australia	1,490	4,848	3,579	3,847	3,856	3,231	3,793	5,055	2,905	3,941	4,359	7,091	5,370	6,377	7,805	7,612
Bangladesh		206	7	37	256	396	17	1,250	2,528	3,349	1,953	1,755	2,147	615	2,286	4,850
Singapore	3,423	2,030	4,024	3,488	1,391	7,735	12,033	5,233	1,394	4,556	9,001	8,553	10,146	2,513	4,668	4,314
Thailand	674	2,277	166	1,255	321	1,002	1,205	3,108	266	5,155	7,289	14,776	7,059	1,896	1,381	2,248
Indonesia	80	49	506	625	491	1,112	553	936	547	2,119	1,764	336	1,224	255	3,343	1,011
Malaysia	792	244	575	282	420	959	7,369	2,604	63	7,160	7,208	5,799	6,221	11	1,221	775
Iran	3	88	149	7			12	37	1	26	37	66	9	18	382	764
Sri Lanka	57	1,061	618	2,450	1,078	1,400	1,065	2,572	1,393	668	366	2,839	1,562	1,422	1,736	716
Oman	26	319	446	54	77	916	140	911	110	4,206	297	463	692	205	582	537
Yemen					10		25					8				
UAE	118	60	2,205	1,919	2,044	1,382	4,092	28,260	686	247,159	78,682	63,894	5,777	2,630	3,590	3,870

Source: Compiled using UNCOMTRADE data in WITS database.

Appendix 14. Mauritius imports from non-African IORA member ('000 US$)

Country	*1994*	*1996*	*1998*	*2000*	*2002*	*2004*	*2005*	*2006*	*2007*	*2008*	*2009*	*2010*	*2011*	*2012*
Malaysia	45,127	53,652	62,139	63,505	61,383	82,899	90,354	93,874	101,263	120,541	107,544	112,986	115,878	152,625
Australia	57,190	100,895	74,171	72,042	86,477	103,197	91,337	97,849	88,672	112,661	105,299	138,142	134,387	129,319
Thailand	17,151	14,979	22,607	31,179	32,546	42,374	51,841	52,851	69,170	110,012	98,307	101,323	111,018	115,241
UAE	1,410	1,677	5,083	24,452	57,822	63,028	121,429	104,284	47,737	20,283	25,311	37,874	69,363	100,986
Indonesia	16,482	24,877	46,140	45,603	41,667	56,543	71,496	73,907	91,156	108,423	94,122	97,421	103,339	100,537
Singapore	55,340	48,307	48,685	40,708	47,237	42,638	53,688	34,771	42,943	38,694	31,278	33,956	35,682	38,263
Bangladesh	2	13	53	105	75	113	237	271	480	1,956	1,371	2,081	3,135	4,443
Sri Lanka	846	1,068	1,282	1,594	2,299	4,458	2,964	2,473	2,529	2,237	2,229	3,962	3,894	4,031
Oman	18	733	1,335	1,260	1,318	1,747	1,181	9,850	1,088	1,873	2,052	2,885	1,903	2,376
Iran	2,476	400	312	566	5,776	7,044	1,994	2,378	2,865	4,399	23,378	8,965	6,747	650
Yemen					1,207	1,020	989	79	351	821	436	128	142	16
India	128,104	201,564	202,266	182,616	157,809	253,565	218,666	494,573	825,945	1,116,639	703,226	983,630	1,207,848	1,301,552

Source: Compiled using UNCOMTRADE data in WITS database.

Appendix 15. Madagascar's exports to non-African IORA member ('000 US$)

Country	*1990*	*1992*	*1994*	*1996*	*1998*	*2000*	*2002*	*2003*	*2004*	*2005*	*2006*	*2007*	*2008*	*2009*	*2010*	*2011*	*2012*
India	1,598	2,632	1,662	2,175	1,570	774	1,644	4,103	6,347	12,054	11,937	17,859	10,216	18,421	20,241	62,883	66,529
Singapore	17,836	5,220	7,115	4,703	6,427	37,869	21,242	24,863	23,927	13,923	19,585	19,941	22,700	23,549	18,121	101,060	48,068
Indonesia				293	837	5,264	534	153	1,193	778	2,109	2,797	3,967	3,431	6,443	24,406	20,856
UAE	12	5,491	444	41	159	638	102	1,017	714	1,093	1,787	5,580	4,116	5,135	3,563	7,421	10,667
Thailand	14	189	369	903	2,238	12,785	6,757	8,979	3,712	10,533	15,669	4,943	1,550	1,336	2,004	7,579	8,874
Malaysia			110	18	311	67	210	480	202	255	72	354	386	381	709	549	4,317
Australia	327	138	156	347	72	346	185	321	191	209	320	260	377	579	514	2,382	1,462
Bangladesh		380	5	10	16		0	0	0	1	221	263	158	522	276	233	574
Yemen				3	15	0	2	0	77	0	59	66	36	171	124	588	374
Sri Lanka		8	3	74	5	190	277	251	1,196	1,197	1,353	941	485	168	2,875	1,535	296
Oman					1,023	3					1		50		9	10	32
Iran			1		26			7	2	4	148	87	48	53	40	83	1

Source: Compiled using UNCOMTRADE data in WITS database.

Appendix 16. Madagascar's imports from non-African IORA member ('000 US$)

Country	*1990*	*1992*	*1994*	*1996*	*1998*	*2000*	*2002*	*2004*	*2005*	*2006*	*2007*	*2008*	*2009*	*2010*	*2011*	*2012*
UAE	179	2,444	40	1,321	710	2,097	79,330	15,205	20,268	13,294	18,633	78,401	55,075	72,733	495,571	389,543
India	6,964	2,701	5,736	8,700	10,913	16,231	21,331	62,093	99,687	51,356	70,176	182,115	124,650	60,445	118,771	129,796
Thailand	4,090	1,590	1,759	4,256	3,473	2,731	3,150	30,834	32,815	26,339	38,451	71,938	578,895	45,786	53,541	50,455
Singapore	5,256	5,028	6,658	11,714	3,516	8,179	3,688	11,127	23,705	6,272	9,351	20,649	81,939	96,585	67,711	38,246
Indonesia				5,194	13,912	18,837	11,827	23,586	20,866	34,539	28,933	72,108	32,887	20,183	38,441	34,503
Malaysia	1,692	2,099	6,598	8,301	5,865	8,351	8,476	22,866	20,811	17,358	24,824	36,310	43,131	32,675	69,496	30,427
Oman	3,160		2		71	56	17	299	565	60	620	701	154	4,488	7,356	25,874
Australia	2,277	1,935	527	2,798	3,686	13,429	2,143	6,229	4,803	8,634	35,119	23,714	19,064	11,144	37,139	18,263
Iran	32,597	13,279	21,969	84,298	44,608	103,346	3,701	9,571	2,794	6,465	6,924	4,732	1,035	1,009	2,121	1,022
Bangladesh	35	43	1	374	66	109	184	265	261	550	531	424	481	321	547	746
Sri Lanka	27	105	12	1	7	276	306	2,924	2,249	712	661	5,001	278	139	207	206
Yemen		2					1,063	68	18	1	2,422	20	17	20	33	

Source: Compiled using UNCOMTRADE data in WITS database.

Appendix 17. Seychelles exports to non-African IORA member ('000 US$)

Country	*1994*	*1995*	*1996*	*1997*	*1998*	*1999*	*2000*	*2001*	*2002*	*2003*	*2004*	*2005*	*2006*	*2007*	*2008*
Sri Lanka							18	0.1		551.1	1,085.90	1,898.80	2,565.70	1,342.20	2,433.00
Australia	101.6	18.8	56.4	73.6	29.8	49.5	29.4	410.6	441.5	61.6	349.6	234.3	269.6	675.6	560.5
Singapore	318.1	604.6	785.6	1,592.30	181.7	84.2	576.3	61.5	202.8	922	369.2	279.1	134.4	335.1	449.4
Malaysia		0		0	0	0	91.4	45.3	62.7	8.7	6.2	12.7	90.2	546	137.8
India	0	0	0	17.4	5.9		40.1	11.7	8.9	10.8	7.6	423.5	44.1	13.3	107.7
Iran							0.3	39.2	233	10.3					67.8
UAE	18.1	11.5	4	291.3	0	0	0	75.1	62.3	37.3	21.7	176.5	15.6	71.4	43.4
Thailand	200.6	75.6			0	0.6	0	0.3	0	0.1	189.1	149.2	18.5		24.6
Indonesia				0	0				34.6			120		41.2	16.2
Oman								15.8	70.7					358.7	6.9
Yemen	0	0	0	0	0								0		

Source: Compiled using UNCOMTRADE data in WITS database.

Appendix 18. Seychelles imports from non-African IORA member ('000 US$)

Country	*1994*	*1995*	*1996*	*1997*	*1998*	*1999*	*2000*	*2001*	*2002*	*2003*	*2004*	*2005*	*2006*	*2007*	*2008*
UAE	910	1,416	2,054	3,878	3,674	3,770	5,831	4,790	6,574	8,025	10,784	25,440	34,306	42,285	170,395
Australia	30,106	37,347	35,120	38,712	38,060	32,983	27,059	24,661	31,142	32,748	35,741	51,582	85,663	73,324	83,888
Bangladesh	2,412	2,887	3,483	3,691	7,435	5,681	7,324	4,618	7,885	4,027	6,239	11,941	11,652	16,949	29,336
Indonesia	3,075	4,962	9,032	8,905	9,875	8,982	12,141	6,220	8,262	9,139	13,002	13,746	15,886	18,561	27,142
India	353	565	488	1,242	2,591	6,581	1,606	2,194	1,639	3,615	2,318	5,126	9,250	6,028	10,566
Iran	3,704	5,030	6,671	8,068	5,729	5,940	3,902	5,161	4,617	5,710	4,187	5,317	9,724	11,144	8,462
Sri Lanka	3,294	3,035	4,839	7,357	15,749	6,955	4,107	3,742	5,988	6,060	4,777	4,381	5,915	15,123	8,148
Malaysia	137	125	267	449	257	488	239	866	199	313	307	1,017	3,046	1,526	4,126
Oman						200	5		319	12	6	1,001	268	53	1,050
Singapore	29,175	40,623	9,287	4,506	29,771	7		4		1	1		187	37	231
Thailand						12	12		1	1	428	4	9	19	174
Yemen							0				3				2

Source: Compiled using UNCOMTRADE data in WITS database.

Appendix 19. Comoros exports to non-African IORA member ('000 US$)

Country	*1995*	*1996*	*1997*	*1998*	*1999*	*2000*	*2001*	*2002*	*2003*	*2004*	*2005*	*2006*	*2007*	*2008*	*2009*
UAE	0.8	180.9	190.5	14.2		25.6	210.5	116.1	4.4	56.0	64.4	191.5	53.6	35.6	189.2
Australia						7.2									
Indonesia					194.6										
India			27.1							26.2	227.3	444.4	104.3	71.9	93.7
Malaysia														0.3	2.1
Oman		16.4													
Singapore	68.7	30.3	129.7		450.5	1083.7	135.6	60.5		155.9	58.4	181.9	112.9	663.0	3013.2
Yemen								0.3	427.3		2.8	14.1	28.3		42.6

Source: Compiled using UNCOMTRADE data in WITS database.

Appendix 20. Comoros imports from non-African IORA member ('000 US$)

Country	*1995*	*1996*	*1997*	*1998*	*1999*	*2000*	*2001*	*2002*	*2003*	*2004*	*2005*	*2006*	*2007*	*2008*	*2009*
UAE	2,214.2	3,696.7	3,376.5	3,564.6	2,901.9	1,794.7	4,090.9	3,259.2	6,093.1	11,252.8	25,959.9	31,070.8	46,464.8	51,688.4	53,254.7
Australia	1.2		6.0	6.7	10.6		0.0					0.0	0.0	0.1	22.2
Bangladesh								4.5						19.9	
Indonesia	3.1	82.0		96.9	748.6	1,491.6	1,126.0	1,266.9	1,230.7	977.8	1,330.1	662.6	387.3	899.7	893.8
India	10,882.6	603.0	2,981.3	1,842.2	1,301.2	468.8	2,014.1	397.9	392.8	4,899.2	3,038.7	5,737.5	1,589.3	5,894.8	5,439.2
Iran						12.6	120.7	2.1			10.5	0.2	439.8		
Sri Lanka													0.1		
Malaysia				19.7	8.2		63.2	440.5	25.3	29.3	260.1	434.3	166.7	2,152.3	3,546.9
Oman		5.2			2.1	0.9	2.7	5.1	44.5	17.3	30.8			73.2	316.6
Singapore	1,352.3	993.4	649.8	895.4	140.8	197.6	140.7	324.3	440.1	1,086.3	799.0	1,292.5	381.2	1,232.8	1,134.7
Thailand	64.9	15.4	17.4	3.5	19.2	60.0	84.7	240.1	277.0	350.4		582.8	339.9	497.1	4,284.8
Yemen	5.3	16.0		5.7	22.6	40.1	6.4	16.4	28.5	104.4	86.9	88.6	104.3	183.9	84.4

Source: Compiled using UNCOMTRADE data in WITS database.

Appendix 21. FDI inflow to African members of IORA from the world (in US$ million)

Country	*2007*	*2008*	*2009*	*2010*	*2011*	*2012*
Comoros	8	5	14	8	23	17
Kenya	729	96	115	178	335	259
Madagascar	773	1169	1066	808	810	895
Mauritius	339	383	248	430	273	361
Seychelles	239	130	118	160	144	114
Mozambique	427	592	893	1018	2663	5218
Tanzania	582	1383	953	1813	1229	1706
South Africa	5695	9006	5365	1228	6004	4572

Source: World Investment Report 2013.

Chapter 7

Trade and Investment Relations in the IORA Area: The Case of India-Tanzania Trade and Investment Flows

Honest Prosper Ngowi

ABSTRACT

The countries forming the Indian Ocean Rim Association (IORA) have had various relations for many years, including cultural, political, diplomatic as well as economic relations. The IORA countries have experienced both trade and investments inflows and outflows with many and far-reaching social, economic and political implications. Using secondary data in this chapter, the author identifies, analyzes and discusses trade and investment flows between India and Tanzania. He then draws conclusions and recommendations with implications not only to the two case study countries but also to the other IORA states.

Key words: Trade, Investment, India, Tanzania.

Introduction

The current 20 Indian Ocean Rim Association (IORA) states have been trading with each other as well as investing in each other over many years. In this chapter the focus is on trade and investment relationships between Tanzania and India as a case study to illustrate the nature of trade and investment among IORA states and implications of the same to the countries involved and the IORA region at large.

Introduction to India and Tanzania Relations

Although the chapter focuses on trade and investment relations between

India and Tanzania, it is important to have an overview of the general relationship between the two countries. This is important in order to be able to locate and understand the trade and investment relationships in a broader and more appropriate context.

According to URT (undated)[1]:

> India and Tanzania are closely linked through diverse geographical, historical, cultural, political, economic, commercial and other ties. Geographically both are neighbours across the Indian Ocean. Evidence shows that even before Vasco da Gama discovered the sea-route to India via the Cape of Good Hope (Cape Town), Indians and East Africans were in close contact with each other through trade and cultural ties. It is said that fishermen off the coast of Tanganyika guided Vasco da Gama in his exploration trip to India in 1498.

According to the Confederation of Indian Industries (undated)[2],

> Tanzania and India have traditionally enjoyed close, friendly and co-operative relations. From the 1960s to the 1980s the political relationship was driven largely by shared ideological commitments to anti-colonialism, anti-racism and socialism in various forms as well as a genuine desire for South-South Cooperation. In recent years Indo-Tanzanian ties have evolved into a modern and pragmatic relationship with greater and diversified economic engagement.

The first Indian Diaspora came to Tanzania shortly after World War I, when the League of Nations designed Tanzania as a British protectorate. Many of the top business establishments of Tanzania are owned by members of Indian origin. This can partly explain why the nature of Indo-Tanzanian trade and investment is the way it is today. Whereas India has a High Commission in Tanzania, Tanzania has an Embassy in India. There have been various visits of individuals and leaders from the two countries to each other over time. According to Tairo (2008)[3], a friendship, technical, economic and scientific cooperation was signed in 1966. In 1975, a cultural agreement was signed, while in 2008, a memorandum of understanding (MoU) on tourism was signed between India and Tanzania.

According to the Ministry of External Affairs of the Government of India (GoI), in 2009, the government of India granted a US$40 million Line of Credit (LoC) to Tanzania for financing the country's agricultural sector (including the export of tractors, pumps and equipment from India to Tanzania). The second Line of Credit of

US$36.56 million for the supply of Ashok Leyland trucks to the Government of Tanzania was approved and the Agreement was signed on 28th March, 2011 on the sidelines of the 7th CII Exim Bank Conclave on India Africa Project Partnership in New Delhi from 27-29 March, 2011. The Ministry has also been involved in several other important agreements between the two countries. These include the Agreement on Avoidance of Double Taxation and Prevention of Fiscal Evasion (2009), Air Services Agreement (2006), MoU for cooperation in the field of Agriculture (2002) and Trade Agreement (2000).

From the above, it can be concluded that the contemporary Indo-Tanzania trade and investment relationships should be understood in the wider context of deep-rooted relations including historical and political ones.

Trade Relations

The Confederation of Indian Industries (undated)[4], shows that the vibrant commercial relationship between India and Tanzania is reflected in the about 40,000 strong Indian community present in the country. Their ancestors came to Tanzania more than 100 years ago as merchants, sailors and labourers employed in railroad building. The Indian community continues to play an important role in trade and industry in Tanzania.

According to Bébien (2011)[5], trade between India and Tanzania amounted in 2009-2010 to 31 billion dollars. The Confederation of Indian Industries (undated)[6], notes that India is a leading trading partner of Tanzania. URT (undated), indicates that the bilateral trade volume between India and Tanzania for the year 2010/11 has increased by about 55% compared to the previous year. In comparison to the 2009/10 ranking, it is observed that during 2010/11 Tanzania remained at the same ranking as India's 5th Major Export destination and improved to become the 12th (from previously the 15th) Major Import Source to India from Africa. It has been reported that bilateral trade between India and Africa stood at 65 billion US dollars, with Tanzania's share estimated at 1.4 billion US dollars.[7]

Tanzania's Imports From India

India is among the largest sources of Tanzania's imports. According to the Confederation of Indian Industries (undated)[8], imports from India to Tanzania grew at average rate of 18.5% between 2006 and 2012. Goods imported from India include mineral fuels, mineral oils and products of their distillation; iron and steel and articles thereof; pharmaceutical products; machinery and mechanical appliances; vehicles other than railway or tramway; plastic and articles thereof; electrical machinery and equipment and parts thereof; sugars and sugar confectionery; articles of apparel and clothing accessories as well as rubber and articles thereof. It is worth noting that Tanzania imports from India a substantial amount of health services by sending its citizens for treatment in Indian hospitals, such as Appolo.

According to the Confederation of Indian Industries (undated)[9], Indian exports to Tanzania have shown a growth of about 65% in 2010-2011 over the previous year, with exports touching almost USD 1.5 billion.

Tanzania's Exports to India

Tanzania exports a range of goods to India including but not limited to edible fruit and nuts; edible vegetables and certain roots and tubers; natural or cultured pearls, precious or semi precious stones; wood and articles of wood; wood charcoal; tanning, dyeing extracts, tannins, pigments etc; oil seed, oceanic fruits, grain, seed fruit; coffee, tea, mate and spices; raw hides and skins as well as iron and steel.

The Confederation of Indian Industries (ibid)[10] indicates that Tanzania's exports to India (India's imports from Tanzania) registered a growth of 37% amounting to $326 million in 2010-11.

India's Imports From Tanzania

It can be seen from the Table 1 and Figure 1 that there has been general increase in India's imports from Tanzania in the time period under consideration. However imports declined in total in two years (2011 and 2006) out of the seven years covered.

Table 1. India's Imports From Tanzania, 2005-2011 (In Million USD)

S/n	*Year*	*Imports*	*Change from previous year*
1	2011	207.99	-21.2
2	2010	226.19	38.61
3	2009	187.58	15.76
4	2008	171.82	93.17
5	2007	78.65	22.09
6	2006	56.56	-7.62
7	2005	64.18	

Source: Confederation of Indian Industry (online at http://www.indiashowtanzania.com/advantage_tanzania.html) and computation by the author.

Figure 1. India's Imports From Tanzania, 2005-2011 (In Million USD)

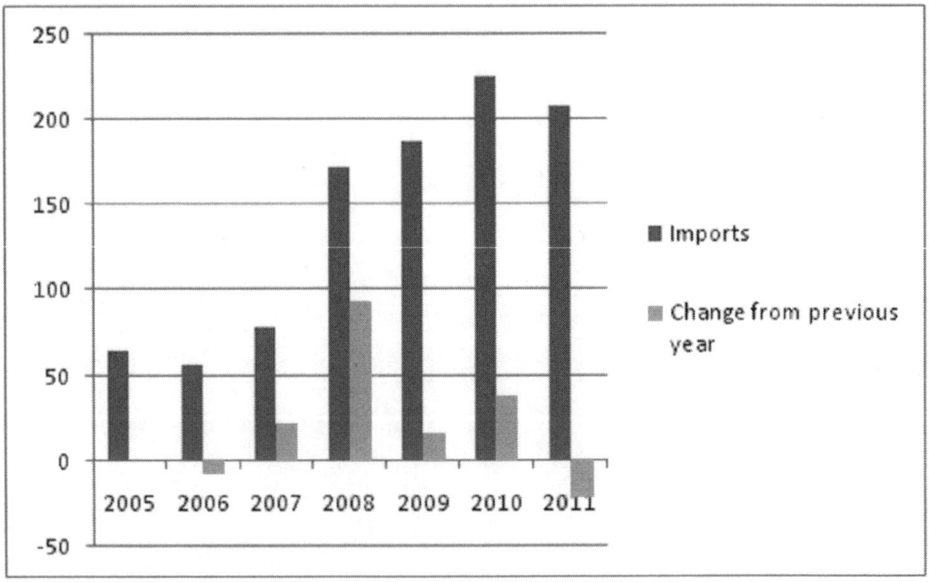

Source: Computed by the author.

India's Exports to Tanzania

According to the Confederation of Indian Industries (ibid)[11], exports from India to Tanzania grew at an average of 41.1% between 2006 and 2012.

Figure 2. Trend of Indian Exports to Tanzania, 2005-2011

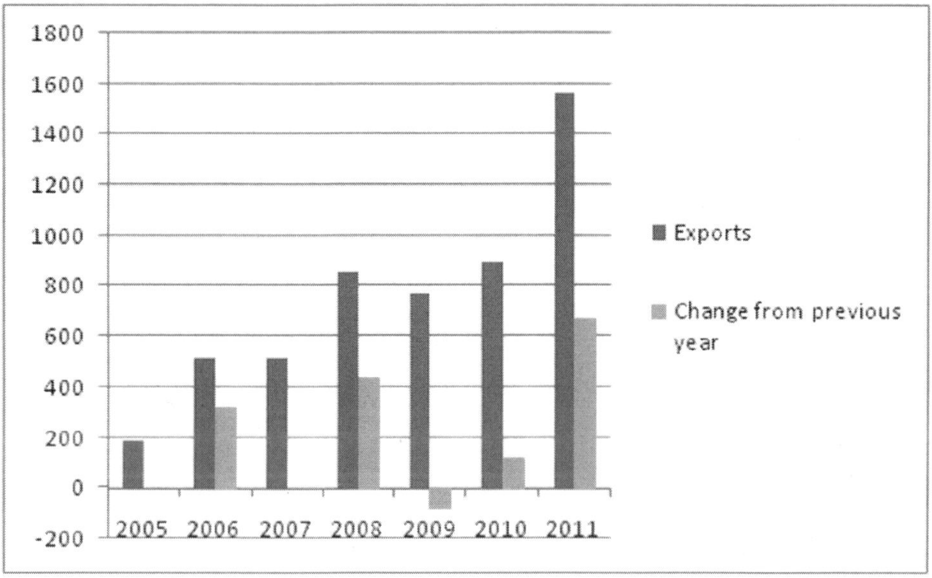

Source: Computed by the author.

Table 2. India's Exports to Tanzania, 2005-2011 (In Million USD)

S/n	*Year*	*Exports*	*Change from previous year*
1	2011	1564.95	669.94
2	2010	895.01	122.14
3	2009	772.87	-87.06
4	2008	859.73	437.33
5	2007	512.40	0
6	2006	512.40	321.19
7	2005	191.21	

Source: http://www.indiashowtanzania.com/advantage_tanzania.html) and computation by the author.

Figure 3 shows that India exported to Tanzania much more than it imported from the country.

The Indo-Tanzania Trade Balance

In order to identify who between India and Tanzania benefits more from Indo-Tanzania trade (exports and imports), the trade balance between the two countries was computed by the author. This is shown in the Table 3.

Figure 3. Combined Graph of Imports and Exports

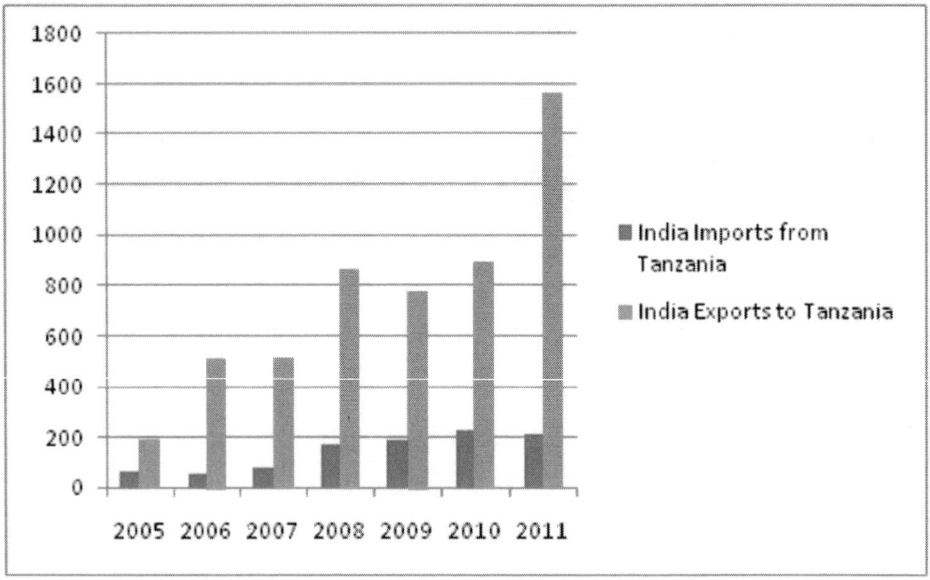

Table 3. The Indo-Tanzania Trade Balance, 2005-2011

S/n	*Year*	*India's Exports (mil USD)*	*India's Import (mil USD)*	*Difference (Surplus)*	*Export as % of imports*
1	2011	1564.95	207.99	1356.99	752.4%
2	2010	895.01	226.19	668.82	395.7%
3	2009	772.87	187.58	585.25	412%
4	2008	859.73	171.82	687.91	500.4%
5	2007	512.40	78.65	433.75	651.5%
6	2006	512.40	56.56	455.84	905.9%
7	2005	191.21	64.18	127.03	297.9%

Source: http://www.indiashowtanzania.com/advantage_tanzania.html) and computation by the author.

Table 3 shows that India has been a net-exporter to Tanzania in all of the seven (7) years under consideration. India has recorded a huge trade surplus in its exports and imports transactions with Tanzania. When India's exports are expressed as a percentage of its imports from Tanzania, it is clearly seen that in all years, the ratios of exports surpass imports by a very large percentage, ranging from a whole 905.9% in 2006 to 297.9% in 2005. This implies that whereas India has been doing very well in its trade relations with Tanzania, the latter has not performed well. This should be a matter of huge concern to Tanzania.

Analysis of Tanzania-India Trade Relations

From the types of imports and exports from and between the two countries, it can be seen that Tanzania imports from India largely finished manufactured industrial goods. These are final products that result from value addition processes in India. On the export front, Tanzania largely exports to India raw materials from unprocessed outputs. These are outputs that have not undergone value addition. The implications for Tanzania are, *inter alia*, export of low price-fetching products. It also implies the export of some employment (for workers who would have processed the exports domestically) and the export of some government revenues that could have been obtained through various fees and taxes related to domestic value addition. It also exports some raw by-products that emanate from value addition process. It would be more economically meaningful for the country to add value domestically for its raw exports. These data also indicate that Tanzania is a net importer from India. This is not favourable from the Tanzanian Balance of Payments perspective. The trade balance is in favour of India as Tanzania is experiencing deficits in its trade with India.

Investment Relations

Investment relations between Tanzania and India have been characterized by the latter receiving investments in the form of Foreign Direct Investment (FDI) in various sectors of the economy. Tanzania has not been investing in India by way of FDI. This can be understood from various perspectives. Firstly, Tanzania's private sector is relatively young and is still in an early stage of development, although notable progress has been made after the major and far-reaching reforms in the management of the economy since mid 1980s. Young, inexperienced and uncompetitive as it has been, the local Tanzanian private sector does not have what it takes to internationalize its operations in the forms of FDI to as far as India.

Tanzania has witnessed a steady and consistent flow of inward FDI during the last decade. FDI increased from US$467m to US$1095m between 2001 and 2011. Tanzania's most significant investors have been of European origin—Denmark, Norway, and Germany. However, India remains an important non-Western economic partner. Without giving figures, Bébien (ibid) argues that India is Tanzania's second largest investor.

Citing Tanzania Investment Centre (TIC), URT (undated), indicates that India is the biggest investor in Tanzania from Asia and is among the top three investors in Tanzania from all over the world by accumulated value for the period 1990-2010. Records show that between 1990-2008, companies with an Indian interest have invested in Tanzania in projects worth USD 1,217.57 Million. Table 4 presents the Indian investments in Tanzania (stock and flows) for 2009, 2010 and 2011.

Table 4. India FDI Stock in and Flows to Tanzania, 2009 -2011 (in Million USD)

S/n	*Year*	*Stock*	*Flows*	*Remarks*
1	2009	49.2	-	Compared to India, about 14 countries had more FDI stocks and flows in Tanzania in the years under consideration. The countries include but are not limited to South Africa, Barbados, UK, Canada, Mauritius, Kenya, Switzerland, Japan, Norway, Botswana, Jersey Channel Islands, France and USA. Apart from Mauritius and India other IORA countries with FDI stock and flows in Tanzania include UAE, Kuwait, Pakistan, Australia, Malaysia, Oman, Yemen, Iran, Saudi Arabia, New Zealand and Seychelles. The grand total of FDI stocks from the 62 countries with stocks in Tanzania for 2009 was 8,066.3 USD, in 2010 it was 8,762.2 USD and 9,278.1 USD in 2011. Grand total FDI flows from the 62 countries in 2009 was 1,813.3 USD and 1,229.4 USD in 2011. This shows increase in the stocks and inflows in the years under consideration
2	2010	63.3	2.3	
3	2011	71	4.9	
Total		183.5	7.2	

Source: Extracted from TIC et al (2013) and remarks by the author[12].

Selected Indian Investments in Tanzania

Among the Indian companies with investments in Tanzania include but are not limited to Reliance Industries Ltd, RITES, Bank of Baroda, Bank of India, Air India, Tata International Ltd, NMDC, Bharti Airtel Ltd, Larsen & Toubro Limited, ONGC Videsh Limited, National Insurance Corporation and LIC of India.

As is the case for trade, Tanzania has been a net recipient of investment inflows from India. No known Tanzanian companies have invested in India. This partly reflects the bigger picture which indicates that Tanzanian companies are yet to go multinational save for a handful of them that are present within a couple of countries in Africa, mainly Eastern and Southern Africa.

NOTES

1. The High Commission of the United Republic of Tanzania, New Delhi
2. http://www.indiashowtanzania.com/advantage_tanzania.html
3. Apoliniari Tairo (26 June 2008). "Tanzania set to strengthen tourism ties with India". *ETurboNews*
4. http://www.indiashowtanzania.com/advantage_tanzania.html
5. Arnaud Bébien (27 May 2011). "Tanzania: India—a Rewarding Relationship". *allAfrica.com*
6. http://www.indiashowtanzania.com/advantage_tanzania.html
7. See http://www.safpi.org/news/article/2013/tanzania-india-trade-could-more-double-2016 for details
8. http://www.indiashowtanzania.com/advantage_tanzania.html
9. http://www.indiashowtanzania.com/advantage_tanzania.html
10. http://www.indiashowtanzania.com/advantage_tanzania.html
11. http://www.indiashowtanzania.com/advantage_tanzania.html
12. TIC, BoT, OCGSZ, NBS and ZIPA (2013), Tanzania Investment Report 2012: Foreign Private Investment and Investor Perception

REFERENCES

Bébien, A. (2011). "Tanzania: India—a Rewarding Relationship". *allAfrica.com*

http://www.indiashowtanzania.com/advantage_tanzania.html (Retrieved on 23rd January 2014).

Confederation of Indian Industries (undated), online at http://www.indiashowtanzania.com/advantage_tanzania.html (Retrieved on 23rd January 2014) .

Tairo, A. (2008), "Tanzania set to strengthen tourism ties with India". *EturboNews,* (26 June 2008).

TIC, BoT, OCGSZ, NBS and ZIPA (2013), Tanzania Investment Report 2012: Foreign Private Investment and Investor Perception.

URT (undated). The High Commission of the United Republic of Tanzania, New Delhi.

Chapter 8

The Geopolitics of Official Development Assistance in Indian Ocean Africa: An Australian Perspective

Dennis Rumley

ABSTRACT

Among other things, the combination of the Global Financial Crisis (GFC) and an increase in nationalist sentiments among some developed states have contributed to a reduction in the amount of official development assistance (ODA) as a percentage of GNI in the budget allocated by many Development Assistance Committee (DAC) states. In addition, and in association, the neo-liberal ODA paradigm emphasises the efficacy of trade and foreign direct investment (FDI) rather than state-derived ODA as a more effective mechanism to facilitate economic development in the less developed states. This 'new paradigm' is bolstered to a considerable degree by the prospect of exploiting the natural resources and energy potential in those states. In addition to these geo-economic considerations, from a donor state perspective, decisions regarding priorities over the spatial allocation of ODA have become increasingly guided by geo-economic and geopolitical imperatives rather than humanitarian concerns, especially since the end of the Cold War.

This chapter explores and describes this ODA paradigm especially in an examination of Australian aid allocations since the end of the Cold War and the relative priority given to Africa in its ODA policy, with special reference to African member states of the Indian Ocean Rim Association (IORA). It is concluded that the trajectory of Australian overseas aid allocations to states has emphasised geopolitical rather than humanitarian considerations and that, in the context of Indian Ocean Africa, this presages a shift to an East Indian Ocean (EIO) regional strategic emphasis. This is also in part a response to Australia's geopolitical constraint of "territorial overstretch".

Key words: Official Development Assistance, Australian ODA, geopolitics of aid.

Introduction

Three principal issues are addressed in this chapter. First, it is intended to provide a very broad background/backdrop for the issue of the geopolitics of overseas aid to Indian Ocean Rim Association (IORA) states. Second, some aspects of the geopolitics of Australian aid, with special reference to IORA states, will be discussed in more detail. Third, the chapter will conclude with some observations on what appears to be the emergent Australian Official Development Assistance (ODA) paradigm that now has the "Indian Ocean Asia-Pacific" (Indo-Pacific) as its principal regional focus.

The Context of ODA in the Indian Ocean Region

Contested spaces in Africa

The Indian Ocean Region (IOR) has had a long history of extra-regional influence and it could be argued that some of the many remaining legacies of this, which are evident around the region, are potential sources of instability. Apart from Indian Ocean states themselves, all major industrial powers and energy suppliers have an innate interest in Indian Ocean security and stability (Rumley 2013a, page 40).

An important question is the extent to which any current extra-regional security presence, while aiming to guarantee regional as well as its own security interests, is also perceived by other states as a source of insecurity. From this perspective, regional and external states are seen to be in a process of competition for influence and resources. However, it should be recognised and accepted that the United States and China, as well as other extra-regional states, have legitimate regional security interests.

If we consider the IOR as an overall 'arena of competing influence', then it is instructive to locate a significant United States and Chinese presence and add tothis the regional presence of India. According to some analysts, we end up with an interesting geographical distribution of what we have called Chinese 'pearls', USA 'diamonds' and Indian 'nuggets', principally reflecting concerns over resources security and secure access to SLOCs (Table 1).

Table 1. Chinese Pearls, USA Diamonds and Indian Nuggets

Chinese pearls	*USA diamonds*	*Indian nuggets*
Bangladesh	Australia	Andaman Islands
Burma	Bahrain	Mauritius
Pakistan	Diego Garcia	Maldives
Sri Lanka	Djibouti	
	Egypt	
	Indonesia	
	Kenya	
	Kuwait	
	Oman	
	Qatar	
	Singapore	
	UAE	

Source: Rumley 2013a.

For the sake of the present discussion and putting aside the veracity of arguments over a 'string of pearls' strategy, China has nonetheless some presence in four northern Indian Ocean rim locations—Chittagong in Bangladesh, Gwadarin Pakistan, Hambantota in Sri Lanka and Sittwe in Burma. Furthermore, according to the US Department of Defense Base Structure Report, the United States has some presence in 12 Indian Ocean locations—the centrally-located Diego Garcia, five in the Persian Gulf (Bahrain, Kuwait, Oman, Qatar and UAE), three in Africa (Egypt, Djibouti and Kenya) and a further three on the easternrim (Australia, Indonesia and Singapore).

If we add to these India's sovereignty of the Andaman Islands and its presence in Mauritius and Maldives, we are left with a number of what might be called 'contested spaces'—that is, they remain competitive arenas that have yet to be incorporated into the influence of powerful external states. These include the failed states of Somalia and Yemen and much of Oceanic Africa (Rumley 2013a, page 41). In the case of the latter, given the orientation to France of Comoros and Seychelles and the 'Western' orientation of South Africa, then Madagascar, Mozambique and Tanzania—the region's three poorest states—remain important potential contested spaces in IORA. Official Development Assistance and private and state-sponsored investment are among the various soft power options used to garner influence and to obtain access to raw materials and energy in Indian Ocean African states.

Indeed, as has been recently pointed out: "foreign aid is an essential element of foreign policy for many countries" (Milner and Tingley 2013a, ix), and this has been the case for many years.

Security and stability in Indian Ocean Africa

The relationship between economic insecurity and political conflict is evident both among and within states in the IOR. The potential for conflict among states is also exacerbated due to the global environment of increasing competition over diminishing natural resources. The attempt by states to achieve resources security and maintain energy security is in part propelling a new geopolitics of resources and creating new regional tensions. Within states it has been noted that economic insecurity has become part of a process of deepening social divisions and increasing political instability. Under conditions of increasing fragility it has been suggested therefore that the state faces the threat of losing control not only of its capacity to provide basic services but also of its monopoly over law and order and its political legitimacy (Rumley 2013, page 49).

It has often been said that a post-Cold War global North-South division has replaced the former East-West division as one of the principal dimensions of global conflict. In this new paradigm there is a danger of prioritising the security agenda of the North at the expense of the South. Regional security threats can arise because of the instability of states with problems of economic, social and political viability. In addition, resources scarcity and resources competition constitute threats, especially when they are linked to food and energy insecurity. Indeed, it has been argued that in the years ahead, "resource wars" will become "the most distinctive feature of the global security environment" (Klare 2002, page 212). Furthermore, states that 'fail' due to basic problems of good governance and corruption, and are incapable of asserting authority within their own territories, are seen to be "troubling to world order" since they may become sources of instability, mass migration and terrorism. In short, state and regional stability are jeopardized both by deep economic imbalances among states and deep economic insecurity within states.

Clearly, economic insecurity is common among many Indian Ocean states. Low levels of human development and high levels of economic underdevelopment contribute to significant levels of political instability. The IOR includes only six states that fall into the global category of "very high human development"—Australia, Singapore, Brunei, Kuwait, Qatar and UAE—while the majority of regional states are classified as having "medium human development". Sustainable developmental strategies are especially needed for the "low human development" states, nearly all of which are in Africa.

The context of Indian Ocean underdevelopment and ODA

Official Development Assistance is defined as those flows to countries and territories on the DAC List of ODA Recipients and to multilateral development institutions that are:

> (i) provided by official agencies, including state and local governments, or by their executive agencies; and
>
> (ii) each transaction of which:
>
> (a) is administered with the promotion of the economic development and welfare of developing countries as its main objective; and
>
> (b) is concessional in character and conveys a grant element of at least 25 per cent (calculated at a rate of discount of 10 per cent) (OECD 2008)

The goals and motives of providing aid to economically less developed states clearly vary widely from the pure humanitarian (to meet basic needs and more of recipient states) or idealist perspective to one of economic and/or geopolitical self-interest (aid is an instrument of a donor state's foreign policy) or a realist viewpoint. Enabling economic security for less developed states invariably has a positive impact on state stability. ODA is obviously one mechanism for enabling the implementation of the Millennium Development Goals, but, according to the OECD, development aid has been declining in real terms in recent years:

> Development aid fell by 4% in real terms in 2012, following a 2% fall in 2011. The continuing financial crisis and Euro zone turmoil has led several governments to tighten their budgets, which has had a direct impact on development aid. There is also a noticeable shift in aid allocations away from the poorest countries and towards middle-income countries. However, on the basis of the DAC Survey on Donors' Forward Spending Plans, a moderate recovery in aid levels is expected in 2013. OECD Secretary-General Angel Gurría expressed

> concern over this trend. "It is worrying that budgetary duress in our member countries has led to a second successive fall in total aid, but I take heart from the fact that, in spite of the crisis, nine countries still managed to increase their aid. As we approach the 2015 deadline for achieving the Millennium Development Goals, I hope that the trend in aid away from the poorest countries will be reversed. This is essential if aid is to play its part in helping achieve the Goals (OECD 2013).

As OECD Secretary-General Gurria (2013) recently observed: "Africa will probably be the only developing region not to reach the Millennium Goal of halving poverty by 2015, and will struggle to reach the other goals as well".

In the annual letter of the Bill and Melinda Gates Foundation, overseas aid is described as "a phenomenal investment. Foreign aid doesn't just save lives; it also lays the groundwork for lasting, long-term economic progress" (Gates and Gates 2014). While the question of aid-dependency has been problematical in the past, in Africa 2011, only 8 states continued to receive more aid per capita than tax raised per head of population (OECD 2013).

The majority of aid delivered to African states since the end of the Cold War has been from the 27 states of the UN Development Assistance Committee (DAC). However, the aid revenue stream has traditionally been dominated by a small number of states. In 2011-12, for example, five states—USA, Germany, UK, France and Japan—supplied more than 60% of all DAC allocations.

However, of these five key states, only one—UK—registered an increase in ODA as a proportion of GNI since the end of the Cold War. Indeed, half of the DAC states registered a decline in this percentage. Furthermore, both France and Japan have contributed less of the overall DAC budget—France from 13.2% in 1991 to 9.8% in 2011, and Japan from 16.4% in 1991 to 8.2% in 2011.

The role of the DAC in aid to sub-Saharan Africa

Since the end of the Cold War, there has been an overall decline in ODA to Sub-Saharan Africa:

> ODA to sub-Saharan Africa has followed a similar pattern, trending downward from the early 1990s (see Figure 2). After reaching a pre-

> 2000 peak of $US17.3 billion in 1990, it fell substantially in the mid-1990s, falling from $16.9 billion in 1994 to 11.6 billion in 1999. 11 This trend was reversed in 2000, with ODA reaching a post-1960 high of $17.7 billion in 2002. While the rises in ODA from 1999 should obviously not be overlooked as a very positive signal, the reality is that sub-Saharan Africa has received $1.4 billion less of this aid during 1993 to 2002 than during 1983 to 1992. The declines in total ODA are also evident in aid allocated bilaterally and via multilateral agencies: both forms of aid tend to follow trends in total aid. Shares in world ODA to sub-Saharan Africa have also fallen sharply in most years between 1990 and 1999 (see Figure 3). There has since been some recovery in these shares, with total and bilateral ODA shares rising since 1999 and multilateral since 2000. The main point, however, is that the decline in aid amounts to sub-Saharan Africa during the 1990s was not entirely due to an overall contraction in world aid; donors actually allocated away from the region. Donors, it seems, have favoured less impoverished countries in other parts of the world. (McGillivray, nd)

Given that five states dominate the global distribution of aid through the DAC, it is no surprise that many of these dominate the overall pattern of aid of Africa. In the case of the 9 African IORA states, however, donor priorities vary significantly across recipient states (Table 2).

Table 2. Principal DAC ODA Donors IORA African States 2010-11 (US$M)

Comoros	France (US$23 of US$52)
Egypt (DP)	USA, France, Kuwait, Japan, Arab Fund, EU Institutions (all >100M)
Kenya	USA, IDA, IMF, Japan, AFDF, UK, Germany, France, EU Insts (all > 100M)
Madagascar	France, USA, IDA (all > 50M)
Mauritius	France, EU Institutions (all > 50M)
Mozambique	USA, Portugal, EU Insts, UK, IDA, Canada, Denmark (all > 100M)
Seychelles	France, UAE (each > 10M)
South Africa	USA, EU Insts, France, Germany (all > 100M)
Tanzania	USA, IDA, UK, EU Insts, AFDF, Global Fund, Denmark, Norway, Germany, Japan (all > 100M)

Source: DAC Statistics.

The United States is the lead donor state in Egypt, Kenya, Mozambique, South Africa and Tanzania, while France is especially important in Comoros, Madagascar, Mauritius and Seychelles. Japan has had a long-standing interest in aid to African states and remains an important donor especially to Egypt, Kenya and Tanzania. However, in 2011-12, the Democratic Republic of Congo (DRC) was the only African state represented in Japan's top 10 aid recipients (DAC statistics). UK African IORA state aid priorities are with Kenya and Mozambique. Germany is also an important aid donor to Kenya and also to Tanzania. Interestingly, both Germany and Denmark appear more than once on this Table.

It is not unreasonable to conclude that this variability in donor state priorities implies an aid strategy that is not simply targeted at meeting humanitarian goals, since, for the 9 African IORA states, the amount of aid delivered as a proportion of the total given to all African states is not a reflection of need. If we take a poverty index as percentage population with an income below US$2 and correlate this with recipient state aid as a percentage of total African aid, then we can see that the poorest regional state (Madagascar) by no means receives the largest proportion of aid (Table 3).

Table 3. Poverty and Proportion of Total African Net ODA to IORA States 2006-2011

	% below US$2 income (rank)	*DAC Category*	*2006*	*2011*
Comoros	65.0 (6)	LDC	0.07	0.1
Egypt (DP)	15.4 (9)	LMIC	2.0	0.8
Kenya	67.2 (4)	OLIC	2.1	4.8
Madagascar	92.6 (1)	LDC	1.8	0.8
Mauritius	n. a. (7)	UMIC	0.04	0.4
Mozambique	81.8 (3)	LDC	3.7	4.0
Seychelles	65.8 (5)	UMIC	0.03	0.04
South Africa	31.3 (8)	UMIC	1.6	2.5
Tanzania	87.9 (2)	LDC	4.2	4.8

Source: African Economic Outlook 2013, Statistical Annex.

Even the least poor state on this index receives the same proportion of aid as Madagascar. This is one of the reasons why the United Nations Economic Commission for Africa, in its *African Economic Outlook 2013* raised the concept of "under aided countries" as being states that should have received more aid according to needs-based allocation criteria (UNECA 2013, pp. 55-6):

> There is no agreed definition of what constitutes an under-aided country. It can be in absolute or relative terms. Receiving insufficient aid in absolute terms means not being able to finance needs to meet the Millennium Development Goals (MDGs) or other development goals—a situation many countries face. The OECD-DAC instead determines which low-income countries are under-aided in relative terms—that is, receiving less aid relative to others that have similar needs and characteristics.
>
> Some countries are under-aided in part because of inadequate co-ordination amongst donors of their individual incentives, frameworks and priorities. Development assistance providers rarely take into consideration the decisions of other actors when making their own allocations. The recent decision by several donors to focus development assistance on fewer countries has aggravated the situation, with donors exiting from some of the same countries. Besides, there is no commonly agreed framework or co-ordination mechanism for development providers to seek analysis of aid allocation patterns. (UNECA 2013, p. 54).

DAC and non-DAC aid—the rising importance of Chinese aid and Japanese influence

One interesting development in the geopolitics of aid is that, since the end of the Cold War, there has been a significant growth in aid provided by so-called "non-DAC" states, including China, India, Saudi Arabia and the UAE. It has been suggested that the entry of new donors operating outside of pre-existing OECD guidelines not only implies the existence of differential goals between DAC and non-DAC states, but also tends to encourage a competitive process for influence (Milner and Tingley 2013a, x-xviii). For example, it has been argued in the case of China that aid is being used, especially in Africa, as part of a "charm offensive". With 45.7% of its aid directed towards Africa in 2009, it has been noted that China has developed 1700 projects since 2000 worth some US$75B. It has been suggested that this geopolitical strategy has been aimed principally at resource-rich African states: "the dominant narrative has been one of China's insatiable desire for resources". While it still seems to be somewhat unclear as to whether all of the money involved can be classified as ODA according to OECD guidelines, what does seem to be clear is that "China is an important emerging player in development finance" (Provost and Harris 2013).

Also, in the past couple of years, Japan, as one of the other IORA Dialogue Partners, has been in the process of reassessing its Indian Ocean policy, including its Africa strategy in order to "contribute to stability and prosperity in the IOR" (Hattori 2013). Indeed, some commentators will have observed the number of senior Japanese and Chinese officials crisscrossing Africa since the beginning of 2014, indicating that Africa has a growing strategic importance for both the Chinese and Japanese governments. Over the next several years, Japanese economic and political influence is likely to grow throughout the Indian Ocean Rim.

Some commentators have gone so far as to portray this behaviour as a form of geopolitical competition for influence linked closely to the potential availability of energy and raw materials. For Japan, it seems that Mozambique is one important priority due to the recent discovery of significant deposits of natural gas (Brothers 2014).

The geopolitics of Australian ODA with special reference to IORA states

Australian Official Development Assistance Policy

Australia could be regarded as an aid donor of 'average' proportions among DAC states. In 2011-12, for example, its ODA budget was just above the average, was less than that of Canada and slightly more than Norway and amounted to 3.9% of the total DAC budget.

Australia's ODA policy had formerly been managed by AusAID, an Australian Government agency that was created by the Labor Federal Government in 1995. However, on 31 October 2013, it ceased to be an executive body and was integrated into the Australian Department of Foreign Affairs and Trade (DFAT). The Australian decision came only a few months after the Canadian Government had enacted a bill to amalgamate the Canadian International Development Agency (Cida) with its Department of Foreign Affairs and International Trade into a new Foreign Affairs, Trade and Development Canada (FATDEC).

Australia's ODA agency has existed in a variety of names and formats. It was founded in 1974 under the Whitlam Laborgovernment as the Australian Development Assistance Agency (ADAA) to fulfill a role that had previously been the responsibility of several departments. It was renamed the Australian Development Assistance Bureau (AIDAB) following the publication of the Jackson Report in 1984, before being given its current name by the Labor Keating government in 1995.

Throughout this period, the prime objective of the Australia's aid program has been "to assist developing countries to reduce povertyand achieve sustainable development, in line with Australia's national interest" and "to promote the economic and social advantage of people in developing countries" (Rumley 1999, pp. 182-3).

Australian ODA goals

As has been argued elsewhere, in the post-Cold War period, Australia's ODA has been directed at four main policy goals. First, it has represented an important element of what Gareth Evans referred to as Australia's multidimensional security policy. Second, there has been an explicit attempt to incorporate the idea of ecologically sustainable development. Third, Australian ODA has been used as a mechanism for promoting Australian business interests—an issue not uncommon among DAC member states. Fourth, the post-Cold War geopolitical orientation of Australian ODA has increasingly focussed towards states in the Asia-Pacific region. As a result, in the post-Cold War years, almost 90% of Australian bilateral aid has been directed towards the Southwest Pacific, East Asia and South Asia. Nearest neighbours, Papua New Guinea—due in part to historical-colonial ties, as well as proximity—and Indonesia have since remained Australia's largest individual ODA state recipients (Rumley 1999, pp. 183-5).

An analysis of Australian ODA data for 1998 showed that there was no overall relationship between per capita aid allocations and development need, using the Human Development Index (HDI) as the indicator of need. It was shown, for example, that states such as Nepal and Pakistan were 'disadvantaged' on the basis of their ODA per capita aid allocation while Papua New Guinea and Indonesia were found to be 'advantaged' on the basis of their allocations. In short, geopolitical considerations rather than need were more important in the geography of Australian ODA (Rumley 1999, page 187).

The highest per capita Australian ODA allocations define what has been referred to as an "aid front" in the Southwest Pacific, the only region in the world that has been regarded as Australia's traditional sphere of influence. This was expressed in the form of an "Australasian Monroe Doctrine" which emerged in the latter part of the 19th Century and which viewed the South Pacific Islands as an Anglo-Saxon preserve in which "other 'powers' should not trespass" (Rumley 1999, page 188).

Thus, it has been argued, that during the post-Cold War period, Australia's regional relations have been developed along four principal fronts—a cooperative security front to the north; an aid front to the east; an environmental security front to the south; and, a trade front to the west. In short, the western Indian Ocean, rather than being viewed as a strategically important region for Australia, and rather than being perceived as the region of greatest development need, was regarded as a potential "trade front" (Rumley 1999).

Australian ODA to Africa

"Africa has long been at the margins of Australian public policy and scholarship alike", although with Kevin Rudd's election as Prime Minister in November 2007, there was promise of a greater developmental engagement aimed at meeting the Millennium Development Goals (Hawker 2009, page 25). The so-called United Nations Security Council (UNSC) Africa "controversy" is an interesting illustration of the geopolitics of Australian ODA to Africa. An undated and highly censored letter from former Foreign Minister, Stephen Smith, to then Prime Minister, Kevin Rudd, refers to a conversation they had on 20th March 2008. It proposes that Australia announce its candidacy for the October 2012 election to be a non-permanent member of the UN Security Council (UNSC), with Australia's opponents being Finland and Luxembourg. Stephen Smith points out that "running a successful campaign" would be "very challenging" and "would involve a whole-of-government approach" as well as "extensive representation activity and promotional travel" (DFAT 2008).

The resultant public relations "campaign", among other things, involved the use of the Australian Governor-General (G-G), who visited 9 African states in March 2009. This was the first ever visit by an Australian Head of State to southern and eastern Africa (Hawker 2009, page 27). In addition, two Special Envoys to Africa were appointed for the length of the bid to facilitate Australia's UNSC case, announced in a media release in October 2010 by then Foreign Minister, Kevin Rudd. Former Federal Minister, Bob McMullan, was appointed as Special Envoy for Anglophone Africa, and Bill Fisher, a former Australian Ambassador to France, was appointed as "Special Envoy to La Francophonie" (Rudd 2010).

Australia's campaign for a seat on the UNSC has been portrayed as being somewhat costly (estimated at A$23.59 million—Rose 2012), controversial, and even cynical by some commentators. One of the elements of criticism is that Australia's ODA policy had become (geo)politicised in that aid was being used essentially to buy votes in Africa for the Security Council bid (Sheridan 2013). Some have argued that Africa, with 53 votes, was regarded as a major vote bank in the bid to reach the necessary target of 129 votes. Caribbean states apparently were another vote bank target—for example, the new Parliament House in Grenada has been portrayed as part of the vote buying exercise (Sheridan 2014a). One ANU academic, Raoul Heinrichs, has argued that Australia's aid funding "had been skewed to win support" and that votes may have even been bought more than once (Cooper 2012). Others have argued, however, that, while Australia's UNSC bid contributed to an increase in ODA to Africa, it was only one factor among many (Colebatch 2012). Yet one other line of criticism and concern is that the campaign for the UNSC seat had become a "personal obsession of Kevin Rudd" (Cooper 2012). The then Shadow Foreign Minister, Julie Bishop, claimed in the Australian Parliament that it was "obvious that Kevin Rudd is diverting funds from the foreign aid budget to buy votes for *his* campaign" (emphasis added) (Lewis 2010). The level of media and political reaction to what was broadly perceived as a blatant vote-buying exercise resulted in an extraordinary DFAT press release in an attempt to diffuse the debate and clarify the government's role in this matter. Among other things, the press release noted that:

1. The Australian Government has not allocated aid according to partner countries' UNSC voting intentions
2. There has been no change in regional aid focus
3. It is completely appropriate that the Government would assist some of the poorest and most vulnerable countries
4. Decisions on the aid budget are not made on the basis of the UNSC campaign
5. The Government is not cutting the aid program (Rose 2012)

Keen observers of the apparent vote buying exercise, however, will refer to the proportion of Australian bilateral ODA devoted to Sub-Saharan Africa during this century. In the early years this proportion declined and then began to rise again in 2008. It continued to rise until success had been achieved in the UNSC bid in 2012 and then began to fall again (Figure 1).

Figure 1. Percentage Australian Bilateral ODA to Sub-Saharan Africa 2001-2013

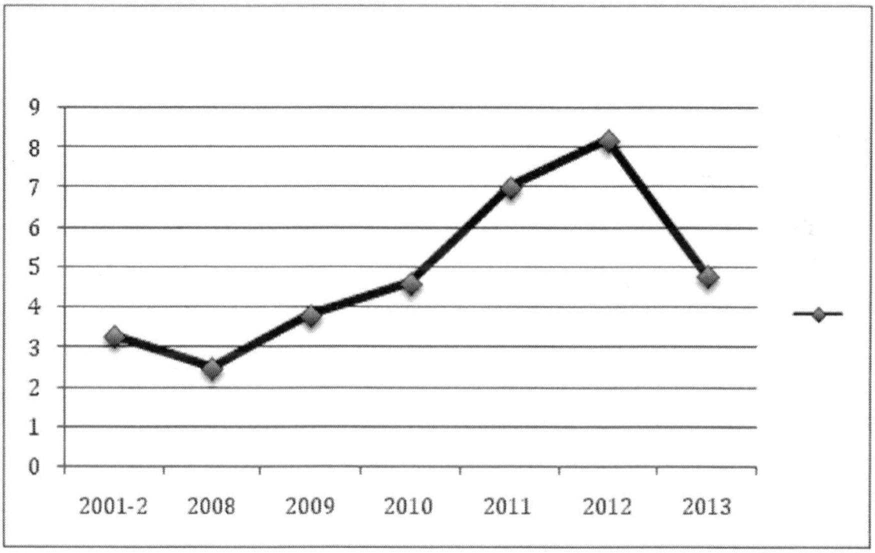

Source: DAC Statistics.

Australian ODA to IORA States

Australian Official Development Assistance to IORA states since 1997 can at best be described as quite modest. For 2008-9, for example, the Pacific Islands States received 14.4% of Australian aid, compared with 11.4% to Indonesia, 10.1% to PNG, 9% to South Asia and 4.5% to Sub-

Saharan Africa. While IORA states received 22.7% of Australian aid in 2008-9, the five poorest IORA states received just 2.2% of Australian ODA (Rumley 2012, page 101). In short, not only is the region of greatest global need not the highest Australia ODA priority, those states most in need within that region received very little humanitarian assistance.

For the IORA states in the 21st Century, this pattern has become more pronounced. Australian ODA to sub-Saharan Africa is declining and aid to IORA states represents a minor percentage of total DAC aid (Table 4). Furthermore, IORA states with the greatest need—that is the poorest states—especially Madagascar, Mozambique and Tanzania—on average have not received the greatest assistance. Indeed, less poor states, such as Egypt and South Africa, have on occasion received more aid than the poorest states (Table 4). Madagascar again emerges as a state that can be described as being "under-aided".

Table 4. Australian ODA to IORA African States, 2000-2013 ($'000)

	2000		*2005*		*2010*	
	Australian ($'000)	*% DAC*	*Australian ($'000)*	*% DAC*	*Australian ($'000)*	*% DAC*
State (poverty rank)						
Comoros (6)	7	0.02	n. a.	n. a.	80	0.001
Egypt (DP) (9)	17985	2.0	13082	1.45	8366	1.42
Kenya (4)	2916	0.31	5106	0.54	17140	1.05
Madagascar (1)	321	0.4	n. a.	n. a.	518	0.11
Mauritius (7)	518	2.73	209	1.1	664	0.53
Mozambique (3)	12493	0.76	7758	0.47	24745	1.27
Seychelles (5)	108	0.77	n. a.	n. a.	n. a.	n. a.
South Africa (8)	10947	1.53	8738	1.22	7199	0.70
Tanzania (2)	3347	0.18	3349	0.18	13790	0.47
Sub-Saharan Africa	56038	0.35	76853	0.31	264241	0.93

Sub-Saharan Africa change in ODA 2012-13 to 2013-14: from 211200 to 133000 (a reduction of 37%)

The emergent Australian ODA paradigm

The closure of AusAID and its incorporation into the Australian Department of Foreign Affairs and Trade (DFAT) has been referred to as a "*good day for diplomacy*" (emphasis added). One view is that this outcome will give DFAT a stronger and more effective role as ODA will be more able to satisfy both humanitarian needs and Australia's national interests (Sheridan 2013). However, the decision in part reflects the ongoing tension in Australian aid policy which has been portrayed as a "contest between the foreign policy demands that aid must serve the national interest (defined with a focus on security) and an increasing cognisance among aid bureaucrats, and some politicians, that effective 'development' may be stymied by these demands" (Davis 2011, page 402). The tension in the balancing of business goals with developmental and humanitarian goals has been ongoing (Hawker 2009, page 25).

On the other hand, the AusAID decision was made in the context of the Government's ongoing determination to reduce public expenditure as well as to eradicate inefficient and wasteful spending. Furthermore, Australian aid agencies have been criticised from a number of perspectives and thus AusAID was vulnerable, given the Government's ideological and expenditure priorities. As Davis has also put it:

> Taken together, these narratives tell a story of foreign aid institutions that are dominated by foreign policy concerns, elites and bureaucracies, yet also attempt, unsuccessfully as a rule, to grapple with the political complexity of development. This has helped to produce a policy conceptualisation of aid relationships with recipient countries that de-emphasises, or simply avoids, acknowledgement that 'the South' is a valid entity within global development debates (Davis 2011, page 403).

However, the volume of aid that is directed to Africa is more than balanced by the amount of international trade that is in favour of Australia (Hawker 2009, page 27). On the basis of merchandise trade, in 2012, Australia had a trade surplus with all African IORA states (Table 5). However, there was a substantial range—the largest surpluses were with South Africa (A$526M), Egypt (A$452M) and Mozambique (A$383M); the lowest was with Comoros (A$19,000). For the region's poorest states, the trade surplus-aid equation was:

Madagascar	trade surplus 2012 A$14.1M;	Australian ODA 2010 A$518,000
Tanzania	trade surplus 2012 A$112M;	Australian ODA 2010 A$13.8M
Mozambique	trade surplus 2012 A$383M;	Australian ODA 2010 A$24.7M

On the other hand, while Australian investment was negligible in some states—Comoros, Madagascar, Mozambique and Seychelles—the overall balance of Australian investment in IORA African states was strongly in the region's favour, especially for South Africa, Mauritius,

Tanzania and Egypt. Furthermore, total regional net investment gain from Australia closely matched Australia's total regional trade surplus—that is, for all IORA African states, Australia's merchandise trade surplus in 2012 was A$1.66 Billion; the net investment gain on the other hand was A$1.59 Billion.

Table 5. Australian Trade and Investment with IORA Africa 2012

Comoros	
Exports to Comoros	A$116,000
Imports from Comoros	A$97,000
Australia's investment in Comoros	NIL
Comoros' investment in Australia	NIL
Egypt	
Exports to Egypt	A$511M
Imports from Egypt	A$59M
Australia's investment in Egypt	A$218M
Egypt's investment in Australia	A$17M
Kenya	
Exports to Kenya	A$114M
Imports from Kenya	A$20M
Australia's investment in Kenya	NIL
Kenya's investment in Australia	A$7M
Madagascar	
Exports to Madagascar	A$17.6M
Imports from Madagascar	A$3.5M
Australia's investment in Madagascar	NIL
Madagascar's investment in Australia	NIL
Mauritius	
Exports to Mauritius	A$90M
Imports from Mauritius	A$11M
Australia's investment in Mauritius	A$435M
Mauritius' investment in Australia	NIL
Mozambique	
Exports to Mozambique	A$391M
Imports from Mozambique	A$8M
Australia's investment in Mozambique	NA
Mozambique's investment in Australia	NA
Seychelles	
Exports to Seychelles	A$3.8M
Imports from Seychelles	A$2M
Australia's investment in Seychelles	NIL
Seychelles' investment in Australia	NA

South Africa	
Exports to South Africa	A$1,380M
Imports from South Africa	A$854M
Australia's investment in South Africa	A$3,024M
South Africa's investment in Australia	A$2,310M
Tanzania	
Exports to Tanzania	A$119M
Imports from Tanzania	A$7M
Australia's investment in Tanzania	A$257M
Tanzania's investment in Australia	NA

Source: DFAT fact sheets from DFAT website 2014.

However, current Australian government policy "is directing attention to the Asia-Pacific and Indian Ocean and away from Africa and the Middle East" (*sic*) (Hepworth 2014). Australia's "region" has been "shielded from aid cutbacks" and thus ODA has been "protected" for Indonesia, PNG, Philippines and Nauru. Australian Foreign Minister, Julie Bishop "believes that there is a natural division of labour in the aid sphere"—Europe takes care of Africa, the United States takes care of its South and Australia concentrates its efforts in the Asia-Pacific region (Sheridan 2014a). In short, current Australian government ODA policy appears to support a quasi-pan region geopolitical organisation of global space (Rumley 1999, page 25).

Australia is also in the process of developing and implementing a 'new philosophy of aid' that seeks to go well beyond the traditional aid donor-aid recipient quasi-dependent relationship (Smith 2013). This approach comprises a number of elements that are primarily aimed at using aid as a "tool of diplomacy and national policy" that will focus on key issues of education, health, good governance and empowering women (Sheridan 2014a). It is argued that this new philosophy of aid will lead to "a more effective aid dollar" with a greater emphasis on accountability and performance (Sheridan 2014b).

One other element underpinning this emerging Australian ODA paradigm is a view that reducing or removing trade tariffs will have a greater impact on economic development than large ODA transfers. From this perspective, it is expected that the merger of AusAID into DFAT will actually encourage private sector growth (Hepworth 2014). Indeed, Australian strategy towards the western Indian Ocean region is to increasingly view it as a "trade front". Furthermore, part of the future for Australian exports will entail a greater concern for energy and food (Rumley 2013b).

In the dying days of the Cold War, Paul Dibb identified Australia's "region of primary strategic significance" (ROPSI) stretching from the Cocos Islands in the west eastwards in an arc around to New Zealand and to the South Pacific Islands (Dibb 1987). Critics of Dibb noted that this huge area, which comprised about 10% of the earth's surface, would be impossible to defend in a traditional sense and that non-military strategies would more likely guarantee Australia's long-term security (Rumley 1999, page 170).

Such criticisms notwithstanding, however, as far as the Indian Ocean Region is concerned, there exists an ever-present geopolitical constraint which has been referred to as "territorial overstretch"—that is, given the nature of Australia's regional relations and the enormous extent of its maritime boundaries, that, with limited resources, it is extremely difficult to attempt to undertake too much engagement across too great a span of territory on too many issues (Rumley 2012, page 103). In short, sub-regional priorities need to be identified for appropriate policy frameworks. One geo-economic and geopolitical outcome of this is to concentrate ODA in Australia's most immediate 'region'.

This point touches on a related issue of the prospect that Australia, rather than emphasising Indian Ocean-wide security (broadly-defined) issues, might give greater weight to sub-regional matters in the East Indian Ocean Region. The recently initiated Trilateral Dialogue on the Indian Ocean (TDIO) in Delhi involving Australia, India and Indonesia is indicative of this future prospect. It may well be that this Dialogue process develops further to involve other regional states and/or states with a vested interest in a secure East Indian Ocean such as Japan.

The Western Australian State Premier, Colin Barnett, visited Africa in January 2014 to sign an MOU formalising closer links with the Common Market for Eastern and Southern Africa (COMESA) with a view to strengthening investment and exporting WA experience to the African mining sector (Bergin 2013b; Parker 2014). It has been estimated that current Australian investment in African resource projects is in the order of A$40 Billion and will likely continue to grow. In addition, Australian expertise in mining governance, skills and technology, as well as in associated environmental impacts, are seen to be potentially valuable export items (Bergin 2013a).

On 9 December 2013, the Australian Senate referred the following matter to the Foreign Affairs, Defence and Trade References Committee for inquiry and report on:

> Australia's overseas aid and development assistance program in light of the Government's $4.5 billion cut to international development assistance, with particular reference to:
> (a) Australia's ability to deliver aid against stated policy objectives and international commitments;
> (b) Australia's ability to maintain its international development priorities, including sectoral, regional, bilateral and multilateral international relationships;
> (c) the integration of AusAID into the Department of Foreign Affairs and Trade and the freeze in international development assistance funding;
> (d) any unintended consequences of these changes; and
> (e) any other related matters.

Submissions were to be received by 7 February 2014 with the official Committee reporting date set for 20th March 2014. The Senate Report contains 24 recommendations, probably the most important of which is recommendation 2—

> The Committee recommends the Australian Government undertake a white paper process to refine the long term strategic objective of Australia's aid program and identify measures to achieve these objectives (Commonwealth of Australia 2014, page 94)

The Report also contains one especially important recommendation regarding the geopolitics of Australia's aid delivery—that is, recommendation 6:

> The Committee recommends that the Australian Government promote the interests of developing countries in the Asia-Pacific. Given the Australian Government's stated intent to refocus the aid program on *'reducing poverty in the Indo-Pacific region'* (Commonwealth of Australia 2014, page 95—emphasis added)

It would seem that the Senate Committee is interpreting and reinforcing the current Australian Government's aid policy as indicating a kind of "aid pivot" reorientation. Nonetheless, the Committee did note that: "it is also important for Australia to continue its development engagement with Africa" (Commonwealth of Australia 2015, page 95).

The current conservative Abbott Government's response to the Senate Report on ODA is in the process of being fully articulated through its "new aid paradigm". The Government's first budget, released on Tuesday 13th May 2014, advocated the stabilisation of Australia's foreign aid outlays to A$5billion for two years resulting in a A$2billion saving in 2017-18. Critics of these significant cuts in ODA have argued that the Australian Government "has effectively junked its commitment to the Millennium Development Goals". Furthermore, Oxfam has stated that: "Australia was looking to balance its Budget on the backs of the world's poorest people" (Butterly 2014).

Conclusion

The Australian Foreign Minister, Julie Bishop, in a major speech in June 2014, elaborated on the essential elements of the "the new aid policy and performance framework", or "the new aid paradigm". As implied earlier, this new approach was prompted in part by a combination of a change in the global environment for financing development, Australia's budgetary constraints, a determination to increase performance based measures and a renewed focus on "economic diplomacy". The principal focus for aid allocations would be on Australia's region—"the Indian Ocean Asia Pacific"—while at the same time maximizing Australia's national interests. The new aid paradigm would deal with six core priority areas—infrastructure and trade, agriculture, fisheries and water management, effective governance, education (a "new Colombo Plan") and health, an increase in humanitarian assistance, and sixthly, women's economic empowerment (Bishop 2014).

References

Balogh, S. (2014), 'Regional emphasis in reduced spend', *The Australian* newspaper, 14 May, page 12.

Bergin, A. (2013a), 'Bread and stones: Africa-Australia opportunities', *The Strategist*, 5 September, and available at: http://www.aspistrategist.org.au

Bergin, A. (2013b), 'Mining unites Western Australia and Africa', *The Strategist*, 23 September, and available at: http://www.aspistrategist.org.au

Bishop, J. (2014), 'The new aid paradigm', speech to the National Press Club, Canberra, 18 June.

Butterly, N. (2014), 'Defence spending up, foreign aid cut', *The West Australian* newspaper, 14 May, page 11.

Channer, H. (2013), 'Announcing the first Australia–Africa Leadership Dialogue', *The Strategist*, 18 March, and available at: http://www.aspistrategist.org.au

Colebatch, T. (2012), 'Aid to Africa doubled but is it a vote winner?', *Sydney Morning Herald* newspaper, 26 September.

Commonwealth of Australia (2011), *Inquiry into Australia's relationship with the Countries of Africa*, Canberra: Joint Standing Committee on Foreign Affairs, Defence and Trade.

Commonwealth of Australia (2014), *Australia's Overseas Aid and Development Assistance* Program, Canberra: Joint Standing Committee on Foreign Affairs, Defence and Trade.

Cooper, H. and staff (2012), 'UN votes on Security Council bid', ABC News, 19 October, available at: http://www.abc.net.au/news

Davis, T. W. D. (2011), 'Foreign aid in Australia's relationship with the South: institutional narratives', *Round Table: The Commonwealth Journal of International Affairs*, Vol. 100 (415), pp. 389-406.

Development Assistance Committee (DAC) Statistics.

DFAT 2008, 'Letter from Stephen Smith to Kevin Rudd', declassified censored version.

Gates, B. and M. (2014), 'World poverty will almost be a thing of the past in two decades', *The Australian* newspaper, 21st January, page 10.

Gurria, A. (2013), 'Realising Africa's potential', *OECD Observer*, No 296, Q3, page 3.

Hattori, K. (2013), 'The Indian Ocean Rim', Japan External Trade Organization (JETRO), Dubai policy paper, May.

Hawker, G. (2009), 'Australia's new deal for Africa', *Australian Quarterly*, Vol. 81 (6), pp. 25-32.

Hepworth, A. (2014), "Trade before aid' is what region needs', *The Australian* newspaper, 23 January, page 2.

Lewis, S. (2010), 'Aid to Africa doubles in UN seat bid', *The Advertiser* newspaper, 25 May.

McGillivray, M. (n.d.), 'Is aid effective?', draft paper, WIDER, Helsinki, Finland.

Milner, H. V. and Tingley, D. (2013a), *Geopolitics of Foreign Aid, Volume I*, Cheltenham: Edward Elgar.

Milner, H. V. and Tingley, D. (2013b), *Geopolitics of Foreign Aid, Volume II*, Cheltenham: Edward Elgar.

Ministry of Foreign Affairs (2013), *Japan's Official Development Assistance White Paper 2012*, Tokyo.

Negin, J. and Denning, G. (2011), 'Study of Australia's approach to aid in Africa', Commissioned study as part of the Independent Review of Aid Effectiveness, 21st February.

OECD (2008), 'Is it ODA?', November, available at: www.oecd.org/dac/stats

OECD (2013), 'Aid to poor countries slips further as governments tighten budgets', 3 April.

Parker, G. (2014), 'Africa our new frontier: Barnett', *The Weekend West*, newspaper, 25 January, page 14.

PRC (2011), *China's Foreign Aid*, Beijing: Information Office of the State Council.

Provost, C. and Harris, R. (2013), 'China commits billions in aid to Africa as part of charm offensive', *Guardian* newspaper, 29th April.

Redden, J. (2014), 'Bishop means business: binding aid to trade leaves everyone a winner', *The Australian* newspaper, 7 February, page 12.

Rose, E (2012), 'Multilateral organisations—UN Security Council bid', DFAT statement 15.07 to Senate Estimates Hearings, October; released as part of a Freedom of Information request, February 2013.

Rudd, K. (2010), 'Appointment of Special Envoys', Media Release, 12 October, Brisbane.

Rumley, D. (1999), *The Geopolitics of Australia's Regional Relations*, Dordrecht: Kluwer.

Rumley, D. (2012), 'Refloating IOR-ARC: Australian Perspectives', in Sakhuja, V. ed., *Reinvigorating IOR-ARC*, New Delhi: Pentagon Press, pp. 87-105.

Rumley, D., ed. (2013a), *The Indian Ocean Region: Security, Stability and Sustainability in the 21st Century*, Melbourne: Australia India Institute.

Rumley, D. (2013b), 'Western Australia: peripheral State and Indian Ocean orientation', *The Otemon Journal of Australian Studies*, Vol. 39, pp. 7-20.

Rumley, D., Doyle, T. and Chaturvedi, S. (2012), "Securing' the Indian Ocean: Competing regional security constructions', *Journal of the Indian Ocean Region*, Vol. 8 (1), pp. 1-20.

Sharma, Y. (2014), 'Aid mergers in Australia and Canada could hit poor regions, experts warn', *The Guardian*, SciDev. Net, 8 May.

Sheridan, G. (2013), 'AusAID shake-up good for diplomacy', *The Australian* newspaper, 19 September.

Sheridan, G. (2014a), 'Region shielded from aid cutbacks', *The Weekend Australian* newspaper, 18th January, pp. 1 and 6.

Sheridan, G. (2014b), 'A more effective aid dollar', *The Weekend Australian* newspaper, 18th January, page 18.

Smith, S. J. (2013), 'Australia helping to facilitate Africa's 'third liberation'', *The Strategist*, 20 September, and available at: http://www.aspistrategist.org.au

United Nations Economic Commission for Africa (UNECA) (2013), *African Economic Outlook 2013*, available at: www.africaneconomicoutlook.org/en

UNCTAD (2013), *Economic Development in Africa: Intra-African Trade: Unlocking Private Sector Dynamism*, Geneva.

Chapter 9

The Indian Ocean Region and Opportunities for Global South-African Development

Siphamandla Zondi

The oceans of the Southern Hemisphere provide exciting opportunities for linking Africa, the Indian Subcontinent, Latin America and Australasia in ever-closer ties that promise many rewards. Ultimately this will enhance the contribution of the South, in partnership with the rest of the world, towards a more peaceful and prosperous future for humanity.

***—Nelson Mandela*, 1997[1].**

ABSTRACT

This chapter contends that the recognition of the strategic significance of the southern oceans on either side of southern Africa—the Indian Ocean and the South Atlantic—is crucial in efforts to boost regional integration and development as well as in translating South-South cooperation from solidarity to concrete cooperation across southern regions. It suggests that a serious African oceans policy agenda is slowly emerging after decades of experimentation in sectoral policies and programmes and following a lull in oceans dialogue within Africa. This lull is partly as a result of the growing importance of oceans as zones of peace and development in the global South generally, partly because of the championing of maritime issues by African island and other littoral states, and partly because its time has come. The interest in intensifying regional integration in southern Africa especially, and the efforts to upgrade South-South cooperation through region-to-region partnerships such as that between Africa and Asia, the New Africa Asia Strategic Partnership (NAASP) has come together to become mutually reinforcing with a potential to boost human and economic development and stability across the Indian Ocean Region. This is happening also at the time when there is growing interest in promoting the 'regionness' of the Indian Ocean Rim on the part of key Indian Ocean powers and intellectuals writing on the region.

Keywords: South-South cooperation; African oceans policy agenda; regional integration; regionness.

Introduction

As Nelson Mandela's speech to the World Oceans Commission in 1997 suggests, South Africa and the rest of Africa had by the mid-1990s come to realize the precious opportunities for linking Africa and Asia through the Indian Ocean and Africa and Latin America through the South Atlantic, thus adding a new and an exciting dynamic to South-South solidarity. This also has the potential to benefit South Africa, the rest of Africa, the global South and the rest of humanity in ways that makes the age-old dream of a prosperous humanity possible. One implication of this is that the rejuvenation of the Indian Ocean Region should involve a clear understanding of the region's location in the modern world system and its succession of orders since the 1490s, so that it is made clear how the revitalization process would also contribute to decolonizing the world system and the ideologies of humanism that it has entrenched as it bifurcated humanity into beings and non-beings, the dominant and the dominated, the first and the third world and so forth.

South-South cooperation for development[2] offers great opportunities for poor countries, including African littoral states, to become dynamic economies and states able to respond successfully to their deep developmental challenges. Recognising the fact that they were victims of global progress, to use Shiva's phrase and the fact that the global economy that enabled countries of the North to prosper was producing underdevelopment in the global South, then South-South cooperation is a commitment to increase cooperation among Southern states in order to overcome their shared wretchedness in the world and to raise their bargaining power in international negotiations[3].

This kind of cooperation promotes self-reliance, solidarity, policy sovereignty, knowledge-sharing, Southern agency and other principles that North-South development aid tends to weaken, neglect or distort in practice. This chapter contends that, for African littoral and island states, the development promise of the Indian Oceanic Region lies in the pursuit of principles and practices of South-South cooperation both in the form of strategic bilateral cooperation among key countries of the region and through regional cooperation among international organisations in the Region. The first part of the chapter outlines the development promise of the Indian Ocean Region, followed by a discussion of the changing nature of international development and its bearing on the Indian Ocean geopolitical space. This leads into a section outlining ways in which development cooperation in the Region could be rethought and reorganized with special emphasis on developing and island states that are particularly in need.

On The Contested Idea of International Development

The concept of development or international development is generally associated with paradigms, thoughts, actions and ideologies driven by development agencies of the global North. Obviously, this arises because the structure of global power in the past five centuries has produced modern orders of European origin that have reproduced ubiquitous ghosts of *alterity*—the world without others. The modern concept of societal progress took the form of modernity from the West after the 15th century as a civilizing mission of the West towards others. Later it was a colonial/Christian mission to save others from their wretchedness or damnation, and more recently the globalisation of the ways of the West in order to make others in the image of Western civilisation, which includes culture, ideologies, political economy and knowledge[4]. The world moved from one that was polycentric and non-capitalist before the 16th century, a world with many centres of civilization and knowledge, a world where the Chinese dynasties co-existed with the Roman Empire and traded with Swahili polities off the east coast of Africa, to a single world system with the region of North America and Western Europe as the dominant centres able to extend their power and influence to the point where they globalised their ways in order to build what became known as the global village. This transformation was made possible first by the European renaissance, the awakening of the Western person that led to the rise of modern capitalism and the gradual emergence of the West as a geopolitical idea/invention—the first world empire[5].

The capitalist economic system was able to expand to other parts of the world, not because of expansion in transport and communication systems and technology, but also because of imperialism, colonialism and neocolonialism. In this sense, while at the point of departure in Europe, it was an unproblematic economic system of production and consumption at the point of arrival, and it was also a system of exploitation, crass materialism, proletarianisation, underdevelopment and homogenization of political economy through the destruction of pre-existing systems of economic production. The underlying power relations between the metropolis and economic colonies throughout the process of worldwide expansion of capitalism produced amazing development for some and underdevelopment for others. While modernity would promise to the periphery the replication of the economic and development experiences of the highly industrialised states of the West, it produced conditions of poverty, inequality, despair and violence not seen by Western countries in the development of modern capitalism. This underdevelopment turned out to be an essential part of the structure of the modern capitalist system where the diffusion of capital, institutions and values of the capitalist metropoles thought essential for the development of the peripheral areas produced poverty and inequality on even broader scale than before[6].

In celebration of Western hegemony over the world civilization, John Headly writes in *Europeanisation of the World* that, "For however remote, tangential, and irrelevant sixteenth-century Europe may appear to some, it is one of the main tenets of this analysis that the Renaissance decisively and effectively prepared the global context for the European engagement of the world's peoples."[7] It enabled Western Europe as a geopolitical construct to remake the world's economic, political and social geography after its imaginations of the Enlightenment period a century earlier. Headley establishes this point that has been made by decolonial thinkers on the periphery for sometime, that globalisation and what he calls the American Century are an outcome and the culmination of processes to be traced back to 16th century Western Europe. For this reason, "If globalization has become the major focus of social studies and the new frontier for historians, the European Renaissance then provides the proper moment to begin examining a process that increasingly enfolds us all."[8] Globalisation demonstrated the success of Western civilization to homogenise others, making them after its own image, fusing every culture for its own ascendance and thus forging as a mask what is called 'modern civilization'.

It is on this basis that Walter Mignolo contends that modernity is a mask that conceals something a lot more problematic for thinkers and peoples on the periphery of this making of the modern system. He argues that understood and explained the way Headley does, the idea of modernity privileges the positive message of improvements in humankind's control over time and space above the fact that in the process others also encountered its darker side, coloniality[9]. The expansion of Western modernity, first through the Iberian agency in the 1500s to the 1700s, touched the Americas and then by what Georg Hegel called "the heart of Europe" to which England, France and Germany were central as they took Western modernity to all parts of the world. These areas outside of Europe were considered by Europeans to be a New World which they discovered. In their idea of common humanity, which Headley gloats about as a major innovation of Western civilization enabling it to spread itself throughout the world, the West masked the processes of enslavement, conquest, colonial domination, capitalist exploitation, cultural imperialism and epistemic injustice[10]. The idea of a "single moral, biological totality" joined together the "Western notions of rationality and individuality"[11] masked under the rhetoric of universal knowledge/innovation and human rights respectively with the imposition of European ways of living masked under the rhetoric of salvation, progress and improvement that had their origins in Christian moralizing discourses of Renaissance.

The most recent phase of this process of building a common idea of humanity with Western civilization as its engine happened in the period after the Second World War, driven by the United States. The task started by the Portuguese and the Spanish in the 15th century and continued by Western Europe from the 17th century passed on to the Anglo-Saxon part of Americas, itself a product of the "discovery" moment in European history. Thus, through slavery, colonisation and capitalist expansion, a global order, a polycentric world interconnected by the same type of economy and marked by an increasingly similar culture, knowledge and controlled to a large measure by men from the North Atlantic region of the world (Western Europe and North America) emerged over a five century period[12]. As Headley explains, "It was not until the late nineteenth century that the term 'West' came to displace 'European'—undoubtedly a process reinforced by America's increasing prominence—and to represent the entire collectivity of our civilization." Of course, in the process, geographically eastern countries like Australia and New Zealand would be incorporated into this not least because of the peopling of these areas by a white race, for, inspite of its integration into and submission to the North Atlantic powers, Japan remains a non-Western power, while Australia and New Zealand are commonly accepted as Western. Thus, the term 'West' became a geopolitical construct for the hard and soft power of the North Atlantic as the dominant core of the modern world system.

These processes were accompanied by modernity's invention of traditions, the invention of Europe as a seat of civilization, the centre of the world system, as well as the invention of non-European traditions where modernity meant conversion civilization and later development. In the latter case, "[T]he rhetoric of salvation by conversion to Christianity was translated into the rhetoric of salvation by the civilising mission."[13] It was complemented with the idea of progress through the Iberian and Western European phases of the global expansion of modernity. Development and modernization would be added to the vocabulary during the US-led phase after the Second World War. More recently, salvation by development has acquired a new rhetoric - globalisation and free trade. The point is that the rhetoric of modernity (newness, salvation, progress and development) always had a darker underside, which AnibalQuijano terms 'coloniality'[14]. This is best illustrated by Artuto Escobar when he contends that the idea of development in the post-War period means replicating in Asia, Africa, the Caribbean and Latin America "the conditions that were supposed to characterize the more economically advanced nations of the world—industrialisation, high degrees of urbanization and education, technification of agriculture, and widespread adoption of values and principles of modernity including particular forms of order, rationality and individual orientation."[15] In this sense, subjects from developing countries are recognised as being different and development is seen as a way to remove this difference. Thus, development came to mean a simultaneous recognition and a disavowal of difference. No wonder that after centuries of efforts, the world simply failed to register lasting social, cultural and economic improvement in the situations of the developing world.

The developed/developing world distinction remains intact. The former continues to produce the science and practice of development in places like Africa. Such development continues to take the form of replicating in Africa, Latin America and Asia conditions assumed to characterize the developed world. Through development aid or assistance and powerful global governance institutions like the Bretton Woods Institutions—the International Monetary Fund and the World Bank—ideas produced by Western neo-classical economics are nested and championed. The discourses around the question of development internationally, including and especially multilateral international discussions about the question of development, continue to take the form of a dialogue of the deaf because of divergent understandings of what is meant by development. When the United Nations placed the question of development as the central plank for building the international community, declaring the 1960s to be the first development decade, the developing world hoped for deep structural reform of the world system to rid of its poverty-reproducing character, while developed countries salivated in the prospect for even easier replication of their own experiences in the periphery through development aid and trade/ investment interventions. Thus, a keen observer of international development over time says of the UN efforts to champion the idea of development as a better life for all: "With the benefit of hindsight, one can see not only that the UN has often led the way but that it has often also been right when others—in particular, the Bretton Woods institutions—have opposed, doubting or reluctant to follow."[16]

While the agenda of placing development at the centre of international affairs was born out of moral awakening about the injustice of having one part of humanity living well and another, mostly from the newly-independent former colonies, lived in abject poverty, global power considerations went beyond, using poverty as a weapon in building geopolitical alliances during the Cold War[17]. Having cast off colonial rule, the new countries were confronted with the need to cast off the chains of poverty, and development aid was accepted as a major contribution by the developed countries to building common humanity.

It is this global reality, the *imperiality* of the international system produced out of global colonial projects that justifies counter-modernities that South-South Cooperation is born out of. This includes what Kishore Mahbubanirefers to as the 'de-westernisation of modernity' through a defiant process of its appropriation that enables it to loose its imperiality[18]. This epitomises the development miracle of Asian countries in the post-World War II era, the rise of the Orient as Niranjan Rajadhyaksha[19] puts it, and makes it reasonable to argue that the 20th century was the Asian Century. There is also a range of options that sees de-westernisation as the de-imperialisation of the world system, which entails establishing a new world order, decolonial cosmopolitanism and a world for all[20]. This means a rejection of or rebellion against the coloniality of Western modernity and its genocidal reason. South-South cooperation and regional cooperation/regionalism are two of the key Southern inputs into the pursuit of a polycentric political order, pluralistic economic development, and decolonial cosmopolitanism. Ideas on the potential for development partnerships within the Indian Ocean Region have meaning for countries of the South in this area, especially African countries, if they are linked to what these countries are pursuing as a part of the greater developing world.

There is no better way of unpacking the Indian Ocean-based development efforts as a contribution to changing South-South cooperation than recalling the meaning and implications of the declaration of the first Africa-Asia Solidarity Conference in Bandung, Indonesia, in 1955. The Conference placed the question of development at the centre of South agency by underlining the urgency of economic development in the developing world and agreed that it would come from three sources: the first and the most important was economic cooperation among countries of the South including trade and investment within the South; the second was economic cooperation with developed countries expected to invest in economic opportunities that would help developing countries overcome their problems; and third, development cooperation both among developing countries and with developed countries[21]. Out of this would evolve three important principles of South-South development cooperation—collective self-reliance, endogenous development and solidarity in pursuit of a better life for all. It is these big ideas and principles that would need to be anchored strongly in Indian Ocean affairs within the ambit of the inter-state formations like the Indian Ocean Rim Association (IORA) and the Indian Ocean Commission (IOC).

In his 1997 address to the 5th Session of the Independent World Commission on the Oceans, South Africa's President, Nelson Mandela, argued that the growing 'regionness' of southern oceans in general, and the Indian Ocean in particular, presented huge opportunities for linking

Africa with Asia and Latin America in order to harness opportunities for trade, investment, development cooperation, scientific innovation and so forth. This, he said, "will enhance the contribution of the South, in partnership with the rest of the world, towards a more peaceful and prosperous future for humanity."[22] Speaking in Malaysia on South Africa-Malaysia relations in the same year, Mandela suggested that relations between African countries and Asian countries were much more significant than ordinary bilateral cooperation because in the long-term they could transform the Indian Ocean into a zone of human development, economic vitality and political stability[23]. Thus, Mandela took a view that stronger bilateral relations were crucial for strengthening the 'regionness' of the Indian Ocean and that this 'regionness' would in turn find expression in effective economic growth and development among Indian Ocean states.

Although southern Africa and the rest of Africa cannot be said to have developed by 1997 a clear and elaborate vision and strategy regarding the Indian Ocean, they had, since the 1974 African position on the Indian Ocean as a Zone of Peace, taken a view that emphasises solidarity with Asian countries, rejecting the hegemonic agenda of non-Indian Ocean powers on the basis of the principle of sovereignty, and foreseeing a balance between resource exploitation and presentation[24]. Of course, various decisions relating to one or another aspect of ocean affairs, from transport through fisheries to security, have since elaborated this position. This includes decisions to adopted integrated strategies for protecting water and water-based resources from illegal use and exploitation by other countries traced back to 2004-5 and reiterated in an AU Summit declaration in 2009[25]. This decision was informed both by security considerations relating to growing criminality in Africa's sea waters as well as greater sensitivity to the full extent of the economic value of its water resources including the oceans around it. It was this understanding that the continent is a big island surrounded by an abundance of water that was apparent as early as the 1970s, although between then and the 2000s, very little was done to translate this awareness into a policy agenda. This was the basis on which African thinkers proposed in the early 1970s a continental energy mix one component of which facilitate energy to be generated by the continent's sea, what Cheik anta Diop called tidal energy[26]. Decisions in support of or to ratify international conventions, treaties and decisions on ocean affairs, including the decisions taken by the International Maritime Organisation (IMO), were out of he realization of the importance of ocean governance, development and security for Africa's long-term goal, although the failure to develop concrete comprehensive plans regarding the oceans made these decisions look more routine than strategic. As the IMO itself noted, African countries grew more and more interested in their ocean affairs, especially in respect of security and maritime transport. The latter was given impetus by the establishment of the African Ministers' Conference on Maritime Transport[27].

The Maritime Domain and African Development

Formal discussions among African states regarding the contribution of the maritime domain to Africa's development, its "present and future prosperity" became part of the emphasis on development in African multilateral diplomacy in the 1990s. Still this tended to focus a bit more on transport dimensions associated with the maritime domain, including the development of ports and shipping and the protection of these from foreign control inspired by the 1999 Abuja Memorandum of Understanding on Port State Control. The Abuja MoU is an outcome of a Conference of Ministers from West and Central African regions co-organised by Nigeria and IMO to facilitate the implementation of IMO resolutions relating to maritime transport. The MoU recorded the agreement of these countries to harmonise state port control procedures and practices; to eliminate substandard shipping in the two regions in order to improve maritime safety, pollution and other harmful practices; and to facilitate regional cooperation to improve shipping enterprise in the region. Through the MoU, the signatories sought to position the Gulf of Guinea area and the rest of the west and central African littoral to be attractive to lucrative shipping business[28]. Incidents of oil spillage, shipwrecks, substandard living conditions for sailors, poorly maintained ships, poor shipping services and other problems prompted these states to recall the IMO decisions on regional cooperation on maritime affairs. Of particular concern was the growth in the incidence of accidents off African coasts with small ferries involved in intra-African trade and used for passenger transportation. Like the Abuja MoU, the Indian Ocean MoU, developed between the 1997 meeting of the member states of the then Indian Ocean Rim Association for Regional Cooperation

(IORARC) and the ministerial committee of 18 initial signatories in India in 1999[29], also helped shine the spotlight of African continental diplomacy on the importance of the oceans for development and regional integration. A number of African littoral states belonging to the Indian Ocean Region formed part of this initiative, which according to the IMO, laid the basis for African regions to harness the maritime domain for development[30]. One of the developments coming out of these initiatives were projects promoting regional responses to the pollution of the environment as a result of shipping, especially in oil-rich areas like the Gulf of Guinea as well as South Africa, where the intensity of maritime trade exposes the marine environment to pollution.

Of course, also of importance was the participation of the islands of Comoros, Madagascar, Mauritius and Seychelles in the Indian Ocean Commission, created in 1982 to foster the spirit of solidarity and the practice of regional cooperation among Indian Ocean states. It has sensitized these countries even more about the need for ensuring the sustainable use of marine resources, improving the living conditions of the peoples of the area and strengthening the capacity of island and small developing states to negotiate their interests in international forums. These countries have been key champions for a greater embrace by mainland Africa of the strategic value of the oceans. Mauritius and Seychelles played an proactive role in the adoption of the SADC Protocol on Fisheries with a strong emphasis on the sustainable use of aquatic resources, coordination of the activities of fishing vessels especially in the high seas, as well as cooperation between Port States and Flag states within the framework of international law[31].

Otherwise, the impetus for a southern African focus on ocean affairs comes from SADC's instrument for collective security cooperation— the SADC Inter-State Defence and Security Committee (ISDSC) -which established in 1995 a Standing Maritime Committee. However, lacking in navy capabilities and having no culture of maritime security in general, SADC states kept their work on ocean affairs to a minimum until 2007 when the first Ministerial Conference on Maritime Security was held to reflect on the growing incidence of piracy, illegal fishing and other forms of criminality along the coast of Southern Africa[32]. Besides the Indian Ocean island states, South Africa and Mozambique that hosted the 2007 and 2010 conferences respectively, were particularly enthusiastic about maritime affairs because insecurity in the Indian Ocean was negatively affecting or threatening to affect their economies.

Not only because it has the most advanced maritime facilities in Africa and large exclusive economic zones in the Indian Ocean and the Atlantic, but also because it has a long tradition of involvement in maritime affairs, South Africa underwrites the SADC oceans agenda by leading many maritime initiatives which it also mostly funds[33]. While it too has not evolved a comprehensive oceans policy combining security, economic, development and political interests, comparatively speaking it has a generally more advanced involvement in maritime affairs. It has a relatively developed naval power over the southern oceans, qualifying it to be regarded as one of the few African sea powers with necessary capability to underwrite the continent's maritime security and governance. It is also an ocean power because it has the capacity to increase maritime trade across both the Atlantic and Indian Oceans by leveraging strategic relationships it has with regional and sea powers across both oceans—India, Indonesia and Australia, on the one hand, and Brazil and Argentina, on the other. There is no gainsaying that a number of South African universities and research institutes involved in scientific research on ocean affairs—oceanography in Durban University of Technology and the University Cape Town; security and diplomacy at the University of Witwatersrand and the Institute for Global Dialogue and ocean biology and technology at the Centre for Scientific and Industrial Research (CSIR) and Tshwane University of Technology, to name just a few examples—gives it some advantage in any race to dominate research and knowledge production, a race that would involve other regional states such as Australia, India, Indonesia and Singapore. If it is accepted that in the post-Cold War world science and innovation is an important source of advantage in taking up opportunities in the world economy in the pursuit of national development and security, then this is no small factor in South Africa latent potential to lead African efforts to reprioritize ocean affairs. It stands to benefit immensely, perhaps much more than others, from fully developed southern oceans governance because its capacity to absorb the benefits of growth in trade and commerce, improved stability and security, increase in aquaculture and enhanced human development cooperation and innovation across the oceans.

In what had become a typical focus, the President of Seychelles, James Michel, urged the African Union as recently as 2012 to develop a comprehensive approach to ocean affairs on the basis of oceans as zones for peace, economy, human development, environmental governance and knowledge production. He said:

> [W]e Africans need to take ownership of our Blue Economy by seriously paying attention on our inland waters, our Seas and Oceans as the opportunities inherent in these geostrategic spaces belong to us; and only us have the sole right and duty to design creative frameworks able to develop such an immense source of resources that has, unfortunately, for quite some time, been virtually neglected, under-developed, but which remains a source of incommensurable wealth and a synonym of enhanced dignity for future African generations.

Speaking at the launch of the joint summit of the Economic Community of West African States (ECOWAS) and the Economic Community of Central African States (ECCAS) on maritime safety and security in Malabo, Equatorial Guinea in June 2013, Dr Nkosazana Dlamini-Zuma, in her capacity as the AU Commission Chairperson, announced that the time had come for Africa to move its focus on ocean affairs from a number of sectoral policy positions with gaps inbetween to what she called "an African-driven comprehensive long term multilayered common Vision to tackle the cross-cutting geostrategic and geopolitical challenges and opportunities that we face in our Maritime Domain."[34] She recalled that the adoption of the Maritime Transport Charter in 1994, the Plan of Action on Maritime Transport of 2007, the Durban Resolution on Maritime Safety and Security and the Protection of Environment of 2009 and a host of initiatives at sub-regional and national levels all sought to advance African interests in the maritime domain. But none of these were in and of themselves adequate. The time had thus come for Africa to "better understand our Maritime Domain so as to strategically innovate winning frameworks that would help us to take advantage and maximize the wealth opportunities provided to us by our inland waters, Seas and Oceans." As the continent understood better how its maritime resources were being plundered, polluted and under-utilised, she said: "Blue Economy must now become the new frontlines of our fight and struggles for Africa's economic rise and prosperity." It is the struggle for human solidarity and intra-African cooperation and coordination with others to enable the continent to rise and occupy its rightful position in world affairs. It is a struggle against marginalisation in a global power system that made it normal for Africa to be resource-endowed and yet poverty-stricken as well as it was the struggle against ignorance in respect of ocean affairs.

The Indian Ocean Region, Africa and the Question of Development

The growing literature on the geostrategic dynamics of the Indian Ocean has all but made the case for the geopolitical significance of the Indian Ocean as a zone for security, development and culture[35]. Scholars have underscored the need for strengthening regional identity or 'regionness' of the area because this has a potential to lift many out of poverty and achieve region-wide prosperity and stability, while enhancing the role of the Indian Ocean Region as an actor in changing international relations. Consistent with the literature in search of alternatives to dominant paradigms of development, the Indian Ocean literature has also identified key drivers of change for transforming the region into a major cultural, political and economic order in a changing world.

Two of the drivers identified, which we discuss below—cosmopolitanism and regionalism- are fundamental for turning the development promise of the Indian Ocean Region into a lived reality, especially for African littoral states and sub-regions like East Africa and Southern Africa. If it is accepted that the successive orders of Western world modernity culminating in globalisation brought so much good for the world in the form of growth in prosperity as a whole, while it also produced slavery, colonialism and today neocolonialism as conditions under which underdevelopment and poverty have persisted, then the development potential of the Indian Ocean from the perspective of Africa will require decolonial cosmopolitanism and regional cooperation and integration. The domination of African states that began with colonial contact as way back as the 1490s, the very inception of Western modernity, required the growth of African nationalism and pan-Africanism the central message of which was unity among the oppressed, or today the disadvantaged, to defend their right to live and to live well. The model of global power discussed above continues to generate the need for unity and integration in Africa as the continent's defence against peripherialisation and as a contribution to the birth of a truly cosmopolitan world where Africa's prosperity is possible[36].

Indian Ocean and Dialogical Cosmopolitanism

We have already stated that Mandela's hope for the birth of a peaceful and prosperous global humanity out of a rebirth of South-South cooperation through ocean affairs can only be realized if it is understood that the current imagination of humanity is born out of ideologies/ philosophy of humanism that are central to the Western modernity project over the past five hundred years. The current condition of Africa and the global South is a product of a modern model of global power in which identity, knowledge and power are used to create a world without others. The African littoral can look to the consolidation of Indian Ocean 'regionness' to work with others to escape the trap of being on the periphery. The one driver of such consolidation is the harnessing of the diversity of the region in terms of cultural, economic, political systems. Here lies the opportunity for redefining global cosmopolitanism by creating opportunities for a post-colonial one. It brings together Western, Asian, Islamic and African cultures of the modern world in an interface with other island cultures spread through the area covered by the ocean. This interface is one of cultures with significant histories and by which a large part of the world population identifies itself. The many countries of Asia, the Arab Middle East, Africa and Oceania that form part of this mega-oceanic region have different political systems, ranging from liberal democracies like Australia to social democracies among African littoral states like South Africa, multi-ethnic complex democracies like Indonesia, fluid democracies in Thailand, non-democracies like kingdoms like Oman and a variety of other political systems. These systems generally vary in the manner in which they drive economic development, manage state-society relations and in their approach to international relations. They are generally similar in their ambitions to become part of a new global era, a new world where all prosper, which in the case of developing countries means escaping the trap of the periphery by undoing the idea of one structural centre. The diversity of economic systems is manifest in terms of how states relate to the major economic question of our time, namely: how does a state organise societal forces in the manner that enables its people to prosper? This leads to the policy question of whether the market forces or something more than those should drive economic prosperity and development. In some cases, economic systems allow significant space for markets to transform society and in others the government has a dominant role. In many more countries the government and the business sector share the leading role in ensuring economic development. It is now common cause that the future of the world hinges on a kind of cosmopolitanism that truly accepts and harnesses the heterogeneity of humanity and no longer one which accepts the basis of the bifurcation of humanity into a zone of beings and a zone of non-beings. Therefore, the Indian Ocean's heterogeneity both represents the objective reality of the world and the aspired nature of the future world, except that it should be marked by shared prosperity and equality.

The Indian Ocean area has well-affirmed sub-regional systems, where sub-regional cooperation and economic integration are growing development outcomes for the peoples of the Indian Ocean region, while enabling parts of the region to enhance their geopolitical standing in world affairs. Indeed, crucial for growth and development in African littoral is how regional groupings like the Common Market for Eastern and Southern Africa (COMESA), the Southern African Development Community (SADC), the East African Community (EAC), and the Intergovernmental Authority on Development (IGAD) enable them to pool their markets, harmonise development policies, stabilize the region and consolidate their geopolitical positions critical for them to negotiate to their advantage internationally. What these sub-regional schemes have in common is that their promotion of regional economic, political and security cooperation as a means by which these countries largely on the periphery of the world system respond to challenges and opportunities produced by a globalising world and economy. African states have always seen regional integration as the most rational and pragmatic response to globalisation. They harmonise economic and development agendas and policies among member countries in the hope of building sizeable economies to compete for and attract international trade and investment. They agreed legal measures to enable the faster movement of goods and services between countries, thus creating new economic values thereby unlocking development potential. They form collective security mechanisms by which they assure common security by anticipating and responding to threats to any of their member states. They pool together their political capital in order to negotiate beneficial relations with other parts of the world, especially the richer regions of the world and thus enhance their agency in international diplomacy. In this sense, they help build geopolitical equilibrium within the region and between sub-regions and external powers that have taken an interest in Indian Ocean affairs.

Ocean-wide regionalism is now formalized in the Indian Ocean Rim Association (IORA), formerly the Indian Ocean Rim Association for Regional Cooperation (IOR-ARC). It is very clear that one of the important developments in the post-Cold War era has been the consolidation of areas into regions with deliberate geostrategic agendas. The Indian Ocean area is no exception. The manifestation of this was the founding of IORARC in 1997, which was the clearest expression of the acceptance by Indian Ocean states that they form part of a region as evidenced by the words "for Regional Cooperation" in the name and the mandate of the organisation. The organization is promoting 'regionness' in ways more concrete than many realize from sectoral initiatives jointly championed by various member states that are funded by the IORA. It is establishing regional institutions like an Indian Ocean University, a statistical body, a business forum and an academic group. As its Perth Communiqué of November 2013 puts it, it sees itself as a premier driver of regional cooperation across the Indian Ocean Region. The Indian Ocean Commission (IOC) is also aware of the importance of oceanic cooperation and so do two major African regional organisations—the AU and the SADC. With the Africans and Asians having decided recently to forge ahead with concretising cooperation between the two regions by implementing the agreements contained in NAASP, the Indian Ocean is well poised to become a catalyst for South-South cooperation and inter-regional cooperation for the benefit of all peoples of the Indian Ocean Region.

Conclusion

Certainly, for Africa and the South powers in the Indian Ocean area, the ocean presents crucial opportunities for achieving their old-held dreams of regional integration and South-South cooperation marked by functional economic and trade relations, developmental partnerships, science and technology cooperation and human development. In this sense, oceanic cooperation emerging in the Indian Ocean with the IORA, the IOC, NAASP and other initiatives as catalysts may contribute meaningfully to the world's wish for the emergence of a world for all, a prosperous common humanity. If regional integration continues to anchor ocean governance by going beyond declarations to concrete actions towards shared sovereignty and to strengthen South-South cooperation through inter-regional cooperation between Africa and Asia, in this case, then the revitalization of the Indian Ocean may just be the driver of the new transition Africa has been waiting for. This chapter contends that this outcome depends also on transforming in deeper ways the very conceptual framework that Eurocentrism has sold to the world, one that masks the coloniality of global power, which is the major constraint on the transformation of humanity and the world in ways that ensures Mandela's dream of prosperity for all.

NOTES

1. Mandela, N. 1997. 'Speech by President Nelson Mandela at the opening of the 5th session of the Independent World Commission on the Oceans, 11 November'. Available at: http://db.nelsonmandela.org/speeches/pub_view.asp?pg=item&ItemID=NMS529&txtstr=Indian%20Ocean (accessed on 27 July 2013).
2. South-south cooperation for development is the fuller term for what is generally known as south-south cooperation as reflected in the Declaration of the United Nations Conference on Technical Cooperation among Developing Countries, held in Buenos Aires, Argentina, on 30 August to 12 September 1978. Available at:www.undp.org (accessed on 2 July 2012).
3. This sentence borrows from Sneyd, A. 'South Commission/South Centre'. Available at: www.globalautonomy.ca/global1/glossary_entry.jsp?id=OR.0045 (accessed on 2 July 2012).
4. There is a rich literature on this, some of it referring to Africa broadly and southern Africa. See, for instance, Jean and John Comaroff, 1991. *Of Revelation and Revolution: Christianity, Colonialism, and Consciousness in South Africa*, Volume 1, Chicago: University of Chicago Press. Mignolo, W. 2005. *The Idea of America.* Oxford: Blackwell Publishing. Aldrich, R. 1996. *Greater France: A History of French Overseas Expansion.* New York: St Martin's Press. Young, C. 1994. *The African Colonial State in Contemporary Perspective*. Yale: Yale University Press.
5. This is the issue that concerns Immanuel Wallerstein in Wallerstein, I. 1976. *The Modern World System: Capitalist Agriculture and the Origins of the European World-Economy in the Sixteenth Century*. New York: Academic Press.
6. This part draws from the work of Andre Gunder Frank and Walter Rodney. See Frank, A.G. 1966. 'The Development of Underdevelopment', *Monthly Review*, 18, pp. 1-12. Rodney, W. *How Europe Underdeveloped Africa.* Dar-Es-Salaam: Bogle-L'Ouverture Publications.
7. Headley, J. 2007. *The Europeanisation of the World*, Princeton: Princeton University Press, p. 1.
8. Headley, *Europeanisation*, p. 1
9. Mignolo, W. undated. 'The Darker Side of Modernity'. Available at: https://

m1.antville.org/files/walter_mignolo_modernologies_eng/ (accessed on 1 May 2012).

10. Headley, *Europeanisation*, p. 2.
11. *Ibid.*
12. Mignolo, 'The Darker Side', pp. 41-2.
13. Mignolo, 'The Darker Side', p. 43.
14. Quijano, A. 'Coloniality and Modernity/Rationality', *Cultural Studies*, 21 (2-3), pp. 155-67.
15. Escobar, A. 1997. *Anthropology and Development*. Paris: UNESCO, p. 497.
16. Jolly, R. 'The UN and Development Thinking and Practice', *Forum for Development Studies*, 1, June: 49- 73, p. 50.
17. See UNICEF, 1996. 'The 1960s: Decade of Development' in *The State of the World's Children* Available at http://www.unicef.org/sowc96/1960s.htm (accessed on 2 July 2012).
18. Mahbubani, K. 2008. *The New Asian Hemisphere: The Irresistible Shift of Global Power to the East*, New York: Public Affairs, 2008.
19. Rajadhyaksha, N. 2008. 'Eye on the new Orient' Mumbai, Mint, 22 February.
20. Mignolo, 'The Darker Side', p. 42.
21. See 'Final Communiqué of the Asian-African Conference of Bandung', 24 April 1955. Available at: http://franke.uchicago.edu/Final_Communique_Bandung_1955.pdf (accessed 4 April 2006).
22. Mandela, 'Speech by President Nelson Mandela at the opening of the 5th session of the Independent World Commission on the Oceans'.
23. Mandela, N. 1997. 'Speech by President Mandela at the Malaysian Institute of Diplomacy and Foreign Relations'. Available at:http://db.nelsonmándela.org/speeches/pub_view.asp?pg=item&ItemID=NMS897&txtstr=Indian%20Ocean (accessed on 1 August 2014).
24. OAU, 1974. 'Resolution on the Indian Ocean as a Zone of Peace'. CM/Res.326 (XXII). AU Library Collections, Addis Ababa.
25. AU, 'Decision on the Establishment of the African Agency for the Protection of Territorial and Economic Waters of African Countries', Doc. Assembly/AU/15(XIII) Add.4. AU Library Collections, Addis Ababa.
26. See the foreword to Diop, CA. 1974. *Black Africa: The Economic and Cultural Basis for a Federated State*, Paris: Presence Africaine.
27. See, UNDESA, 1996. 'Cooperation Between the United Nations and the Organisation of African Unity'. General Assembly, Fifty-First Session, Agenda Item 42. A/51/386. Available at www.un.org/documents (accessed on 1 May 2014).
28. See Abuja MoU, 'Memorandum of Understanding on Port State Control for West and Central African Region, 1999 (amended October, 2012)'. Available on www.abujamou.org (accessed on 3 May 2014).
29. See IOMOU, 'Indian Ocean Memorandum of Understanding on Port State Control'. Available at: www.iomou.org (accessed on 3 May 2014).
30. Mitropulos, E.E. undated. 'The Role of Maritime Transport in Achieving Africa's Development, Address to the Conference of African Ministers of Transport, Abuja, Nigeria.' Available on www.imo.org (accessed on 21 June 2014).
31. SADC, 'Protocol on Fisheries'. Available at http://www.sadc.int/files/5613/5292/

8363/Protocol_on_Fisheries2001.pdf (accessed on 5 May 2014).

32. Coelho, J. P.B. 2011. 'Uneasy Shores: The Indian Ocean and the challenges to SADC's Maritime Security', SADSEM-FES Annual Regional Security Dialogue on Security Cooperation in Southern Africa 27-28 October.
33. Coelho. 'Uneasy Shores.'
34. Dlamini-Zuma, N. 2013.
35. Recent books coming out of the Indian Ocean Research Group and IORARC Academic Group are of particular importance. See, for instance, Rumley, D. and Chaturvedi, S. (eds.) 2004. *Geopolitical Orientations, Regionalism and Security in the Indian Ocean.* New Delhi : South Asian Publishers; Rumley, D. and Chaturvedi, S. (eds.) 2005. *Energy Security and the Indian Ocean Region.* New Delhi: South Asian Publishers; Bouchard C. 2003. ' The Case for Indian Ocean Security and Strategic Matters in the Indian Ocean Regional Cooperation', *Indian Ocean Digest,* 17 (2), pp. 13-21; and Bouchard, C and Crumplin, W. 2010. 'Neglected no longer: the Indian Ocean at the forefront of World Geopolitics and Global Geostrategy', *Journal of the Indian Ocean Region*, 6, No. 1, pp. 26-51.
36. See Mafeje, A. 1992. *In Search of an Alternative: A Collection of Essays on Revolutionary Theory and Politics*, Harare: SAPES, pp. 11-12.

Chapter 10

Law of the Sea: Maritime Security Enforcement and Jurisdictional Issues for the Indian Ocean Rim Association (IORA) Member States

Bimal N. Patel

ABSTRACT

As IORA consolidates as an important regional mechanism to address issues ranging from trade and commerce to strategic cooperation, it is essential that important international legal issues are examined to formulate opinion for the IORA policy-making community. Despite the fact that issues identified in the present chapter are supposed to be known and remain priority concerns for IORA members, the availability of a legal and regulatory framework is rather sparse. Until and unless these issues are subjected to national and international legal scrutiny, substantive cooperation which requires common understanding and position will be difficult to achieve. Dedicated efforts by IORA legal scholars, academicians and policy-community, therefore, are imperative.

Keywords: Maritime Security Enforcement and Jurisdictional Issues in IORA; UNCLOS; International Seabed Authority; International Maritime Authority; International Tribunal for the Law of the Sea.

Introduction

Since the adoption of the Law of the Sea Convention, the world has undergone significant developments. Whether and how the implementation of the Convention, which is otherwise known as the "Constitution of the Ocean" and which emerged as a result of the concept of "package deal", is able to respond to 21st century maritime security threat issues of enforcement and jurisdiction requires continued attention by the scholarly as well as policy-making community. What is the state practice of major maritime states in this regard and whether these state practices are important sources of evidence for IORA member states? What is the congruence and divergence of issues among major maritime and IORA member states? Whether the existing practices in general and implementation of the UNCLOS serve to promote and protect maritime interests of these states? If not, is there a requirement for a comprehensive assessment on part of these states to provide their views to the international community?

It is possible that the implementation, enforcement and jurisdictional authorities of the IORA member states may perceive a particular maritime security threat in many different ways and apply various sources of law depending upon the circumstances and the particular context. These may also give rise to issues of non-compliance, conflicting ways of interpretation and implementation to the existing international and national legal structures between maritime states and IORA member states and also among IORA member-states *per se*. It is considered that maritime security among IORA member states is perceived to be largely a military security issue and therefore scant attention is paid to other equally important issues. In this regard, it is important to identify a list of other maritime security issues among these states and place them in an overall context of each individual state's profile and the IORA member states as a whole group. This policy-oriented research chapter attempts to analyse and offer emerging perspectives based on the state practice of major maritime states on issues concerning terrorism, WMD trafficking, drug trafficking, people smuggling, illegal, unreported and unregulated (IUU) fishing and unlawful damage to the environment in the Indian Ocean Rim.

Although piracy remains one of the most important maritime security issues, this chapter deliberately avoids any discussion on this issue. However, a few remarks are offered based on the latest developments in state practice and the UN resolutions for consideration. It is widely known that the definition of piracy as provided in UNCLOS and the rights and obligations of the international community, including all relevant stakeholders, flowing therefrom itself constitute a source of political and legal controversy and conflict. The fact that the definition is unable to take care of the current menace is beyond dispute. Many IORA members do not have any domestic legislation on piracy that fully reflects the provisions of the Law of the Sea Convention, other treaties, the Security Council resolutions and emerging state practice. There is lack of uniformity, including the definition of piracy and the prosecution process of piracy[1]. To have a uniform approach, it is imperative that IORA creates a group of legal experts who can draft and vet available national implementing legislations.

Terrorism

Since the entry of the SUA Convention and the 2005 SUA Protocol, fears of terrorism on the offshore installations have increased[2]. Despite the weakness of the ISPS code[3], IORA members need to provide regular training to those who are directly involved in the implementation of the Code. This will enormously help to assess the risk that a visiting ship may pose to a particular port and provide a means to allow for preventive measures against security threats[4]. In this regard, it is extremely important to enact laws that could provide for measures to instruct ships to declare private security personnel and store weapons in separate containers for weapons and munitions before entering port limits[5].

In the light of terrorists using sea avenues, it is incumbent that coastal states are empowered by the UN Security Council Resolution 1373 to exercise criminal jurisdiction over a vessel if a terrorist act has occurred or is occurring while the vessel is in the territorial waters of the coastal state. In this regard, it is imperative that IORA member states enact or amend existing legislation expanding the scope of jurisdiction. Undoubtedly, several IORA member states may be wary of the UN Security Council resolution in terms of sovereignty and territorial integrity perception. However, any concerns can be addressed in their legislation in a balanced manner. IORA member states will continue to face jurisdictional problems arising out of the conflict between international and national rights and obligations, if they do not enact necessary legislation at the earliest opportunity. For example, despite India having a robust legal and judicial system, the criminal jurisdictional issue arising in the *Enrica Lexie* case is posing serious challenges to India and Italy. The issue has considerable potentially negative ramifications on bilateral and multilateral relations. If India would have enacted a Maritime Bill which has been languishing in the Indian Parliament for many years, it would have given additional certainty to both states in appreciating and deciding on the jurisdictional issue.

Tracking terrorism-suspected vessels in the EEZ poses a most difficult challenge. On the one hand, the EEZs are conduits and rising sources of potential operations, while on the other hand, intelligence gathering in the EEZ poses operational and international legal challenges. IORA member states, having weak operational and intelligence capacity at large, are unable and can ill-afford to allow other states to conduct intelligence gathering under the pretext of aiding anti-terrorism efforts. There can be no possibility that such controversial state practice will yield desirable cooperation from IORA member states. While the sensitivity of IORA members can be appreciated, the mandatory requirement under the SUA convention for express flag state consent for a right to visit of a suspected vessel and the consecutive weaknesses this matrix poses, are definite challenges to IORA members and in fact reduce their capability to thwart potential terrorist operations emanating from sea. The 26/11 attack in Mumbai is a stark reminder of such a scenario.

WMD Trafficking

Can a coastal state force a foreign-flagged vessel on the high seas carrying WMD material to bring to its port? Can a state without becoming a member of PSI carry out such conduct? Under PSI, participating states can carry out stop and search in territorial waters. One can see an important point in Klein's proposition that, 'while not free from controversy, there is an arguable basis that the illicit trafficking of WMD and related material through the territorial sea of a state is not consistent with the right of innocent passage because that activity is inherently prejudicial to the peace, good order or security of the coastal state, contrary to article 19.1 under UNCLOS, or, depending on the intelligence available, may be viewed as a threat of force, contrary to article 19.2 under UNCLOS".[6] As the SUA Convention has not been ratified by all IOR members[7], the capacity of states to board, inspect and arrest a vessel having reasonable suspicion of carrying illicit WMD and related material in the territorial sea is a large legal challenge. This problem is being compounded by the fact that Security Council resolution 1540 does not provide a blanket authority. Neither does any Security Council resolution provide authority nor does such a right exist under customary international law. Hence, the right to board on a foreign-flagged vessel without the latter's permission under such circumstances continues to pose a major challenge. One model option such as the bilateral agreements concluded by the US with several Caribbean states can be usefully considered.

Drug Trafficking

No disputes exist with regard to a coastal state's criminal jurisdiction in internal waters, territorial waters and contiguous zone on drug trafficking. While IORA members may have few resources to deal with the menace, it is important to keep in mind that under the concept of good order, peace in country, IORA members may use necessary measures to control the problem. To curb the menace of drug trafficking, it is imperative that IORA members work towards a cooperative model agreement similar to the 2003 Caribbean Agreement, putting aside the over-sensitivity to the abstract concept of sovereignty in the larger interests of the IORA community. The Shiprider Agreement in the Caribbean region enables the law enforcement officials of these states to carry out law enforcement activities under the agreement in waters of other states. The agreement aims to provide "effective, efficient, seamless maritime law-enforcement capability throughout the [Caribbean] region, leaving drug traffickers no safe haven".[8] However, concerns such as the US exercising unconditional power within the territorial waters of some Caribbean states, especially their EEZ, have remained a strong source of concern.

It is imperative that IORA members ratify the 1988 Vienna Convention against the Illicit Traffic in Narcotic Drugs and Psychotropic Substances which allow among other issues, under article 17, a procedure whereby a state party may request permission to board a vessel of another state party when the ship is outside the territorial sea of another state. The sheer number of bilateral and multilateral agreements in this area leads to the conclusion that there is a need for IORA members to conclude such an agreement and consider other mechanisms by which IORA members can conduct a right of visit against foreign-flagged vessels at least of IORA members on the high seas.

Smuggling and Trafficking of Persons by Sea

Clandestine migration usually entailing considerable risks, such as from unseaworthy ships or craft, inhumane conditions on board, or from being abandoned at sea by smugglers[9] pose one of the important maritime security threats in the Indian Ocean. Human rights and refugee concerns apart, clandestine migrations may also entail terrorism or criminal attack risks against the potential host state. It would be difficult for a potential host state to identify, verify and carry out the necessary checks if persons intending to carry out terror or criminal attacks are part of otherwise genuine refugee groups.

A state can consider a passage non-innocent if the loading or unloading of persons is contrary to immigration law. Similarly, the coastal state can exercise criminal jurisdiction against a foreign flagged vessel in its territorial waters if the transport of illegal immigrants is a crime the consequences of which extend to the coastal state or is a crime that disturbs the peace of the country or the good order of the territorial sea[10]. The coastal state can exercise necessary control to prevent and punish the infringement of its immigration laws in the contiguous zone. Klein argues that even if the vessel is simply transiting the territorial waters, the very transport of illegal immigrants may disturb the good order of those territorial waters if the vessel is unseaworthy or the conditions of transport are otherwise such that a rescue of those on board may be necessary[11].

The interception of human beings on the high seas poses political and legal challenges to the coastal state, flag-state and ship operators. Striking a balance between, on the one hand, international human rights law, international refugee law and distress at sea, and obligations to ensure peace and good order on the other hand, remains, however, a priority. Although incidents such as the *M/V Tampa*[12] are either not happening in the Indian Ocean or remain unreported, it is imperative that a formal understanding or consultation mechanism is established to alleviate the concerns mentioned here above. The 1998 IMO Measures for Combating Unsafe Practices Associated with the Trafficking or Transport of Migrants by Sea provide useful guidance to IORA states to request authorisation from the flag state to take appropriate measures in regard to that ship. Similarly, ratification and enactment of national legislation to the 2000 Protocol against the

Smuggling of Migrants by Land, Sea and Air Supplementing the Convention against Transnational Organised Crime provide a strong legal avenue to deal with the challenge.

IUU Fishing

Klein makes a convincing argument that IUU fishing can be considered as a threat to the maritime security of a state[13]. She takes organised crime networks dealing with IUU fishing and the aggressive approach of some states to protect their fish resources, economic, social and environmental consequences due to depleted fish stocks as solid grounds for such consideration as well as regarding that this is an important element in achieving overall human security. In view of the heavy dependence of IORA members' populations on fishing as a main source of protein, IUU fishing needs to be viewed as an important maritime security threat. Most IORA members have relatively weak fishing laws as compared to a regional group such as the EU. The weak legal system along with operational incapability places IORA members in a very vulnerable situation vis-à-vis fishing carried out by vessels of flags of convenience.

Port state jurisdiction over convenient-flag vessels for their acts on the high seas is an important legal development in this direction. Similarly, ratification, followed by enactment of national implementing legislation and effective monitoring of provisions of the 2009 Port State Measures Agreement which enables port states[14] to seek information from foreign flagged vessels seeking entry to their ports regarding their catch as well as their fishing and transhipment authorizations, will be the most important international instrument since the 1995 UN Fish Stocks Agreement. Under this agreement, vessels involved in IUU fishing can be denied docking rights and the agreement provides a financial deterrent to owners as they can suffer considerable financial loss. The flag state has a duty to take necessary enforcement action. Reading together article 19(2)(i) and 27(1)(b) of UNCLOS, a coastal state can exercise criminal jurisdiction over IUU fishing because the consequences impact on the good order of territorial waters. Under article 73, a coastal state has the authority to enforce its laws relating to fisheries in the EEZ, including power to board, inspect, arrest and to conduct judicial proceedings against the vessel. Undoubtedly, the arrested vessel can claim a right to prompt release upon posting of a reasonable bond or other security and the initiation of proceedings against the coastal state at the ITLOS. As IORA members may not have the same level and size of fleets and manpower to protect the vast span of the EEZ, coordinated action allocating the competences to prescribe and enforce fisheries laws of IORA members needs to be considered.

The conservation and management of highly migratory species and straddling stocks in the high seas poses a major challenge since cooperation from flag-state vessels is an important corollary to exercise the necessary powers by the states parties on the high seas to prevent IUU. In the case of the Indian Ocean, high seas fishing constitute IUU fishing as the high seas areas and stocks are regulated by the Indian Ocean Tuna Commission (IOTC). These enable states to take various enforcement measures in consonance with the 1995 Fish Stocks Agreement. Accordingly, when there are clear grounds for believing that a vessel has engaged in activity contrary to applicable conservation and management measures, the inspecting state must promptly notify the flag state. If the flag state does not act, and there are clear grounds for believing that a serious violation has been committed, the inspectors may remain on board the vessel and secure evidence, which may include requiring the vessel to proceed to the nearest appropriate port. However, at each stage, the flag state's authority to conduct enforcement action holds sway over the actions of the inspecting state. Various proposals made by the Regional Fisheries Management Organisations (RFMOs) in general and the IOTC in particular to overcome this weakness need to be pursued by international organisations, including the FAO.

As Klein concludes, the

> legal framework for IUU fishing has thus sought to move away from dependence on and respect for the exclusive jurisdiction of the flag state and instead emphasizes cooperative endeavours and a reallocation of competences that provides greater authority to port states and inspecting states. As this reallocation is dependent on participation in the relevant treaty regimes, a risk of inconsistent enforcement jurisdiction may [does] arise. Moreover, whether a state is a member of an RFMO or party to a particular treaty may encourage further registry or port shopping as those involved in IUU fishing seek to avoid regulation and policing"[15].

It is advocated that IORA members need to go beyond traditional approaches to conservation measures and explore new approaches which can directly contribute to the overall enhancement of the efficiency and effectiveness of resources. In this regard, it is useful to follow the European Union model. Undoubtedly, the European Union may have reservations if the IORA members strictly follow the EU model and enforce the measures. Recognising the heavy dependence of IORA coastal states on fisheries[16] and IUU fishing by non-IORA members and vessels, the protection of fish on the high seas will be an important consideration for these states. A broad interpretation of article 7 of the UNCLOS would suggest that, in certain circumstances, the coastal state can take unilateral conservation measures appropriate to any stock of fish or other marine resource in any area of the high seas adjacent to its territorial waters. Fishing states are obliged to apply the measures unilaterally adopted by the coastal states to their own nationals. As Judge Oda argued, article 7(1) of the UNCLOS does not disturb the exclusivity of the flag state jurisdiction over vessels flying its flag[17]. The obligations to conserve living resources in the EEZ remain weak[18], and therefore, the concerns of IORA developing state members need special consideration and measures. In addition to legal instruments dealing with fisheries, the lack of effective legislation and enforcement mechanisms with regard to various marine mammals among the developing states of IORA may attract encroachment by powerful industrialised states and become a cause of dispute especially when these industrialised states may use the absence of domestic legislation to benefit their claims.

The Marine Environment

Due to the prevailing ambiguity in international environmental law concerning maritime areas, port states and coastal states need to exercise more control and jurisdiction over various maritime zones. Wherever treaty law is silent, these states need to initiate state practices which ensure the long-term protection and promotion of their interests, especially to prevent flag of convenience states from further endangering the environment. UNCLOS enables port states to undertake investigations, and, where the evidence so warrants, to institute proceedings in respect of any discharge from a vessel that has voluntarily entered the port when the discharge is in violation of international standards, and has occurred outside the internal waters, territorial sea and EEZ of that port state[19]. It is clear that any intentional violation can trigger a coastal state to deny the right of innocent passage and enable, depending upon the gravity of the matter, the exercise of criminal jurisdiction as per article 19(2)(h) and 27 of UNCLOS. The enforcement powers and authorities of coastal states on vessel-source pollution and other sources of marine pollution are well settled in UNCLOS. It is important to note that these controls and jurisdiction powers bestowed upon the coastal states do not encroach on the freedom of navigation in any way. Rather, it is incumbent upon flag-state vessels to ensure and comply with the exercise of the rights of coastal states concerning maritime environmental control and jurisdiction. As far as the high seas are concerned, the laws are silent. Nevertheless, using the soft law resort[20], depending upon the gravity of marine pollution to affect the EEZ and subsequently contiguous zone and territorial waters over a period of time, no law prohibits states from undertaking necessary means and measures at its disposal to prevent pollution reaching its waters. The 1988 SUA Convention and 2005 SUA Protocol enable the right of visit by coastal states should the damage fall within the list prescribed by these instruments. One would agree with Klein that "there has been insufficient concern regarding damage to the marine environment outside national jurisdiction to warrant any reallocation of policing powers on the high seas at this point"[21].

Marine Biodiversity

It is well-known that Asian and African states possess a high concentration of marine biodiversity which can in turn play a crucial role in achieving sustainable development. However, due to a lack of knowledge, technological capacity, financial resources, political will and assistance from developed states, these states are unable to assess the individual and cumulative impacts of various human activities in the Indian Ocean which are increasingly putting at risk the very basis upon which the economies of many countries depend. It is also understood that the "loss in marine diversity and productivity of marine ecosystem will hamper efforts to meet development goals"[22]. The UN in recent years has been heavily emphasising the conservation and management of marine biodiversity and ecosystems[23]. As per the latest development in this regard, as Mathias has noted, UN Member States agreed on significant steps, "including on the initiation of a process aimed at ensuring that the legal framework for the conservation and sustainable use of marine biodiversity in areas beyond national jurisdiction effectively addresses those issues. To that end, such a process will identify gaps and ways forward, including through the implementation of existing instruments and the possible development of a multilateral agreement under UNCLOS." This analysis suggests (1) a need for IORA members to enact new or amend existing legislation appropriately and, (2) a coordinated instrument, at IORA level, to achieve a region-based approach. As the UN has deliberated issues in the last two years on international cooperation and coordination as well as capacity-building and the transfer of marine technology, the IORA should actively tap the benefits offered under these outcomes. It is also important that IORA take a clear approach on the legal status concerning the issue of jurisdiction of marine and genetic resources as there is a sharp division currently among governments[24]. While discussing the issue of marine biodiversity and ecosystems, it is important to realise that "there is no multilaterally agreed legal regime for the establishment of MPAs in areas beyond national jurisdiction. And that MPAs could not be established unilaterally or by a group of States only." Although the dilemma prevails over the legitimacy and legality of the establishment of MPAs in areas beyond national jurisdiction, an IORA initiative of an informal understanding nature is essential. Such an understanding will give a form of framework to IORA members to protect and promote their interests while a multilateral instrument under the UN auspices or otherwise takes shape. Such approach will help to fill the current governance and regulatory gaps[25]. As September 2015 approaches, whereby an international instrument will be concluded and which will take care of key issues on this critical area of marine biodiversity and ecosystem, an IORA specific approach is essential. An IORA position will help to give vital input to the current negotiation and drafting process.

While suggesting an IORA-specific approach in the marine biodiversity area, it is important to also underline an IORA position on the better benefit sharing provisions under the Nagoya Protocol which deals with genetic resources and access and benefit sharing of genetic resources. Individuals and institutions dealing with the regulation of genetic resources in IORA members also need an awareness regime which can delineate legal rights and obligations flowing under national jurisdiction and different treaties which regulate these resources beyond national jurisdiction—the common heritage of humankind. An associated issue is the terms and conditions known and available for the exploitation of flora and fauna available in IORA members. Finally, IORA members need to study the application of the ABS protocol not only for areas within national jurisdictions but also areas under other international treaty regimes and processes and how to build the capacity of IORA members in this area[26]. As far as IORA is concerned, one can discern that the region needs legal instruments to protect all types of marine areas within it. An effective regional institutionalised compliance mechanism is, therefore, a need of the day for IORA members[27].

Conclusion

One of the important contributions that can be made by IORA to its member states is to promote the ratification of important instruments and provide assistance to enact or amend existing legislation which can directly contribute to the achievement of IORA goals. In the area of the law of the sea and maritime laws, there are various instruments which require ratification and effective national implementing measures. The legal expert group of the IORA could compare the domestic legislation of IORA members and recommend necessary measures through the IORA to the member states. This would also help in compiling and understanding the best practices among IORA members.

Unauthorised broadcasting: Unauthorised broadcasting is one of the important security, peace and order-related issues which pose challenge to IORA members for a variety of reasons. In this regard, it is important to note that non-flag states can exercise jurisdiction over unauthorised broadcasting. States are obliged to cooperate under article 109(1) of UNCLOS. Furthermore, article 109(3) provides for the prosecution by flag state of the ship, state of registry of the installation, state of which the person is a national, any state where the transmissions can be received or any state where authorised radio communication is suffering interference. A state which has jurisdiction in accordance with article 109(3) read with article 110, can arrest any person or ship engaged in unauthorised broadcasting and seize the broadcasting apparatus in accordance with article 109(4) on the high seas. It can be concluded that article 109 does not provide for a universal jurisdiction for the suppression of unauthorised broadcasting, unlike piracy.

Ship without nationality: This is another important issue which needs serious attention by IORA members. As per customary law, a ship without nationality is without protection. However, it is important to remember that UNCLOS does not provide for universal jurisdiction over a stateless vessel.

The right of hot pursuit: In view of the increasing incidence of encroachment of foreign vessels, it may be emphasised that the right of hot pursuit is not limited to actual commitment of offence but also attempted offences[28]. Hot pursuit may also continue in the EEZ of a third state[29].

International Seabed Authority: As the "Area" becomes more and more important with regard to exploration and exploitation of resources, it is important to be kept in mind that the ISA can directly exercise jurisdiction over natural persons, in other words, a supranational jurisdiction.

NOTES

1. Ticy Thomas while analysing the comparative legislation states that, "domestic laws countries like Singapore, Thailand, Kenya, US and UK have laws that define piracy as something that occurs on the high seas, consistent with UNCLOS…[in case of Japan), it is defined that piracy occurs in territorial waters as well as high seas…[in case of the Philippines], it recognises piracy only in territorial seas….[in case of Scotland and France], piracy is recognised in both territorial and high seas…[in case of Belgium], it recognises piracy committed for other ends and not just the private ends…[South Korea] recognises attempts to commit piracy. Ticy Thomas, 'The Legal Regime of Maritime Piracy: Problems and Progress', *AALCO Verbatim Record of the Legal Experts Meeting to Commemorate the 30th Anniversary of the United Nations Convention on the Law of the Sea (UNCLOS)*, New Delhi, India, 5 March 2013, p. 54.
2. http://www.ogj.com/articles/print/volume-102/issue-17/general-interest/terrorists-attack-iraqs-persian-gulf-terminals.html accessed on 8 February 2014
3. ISPS code applies to passenger and cargo ships of at least 500 gross registered tonnage, and so does not assist in identifying the risks posed by smaller vessels, especially as those craft that have been used in terrorist attacks against vessels and ports so far. However, as the weakness is known, states can suitably modify the techniques suggested in the ISPS code for the purposes of mitigating the weaknesses while providing the trainings.
4. Nathalie Klein, *Maritime Security and the Law of the Sea*, Oxford University Press, 2010, p. 306
5. Malaysia is creating a law whereby the Marine Department of the Ministry of Transport will instruct measures in this regard. See Dato Zulkifli Adnan, Director General of Maritime Affairs Department, Ministry of Foreign Affairs, Malaysia, "Implementation of Relevant Provisions on Maritime Security", See *AALCO Verbatim Records 2013* above, p. 50.
6. Klein, p. 310.
7. Indonesia, Malaysia and Thailand are yet to ratify the Convention.
8. http://jamaica-gleaner.com/gleaner/20040208/cleisure/cleisure2.html accessed on 11 February 2014.

9. UN Document A/63/63, para. 89 dated 10 March 2008.
10. UNCLOS Art. 27(1).
11. See Klein, p. 313.
12. Donald R. Rothwell, "The Law of the Sea and the MV Tampa Incident: Reconciling Maritime Principles with Coastal State Sovereignty", 13 *Public Law Review* (2002).
13. Klein, p. 315.
14. Indian Ocean MOU has nineteen member countries: Australia, Bangladesh, Djibouti, Eritrea, France (La Reunion Island), India, Iran, Kenya, Maldives, Mauritius, Mozambique, Myanmar, Oman, Seychelles, South Africa, Sri Lanka, Sudan, Tanzania, Yemen.
15. Klein, pp. 317-18
16. IOR states have over 90% of all commercially exploitable fish stocks within 200nm of their coasts.
17. Yoshifumi Tanaka, *The International Law of the Sea*, Cambridge University Press, 2012, p. 221 quoting S. Oda, "Fisheries under the United Nations Convention on the Law of the Sea" (1983) 77 *AJIL* p. 740.
18. Tanaka at p. 224.
19. Art. 218(1).
20. General Assembly Resolution 37/7 of 28 October 1982.
21. Klein, p. 319
22. Stephen Mathias, Assistant Secretary-General for Legal Affairs, UN, Inaugural address at the AALCO Legal Experts Meeting to commemorate the 30th anniversary of the UN Convention on the Law of the Sea, 5 Marcy 2013, p. 18.
23. See also UN General Assembly Resolution, 66/288 "The Future We Want" and 67/78—"Oceans and the Law of the Sea". Ibid at 18.
24. As Luther Rangreji identifies, the "positions of governments are sharply divided between those who consider that they are regulated by Part VI of UNCLOS relating to the High Seas, and those who contend that they are governed by Part XI relating to "the Area", namely the deep-seabed beyond areas of national jurisdiction. The former view is based essentially on the literal interpretation of UNCLOS provisions. According to this view, marine resources in areas beyond national jurisdiction are living resources, and thus fall under the region of the high seas. Part XI of the regime applies only to resources in the Area, which is explicitly defined in Article 133 as mineral resources and thus excludes living resources. The activities relating to genetic resources are therefore governed by the freedom of the high seas.", Luther Rangreji, "Issues for Developing Countries under the Nagoya Protocol", in *AALCO UNCLOS Verbatim Records 2013*, p. 32.
25. Rangreji, at p. 34.
26. Rangreji, at p. 39.
27. It is worth suggesting that IOR shall carry out empirical research on pollution from land-based sources, seabed activities subject to national jurisdiction, activities in the Area, by dumping, by vessels and from or through the atmosphere.
28. O'Connell, *The International Law of the Sea*, pp. 1088-1089.
29. Tanaka, at p. 164.

Chapter 11

Myriad Maritime Threats and Multilateral Approaches: the Indian Ocean and East Africa

Vijay Sakhuja

ABSTRACT

The Indian Ocean is a large body of water and spans from the east coast of Africa along the Persian Gulf, South Asia, and maritime Southeast Asia to the west coast of Australia. Its economic vitality is best exhibited by the volume of trade which passes through its waters: nearly 50 per cent of the world's container traffic, about 30 per cent of global trade is handled by the regional ports and around 66 per cent of the world's traded oil carried on board tankers transit through the Indian Ocean. Further, about 55 per cent of known oil reserves and around 40 per cent of gas reserves are known to exist in the littoral countries of the Region. Given its economic vitality, the sea lanes and the choke points such as the Straits of Malacca, Strait of Hormuz and Bab-al-Mandab are strategically important for maritime commerce and global economy. At another level, the Indian Ocean is confronted with a number of maritime asymmetric threats and challenges that can potentially undermine the economic potential of the Region. The intensity of these threats and challenges varies depending on the ability of the littoral state to counter the perpetrators.

In the above context, this chapter attempts to highlight the sea-based threats and challenges in the western Indian Ocean and sea areas adjoining the east coast of Africa. The chapter showcases the proactive measures taken by Indian Ocean states at the national, bilateral and multilateral levels including dialogue, joint naval exercises, information sharing and capacity building which have helped to enhance maritime security in the Indian Ocean.

Key words: maritime threat, maritime security, African littorals.

Littorals: Threats, Challenges and Responses

In the contemporary strategic literature, littoral is defined as a space where sea and land converge. In maritime economic lexicon, the littorals are where maritime trade originates or where it enters the market. Therefore littoral regions are extremely important for the economic and social wellbeing of societies. In security terms, the littorals are strategic spaces where national forces should be deployed to protect the economic hubs. Littoral spaces witness two significant phenomena—congestion and contestation. In the first case, dense shipping, port operations, fishing, and other maritime activities thrive thus providing the critical ballast for economic growth and wellbeing. In the second case, poor governance and the absence of robust security systems result in favourable conditions for the growth of a number of non-state actors who engage in illegal activities. In essence, ambient conditions prevail in the littorals for opportunities for economic growth as well as for insecurities wherein non-state actors pursue their activities with total impunity. These activities are in the form of maritime piracy, terrorism, drug smuggling, gun running, and illegal and forced human smuggling.

In recent times, piracy in the Gulf of Aden-Somali coast has attracted international attention due to the phenomenal increase in the number of piracy attacks on international shipping since 2008. In the wake of the rise in piracy attacks in the Gulf of Aden, the UNSC adopted Resolution 1816 in June 2008 that authorized states to deploy warships in Somalia's territorial waters and conduct counter piracy operations[1]. Thereafter, several UN resolutions have been adopted calling upon states to provide assistance to Somalia, to deploy naval forces, and to protect Somalia's EEZ and prevent illegal fishing and the dumping of waste.

Navies from a number of countries are currently engaged in counter-piracy operations in the Gulf of Aden; important among these include the US-led Task Force 151, EUNAVFOR through Operation Atlanta, and NATO in support of Operation Ocean Shield. Warships from India, Iran, Japan, Pakistan, Malaysia, Singapore, and the Republic of Korea are also deployed. China has deployed a naval task force (CTF 525) and more than 25 warships in rotation have provided escort to over 4,500 vessels including Chinese flagged ships[2]. These forces have escorted merchant ships, prevented attacks, challenged/intercepted pirate boats/ships and even incapacitated the equipment used for conducting pirate attacks.

A number of organizations in the shipping industry have supported international efforts to fight piracy and include the Baltic and International Maritime Council (BIMCO), IMB Piracy reporting Centre (IMB PRC), International Association of Dry Cargo Ship-owners (INTERCARGO), International Chamber of Shipping (ICS), Oil Companies International Marine Forum (OCIMF), The Society of International Gas Tanker and Terminal Operators (SIGTTO), Maritime Piracy: Humanitarian Response Programme (MPHRP), Mission to Seafarers, Save our Seafarers, Seafarers Rights international (SRI)[3] to name a few. Likewise, the shipping industry has taken a number of operational initiatives such as the best practices for navigation through piracy-infested waters, standard operating procedures for piracy response, onboard protection systems, and requisitioning private maritime security personnel for self-defence. These have contributed to a decrease in the number of hijackings.

A number of multilateral responses to counter piracy have also been instituted. These include the Shared Awareness and Deconfliction (SHADE)[4] and the Contact Group for Piracy off the Coast of Somalia (CGPCS)[5] which are an interface between the government and industry. Under SHADE, country force commanders share tactical intelligence, information on threats and challenges, deployment of forces and other operational details relevant to counter piracy operations. Likewise, the CGPCS provides a common platform for the military, industry, legal experts and other interest-based groups to deliberate and share information relating to counter-piracy operations. The CGPCS meets three times annually at the United Nations and the five Working Groups meet on a regular basis to strategize international counter-piracy policies and programmes. There have been some attempts to take a sub-regional approach to address common maritime security concerns. For instance, the Djibouti Code of Conduct (DCoC) is an initiative aimed at the Repression of Piracy and Armed Robbery against Ships in the Western Indian Ocean and the Gulf of Aden and was signed in January 2009[6]. It also envisages technical co- operation and assistance and enhancing training in the Region.

An Asian counter-piracy multilateral initiative involves China, India Japan and South Korea under which their navies share information and engage in coordinated escort duties through the Internationally

Recommended Transit Corridor (IRTC),[7] a recommended passage corridor in which the warship undertakes patrolling and escort duties to provide cover to the international shipping which is generally arranged in convoy formations. One of the navies is designated as a 'Reference Navy' for a period of three months, which announces its escort schedule. The information on the timings of the escort convoy is transmitted by e-mails through secure servers.

Terrorism

The phenomenon of maritime terrorism has been gathering momentum and several terrorist groups have built a capability to attack targets 'at sea', 'from the sea' and 'under the sea'. It is estimated that there are over a dozen terrorist groups that possess a capability to attack targets at sea. In the Indian Ocean, the Liberation Tigers of Tamil Eelam (LTTE) in Sri Lanka, Al Qaeda in Pakistan-Afghanistan with strong links with Al Shabab in Somalia, and Lashkar-e-Taiba (LeT), a group based in Pakistan, have demonstrated or possess some capability to successfully attack targets in the littorals.

Among these, the LTTE (decimated by the Sri Lankan military in 2009) possessed enormous human and tactical capabilities to challenge the Sri Lankan Navy[8]. The LTTE was known to operate an ocean-going fleet, has built a global trading network that supported its economy, had control over ports and harbours in northern Sri Lanka, a fishing fleet, ship/boat building yards, and a navy. The LTTE navy, also called as 'Sea Tigers', had skillfully engaged in wolf pack attacks using high-speed boats against the Sri Lankan Navy. Its underwater capability was built around trained divers deployed as saboteurs to carry out attacks against naval ships by using improvised sea mines similar to limpet mines, semi-submersible to replicate as a "human torpedo" and submersible platforms such as mini-submarines.

The Al Qaeda is best known for its spectacular attacks in 2000 against the USS Cole and on the French tanker MV Limburg[9]. The Al Qaeda operatives possessed a sophisticated knowledge of naval warfare as was revealed from its naval manual which provides details for the use of limpet mines, the procedure for attaching these to the ship's hull, the location for best effect in different types of ships, and also the amount of explosive to be used[10].

The LeT's maritime capability was revealed after its successful attacks in India. The LeT operatives embarked on board inflatable craft and landed on the unsecured waterfront of south Mumbai. Before reaching the Indian coast, the terrorists had left Karachi in an unknown vessel, hijacked an Indian fishing craft, killed some of the crew and threw the bodies overboard[11]. Their plans included using hostages as shields to escape by the sea route. The 2008 Mumbai terror attacks left 188 people dead, including 28 foreign nationals, and hundreds injured.

It is quite evident from the above that terrorist groups have exploited the littorals to attack targets ashore; this is notwithstanding the fact that the sea is a complex medium, highly opaque, and requires greater mastery to conduct attacks.

Trade in Contraband: Drug Smuggling and Gun Running

The Indian Ocean maritime security environment is also challenged by contraband trade—that is, drug smuggling and gun running. The burgeoning trade in natural and synthetic drugs from the Golden Crescent (Afghanistan-Pakistan) and the Golden Triangle (the Golden Triangle comprises Northern Thailand, Shan and Kachin states in Myanmar and Western Laos) has been a feature that is causing growing concern both regionally and internationally. It is contributing to social instability and plays a key role in undermining and weakening vulnerable regimes by encouraging corruption and the spread of deadly diseases like AIDS.

It is pertinent to mention that bulk drug consignments are moved over the seas, but only few interceptions have been made in the Indian Ocean. In the case of the Golden Triangle, heroin produced by Myanmar is largely trafficked through unmarked transit land routes and then to ports and onward through sea routes; drugs from Afghanistan are moved through ports in Pakistan and other South Asian countries. For instance, in a recent incident, the narcotics Division of Sri Lanka's Customs Department recovered 100 kilograms of heroin from the Orugodwatta container yard[12]. The consignment was hidden inside industrial grinding machines imported from Karachi, Pakistan.

In the case of east Africa, there have been a few intercepts. In April 2014, the Australian Navy ship, HMAS Darwin, while on patrol off the coast of Africa, seized more than one tonne of heroin valued at US$290 million from a sailing boat[13]. The consignment was concealed among bags of cement. In July 2014, the Kenyan police recovered some 342 kilograms of heroin from a ship that was intercepted off Kenya's territorial waters in Lamu[14].

Likewise, gunrunning by ships is by far the 'safest' method. The LTTE had established a network of gun running and these consignments were sourced from Southeast Asian countries, Africa and also from the Gulf region. Perhaps one of the largest interceptions of arms took place in Chittagong harbour in Bangladesh when the police seized a huge consignment of 1,500 boxes of weapons and ammunition, "good enough to arm an entire military brigade"[15]. In 2014, 14 people were awarded the death sentence over the 2004 Chittagong arms haul.

Illegal and Forced Migration

There has been a huge exodus of Rohingya who are escaping the growing tensions between the Buddhist and Muslim communities in the Burmese state of Rakhine. Nearly one million Rohingya live in Burma and are considered illegal Bangladeshi immigrants by the local authorities. They are a minority in the predominantly Buddhist state and have been denied citizenship. There are reports which suggest that the Rohingyas are ill treated and live in makeshift camps without access to proper food, clean water and healthcare. According to the United Nations, in 2012, nearly 13,000 people fled Burma to escape isolation and religious persecution and while undertaking perilous voyages as many as 500 may have perished at sea[16].

Likewise, in 2013, the Thai security forces intercepted an overcrowded boat carrying 73 Rohingya migrants including women and young children, near Bon Island in Phuket province[17]. The Thai authorities brought these people ashore and transported them to Ranong province for deportation to Burma. Not very long thereafter, towards the end of January, Thai authorities intercepted another boat carrying 200 people near Raja Noi Island in the Andaman Sea off Phuket province, a popular tourist destination[18]. These people were not allowed to land ashore and were pushed back to sea with some water and food. The Sri Lankan Navy rescued 38 Burmese nationals from a boat that was discovered by fishermen drifting 400 kilometers off the east coast.

This was the second instance that the Sri Lankan navy had rescued a boat carrying illegal migrants. Likewise, the Indonesian authorities reported that their fishermen had found adrift 121 Rohingya, including women and children, 25 kilometers from Cot Trueng, in Aceh province. In 2009, the Thai security forces were accused of turning away the boat people and some of them were towed out to sea and left to die without adequate supplies. A number of these had arrived on Indian shores in the Andaman and Nicobar Islands.

Similar conditions prevail in the Gulf of Aden and the Red Sea. Numerous boats carrying hundreds of Somalis, Ethiopians and Eritreans escaping the political turmoil, civil war and poverty are smuggled over by boats to Yemen. According to the UNHCR, over the last five years, nearly half-a-million people were transported in boats[19]. The data released by the UNHCR for the first quarter of 2014 are encouraging and show that only 16,500 refugees arrived by boat and landed along the Yemeni coast compared to 35,000 in the same period in 2013[20]. There are large numbers of undocumented casualties and the smugglers are reported to have thrown passengers overboard to prevent capsizing or to avoid detection. Some of the migrants have been spotted as far as Australia. For instance, in January 2014, the Royal Australian Navy intercepted boats carrying illegal immigrants from Africa and the Middle East (Sudan, Eritrea, Somali, Ghana, Egypt, Yemen and Lebanon) and prevented them from entering Australian waters[21].

WMD Proliferation

There have been a few incidents involving the transportation of WMDs through the Indian Ocean. In December 2002, a Spanish frigate seized *So San*, a North Korean vessel, about 600 miles off the Horn of Africa in the Indian Ocean[22]. The vessel's cargo included 15 Scud missiles for Yemen and, according to Spanish sources, *So San* sailed under a Cambodian flag but had no identifying marks on it and therefore was a fit case for being a pirate ship[23]. However, the Yemen authorities defended their consignment and declared that it was legal and that it was meant for a sovereign state. Another interesting case relates to the seizure of the ship *BBC China* that was carrying uranium enrichment equipment bound for Libya[24]. The capture of the ship apparently resulted in Libya's decision to come clean with its WMD activities. Similarly, a nerve-agent precursor destined for North Korea was confiscated in Taiwan. In 1999, the Indian customs authorities impounded a North Korean vessel *M V Ku Wol San* at Kandla Port for carrying equipment for the production of tactical surface-to-surface missiles that was suspected to be bound for Pakistan or Libya[25].

A number of Indian Ocean countries have cooperated to in order to prevent rogue states and non-state actors from acquiring WMD, interdicting shipments at sea, in the air, and on land and have endorsed the Proliferation Security Initiative (PSI), first announced in 2003. The PSI now plays a central role in overall efforts to counter WMD proliferation.

Private Maritime Security Companies

The rise of piracy off Somalia also stimulated commercial activities by escort companies and private security agencies that supply trained personnel for onboard security duties. According to a recent report, the shipping industry spent US$1.1 billion for security equipment and armed guards[26]. Interestingly, nearly 120 companies are operating and are popular among shipping companies. Apparently, they 'make more money than the pirates'. Firms such as Hart Security of Britain and Templar Titan of the United States provide security guards for 1,500 voyages every month and generate a monthly revenue of some $55.2 million[27]. Similarly, the Convoy Escort Programme Ltd. charges a fee of $30,000 per ship to escort ships across the Gulf of Aden[28]. According to the Director of the UK Security Association for the Maritime Industry: "Piracy is a lucrative business not only for Somali pirates but to many profiteers who make more money than the pirates themselves...some of them are cowboys...they have no proper security training, they're inefficient, incompetent and they want money."[29] Also, "there are rich pickings to be had for the expanding security outfits" and "Some of the big maritime security companies have improved their turnover by 350 percent in the last year."[30]

According to a report entitled *Economic Cost of Somali Piracy 2012* (ECoP 2012) published by Oceans Beyond Piracy (OBP), a project of the One Earth Future Foundation (OEF), there is greater acceptance of armed guards by both flag states, ship owners and operators[31]. Further, 25% of the ships transiting the Gulf of Aden-Somali coast employed a team of armed guards at an estimated cost of US$530.6 million in 2011 which increased to US$1.15–$1.53 billion in 2012[32].

However, escort companies and private security agencies have not been trouble free. There are two notable cases which merit attention. In the first case, Italian Sea Marshals deployed on board the *M V Enrica Lexie*, fired and killed two Indian fishermen. The incident led to a diplomatic fall-out between India and Italy and the case is still pending in the Indian courts. With more governments allowing their national flagged vessels to position security guards on board ships, it is time to rethink the issue of arming merchant vessels with either trained or untrained security guards. A number of issues such as rules of engagement, right of self defence, the politico-diplomatic fallout of such incidents, and, of course, the legal-jurisdictional understanding of the dynamics of affairs at sea , all remain to be addressed.

In the second case, in October 2013, the Indian Coast Guard intercepted *Seaman Guard Ohio,* a Sierra Leone-flagged vessel, after it was detected in Indian waters. The vessel was being operated by PMSC AdvanFort, a US-based company, and was charged by the Indian authorities as "unauthorized entrance into Indian waters while being in the possession of firearms on October 13, 2013"[33]. The ship owners approached the Indian High Court "to quash the criminal proceedings initiated against the crew by the Indian Coastguard, ...contending that the ship was arrested while it was outside the Indian territorial sea and that the ship only aimed to refuel after the strong cyclone Phailin caused the vessel to be nearly out of fuel, also proving that all the firearms on board were legally purchased and properly documented." Unlike the *M V Enrica* case, after an eight-month long legal process, the charges against the ship and its crew were 'quashed' by the Madras High Court who did not "find any offense against the crew and guards of the US-based private security firm AdvanFort."

India is concerned about the unregulated 'floating armouries' and "this has very serious security implications for us including the infiltration of terrorists". The Indian Navy Chief has observed that: "If there are unregulated arms and ammunition on a vessel, the existence of weapons is not known as also where guards are transferring them and this could lead to such a situation on anybody's soil"[34]. Further,

"There are close to 140 private security companies operating in North Indian Ocean, which hire out privately contracted armed security personnel. These personnel shift between vessels at sea, without entering any port or coastal state regulated maritime territory,"[35]

Towards a Multilateral Maritime Security Architecture for Indian Ocean

There have been attempts to develop Indian Ocean regionalism and a number of bilateral and multilateral arrangements among the Indian Ocean states have emerged. The Indian Ocean Rim Association of Regional Cooperation (IOR-ARC), set up in 1997, now rechristened as the Indian Ocean Rim Association (IORA), is the only pan-Indian Ocean economic grouping, which brings together countries from Africa and Asia plus Australia. Since its inception, the IORA has focused on economic cooperation based on the principle of open and inclusive regionalism.

The inclusion of security issues in the agenda of the IORA is a recent development and was highlighted during the IOR-ARC meeting in Bengaluru in 2011. The 12th meeting of the Council of Ministers of IOR-ARC issued the Gurgaon Communiqué 'IOR-ARC at 15—The Next Decade' that stated:

> Piracy is an increasingly serious concern, posing a threat to maritime commerce and the safety of sea farers, making insurance costlier and adding to the costs incurred by the shipping industry in the Indian Ocean Region. Weak governance and instability in parts of the region have contributed to its degeneration into transnational organised crime. We welcome the emphasis that our Association has placed on cooperation in maritime security issues in the Indian Ocean and reaffirm the importance of maintaining freedom of navigation and safety and security of Sea Lanes of Communication in the Indian Ocean.[36]

In November 2013, the IOR-ARC was rechristened in Perth as the Indian Ocean Rim Association (IORA) and Paragraphs 5 and 6 of the Perth Communiqué of December 2013 state:

> IORA is the lead body for promoting regional collaboration across the Indian Ocean rim. We will take forward IORA's role in addressing the development, security, resource and environmental challenges that face our region through policy-oriented consideration of opportunities

and risks and high-quality projects in the six priority areas we identified at our meeting in Bengaluru in 2011...

...We wish to broaden and deepen efforts through IORA to bolster maritime security and safety, particularly in light of continued threats to maritime commerce, and freedom of the high seas, consistent with the UN Convention on the Law of the Seas (UNCLOS); as well as on the safety of sea farers. We look to the upcoming Indian Ocean Dialogue in India to explore, inter-alia, concrete options to enhance counter-piracy cooperation, including through improved maritime information-sharing arrangements and stronger national legal capacity and laws.[37]

The other major pan-Indian Ocean security apparatus is built around the Indian Ocean Naval symposium (IONS) that was initiated in 2008 and can be attributed to the Indian Navy's desire to play an important role in the Indian Ocean. IONS aims to "generate a flow of information between naval professionals that would lead to common understanding and possibly agreements on the way ahead"[38] and address maritime security issues confronted by the Indian Ocean Region. IONS draws liberally from another maritime security construct—the Western Pacific Naval Symposium (WPNS)—for the Asia-Pacific Region. The host country holds the Chair for two years. The 35-member grouping is built around four sub-regions covering the entire Indian Ocean rim. The inaugural IONS was held in New Delhi, India on 14 February 2008; the 2nd in Abu-Dhabi from 10-11 May 2010: and the 3rd in Cape Town, South Africa from 10-14 Apr 2012; and the last meeting was held in March 2014 in Perth, Western Australia.

While IORA and IONS are useful models of regional cooperation, they have witnessed varying degrees of successes. The Perth Communiqué also noted:

"All IORA Member States have a stake as invited participants in the Indian Ocean Naval Symposium (IONS). We consider it important that IORA's work on maritime security and safety and disaster management align with and complement possible IONS initiatives in these areas, including in information-sharing and other activities with both civilian and non-civilian dimensions."

However, there is lack of communication between these multilateral institutions given that economics and security has been the significant feature of transactions among the Indian Ocean littorals. Furthermore, the sub-regional approach to addressing common maritime security concerns has been a priority among regional states. Interestingly, Somali piracy in the Gulf of Aden offered a unique opportunity for IORA to take note of security issues but it did not make any significant effort to bring regional countries to come together and address this menace.

Concluding Remarks

The Indian Ocean has its fair share of maritime asymmetric threats and challenges that can potentially undermine the peace and stability of the Region. The existing maritime cooperative initiatives in the Indian Ocean are noteworthy and contribute significantly to the economic potential of the Region. They have played an important role and are successful initiatives for cooperation that can serve as a model for any other cooperative engagements among the Indian Ocean littorals to address other maritime security challenges.

It is without doubt that there is a realization of the relevance and importance of multinational cooperation among Indian Ocean littorals that is visible in their economic, foreign and security policies. In addition, common security concerns are being addressed through the prism of 'maritime multilateralism' that is a new paradigm of security cooperation. It would be prudent for all Indian Ocean states to continue to invest in additional diplomatic and human capital to make these institutions more robust and capable.

NOTES

1. "Resolution 1816 (2008) Adopted Unanimously with Somalia's Consent; Measures Do Not Affect Rights, Obligations under Law of Sea Convention", http://www.un.org/News/Press/docs/2008/sc9344.doc.htm accessed June 17, 2014.
2. Vijay Sakhuja, "Increasing Maritime Competition: IORA, IONS, Milan and the Indian Ocean Networks" http://www.ipcs.org/article/china/increasing-maritime-competition-iora-ions-milan-and-the-indian-ocean-4320.html accessed on July 14, 2014.
3. "Best Management Practices to Deter Piracy in the Gulf of Aden and off the Coast of Somalia", http://www.skuld.com/upload/News%20and%20Publications/Publications/Piracy/MC(09)24%20-%20Annex%20A%20-%20 Piracy%20BMP%20V2%207%20Final.pdf accessed June 17, 2014.
4. For details see "Shared Awareness and Deconfliction (SHADE)". http://oceansbeyondpiracy.org/matrix/activity/shared-awareness-and-deconfliction-shade accessed June 17, 2014.

5. Contact Group for Piracy off the Coast of Somalia (CGPCS). http://www.thecgpcs.org/main.do?action=main accessed June 17, 2014.
6. "Protection of Vital Shipping Lanes", http://www.imo.org/OurWork/Security/PIU/Documents/DCoC%20English.pdf accessed June 17, 2014.
7. "Piracy and Armed Robbery against Ships in Waters off The Coast of Somalia Information on Internationally Recommended Transit Corridor (IRTC) for Ships Transiting The Gulf of Aden". http://www.imo.org/OurWork/Security/PiracyArmedRobbery/Guidance/Documents/SN.1-Circ.281.pdf accessed June 17, 2014.
8. "Humanitarian Operation Factual Analysis: July 2006—May 2009", Ministry of Defence, Democratic Socialist Republic of Sri Lanka, July 2011
9. Vijay Sakhuja , "Security threats and challenges to maritime supply chains", http://www.peacepalacelibrary.nl/ebooks/files/UNIDIR_pdf-art2959.pdf accessed June 17, 2014.
10. Stefano Ambrogi, "Iraq War Could Spur al Qaeda Sea Attacks in Gulf", *Reuters,* February 21 2003.
11. "Mumbai Terror Attacks—Dossier of Evidence", available at http://www.hindu.com/nic/dossier.htm accessed June 17, 2014.
12. "Large heroin haul of over 100 kg seized in Sri Lanka", *Colombo Page*, July 21, 2014.
13. "Australian Navy seizes $290 million of heroin from boat off Kenyan coast", http://www.abc.net.au/news/2014-04-25/australian-navy-seize-290-million-of-heroin-from-boat-off-kenya/5412108 accessed on July 18, 2014.
14. "342kg of heroin found on Mombasa boat", *Capital News* [Nairobi], July 15, 2014.
15. "2004 Chittagong arms haul case exposes many terror links", *The Economic Times*, February 6, 2014.
16. Various sources http://www.thestateless.com/2013_02_18_archive.html accessed on July 10, 2014.
17. Vijay Sakhuja, "ASEAN Must Address the Rohingya Issue", http://www.emergencyscene.com/2013/03/asean-must-address-the-rohingya-issue/ accessed on July 10, 2014.
18. Ibid.
19. "Red Sea tragedy leaves 62 people dead in deadliest crossing of the year", http://www.unhcr.org/5391c1e56.html accessed July 19, 2014.
20. Ibid.
21. "Australia navy drives boat people into Indonesian waters", *The Jakarta Post*, 6 January 2014.
22. Sue Chan "Suspect Scuds Sailing On To Yemen", http://www.cbsnews.com/news/suspect-scuds-sailing-on-to-yemen/ accessed July 19, 2014.
23. Peter Symonds, "The strange affair of the Yemeni Scud missiles", http://www.wsws.org/en/articles/2002/12/scud-d14.html accessed on July 14, 2014.
24. Paula A. DeSutter, Assistant Secretary for Verification and Compliance, "Contending with a Nuclear-Ready Iran", Conference Held at the Wyndham City Center Hotel, Washington, DC, March 7, 2004.

25. "Indian agencies to investigate North Korean ship's entry", *The Economic Times*, August 9, 2009.
26. "Somali piracy begets new security industry", http://www.terradaily.com/reports/Somali_piracy_begets_new_security_industry_999.html accessed on 15 June 2014.
27. "Security Industry- Somali piracy begets new security industry", http://maritimesecurityasia.blogspot.in/2012/02/security-industry-somali-piracy-begets.html accessed on 15 June 2014.
28. Michelle Wiese Bockmann "Somalia Piracy Spurs Private Gulf of Aden Navy to Start Within Five Months", http://www.bloomberg.com/news/print/2011-11-07/somalia-piracy-spurs-private-gulf-of-aden-navy-to-start-within-five-months.html accessed on 15 June 2014.
29. "Somali pirates spawn lucrative security trade", http://www.ft.com/cms/s/0/410d1b40-45b0-11e1-acc9-00144feabdc0.html#axzz38JB55jSq accessed on 25 June 2014.
30. "Somali piracy begets new security industry", http://www.upi.com/Business_News/Security-Industry/2012/02/14/Somali-piracy-begets-new-security-industry/UPI-49371329256394/ accessed on 25 June 2014.
31. "Economic Cost of Somali Piracy 2012", http://oceansbeyondpiracy.org/cost-of-piracy/economic accessed June 18, 2014.
32. Ibid.
33. "Charges against MV Seaman Guard Ohio Crew & Guards Quashed by Indian HC", http://www.advanfort.com/Charges-against-MV-Seaman-Guard-Ohio-Crew-Guards-Quashed-by-Indian-HC.pdf accessed on 25 June 2014.
34. "Floating armouries risk 26/11-type attacks: Navy Chief DK Joshi", http://zeenews.india.com/news/nation/navy-chief-warns-unregulated-private-armoury-ships-can-risk-another-26/11_894052.html accessed December 4, 2013.
35. "Navy sounds alarm on 'floating armouries", *The Times of India*, 4 December 2013.
36. "Gurgaon Communiqué—IOR-ARC at 15—The Next Decade" announced at the 12th Meeting of the Council of Ministers of IOR-ARC, Ministry of External Affairs, Government of India, November 2, 2012.
37. "The Perth Communiqué", https://www.dfat.gov.au/geo/indian-ocean/perth-communique-2013.html accessed on July 17, 2014.
38. "Indian Ocean Naval Symposium' (IONS)", http://ions.gov.in/?q=about_ions accessed on July 12, 2014.

Chapter 12

Maritime Security and Its Impact on Trade in the IORA Region

Nancy Karigithu

The Indian Ocean Region: basic data

- Half of the world's container ships, one third of the bulk cargo traffic and two-thirds of the world's oil shipments;
- A lifeline of international trade and economy;
- Commands control of the major sea-lanes;
- Massive market (2.7 billion people)—rich in strategic and precious minerals, metals and other natural resources—food fisheries, raw material and energy;
- Abundant agricultural wealth in terms of the variety and mass of arable land, significant human resources and technological capabilities;

Maritime Domain Security

Security is the protection of persons, property or an organization from an intentional attack by a person or persons.

Motivation for attack may vary and may involve terrorism, sabotage or subversion—meant to cause maximum fear, panic and despondence.

It follows then that where there is no security there will be no vigorous trade as trade thrives in a conducive atmosphere without fear, despondence or panic.

Maritime security in the seaborne trade encompasses all the supporting maritime clusters within the maritime logistics supply chain.

Maritime Domain Concerns

- Management of marine resources;
- Transportation;
- Maintenance of territorial integrity;
- Protection and preservation of the maritime environment;
- Prevention of illegal activities in the EEZ
- Safety of life at sea;
- Security for vessels and port facilities.

Key Maritime Security Concerns

- Security of port facilities and associated infrastructure.
- Security of vessels.
- Security of crew and passengers.
- Security of cargo.
- Drug trafficking.
- Human trafficking.
- Illegal, Unreported and Unregulated (IUU) fishing.
- Illegal dumping of toxic waste.
- Illegal arms smuggling.

Maritime Insecurity

Exposes global supply chains to risks that have significant impact on production—inventory shortfalls or even production flow shutdowns.

Disrupts supply chains resulting in catastrophic costs to the shipping industry with negative impact on maritime supply chains that need effective risk management solutions to overcome;

Costs of Somali Piracy at its Peak (2010)

Average Ransom in the range of $3.4m to $5.4m per vessel totaling $238 million

Excess insurance premiums for Kidnap & Ransom $540 m

War Risk Premium Surcharge—$4.05 billion;

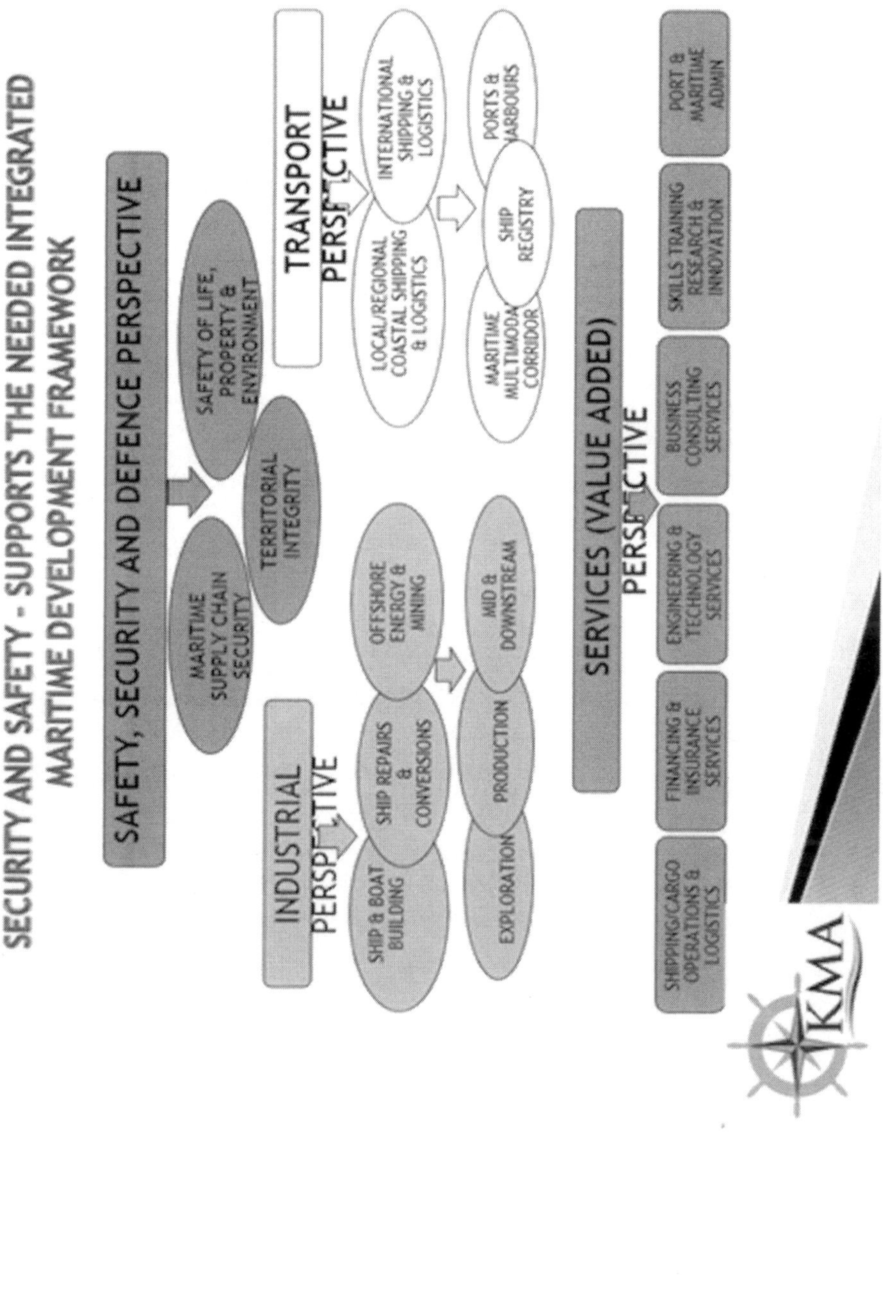
SECURITY AND SAFETY - SUPPORTS THE NEEDED INTEGRATED MARITIME DEVELOPMENT FRAMEWORK
SAFETY, SECURITY AND DEFENCE PERSPECTIVE
MARITIME SUPPLY CHAIN SECURITY
TERRITORIAL INTEGRITY
SAFETY OF LIFE, PROPERTY & ENVIRONMENT
INDUSTRIAL PERSPECTIVE
SHIP & BOAT BUILDING
SHIP REPAIRS & CONVERSIONS
OFFSHORE ENERGY & MINING
EXPLORATION
PRODUCTION
MID & DOWNSTREAM
TRANSPORT PERSPECTIVE
LOCAL/REGIONAL COASTAL SHIPPING & LOGISTICS
INTERNATIONAL SHIPPING & LOGISTICS
MARITIME MULTIMODAL CORRIDOR
SHIP REGISTRY
PORTS & HARBOURS
SERVICES (VALUE ADDED) PERSPECTIVE
SHIPPING/CARGO OPERATIONS & LOGISTICS
FINANCING & INSURANCE SERVICES
ENGINEERING & TECHNOLOGY SERVICES
BUSINESS CONSULTING SERVICES
SKILLS TRAINING RESEARCH & INNOVATION
PORT & MARITIME ADMIN
KMA

Cost of deterrent measures

Licensed Security Guards $80,000 per trip

Sonic Deterrent Equipment $1,250

Barbed/Razor Wire $12,000

Sandbags $1,200

Electric Fences $40,000

Total Per Ship in a trip $134,450

Maritime Security Risks on Shipping

Impacts of piracy on the maritime security chains

1. Re-route issues
   Continue transit
   Faced increased risks and higher costs
   Re-route—face increased costs for both ship and cargo
2. Re-route—effect on regional economies
   Suffer significant loss of foreign currency
   Negative impact on GDP
   Lose operating earnings including unemployment
   Decline in ship calls plus size
   Decline in transshipment/transit cargos—strong decline in revenues
   Increased total operating expenditures
   Decreased carrying capacity
   Impact of costs would possibly be passed on to cargo owners
   Price increases and longer transit and delivery times
   Additional voyage costs
   Higher bunker costs
   Additional cargo inventory plus additional equipment costs

Cost of re-routing vessels away from piracy risk zones

Costs of Re-Routing, Selected Ships Ship Cost: Hire and Fuel

300,000 DWT VLCC Charter Hire	
Cost per day	$30,000
Excess cost for 10 day voyage	$300,000
Cost if 10% of ships re-route	$900 million

10,000 TEU Containership Charter Hire	
Cost per day	$40,000
Excess Cost for 10 day voyage	$400,000
Cost if 10% of ships re-route	$1.2 billion
10,000 TEU Containership Fuel	
Cost per day	$58,200
Excess Cost for 10 day voyage	$582,000
Cost if 10% of ships re-route	$1.75 billion

Naval deployments in piracy hot zones

One U.S. navy vessel costs $82,794 to operate per steaming day totaling $1.3 billion per year with the estimate of 43 vessels deployed;

The administrative budgets of the three major missions deployed in 2010- $2 billion per year.

Total Cost of Prosecutions 2010

Indian Ocean Region	$25,116,000
Europe	$5,166,000
North America	$1,007,199

It is a fact that an estimated 95% of trade by volume is carried out via the sea.

Maritime transport needs efficient and safe infrastructure in port services and land transfers—most significant being rail transport.

Legal Frameworks for Security

The United Nations Convention on the Law of the Sea—rights and obligations of flag states;

International Convention for the safety of life at sea (SOLAS), 1974 as amended (chapter XI-2 on special measures to enhance maritime security)

International Ship and Port Facility Security (ISPS) Code;

Merchant Shipping Acts;

National Regulations;

The IMO/ILO Code of Practice on Security in Ports, which:
Extends the consideration of port security beyond the area of the port facility into the whole port; and applies security guidelines to all areas and functions of the port, and those working in, having business with and requiring access to the port or transiting through the port.

This includes port workers and other port personnel, seafarers, passengers and passengers' baggage, cargo, material and stores, vehicles and equipment originating from within and outside the port area.

The Convention for the Suppression of unlawful Acts against the Safety of Maritime Navigation (SUA) 1988.
It was intended to improve measures for dealing with incidents such as terrorists' attacks on commercial shipping. It entered into force in March 1992.

The above instruments may not deal with all aspects of maritime security especially the following: security of ships not covered under the Code; and the security of the cargo/supply chain.

Conclusions

As states surrounding the Indian Ocean Rim, we must be prudent and cooperate in:

1. Looking after our maritime domain;
2. Knowing that supporting any one cluster in the maritime sector has a multiplier effect in others;
3. Looking at the inherent security framework needed to sustain stability and calm in the undertaking of various maritime economic activities in the region.
4. Understanding that the negative impact of maritime insecurity on trade is enormous and cannot be overemphasized. Any perception of lack of maritime security will send potential business away while good maritime security will attract a lot of business.

Chapter 13

Silences on Maritime Security in Existing Regional Security Architecture: the case of East African and Indian Ocean Waters

Paul Wambua

ABSTRACT

As the global geopolitical map keeps shifting to the East, there has been an increase in the strategic value of the waters of Indian Ocean. Global trade and energy relies heavily on the critical sea lines of communication in these waters. The increase in strategic value is commensurate with threats and vulnerabilities. The Somali coastline piracy scourge raised the global alarm on the need to secure the waters with both littoral and landlocked countries involved over time and space. Regional security mechanisms are the preferred approaches but the existing frameworks are at +be*ad hoc*, and at worse, are silent on maritime security.

In order to objectively discuss the place of regional mechanisms, and the existing gaps, we use the concepts of Maritime Security, Securitization and Regional Security Complexes, borrowing heavily from the Copenhagen School. In constructing a conceptual framework for the discussion the study adopts an expanded meaning of "security" as a concept involving not just states, but also individuals and the wider environment in which the state operates.

This chapter proposes the tightening of the conceptual framework of regional mechanisms on maritime security and the legal tools deployed to hold the states together in such a framework. Developmental (horizontal) infrastructure as opposed to extractive (vertical) infrastructure promises to fundamentally alter the security patterns of the region, lessening conflicts and insecurities, maritime security included.

Key words: Maritime Security, Securitization and Regional Security Complex, Indian Ocean.

Introduction

The Indian Ocean (IO) geostrategic value lies in its centrality to key nodes of global significance. The IO connects the Middle East, East Africa and East Asia with Europe and the Americas. Its waters connect slightly over eighty percentage of the global population for commerce, energy, food, transport and communication. It is the global crossroads and with the continued economic rise of the Asia-Pacific and energy resource discoveries in Africa, its prominence in global cognizance is greatly enhanced.

The increasing strategic value of the Ocean comes with rising threats and vulnerabilities. Global, regional and national responses have increased to counter the threats on the critical space of the IO. However, it is clear that, at present, this is dominated by extra-regional powers. For the Eastern Africa states, a region dependent on the IO for its survival, inward-looking security imaginations and resultant design have limited its response capacity. Existing regional maritime security architecture and innovations point to a growing interest, albeit with conceptual deficiency. This chapter hopes to bring to the fore this deficiency and offer 'patches' to the existing designs.

To achieve this, the chapter begins with a conceptual appreciation of maritime space, securitization and regional security cooperation. This will inform the perspective to examine the geostrategic value of the Indian Ocean and inherent threats. A critical examination of the security responses from global, regional and national actors will facilitate an analysis of deficiencies in regional security architecture in the Eastern Africa region. Hopefully, this will permit proposed 'patches' to the existing designs if the region is to manage current maritime vulnerabilities and be flexible enough to anticipate mutating threats over time and space.

Maritime Space Theory, Securitization and Regional Security Complexes

The need for a conceptual framework in this study is necessitated by the complex nature of phenomena with which we will be dealing. There needs to be some sense of structure for consistency in describing and explaining the status of the region, predicting and prescribing options looking into the future. Just like the Prussian military strategist and theorist, Carl von Clausewitz, notes, theory "gives the mind insight into the great mass of phenomena and of their relationships, then leaves it free to rise into the higher realms of action."[1]

Maritime Space

The maritime domainis the Earth's greatest defining feature, with four principal divisions—Atlantic, Arctic, Indian, and Pacific. They are classified as global commons under no single state's jurisdiction while being open to all states for utility.

The maritime domain is defined as all areas and things of, on, under, relating to, adjacent to, or bordering on a sea, ocean, or other navigable waterway, including all maritime-related activities, infrastructure, people, cargo, and vessels and other conveyances[2]. Maritime security is thus understood here as efforts employed to ensure the freedom of the seas, to facilitate freedom of navigation and commerce, to advance prosperity and freedom, and to protect the resources of the ocean[3]. The task of securing the maritime domain has historically been assumed to fall on the littoral states, the opportunity cost they pay for the strategic value they gain over the landlocked ones.

National perspectives have tended to focus on naval theory, which deals with ships, shipbuilding, war at sea, and allied military forces[4]. Moreover, naval theory is primarily concerned with the means and methods of employing force at sea to achieve national goals while increasing national power and prestige on land. This focus on offshore activities results in a narrow view of the maritime space and as such strategic plans omit operations on shore that have direct bearing on the waters. The Somali piracy case exposes this scenario—the collapse of the on-shore state created direct threats to the offshore space. This conceptual gap—failing to encompass the interaction and interdependence of other environments—is filled by the expansive maritime theory.

Maritime theory covers the whole range of activities and interests regarding the seas and oceans, and their interrelationships: science, technology, cartography, industry, economics, trade, politics, international affairs, imperial expansion, communications, migration, international law, social affairs, and leadership[5]. Additionally, maritime theory especially includes the interaction between sea and land. From this perspective, naval theory, therefore, is but a subset of maritime theory.

The geostrategic thinking of Alford Thayer Mahan and Mackinder has had a lasting legacy on modern maritime thinking. Mahan, in *The Influence of Sea Power Over History: 1793- 1782,* for instance, evolved maritime theory that sought to explain the evolution of power on land through exploitation of the sea. He sought to highlight value derived out of maritime domains through the Command of the Sea (COS), a function of naval superiority and utilization of maritime domain elements. Success on the waters translated into power on land.

According to Mahan, the naval strategy and sea power of a state is conditioned by certain fundamental natural phenomena. They include: geographical location of a state; its physical conformation; the extent of its territory; the size of its population; the national character; and, the character and policy of the government[6]. The differentiated extent to which these factors are aligned towards maximizing the utility of the waters while minimizing threats explains why some states (and regions) boast stronger sea power than others. At the centre of it all is the presence of strategic and objective political leadership to allocate resources for implementing such a maritime strategy.

Zanzibar, for instance, rose as a maritime power due to its leadership's control of strategic sea lines of communications along the east coast of Africa[7]. The destruction of its navy by the British and German navies equally marked its demise as a state. The same can be said of the Buganda kingdom whose growth and collapse was equally rooted in its Lake Victoria navy[8]. The very existence of this pioneering force is a testament to the salience of maritime domains in the Eastern African region. If we are to regionalise Mahan's conception of land-sea-interdependence and its implication on national power—that is, if events at sea can bring some influence to bear on land, then it should be possible for events on land to bring some influence to bear on the sea positively or negatively, and then we can derive a regional maritime strategy. Extrapolating this to the regional level implies the presence of a strategic and objective regional political leadership to align resources with the means to achieve desired maritime goals primarily of commerce and security.

The converse of the principle above holds—the failure to match regional capacity over the control of the land will have a bearing on the maritime space under jurisdiction. Regional political leadership is manifested in the regional bodies organized around security and governance. Limitation in capacity, be it on political authority or resource provision, implies enhanced maritime threats. This is the assertion we seek to probe. To what extent is the apparent vulnerability of the Western Indian Ocean a function of the limited potency of regional security bodies in Eastern Africa? Of importance though are the differentiated imaginations of access to maritime resources among the states of this region. How does this explain the commitment of political capital and military resources?

Mackinder's counter thesis to Mahan in the book *Democratic Ideals and Reality* (1904) finds relevance here. Appreciating the differentiated impacts of resource endowments, Mackinder was interested in political motion underpinned by the differentiated spatial distribution of resources[9]. Mackinder forewarned of the impact technology would force a revaluation of both spatial concepts and military strategies. Technology, he contended, would reduce distance on the continent and in the process open it up including its resources, thus providing continental states with a preponderance of power that technologies over seas had given insular states[10]. According to Mackinder, the railway, internal combustion engine, the construction of the modern highway and road networks would spawn rapid transportation over land opening up both human and natural resources. Wars would shift from the sea back to the hinterland (interiors) in a struggle for power. From this he evolved his notion of the pivot area whose control availed strategic resources critical for assuming control over the world islands of Europe and Africa. The strategic advantage here is that it is defendable and hard to conquer, hence his heartland theory that ultimately fed colonial conquest imaginations. Little appreciation was spared in conceiving the impacts of resource extractions, especially in spaces overseas. Core here being, the fabrication of the non-viable states, a process animated by the construction of vertical macro infrastructures of communication devoid of corresponding horizontal social, economic and political infrastructure. The negative effects of the lack of infrastructure to African economies and modern forms of violence such as those mediated by pirates or bandits are predicated in the sustenance of the colonial operationalization of Mackinder's closed space thesis.

The seriousness with which the British took Mackinder's thesis was brought to the fore by British strategic behaviour in Africa. Not only did they seek to control the source of the Nile, but also that through the Nile achieved the strategic and effective control of Alexandria. This called for the coupling of Sudan to Egypt and the control of Uganda. This has had a lasting legacy on the existing Nile conflict being addressed by the states sharing the waters of the river.

The continent was undermined by the fact that the multiple infrastructures had limited horizontal integration logic within and across the new entities created by colonial actors. Succinctly put, corridors of infrastructure that are extractionist in nature underpin conflicts. Wallerstein's construction of the world systems theory finds rationale here. In his *World Systems Theory*, Wallerstein perceived the world system in terms of social systems with boundaries, structures and actors with rules of legitimation and coherence. Pointing to the world economy that had evolved in Europe in the 16th century and made possible by what he called a functional and geographically defined division of labour, Wallerstein identified three sites: what he called the technologically advanced and capital endowed core that exploited the rest, semi-periphery and under-developed, and exploited periphery. The periphery, where Africa is categorized in this model, was designed for extraction and even after colonialism, the legacy of extraction spawning conflicts is infrastructural design is enduring.

The Mackinder effects on land-locked states with changing demographic pressures like Rwanda, Burundi, and Uganda was telling. Without an alternative outlet to the sea, they were immediately tied to Kenya engendering the first level insecurity generating dependency. They were captive to Kenya's port and infrastructure inefficiency. However, like Kenya, given the prevailing state-centric lens within which they perceived reality, the notion to conceive these and the securitization of the sea as a common regional space was never considered as an option. They had to constantly grapple with tensions and dreams for alternatives.

Securitization

As the debate on whether to broaden, deepen or keep the norm rages, the Copenhagen School continues to capture the middle ground between the extremes of classical realists who argue for a strict state-centric approach and the neoliberals who call for a wide spectrum of actor-specific issues in security management.

With roots in epistemology and classical Schimittian understanding of the state and security politics[11], the normative implications of security discourse on reality has been a central concern. Combining these influences, the general concept of "security" is drawn from its constitution within national security discourse, which implies an emphasis on authority, the confronting—and construction—of threats and enemies, an ability to make decisions, and the adoption of emergency measures[12]. Security has a particular discursive and political force and is a concept that does something—securitize—rather than an objective (or subjective) condition. "Thus the exact definition and criteria of securitization is constituted by the intersubjective establishment of an existential threat with a saliency sufficient to have substantial political effects"[13].

As Buzan notes, security "frames the issue either as a special kind of politics or as above politics" and a spectrum can therefore be defined ranging public issues from the *nonpoliticized*—"the state does not deal with it and it is not in any other way made an issue of public debate and decision," through *politicized*—"the issue is part of public policy, requiring government decision and resource allocations or, more rarely, some other form of communal governance," to *securitization*—in which case an issue is no longer debated as a political question, but is dealt with at an accelerated pace and in ways that may violate normal legal and social rules[14].

These categories have a bearing on the notion of political will, inferring enlightenment, on what needs urgent attention, planning or toleration. It can be asserted here that the apparent lack of capacity within the Eastern Africa region to securitize the Indian Ocean before the piracy attacks was essentially a lack of political enlightenment on the strategic value of the waters.

Regional maritime security enlightenment is a requisite starting point to ensure the freedom of the seas, to facilitate freedom of navigation and commerce, to advance prosperity and freedom, and to protect the resources of the ocean. Since all states benefit from this collective security, all states must share in the responsibility for maintaining maritime security by countering the threats in this domain.

Regional Security Complex

A Regional Security Complex (RSC) is a concept introduced by Barry Buzan to the study of International Security referring to the set of units whose major processes of securitization, de-securitization or both are so interlinked that their security problems cannot reasonably be analyzed or resolved apart from one another[15]. The appreciation here is the idea that most political and military threats travel more easily over short distances than over long ones, with insecurity often associated with proximity. In Eastern Africa, comprising the sub-systems of The Horn of Africa and The Great Lakes Region, the formation of an RSC is mandated by the interaction of anarchy with geographical factors.

Rwanda and Uganda's task of nation-building and sovereignty crisis pushed the countries to the edge in the decades after independence. Others like Ethiopia and Sudan bifurcated, creating Eritrea and South Sudan respectively. Somalia's case, a classic case of state and social collapse, saw its mutilation into Somaliland, Puntland and numerous sections down south under no clear control between Mogadishu and Al-Shabaab. In the Great Lakes, Uganda, Rwanda and Angola allied against the Mobutu regime in D.R. Congo and its Sudanese allies. The second wave of intervention saw Rwanda and Uganda undermine the Kabila regime they helped to install, and its allies; Angola, Zimbabwe, Namibia. Eritrea and Ethiopia worked again with Rwanda and Uganda to aid the Sudanese People's Defence Force (SPLA) against Sudan. Kenya had to invade Somalia to impede Al-Shaabab's incursion into the coastal region. The complex interdependence among these makes the case for a regional response to their insecurity problem. There are states advantaged by water and energy reserves but are challenged by their lack of access to ocean-fronts such us Uganda and Ethiopia[16]. The converse is the case for littoral states, which are challenged by energy paucity despite their communication infrastructure such as Kenya and Djibouti. Given the apparent security-generating dependencies, these have been evolving into platforms of mutual insecurities.

The Evolution of the Indian Ocean's Global Strategic Value to the Region

The Geography

The Indian Ocean (IO) comprises approximately 20% of the Earth's water surface area. It is bounded on the north by Asia, on the west by Africa, on the east by Indochina and Australia; and on the south by Antarctica.

Access to the Indian Ocean is only available via seven critical chokepoints, including the Cape of Good Hope (South Africa), the Suez Canal (Egypt), Bab-el-Mandeb (Djibouti-Yemen), Strait of Hormuz (Iran-Oman), Strait of Malacca (Indonesia-Malaysia-Singapore), the Sunda Strait (Java-Sumatra) and the Lombok Strait (Indonesian islands of Bali and Lombok).

The waters of the IO are calmer than those of the Atlantic or Pacific, allowing maritime trade to develop much earlier than other areas of the world.

The Indian Ocean Region (IOR) is comprised of 33 countries, with two extra-regional states maintaining territory within the region. The 33 countries include (clockwise) Mauritius, Seychelles, Madagascar, Comoros, South Africa, Mozambique, Tanzania, Kenya, Somalia, Djibouti, Eritrea, Sudan, Egypt, Saudi Arabia, Yemen, Oman, United Arab Emirates, Qatar, Bahrain, Kuwait, Iraq, Iran, Pakistan, India, Maldives, Sri Lanka, Bangladesh, Burma (Myanmar), Thailand, Malaysia, Singapore, Indonesia and Australia. The two extra-regional countries maintaining territory within the IOR include France (primarily the overseas region of Réunion) and the UK (British Indian Ocean Territory consisting of the atolls of the Chagos archipelago, including Diego Garcia).

Historical Context

The IOR has been an historic international crossroads of commercial, intellectual and cultural exchange for millennia. The world's earliest civilizations developed near the Indian Ocean, in the Nile, Euphrates, Tigris and Indus river basins[17].

In 1487, Portuguese explorers established a new route to the Indian Ocean, around Africa and the Cape of Good Hope, the same route that Portuguese Vasco da Gama used when he sailed to India in the late 15th century[18]. Portugal dominated trade in the western Indian Ocean for a short period with its armed ships through conquest of critical ports. With the arrival of the other Europeans, the IOR gradually became a contestation ground for foreign imperial ambitions. Britain, France and Holland were the main powers seeking to control the waterways. Britain eventually prevailed when the expansion of the British Empire allowed it to control much of the surrounding landmass by 1815[19]. The development of the Suez Canal in 1869 provided a critical trade linkage between the states of the IOR and the West. After the end of World War II, no other state has unilaterally dominated the IOR. The United States, even at the height of its power, placed primacy of focus on the Pacific and Atlantic.

The IOR has always been a vital crossroads of commercial, intellectual and cultural exchange, and one of the world's most important bodies of water. The rise of United States domination after World War II never saw an immediate focus on the Indian Ocean, arguably due to distance and the focus on both the Atlantic and Pacific. The Cold War saw a quiet entry to key security choke points that had direct geopolitical implications, especially for energy and economic security. The Suez and the Arabian Gulf were such classic examples. Controlling them or at least denying the adversary their access was the logic behind their securitization and strategic planning.

After the Cold War and the effect of diminished security tensions with the Soviets, the Indian Ocean tides calmed briefly. All along, African states using its waters never considered mega securitization efforts. They were absorbed with domestic crises that left them too economically weak and politically strained to engage in such mega projects. There existed navies and regional formations to safeguard the waters but they were too weak in design, form and capacity to deter any aggression on the high seas.

It was after the sustained piracy incidences between 2005 and 2008 in the western IOR on the African SLOCs that global attention turned to the Indian Ocean.

Strategic Importance

There are many reasons for the Indian Ocean's strategic importance, but the most compelling is its centrality to world trade. The IO connects the Middle East, East Africa and East Asia with Europe and the Americas, and links the world with the oil-rich Arabian Gulf area, an especially crucial function for a world largely dependent on hydrocarbon energy. The economic rise of the Asia-Pacific has also turned the IOR into an economically vibrant area, and reinforces the ocean's vital role as a global trade crossroads.

Over 90% of international trade is carried by sea, and of that, over half traverses the Indian Ocean[20]. In monetary terms, over US$7 trillion in international trade crosses the IO every year on more than 23,000 ships, accounting for 50% of all container traffic and a full 70% of global oil and gas exports[21]. For this reason, its SLOCs are strategic to the global economy as a whole, especially for the proximally-placed Africa, Middle East and Asia for imports and exports. About 40% of the world's population is directly served by its waters. In addition, two of the world's rising powers (China and India) are highly dependent on to the Indian Ocean.

The Eastern Africa region is centrally placed between the West and East. Energy and finished goods are transported through these key SLOCs. Additionally, the Information Age has seen a fast intercontinental connection with the Western IOR being a critical seaboard for connecting the space between Asia with the Europe. It is this increased strategic value that stimulates the interest of all manner of actors.

Maritime Threats in the IOR

The increased strategic value of the IOR, real and imagined, by most global actors has brought with it intense threats. They can be classified broadly into two—the existing (traditional) and the new threats (non-traditional). The traditional have been amplified while the non-traditional are making inroads.

They overlap and it would be a task in vain to demarcate out each but for the purpose of clarity in developing policy choices, it would be fitting to tabulate where the main ones are located. These essentially are environmental degradation, piracy, uncontrolled exploitation of marine resources and maritime terrorism.

Environmental Degradation

Coastal zones, where the land meets the sea, are the most dynamic of the natural ecosystems. In the *2005 Millennium Ecosystem Assessment Report* the inland extent of the coastal ecosystem is defined as the line where land-based influences dominate up to a maximum of 100 km from the coastline or 50m elevation and with the 50m depth contour as the outward extent[22]. Since most of the population centres in the states bordering the Indian Ocean are situated in this coastal zone, changes in ecosystems in this zone, however minor, will have serious and potentially disastrous impacts on the population in general.

The Indian Ocean coastal region is a key area of vulnerability in the case of global warming. Several of its component sub-regions have regularly been identified as among the most vulnerable to climate change, now and in the future. All of the coastal areas in Asia and Africa are facing an increasing range of stresses and shocks, the scale of which now poses a threat to the resilience of both human and environmental coastal systems, and which are likely to be exacerbated by climate change. Corals, sea grass beds, mangroves and coastal wetlands are some key environmental regions that are being seriously affected[23].

The Inter-Governmental Panel on Climate Change Report of 2007 noted that the Indian Ocean, especially around the equator, will face higher temperature rises than average increases in other areas of the world. This phenomenon will bring about harsh climatic conditions including frequent storms, heavier rains and longer spells of droughts, impacting people living in countries around the Ocean.

Another concern here is marine pollution, defined as the introduction by humans, directly or indirectly, of substances or energy to the marine environment resulting in deleterious effects such as hazards to human health, hindrance to marine activities, impairment of the quality of seawater for various uses, and the reduction of amenities. Land-based marine pollution causes the biggest damage. Industrial and agricultural wastage, plastic particles, chemicals and municipal sewerage are entering the marine ecosystem through rainwater drains, rivers and are also wind-blown from the land to the sea. This has a dangerous impact on coral reefs, mangroves, aqua life, birds and food webs and in turn the fish stocks. Eighty per cent of the non-biological marine pollution comes from land-based activities. On-shore policies on environmental management will have a direct bearing on off-shore ecosystems.

Piracy

As noted above, piracy is traditional in the sense that it is *as old as the sea* but it can be argued here that the mutating nature of the current practice places it as a non-traditional form due to the sophisticated nature of its operations. In 2011, in the peak season of Somali Piracy off Eastern Africa, 237 incidences were reported. By comparison, throughout the rest of the world only forty incidents were reported[24].

After many failed attempts to contain the threat, even from the highest organs of the United Nations Security Council (UNSC), the incidence of piracy in Eastern Africa waters had declined to a low of 15 incidents in 2013. Only two vessels were actually hijacked and were released in a day[25]. This can be attributed to the heightened naval surveillance and technical preparedness, such as the use of hardened vessels but most importantly the stabilizing influence of Somalia's central government. This is classic Mackinder theory embodiment praxis—bringing onshore order to bear offshore—to the most overt threat the IOR faces.

Maritime Terrorism

Although the incidence of maritime terrorism has drastically reduced after the destruction of Sri Lanka's Liberation Tigers of Tamil Eelam (LTTE) in 2009, it cannot be taken for granted that maritime terrorism will not raise its ugly head again in the region. There is no doubt that the methodologies and tactics adopted by the LTTE to smuggle in arms from the high seas could be replicated by other terror organisations. Accordingly, the need is great for continuous cooperation among the states of the Indian Ocean littoral in particular, and the world community at large, to prevent a similar situation occurring elsewhere.

In particular, given the success of the Somali pirates with such poor and rudimentary organisational skills and equipment, it should always be kept in mind how difficult it would be to thwart a terrorist act of a more sophisticated and organised group who would not be looking for a simple ransom but aiming to disrupt world peace. And this threat looms large and real. The introduction of the International Port and Facility Security code and the Suppression of Unlawful Acts Convention and Protocols, however, have diminished this threat somewhat but it can never be completely taken out until the terrorist activities of groups like Al-Qaida in the countries around the Indian Ocean are eradicated.

Uncontrolled Exploitation of Marine Resources

Illegal, unreported and unregulated fishing (IUU) has become a major concern in the Indian Ocean[26]. For example, it has been estimated that 600 vessels are fishing illegally in Sri Lankan waters at any given time. A gradual reduction in fish stocks is increasingly evident in all traditional fishing grounds, mostly due to overfishing, environmental degradation and the use of destructive fishing methods. Fishermen who can afford to use more expensive and better vessels have started going far beyond their home bases and encroaching into economic zones of other countries and are also engaged in unregulated fishing on the high seas. Lack of exclusive economic zone enforcing machinery has allowed these illegal practices to flourish. Although it is the responsibility of individual states to govern their maritime domains, most of the countries in the region do not have the capacity or the resources to do that.

Global warming effects are likely to impact marine resources negatively. IUU is a major challenge in the Indian Ocean and will be aggravated further when fish stocks decrease gradually in the traditional fishing areas.

Responses to Contemporary Threats

Piracy off the Coast of Somalia

Somali piracy can be defined in a few figures: 23,000 ships of every nationality travel every year on the Indian Ocean; 30% of Europe's energy supply passes through the Gulf of Aden; Western naval anti-piracy operations cost two billion dollars per year; and the losses of merchant shipping because of Somali piracy adds up to 7 to 12 billion dollars per year. In January 2012, there were five ships and 125 hostages in pirate captivity. There have been 199 attacks in 2011, of which 23 were successful. 700 pirates have so far been arrested, but 90% have been released for lack of proof or of transfer possibilities for their trial to take place.

International Cooperative Frameworks and Agencies

Following the adoption of UN Security Council Resolutions 1816, 1838, 1846 and 1851 of 2008[27], there have many international agencies, mostly naval in composition, involved in fighting piracy off the coast of Somalia, the Gulf of Aden and the western Indian Ocean. Some of these agencies include the Combined Maritime Forces, which is an initiative of 25 states being commanded by the United States that conduct integrated and coordinated operations in the Gulf of Aden, the Gulf of Oman, the Arabian Sea, the Arabian Gulf, the Red Sea and parts of the Indian Ocean[28], EUNAVFOR Atalanta[29], North Atlantic Treaty Organization (NATO)[30], China, Russia and India. The political coordination of all of these operations is ensured through the Contact Group on Piracy off the Coast of Somalia (CGPCS), established on the 14th January 2009[31]. It is an *ad hoc* international forum where the states and organizations that are fighting piracy off the coast of Somalia and the Gulf of Aden can meet and exchange ideas and information[32].

The CGCPS has also established an International Trust Fund, managed by the United Nations Office on Drug and Crime (UNODC), which is meant to support all counter-piracy efforts in the Horn of Africa. The targeted areas of support have been documented by Working Group 1 and include judicial capacity building, increasing surveillance capabilities and the training of law enforcement officials[33].

After numerous unsuccessful attempts to contain the threat on the Eastern Africa coast, the incidence of piracy in the Eastern Africa waters has declined to a low of 15 attacks in 2013. Only two vessels were actually hijacked and were released in a day[34]. This is heavily credited to the stabilizing influence of Somalia's central government.

The question that interests most analysts is whether it will be possible for Indian Ocean States to cooperate and join efforts to ensure security in the Indian Ocean.

The Indian Ocean and Security Cooperation

There are a number of well-defined and distinct sub-regions in the wider IOR, each having their own expression in relevant regional forums, limiting common understanding or coordination on securing what links them. Their individual capacities do not equate to a collectivity stronger than their sub-regions. This 'state of nature' character of the IOR has denied it the chance to develop organically sustaining security frameworks that have the political muscle and economic capital to secure the waters.

The Indian Ocean region has also been a theatre of strong strategic competition. During the Cold War, it lay in the middle of two superpowers, each vying for a greater say in its affairs. United States military bases, French Islands, Chinese and Russian navy assistance to IOR states are examples of the interest other 'non-regional' states have in securing the waters in line with their national interests.

As calls for local ownership of the securitization agenda increased, India has established the Indian Ocean Naval Symposium (IONS), a forum through which chiefs of all navies of all Indian Ocean bordering states can, through regular meetings, promote the adoption of joint maritime security mechanisms.

The Indian Ocean Rim Association (IORA) called for an enhanced and mutualized maritime cooperation with a view to bringing maritime security in the region under a broad regional umbrella. It reinforces the capacity of all states in the region to take up contemporary challenges and seeks to promote transnational maritime security through interoperability, joint strategies, procedures and organization and logistics assets.

Western Indian Ocean Regional Cooperative Frameworks

East African states have responded by initiating various cooperative frameworks and agencies to combat piracy in the Western Indian Ocean region.

(a) The Djibouti Code of Conduct

The Djibouti Code of Conduct on Piracy, which was signed on 29th January 2009, is a regional agreement that provides a framework for cooperation among the twenty-one signatory states in combating piracy off the coast of Somalia and in the Gulf of Aden[35]. It calls on the signatory states to establish national focal points for exchange and coordination of information. It established three information centres in Mombasa, Dar-es-Salaam and Sanaa[36]. It also established a training centre in Djibouti. The purpose of these centres is to have a synchronized and concerted approach to the fight against piracy. The signatory states are called upon to encourage ships that are entitled to fly their flags to report any incidents of piracy or armed robbery. Furthermore, the signatory states are called upon to embark on a comprehensive review of local legislation to provide for an effective legal framework to fight piracy[37].

The major weakness with this cooperative framework is that it is merely a *code of conduct* and not a binding agreement or treaty as it was to come into force within two years after adoption and after the establishment of national focal points and after further consultations by the state signatories.

(b) The Maritime Rescue and Co-ordination Centres (MRCC)

The Maritime Rescue and Co-ordination Centres (MRCC) are also playing a critical role in maintaining maritime security[38]. The MRCCs were established under the provisions of the International Convention on Maritime Search and Rescue of 1979 (the SAR Convention). Following the adoption of the SAR Convention, the IMO's Maritime Safety Committee divided the world's oceans into 13 rescue regions for which they are responsible. In 2000, an IMO Conference in Florence, Italy, adopted a resolution inviting African states to establish five sub-regional rescue coordination centres and 26 sub-centres around their Atlantic and Indian Ocean coasts[39]. These centres play a critical role in collecting, collating and disseminating information about maritime security including piracy.

(c) Southern African Development Community (SADC) Anti-Piracy Strategy

Following an increase in cases of piracy in the Western Indian Ocean, a SADC regional anti-piracy strategy was adopted on 25th July 2011 following an extraordinary meeting of SADC defence Ministers and a task force formed comprising of navy commanders from Tanzania, Mozambique and South Africa[40]. The task force is expected to establish a zonal centre in South Africa to coordinate information and intelligence on piracy[41].

(d) The Eastern and Southern Africa - Indian Ocean (ESA-IO) Regional Strategy and Regional Plan of Action

In October 2010, the Eastern and Southern African-Indian Ocean (ESA-IO) states adopted the ESA-IO Regional Strategy (RS) and rolling Regional Plan of Action (RPA) at the second Regional Ministerial Meeting on Piracy and Maritime Security in the ESA-IO Region held in Mauritius[42]. The RS provides for a regional framework to prevent and combat piracy, and promote maritime security through a three-pillar approach: (i) The development and implementation of a Somalia Inland Action Plan to counter and prevent piracy; (ii) Encouraging states in the region to prosecute pirates with the financial and technical support of the international community; (iii) Strengthening regional state capacities to secure their maritime zone.

The RPA underpins the Regional Strategy that encompasses the exchange of information, cooperation, joint action, and capacity building as crosscutting principles. The ESA-IO configuration is the Regional Coordination Mechanism and The Inter-Regional Coordination Committee (IRCC) that consists of COMESA, EAC, IGAD, IOC, SADC, and EU serves as the Secretariat of this Regional Coordination platform.

While the implementation of all of the pillars of this approach is crucial in securing the waters, the first pillar is worthy of note since it seeks to address the human and economic root causes of piracy. The Intergovernmental Authority on Development (IGAD) was tasked with developing the first pillar. On 27th January 2012, the IGAD Assembly of Heads of State and Governments endorsed the IGAD Somalia Inland Strategy and Action Plan to Prevent and Counter Piracy during its 20th extraordinary summit held in Addis Ababa, Ethiopia[43].

The strategy makes fifteen primary general solutions to the problem of piracy. The first solution is to help and facilitate Somalis to solve their problems in their own way in order to foster peace, security, the rule of law and governance[44]. Other solutions include preventing illegal fishing and the dumping of toxic waste in Somali waters[45], delimiting and protecting the Somali EEZ by international agencies such as the IMO, similar to air space protection by the ICAO[46].

The strength of the IGAD proposed solutions is that they take into account the human and economic root causes of piracy. They acknowledge that unless the human and economic root causes of piracy (such as the political and security situation in Somalia, IUU fishing and the dumping of toxic in Somalia's territorial waters and EEZ) are resolved, measures aimed at combating piracy off the coast of Somalia cannot succeed.

Challenges to the Cooperative Frameworks and Agencies

Most of the naval agencies and regional cooperative frameworks discussed above operating in the Western Indian Ocean focus more on maritime security strategies aimed at countering piracy at sea (military) and the prosecution of pirates (legal process). These strategies, although laudable, are heavily focused on a constabulary approach in dealing with the scourge of piracy. They do not address the human and economic factors in Somalia that are the root causes of piracy. It should also be noted that the geographical scope of piratical attacks has also widened to waters hitherto unaffected by piracy and outside the remit of the international navies patrolling the waters off the Somali coast. Pirates are now reportedly operating on the high seas even at distances of up to 1,750 nautical miles[47]. It is also reported that pirates are now moving further south towards unprotected parts of the Indian Ocean[48] and also further eastwards towards the Maldives and India[49]. This has resulted in the stretching of the existing navies.

Many attacks have occurred on the high seas and the pirates quickly retreat to Somalia's territorial waters and into the mainland to avoid arrest. The naval forces are forced to pursue the pirates from the high seas into Somalia's territorial waters, thus reversing the concept of hot pursuit[50]. From the foregoing, the major challenges lie in the conceptualization of maritime security and the enforcing mechanisms to achieve regional capacity.

Gaps in Regional Approaches

The Eastern Africa Standby Force (EASF)

The Eastern Africa Standby Force (EASF) is one of five regional military brigades established in May 2003. It finds its philosophical founding in the concept of a 'pan-African army' dating back to the 1960s by Kwame Nkrumah. He had proposed the establishment of the 'common defense system with African High Command'[51].

During its launch in 2003, it was envisioned that the ASF would be ready to conduct all types of missions by 2010[52]. However, the date had been postponed due to the relatively slow progress in some regions and fields of cooperation. According to Roadmap III for the Operationalization of the African Standby Force, the ASF will achieve Full Operational Capability by 2015[53].

Structurally, the EASF lacks a Regional Economic Community covering all 14 countries of the region. In 2004, the Intergovernmental Authority on Development (IGAD) assumed the coordination role in the establishment of the Eastern Africa Standby Brigade (EASBRIG). As IGAD consisted of only seven states (Djibouti, Eritrea, Ethiopia, Kenya, Somalia, Sudan and Uganda), non-IGAD countries of the region protested against this move. As a result, in 2007, the EASBRICOM (EASBRIG Coordination Mechanism)—a separate regional coordination mechanism—has been established. This structure is located in Nairobi, Kenya, as is the Planning Element (PLANELM) and Standby Force Headquarters. The Logistic Base (LOGBASE) and Brigade Headquarters are both located in Addis Ababa, Ethiopia[54]. There are simmering tensions between the preference for IGAD over EASF between Ethiopia and Kenya owing to the coordination opportunity. Ethiopia is in favour of IGAD while Kenya is aligned more with EASF.

Second, the EASF has a relatively weak legal basis: two most important documents are the Policy Framework for the Establishment of EASBRIG (adopted in 2004) and the Memorandum of Understanding on the Establishment of the Eastern Africa Standby Brigade (signed in 2005). As the legal force of these documents is relatively low, the EASF depends largely on the changing political will of the states involved. The signing out of an RM is less problematic and has minor consequences when compared to the suspension or limitation of membership in an REC. Out of 14 members of the Eastern Region, only 10 states take an active part in the EASF. These are Burundi, Comoros, Djibouti, Ethiopia, Kenya, Rwanda, Seychelles, Somalia, Sudan and Uganda. Eritrea—the regional *enfant terrible*—has suspended its engagement in the process due to hostile relations with some of the other countries, most notably Ethiopia. At the same time, Tanzania, Madagascar and Mauritius have chosen to join the Southern region[55].

The third obstacle, in many aspects connected with previous two, has been political tension among regional states. The history of (and current) international relations in Africa is marked by numerous conflicts, crises, changing alliances and support of armed opposition groups in neighbouring countries. Since the concept of ASF (as a multinational armed forces that could be used in any country, sometimes against the national interest of a troop contributor) touches the very core of sovereignty and national security, such an atmosphere 'successfully' limits the commitment of the governments.

The lack of resources and weak state twin-problem could be pointed out as the fourth challenge. This hindrance should be understood broadly, not only as a scarcity of funds, by also as a lack of military, police and civilian experts that could contribute to the project of the EASF. It creates a problem of dependence on external support, undermines local ownership of the Force and as a result calls into question the role of the ASF as an "African solution to African problems".

A very interesting development within the EASF, both in the context of its possible future activities, as well as in the light of possible changes in the main six scenarios of the ASF, is the establishment of a Maritime Cell within the Military Planning Element[56]. It seems that it is a reaction to the problem of piracy, as well as to the broader issue of the growing importance of maritime transport. It is worth mentioning that the construction work in Lamu, northern Kenya, is underway. The port, will serve Kenya, Ethiopia, Uganda and South Sudan. As a result, the ability to react to threats to maritime security in the waters surrounding East Africa will become a crucial one for the countries of the region.

The decision to create the African Capacity for Immediate Response to Crises (ACIRC) at the African Union summit in Addis Ababa in May 2013 as 'a transitional stop-gap measure pending the full formation of the planed Standby Force' is an interesting one...[57] The ACIRC would be a rapid response force 'formed from voluntary contributions of troops, equipment and funds by member states currently in a position to provide these'[58]. This decision could be seen as a part of a larger and deeper conceptual confusion concerning the ASF project.

This shows how limited the EASF is in the conceptualization of maritime security especially because primarily the standby force was designed to respond to unconstitutional practices in African Countries as a form of responsible intervention.

The Intergovernmental Authority on Development (IGAD)

The Intergovernmental Authority on Development (IGAD) is one of the African Union (AU) recognized Regional Economic Communities (RECs), a building block for the African Economic Community (AEC). Established in 1986 as the Intergovernmental Authority on Drought and Development (IGADD), it was transformed into IGAD in 1996 with an expanded mandate that included peace and security as well as economic cooperation and integration. The Organization has seven member states, namely Djibouti, Eritrea, Ethiopia, Kenya, Somalia, Sudan and Uganda. The expanded mandate of the Organization brought into its focus issues of peace and security, with a full-fledged Division created for this purpose at the Secretariat.

However, considering that IGAD's strategic thrust involves collaborating with institutions serving the member states in this region in the peace support operations involving the deployment of military hardware and military personnel, (in particular EASBRIG), IGAD's relationship with the Security Council will be limited to peacemaking and preventive diplomacy areas. IGAD's involvement in peacekeeping or peace enforcement, aside from maritime security, is residual and collaborative with EASBRIG, under a collaborative instrument (such as an MOU) and framework to be developed between the two organizations.

On maritime security, several meetings have been held through the UN International Maritime Organization geared towards enhancing maritime security. The first was held in Sana'a April 2005, Muscat Oman in January 2006 and in Dar-es-Salaam in January 2008. This was followed by the Djibouti meeting between 26-29th January 2009. The Djibouti meeting saw the adoption of a Code of Conduct to facilitate efforts against piracy and armed robbery against ships. It is supposed to anchor closer coordination and cooperation, it envisages the setting up of national focal points for piracy and armed robberies against ships and the sharing of information relating to incidents as reported in Article 8 & 9 of the draft Code of Conduct.

The operationalization of the Code of Conduct allows IGAD states to mount shared operations such as patrol ships and other actions by ship riders. It is therefore imperative that several actions are considered such as operationalizing maritime corridors to enhance bilateral cooperation among IGAD states.

Again, as observed in the EASF, regional frameworks lack the conceptual primacy on maritime security. They are loosely held together by the imagined idea of cooperation and narrowly on piracy. These gaps and silences on maritime threats indicate where the focus should be applied and possibly coordinated around a single body. Duplicity among the various frameworks is an unnecessary luxury.

Regional Maritime Security Policy Recommendations

The ability to achieve maritime security is contingent upon a layered security system that integrates the capabilities of governments and commercial interests throughout the world. The public and private sectors acting in concert can prevent terrorist attacks and criminal acts only by using diverse and complementary measures, rather than relying upon a single point solution.

This layered security is not static, but deters attack by continually evolving through calculated improvements that introduce uncertainty into the adversary's deliberate planning process and efforts to conduct surveillance or reconnaissance. The overall strategy in enhancing maritime security should be seen here as broad and entailing the entire gamut of state-building processes. This should consist of four levels.

The first level is about building a region-centric developmental infrastructure and entails operationalizing the maritime corridors and their respective security-based triangles of growth. The second level is tied up with the first but has more to do with internal institutional capacities and the enhancement of regional bodies as the coordinating mechanism of regional initiatives for enhancing maritime security.

The third level has more to do with the legal frameworks for mediating the processes of enhancing maritime security. The cooperative frameworks need tightening to increase commitment, power and to facilitate laws for states in ensuring ease of prosecuting pirates. The fourth level brings into the fore community participation in maritime security enhancement. The population is the first line of defence in the securitization of this space.

Summary and Conclusions

The Indian Ocean (IO) geostrategic value lies in its centrality to key nodes of global significance. The IO connects the Middle East, East Africa and East Asia with Europe and the Americas. The increased strategic value of the IOR, real and imagined, by most global actors has brought with it intense threats, especially environmental degradation, piracy, uncontrolled exploitation of marine resources and maritime terrorism.

Responses to these threats have been multifaceted, especially after the Somalia piracy scourge attracted global attention. Local ownership of the securitization agenda has seen the establishment of the Indian Ocean Naval Symposium (IONS) and the Indian Ocean Rim Association (IORA) over time. Others include The Djibouti Code of Conduct, The Maritime Rescue and Co-ordination Centres (MRCC), Southern African Development Community (SADC) Anti-Piracy Strategy, The Eastern and Southern Africa - Indian Ocean (ESA-IO) Regional Strategy and Regional Plan of Action.

As observed both in the EASF and IGAD, regional frameworks lack the conceptual primacy on maritime security. They are loosely held together by the imagined idea of cooperation and narrowly on piracy. These gaps and silences on maritime threats indicate where the focus should be applied and possibly coordinated around one single body. Duplicity among the many frameworks is an unnecessary luxury. The overall strategy in enhancing maritime security should be seen here as broad and entailing the entire enterprise of the state-building processes. This should consist of four levels as indicated above.

Notes

1. Carl von Clausewitz, *On War*, ed. and trans. Michael Howard and Peter Paret (Princeton, N.J.: Princeton Univ. Press, 1989), p. 578.
2. See Mahan Alfred T, *The Influence Of Sea Power on History 1600-1783*, Boston, MA: Little Brown and Company.
3. James Hackett (ed.), *The Military Balance 2009*, London: International Institute for Strategic Studies, 2009, 282–283.

4. John B. Hattendorf, "The Uses of Maritime History in and for the Navy," *Naval War College Review* 56, no. 2 (Spring 2003), p. 20.
5. Ibid. p. 19.
6. P.A. Crowel: Alfred Thayer Mahan "the naval historian" in Paret eds *Makers of modern strategy: form Machiavelli to the nuclear age* Princeton NJ 1986 Pg 450
7. Hall, R *Empires of Monsoon*. Harper Collins, London, 1999. Pg 7
8. Kiwanuka, M., *History of Buganda: From the Foundation of the Kingdom to 1900*. Africana Publishing Company, 1972. Pg 160.
9. Mackinder, H., *Democratic Ideals and Reality: A Study in the Politics of Reconstruction*. Faber & Faber Limited, 2011. Pg 27.
10. Ibid.
11. Buzan B. et al., *Security: A New Framework of Analysis*. Lynne Reinner Publishers, 1998, Pg 23.
12. Lene Hansen, Nissenbaum. *International Studies Quarterly* (2009) 53, 1155–1175.
13. Buzan B. et al., *Security: A New Framework of Analysis*. Lynne Reinner Publishers, 1998, Pg 23
14. Ibid.
15. Buzan B: *People, States and Fear: An Agenda For International Security Studies in The Post Cold War Era,* Second Edition, Pearson Longmans New York 1991 Chapter 8.
16. U.S GPO, *Ethiopia and Eritrea: Promoting Stability, Democracy and Human Rights*. New York. 2005. Pg 62.
17. Trigger, B., *Understanding Early Civilizations*. Cambridge University Press, 2003. Pg 345
18. Koestler-Grack, R and Wiliam H., *Vasco da Gama and the Sea Route to India*. Infobase Publishing, 2009, pg 127.
19. Kearny, M., *The Indian Ocean in World History*. Routledge, 2004, pg 98.
20. IMO, *International Shipping Facts and Figures*. Maritime Knowledge Center, 2012.
21. Ibid.
22. Hassan, R. Scholes, R. and Ash N. (eds) (2005) *Millennium Ecosystem Assessment, Ecosystems and Human Well-Being: Current State and Trends*. Washington, DC: Island Press, p. 516.
23. Pallewela, N and Henry L (2010): *Impact of climate change on coastal ecosystems in the Indian Ocean*. Stimson Centre.
24. 2013 Maritime Piracy, International Maritime Bureau, 2014.
25. Ibid.
26. Zahran M., 600 Vessels fishing illegally in SL at any given time. Sunday Times, 19th Feb, p.4.
27. Available at http://www.un.org/News/Press/docs/2011/sc10454.doc.htm last accessed on 14th February 2012.
28. See Report of the Secretary-General pursuant to Security Council resolution 1950 (2010), 25th October 2011 Available at http://www.un.org/News/Press/docs/2011/sc10454.doc.htm (last accessed on 14th February 2012) at page 8.
29. EUNAVFOR ATALANTA is a military mission comprising 8 European Union

member states; Italy, Netherlands, Germany, France, Spain, Belgium, Luxemburg and Greece.

30. On March 24 2009, NATO launched a naval mission dubbed Operation Allied Protector to counter piracy off the coast of Somalia. For more information see http://www.manw.nato.int/pdf/Press Releases 2010/Jan - May 2010/SNMG2 2010 03_18mar10.pdf (Last accessed on 29th March 2010).
31. More than 30 states were represented together with regional organizations and intergovernmental during its establishment.
32. As at October 2011, the Contact Group had over 66 participants, comprised of Member States and international, regional and non-governmental organizations.
33. The targets of the fund have not been achieved; as of March 2010, only two regional states, Kenya and Seychelles, were being provided with the support. Even within the states getting the support there have been numerous reports that the support was too way little to achieve its intended purposes; this culminated in Kenya rejecting to undertake prosecutions of suspected pirates in March 2010, As at 4th October 2011, the Trust Fund had received a total of about $8.3 million since its establishment .
34. 2013 Maritime Piracy, International Maritime Bureau, 2014.
35. Currently 18 countries out of the 21 eligible countries from the Western Indian Ocean, Gulf of Aden and Red Sea areas have signed the agreement. These countries are Djibouti, Ethiopia, Kenya, Madagascar, Maldives, Seychelles, Somalia, the United Republic of Tanzania and Yemen, Comoros, Egypt, Eritrea, Jordan, Mauritius, Oman, Saudi Arabia, Sudan and the United Arab Emirates. The agreement is not legally binding though the state parties are working with a view to making it legally binding within two years of its effective date (article 13) (for its effective date see article 16) ; It can be accessed on http://www.imo.org/OurWork/Security/PIU/Pages/DCoC.aspx (Last accessed on 14th February 2012).
36. Article 8 of the Djibouti Code.
37. Article 11 of the Djibouti Code; Pursuant to this obligation Kenya enacted the Merchant Shipping Act in 2009 which domesticates the relevant international conventions touching on maritime security. The conventions include UNCLOS, the Convention for the Suppression of Unlawful Acts against the safety of Maritime Navigation of 1988 (the SUA Convention), the International Convention for the Safety of Life at Sea, 1974 (SOLAS) and its protocols of 1978 and 1988 as well as the International Ship and Port Facility Security Code (ISPS Code) Available at http://www.kenyalaw.org/klr/index.php
38. The MRCC were initially designed to assist in rescue operations in case of accidents but due to the heightened threat from piracy the IMO adopted a resolution that would facilitate the use of the MRCC's for purposes of fostering security. The Maritime Safety Committee, at its seventy-second session approved a Directive which allows Governments to grant their MRCCs powers to respond to acts of violence against ships. In this way, MRCCs are incorporated in the mechanisms that Governments have to set up to deal with acts of violence against ships, which may occur suddenly and anywhere, See MSC/Circ.1073 10 June 2003, Directives for Maritime Rescue Co-Ordination Centres (MRCCS) on Acts of Violence against Ships

39. There are currently 5 sub-regional centres following the establishment of the Morocco MRCC near Rabat on 3rd March 2011, other sub regional centres are in Mombasa, Kenya, in 2006; in Cape Town, South Africa, in 2007; in Lagos, Nigeria, in 2008; and in Monrovia, Liberia, in 2009 thus Completing search and rescue cover around Africa's coast, see story on http://www.imo.org/MediaCentre/PressBriefings/Pages/09-morocco-MRCC-agreement.aspx (last accessed on 14th February 2012)
40. In December 2010 A Mozambican registered vessel was hijacked in waters off the southern parts of Africa—and a Liberian registered merchant vessel was hijacked in January 2011 See story Region Steps Up Fight Against Piracy 24 Jan 2012 | Madagascar | Source : All Africa News: Madagascar available athttp://allafrica.com/stories/201201240820.html (Last accessed on 14th February 2012)
41. Ibid.
42. For a full text of the resolution see http://www.consilium.europa.eu/uedocs/cms_Data/docs/pressdata/EN/foraff/116942.pdf
43. IGAD Somali Inland strategy and plan of action to prevent and counter piracy 2011-2015
44. Ibid. at page 59.
45. Ibid.
46. Ibid.
47. Ibid.
48. Supra note 23.
49. Supra note 1 at page 8; also See Congressional Research Services Report for Congress on Piracy off the Horn of Africa, April 27, 2011 at page 1 available at.http://fpc.state.gov/documents/organization/162745.pdf
50. Article 111 of LOSC
51. Nkurumah, K., *Africa Must Unite*, Heinemann, London, 1963, pg 219.
52. Cilliers, J., The African Standby Force: An Update on Progress. 2008, pg 14
53. Ibid.
54. Ibid.
55. P.V. Rao, 'Indian Ocean maritime security cooperation: the employment of navies and other maritime forces', *Proceedings*, Indian Ocean Maritime Security Symposium, 47–48.
56. Ibid.
57. African Union, Decisions, Declarations and Resolution, May 2013, Addis Ababa.
58. Ibid.

REFERENCES

Aboagye, F. (2012), *A Stitch in Time Would Have Saved Nine. Operationalising the African Standby Force*, Institute for Security Studies Policy Brief no 34. Available at: http://www.issafrica.org/uploads/ASFPolBrief.pdf [Accessed: 9 Feb 2014].

African Union (2000), *The Constitutive Act of the African Union*, adopted by the Thirty-Sixth Ordinary Session of the Assembly of Heads of State and Government 11 July 2000, Lome, Togo.

African Union (2002), *The Protocol Relating to the Establishment of the Peace and*

Security Council of the African Union, adopted by the 1st Ordinary Session of the Assembly of the African Union, Durban, 9 July 2002.

African Union (2003), *Policy Framework for The Establishment of the African Standby Force and the Military Staff Committee*, adopted by the Third Meeting of African Chiefs of Defence Staff, 16-16 May 2003, Addis Ababa, Ethiopia.

African Union (2012), *Roadmap III for the Operationalization of the African Standby, Force (Draft)*, 2011-2015, Addis Ababa: AU, February 2012.

AMISOM Frequently Asked Questions [Online]. Available at: http://amisom- ?au.org/about/frequently-asked-questions/ [Accessed: 8 Feb 2014].

Bachmann, O. (2011), 'The African Standby Force: External Support to an 'African Solution to African Problems'?', *Institute of Development Studies Research Report 67*, Available at: http://www.ids.ac.uk/files/dmfile/Rr67web.pdf [Accessed: 8 Feb 2014].

Bouhuys, J. (2011), *The Eastern Africa Standby Force. Enhancing Peace and Security in the Eastern Africa Region* [Online]. Available at: http://www.vovklict.nl/intercom/2011/2/27.pdf [Accessed: 9 Feb 2014].

Buzan, B. and Weaver, O. (2003), *Regions and Powers: The Structure of International Security*. Cambridge: Cambridge University Press.

Cilliers, J. (2008), *The African Standby Force. An update on progress*. Institute for Security Studies Paper 160. Available at: http://dspace.cigilibrary.org/jspui/bitstream/123456789/30855/1/PAPER160.pdf [Accessed: 9 Feb 2014].

Cilliers, J. and Potgieter J. (2010), 'The African Standby Force', In: Engel, U. and Porto, J.G. eds. *Africa's New Peace and Security Architecture: Promoting Norms and Institutionalizing Solutions*, Farnham: Ashgate Publishing Group.

Franke, B. (2010), 'Steady but Uneven Progress: The Operationalization of the African Standby Force', In: Besada, H. eds. *Crafting an African Peace and Security Architecture. Addressing Regional Peace and Conflict in the 21st Century*. Farnham: Ashgate Publishing Group.

Jobson, E. (2012), 'Mock military operation in Ethiopia simulates all too real African Conflict', *The Guardian* [Online] 23 November 2012. Available at: http://www.guardian.co.uk/global-development/2012/nov/23/mock-military-ethiopia-african-conflict [Accessed 8 Feb 2014].

Kasumba, Y., Debrah, Ch. (2010), 'An Overview of the African Standby Force (ASF)', In: de Coning, C. and Kasumba, Y. eds. *The Civilian Dimension of the African Standby Force*. Mount Edgecombe: AU & ACCORD.

Maasho, A. (2013), 'African leaders create emergency military force' [Online]. Available at: http://www.reuters.com/article/2013/05/27/us-africa-force-idUSBRE94Q08R20130527 [Accessed: 8 Feb 2014].

Metaferia, G. (2009), *Ethiopia and the United States: History, Diplomacy, and Analysis*, New York: Algora Publishing.

Musili, P. (2008), 'Joining The Dots: Lack Of Good Order At Sea In The Indian Ocean Region And Challenges Facing Landlocked States Off The East Coast Of Africa'.

Nkrumah, K. (1963), 'The People of Africa Are Crying For Unity'. Speech delivered on the meeting of African heads of state and government, Addis Ababa, 24 May 1963. Available at: http://www.newafricanmagazine.com/special-reports/other-reports/10- years-of-the-au/kwame-nkrumah-the-people-of-africa-are-crying-for-unity [Accessed: 8 Feb 2014].

South Sudan: Kenya, South Sudan Move to Fast-Track Lapsset Project. Capital FM 24 May 2013 [Online]. Available at: http://www.capitalfm.co.ke/business/2013/05/kenya- south-sudan-move-to-fast-track-lapsset-project/ [Accessed: 8 Feb 2014]. The Failed States Index 2012, An Eight Annual Collaboration Between Foreign Policy and Fund For Peace [Online]. Available at: http://www.foreignpolicy.com/failed_states_index_2012_interactive [Accessed: 8 Feb 2014].

Chapter 14

A Virtual Open University for the Real Transformation of Regional Cooperation and Trade: Lessons Learned from the Pan-African E-Network Project

K.S. Sukon

ABSTRACT

One of the major barriers to the socio-economic transformation of states remains the shortage of skills. The unavailability of a sufficient number of people with the required competencies hamstrings local businesses in innovating, adopting technology for state-of-the-art manufacturing practices, and harnessing maritime trade. Education has a strong influence on comparative advantage in international trade. This chapter aims at identifying the key ingredients for the setting up of a virtual open university for the countries of the Indian Ocean Region after an analysis of the Pan-African e-Network (PAeN) Project. The PAeN Project, which is a perfect example of south-south collaboration between India and African countries, aims at providing a universal platform for distance learning where Indian Universities can provide courses to students through video-conferencing, with live and interactive lectures transmitted from India to learning centres in Africa. No less than 47 of the African Member States were benefitting from this project worth US$125 million and funded entirely by the Indian Government. The lessons learned are useful in the setting up of an Indian Ocean Rim Virtual Open University (IORVOU) aimed at supporting countries to transform regional cooperation and trade.

Key words: Virtual Open University, educational skills, Pan-African e-Network, distance learning, regional cooperation

Introduction

Over the last decade, South-South trade, which is the main driving force in the promotion of regional integration and economic growth, has witnessed an accelerated growth as evidenced by the increase in Africa's exports to Asia (Soontiens 2002; WTO 2003; OECD 2006; Athukorala and Nasir 2012). South-South trade has increased from 11.2 per cent in 2000-1 to 20.2 per cent in 2009-10 (Athukorala and Nasir 2012). In this context, improving the competitiveness of every state remains a priority, as this is one of the key ingredients to further enhance regional trade, cooperation and investment. Any lack of required skills will clearly form a stumbling block for countries wishing to move to higher levels of development. For instance, without appropriate knowledge and technological capabilities, countries of the Indian Ocean will be unable to harness the potential of business and trade that the Ocean offers. Only a competent human resource base can boost innovation and enable the production of high value, branded and a more diversified range of products and services required by the international market. It can also guarantee stable and qualified exports. Moreover, it can play a pivotal role in making the optimum use of the positive spillover effects that investment from developed states is having in the developing countries (Lu and Li 2010). Undoubtedly, without an effective education and training system, a firm human resource base cannot be established. This chapter aims at identifying the key ingredients for the setting up of a virtual open university for the countries of the Indian Ocean after an analysis of the Pan-African E-Network Project. Based on the lessons learned, an Indian Ocean Rim Virtual Open University (IORVOU) can be set up in order to support countries to transform regional cooperation and trade.

Pan-African E-Network Project

The Pan-African e-Network[1] (PAeN) is the brainchild of former Indian President, Honourable Dr. A.P.J. Kalam, who, during the inaugural session of the Pan-African Parliament held in Johannesburg on 16th September 2004, proposed in his talk a programme to connect all 53 states of the African Union by a Satellite and Fibre Optic Network that would provide effective communication and connectivity among the various states. The network aims at connecting the 53 Pan-African countries and their heads of state primarily in order to provide Tele-medicine, Tele-education, Internet and Voice-Over IP (VOIP) services. It is scalable and supports e-governance, e-commerce, infotainment, resource mapping and meteorological services. The European Institute of Creative Strategies and Innovation awarded the Hermes Prize for Innovation 2010 to PAeN.

The Tele-education and Tele-medicine project was piloted in Ethiopia[2] in 2006/2007 for a total cost of US$2.12 million. After the successful completion of the pilot project, the Union Cabinet of India on 5th July 2007 approved the PAeN project to a tune of US$125 million, which covers the cost of supply, installation, testing and commissioning of hardware and software, end-to-end connectivity, satellite bandwidth, operations and management support, as well as providing tele-education (TE) and tele-medicine (TM) services to 53 African countries. During the pilot project, around 35 students from Addis Ababa University and Haramaya University enrolled in an MBA course from Indira Gandhi National Open University (IGNOU) through tele-education, whereas Black Lion Hospital of Addis Ababa and Nekempte Hospital in Ethiopia received on-line medical consultations from medical specialists of CARE Hospital, Hyderabad.

Tele-Education (TE)

The Tele-education project provides a universal platform for distance learning with a synchronized multimedia delivery on a number of platforms to the remote end through VSAT, Broadband and Internet coupled with collaborative tools, return video and audio, e-learning and campus management system, integrated digital library and content management system as an integrated package under the educational portal. The educational portal, comprising the above-mentioned modules installed at the University centre and a centralized management system, is provided for scheduling, organizing and managing the Tele-education system in coordination with various universities in Africa and India. Through the VSAT-based linkage, African students have access to seven Indian universities including the Indian Institute of Science, Bangalore; the Indira Gandhi National Open University (IGNOU), New Delhi; Amity University, Noida; Indian Institute of Technology, Kanpur; Birla Institute of Technology and Science, Pilani and the Universities of Delhi and Chennai.

How Does it Work?[3]

The lecturer sits in a studio that has been set up within its university compound in India. Instead of giving lectures in front of a group of students sitting in the same room, s/he gives the lectures in front of a camera. The lectures are then transmitted live and simultaneously to all registered sites or virtual classes in Africa. Webcams and voice-over protocol software enable lecturers and students to see and hear each other. Students sitting thousands of kilometres away from the tutor can interact in real time with tutors in India, ask questions and seek any clarification as they would have been able to do in a traditional classroom. Just like a typical classroom scene, a Professor will deliver a lecture and the students might raise their hand to ask questions. However, here the teacher will be in India, while the students will be in Africa. Provisions have been made to download recorded versions of lectures for those who could not attend the live sessions. Assignments can be uploaded on the Pan-African e-Network portal. All courses are examinable.

The Tele-education set up, apart from establishing the communication infrastructure, also includes setting up the five Tele-education studios with post-production setup, non-linear editing facilities at each of the universities and the appropriate data centres for proving the services, including the initial storage, backup facility and one centralized HUB. In addition, a Data centre and Control station, including a portal comprising the universal Tele-education delivery system software which incorporates the e-learning, content management and digital library solutions for each university, are offered as an integrated package. This allows teachers to interact with the selected students in a sequence; they can also collaborate simultaneously with all of the students using the collaborative tools. IP links provide audio, video and data connectivity to the university studio and enable the students to have live interaction. The network has the flexibility that an expert teacher would be able to give a lecture even from a learning centre (Remote Terminal). Each remote location will be able to access the Internet through the VSAT connectivity by providing the Internet connectivity at the HUB. All five studios are controlled and managed by the central hub for management, scheduling, broadcasting, review learning process and associated facilities.

Telecommunications Consultants India Limited (TCIL), a state-run company, has been appointed for the implementation of the project on a turnkey basis. In fact, TCIL has designed the total network solution. The backbone of this project remains the strong undersea cable network and satellite connectivity (C-Band with INTELSAT-904/RASCOM). Regional African Satellite Communications Organization[4] (RASCOM) with its Pan-African satellite provides Band Lease Services (BLS) with a continental connectivity to more than 30 African countries to support the Pan-African e-network for e-health and e-learning. The satellite also supports the transmission of both radio and television broadcasting services. PAeN also uses the latest technology including broadband devices such as Wi-Fi and WiMax. Programmes are relayed from five universities in India to the satellite hub station located in Senegal. From there, services are distributed to tele-centres across Africa.

TCIL is also responsible for providing operations and management support for five years after commissioning of the network, aimed at providing Tele-Education and Tele-Medicine Services in collaboration with Indian universities and Super Specialty Hospitals selected by the Government of India.

Every African country that agrees to join this project has to start by nominating a National Coordinator (focal point) and to prepare the identified sites with necessary civil and electrical infrastructure and other required facilities. The host country or site has to secure customs clearance of all materials imported into the country, including the exemption of customs duties, as well as the necessary clearances from the various regulatory agencies (VSAT, room for X-ray machine, and so on). The country receiving the services is also responsible for meeting the recurring cost of consumables, utilities and security, and the expenses connected with the maintenance of the facilities while arranging skilled manpower (Telecom/IT, Camera Technician, Paramedical staff, and so on). It must also take care of the on-the-job training during installation phase, and for subsequent day-to-day handling of equipment and facilities set up.

Major components of the project include the construction of the Hub Station Building and the supply, installation and commissioning of: the Satellite Hub Station; VSATs in 169 locations in Africa, Data Centre and Studio Set up in the TCIL HQ Data Centre at the Satellite Hub Station; ICT Equipment (Computer hardware, system software, networking equipment, studio equipment and UPS) at 170 locations in Africa (53 LC, 53 PEL, 53 VVIP Node, 5 RUC, 5 RSSH and 1 DC at hub) and 19 locations in India (7 UC, 12 SSH and DC at Delhi); Medical Equipment at 53 Patient-end Hospitals; and Tele-Ed and Tele-Med Application Software. Operation and Management and AMC support for the network for 5 years: Tele-Education and Tele-Medicine services for 5 years; Satellite Hub Station: Operational since April 2008. IPLC end-to-end commissioned in Aug 2008; upgraded to 4 Mbps in March 2009; and Data Centre, India at TCIL Bhawan, New Delhi Operational since September 2008.

Who is Benefiting From it?

As at 30th November 2011, 47 of the African Union member states had signed an agreement with TCIL. The region-wise participation is as follows:

- West Africa: 15 out of 15;
- East Africa: 13 out of 13;
- Southern Africa: 8 out of 10 (missing - South Africa and Angola);
- Central Africa: 8 out of 9 (missing - Equatorial Guinea);
- Northern Africa: 3 out of 6 (missing -Algeria and Tunisia).

The following 103 sites/centres have been commissioned/integrated with the e-Network:

- Satellite Hub Earth Station in Dakar, Senegal;
- Data Centre at TCIL Bhawan, New Delhi;
- Tele-Education set-up in 5 Indian Universities (Selected by MEA);
- Tele-Medicine set-up in 9 Super Specialty Hospitals of India;
- Tele-Education set-up in 3 Regional Leading University Centres in Africa;
- Tele-Medicine set-up in 1 Regional Super Specialty Hospital in Africa viz. Ibadan Super Specialty Hospital, Nigeria;
- 30 Learning Centres;
- 28 Patient-End Hospitals; and
- 25 VVIP Nodes.

More than 2000 students from Africa have been enrolled in various disciplines such as the MBA, Masters in Finance Control, PG Diploma in IT, M.Sc. in IT and Bachelor in Finance and Investment Analysis and many others. Regular Tele-Education live sessions are being conducted from India and students have shown great interest in the courses.

Advantages of the Pan African E-Network

PAeN is been designed in such a way so as to help African countries to minimize the effects of slow and erratic Internet bandwidth, high connectivity costs, intermittent power supply, and inadequate cooperation and coordination at regional levels. It promotes regional collaborative education and research projects as well as global virtual research communities by overcoming ICT challenges—for example, the Pan-African E-network project at Dar-es-Salaam Institute of technology. PAeN also increases access to tertiary education using flexible modes of delivery while allowing African students to benefit from courses offered by prestigious Indian institutions of higher learning. It contributes to the vision of African Governments in preparing their countries towards a knowledge economy.

Tele-Medicine

The Tele-Medicine connectivity enables the ten super specialty hospitals in India to provide specialty services to African hospitals that are fully equipped with medical equipment such as EGC, Ultra Scan, and Echo machine in each location. Tele-Medicine hardware, camera, software to manage the patients, store and forward the medical records and analyse, digitally signed prescription and advice to the remote patients as an integrated package. Data centre to manage and maintain the records, storage and backup facility, and retrieval mechanism for the medical facilities need to be provided at the each super specialty hospitals.

With a set-up similar to that of Tele-Education, the ten Super Specialty Hospitals also provide Continuing Medical Education (CME), training of doctors and paramedical staff in Africa. The network aims at connecting the 116 terminals delivering the envisaged services, but also to be capable of scaling it up to extend the network to the other locations through adding more VSATs as well as broadband and wireless connectivity.

For Tele-Medicine purposes, the 12 Indian institutions considered for the project are: All-India Institute of Medical Sciences (AIIMS), New Delhi; Apollo Hospital, Chennai; CARE Hospital, Hyderabad; Narayana Hrudayalaya Institute of Medical Science, Bangalore; Amrita Institute of Medical Sciences and Research Centre, Kochi; Fortis Hospital, Noida; King Edward Memorial Hospital (KEM), Mumbai; Manipal Hospital, Manipal; Escorts Hearts Institute and Research Centre Limited, New Delhi; Sri Ramachandra Medical College and Research Institute, Chennai; Mool Chand Khairati Ram Hopsital, New Delhi and Santosh Medical College and Hospital, Ghaziabad. The nodal hospitals in the African countries would be provided with PC-enabled ECG, ultrasound and X-ray equipment that would provide inputs directly to the Indian consultants so that rapid diagnosis and medical advice could be rendered.

Pan-African Network in Mauritius[5]

The ex-Mauritius College of the Air (MCA), now the Open University of Mauritius, was designated by the Ministry of Information Technology and Telecommunications-Mauritius as a Tele-Education centre in line with its mandate to promote distance education.

Following the inauguration of the Tele-Learning Centre in February 2009, steps were taken for the implementation of the project. Negotiations started with the following three Universities chosen amongst others to offer degree and postgraduate programmes - University of Madras (UNOM), Amity University and the Indira Gandhi National Open University (IGNOU).

Following the signing of the usual MOUs with the above institutions, the following programmes started coming on stream for delivery as from July 2010 (Table 1).

So far, the following programmes are on offer:

Diploma in HIV & Family Education—IGNOU *(since 12 January 2011)*

Bachelor in Business Administration—University of Madras—*(since July 2010)*

MBA (International Business)—Amity (*since 21 February 2011)*

Bachelor of Finance & Investment Analysis—Amity *(since 21 February 2011)*

Master of Finance and Control—Amity *(since 21 February 2011)*

The delivery is online through both synchronous and asynchronous offerings with institutional support.

Synchronous delivery: This entails attendance in the Tele-Learning Centre at MCA with live interactions with resource persons from the respective Universities. Queries are addressed there and then.

Asynchronous delivery: Those who cannot attend the live sessions have recourse to the archived sessions 24/7. Queries are addressed to the resource persons via emails.

Students contribute a very small sum towards this as they also benefit from additional counselling sessions as and when required. The services of the resources from the Indian institutions come free to MCA/ Open University of Mauritius.

Fees charged: A nominal fee is charged to meet local costs which includes hand-outs, additional counselling sessions by tutors locally, postage, overtime for MCA staff as sessions are run after office hours, and examination costs.

Lessons Learned

Strengths

The Pan-African e-Network is the biggest project in South-South Cooperation. It is giving Africa-India relations a new substance and content. It is not only bridging the digital divide, it is bridging the divide between the haves and the have-nots…The e-network project aims to change the lives of the African people through the use of ICT has several opportunities and challenges.

Africa has the opportunity to use the services of Indian technical experts to improve their ICT connectivity and expand further from their main nodal connections to the remote areas.

Table 1. Programmes offered in Mauritius through Pan African e-Network

Programme	*Institution*	*Minimum Duration*	*Number enrolled*	*Number of Drop out*	*Number who have completed in 2012*	*Number who have completed in 2013*	*Number who are still enrolled*
Master in Business Administration - International Business	Amity University	2 years	38	17	6	8	7 (Expected date of completion is June 2014)
Master of Finance and Control	Amity University	2 years	13	2	5	3	3 (Expected date of completion is June 2014)
Bachelor of Business Administration - Cohort 1	University of Madras	3 years	11	4	-	Awaiting results	
Bachelor of Business Administration - Cohort 2	University of Madras	3 years	32	2	-	-	30 (Expected date of completion is June 2014)
Bachelor of Finance and Investment Analysis	Amity University	3 years	14	4	8	-	2 (Expected date of completion is June 2014)
Diploma in HIV and Family Education	IGNOU	1 year	26	1	18	-	7 Expected date of completion is June 2014.

Weaknesses

Problems at one institution can be a source of major difficulties. For example, examinations in November 2012 were not held. They were postponed four times - November to December 2012, January 2013, February 2013, March 2013). They were finally held in April 2013 after sending constant requests. Students who were supposed to complete the programme in June 2013 have not been able to do so.

Non-uniform rules and regulations at different institutions can lead to major problems. Curriculum and assessment strategies must be adapted to meet the requirements of the local authorities. Examination results are not declared on time. Names are wrongly written on certificates. Sometimes, results appeared with many discrepancies as follows:

- those were present for the exams, appeared as absent
- student assignments are shown not submitted when they have uploaded on the website
- results are partially declared
- results of last semester's modules still appeared on the results for the last exams taken.

The grading structure is not the same at all universities. Interpretation becomes difficult. All recorded videos were not available on portal and some videos were not playing properly. Due to time differences, the organisation of live lectures may be difficult. Course materials often make reference to country-specific issues that are not relevant to students residing in different countries.

The Proposed Model for the IOR Virtual Open University

An Academic Board (AB) needs to be set up by the Indian Ocean Rim Association (IORA). The AB will be responsible for the identification, development and regulation of academic programmes that meet the requirements of member states as well as the appointment of resource persons (drawn from open universities/higher education institutions/ research institutions established in IORA member states) to:

(1) develop the curriculum and programme structure;

(2) develop the open and distance learning (ODL) materials including case studies;

(3) develop video/audio/multimedia materials;

(4) review the materials;
(5) develop assessment strategies; and
(6) develop all other regulations (for example, admission, award, credit transfer, exit points, quality assurance, fee structure, certification, copyright, and so on).

There may be a need to train local experts to develop ODL materials including videos.

Students may be given the possibility to move from one institution to another through an effective credit transfer system.

It is to be noted that institutions that will deliver the programmes locally must provide learner support (for example, counselling, face-to-face sessions and tutorials) as well as necessary the set up to carry out experiments and practical tasks (for example, in fisheries management) wherever required. They must also provide supplementary materials such as videos and case studies that reflect the local context. Library and other logistical facilities must be provided locally.

The assessment and examinations will be prepared, moderated and conducted by local institutions. Examination papers must be sent to an external examiner for quality assurance purposes. The programme must be approved by the local institutions (for example, the Council of the Open University of Mauritius). The award of a degree, diploma or certificate must also be made jointly by the IORA Virtual University and the local institution. This requires that all of the legal aspects of the Virtual University be worked out.

It is proposed to have an independent group of experts who would be responsible to carry out quality audits. After the initial investment by IORA, nominal fees must be charged to finance the ongoing activities of the Virtual University.

The development of the curriculum may take around six months. A similar period of time is required to develop the ODL materials if done for all the modules simultaneously. It is also suggested that a proper survey be carried out initially in order to:

(1) identify the needs of the member states;
(2) understand how ODL programmes are being implemented in different countries;
(3) identify programmes that already being run; and

(4) identify experts who can contribute to the IORA Virtual University in various capacities.

The AB must meet regularly to review the programmes and the related provisions.

Conclusion

Apart from establishing India as a privileged partner to the African Union Millennium Development Goals, PAeN is a vivid example of harnessing the power of ICT in bringing education and skills development to those who need it the most. It does not only increase access to tertiary education and high-tech medical services in Africa, but it also promotes regional collaboration that is vital for the sustainability of such projects. The effective use of ICT will allow African countries to compete globally, drive socio-economic growth, and improve their business prospects. Setting up the Indian Ocean Rim virtual Open University (IORVOU) will be beneficial to all countries in the region. The lessons learnt from form Pan-African E-network project can play a pivotal role in effective implementation of the virtual university.

NOTES

1. http://www.panafricanenetwork.com/
2. http://www.balancingact-africa.com/news/en/issue-no-289/internet/ethiopia-to-be-first/en
3. http://www.africa-union.org/root/ua/conferences/2009/mai/ie/6-7mai/panafrican%20e-network%20project.pdf
4. www.rascom.org
5. http://www.mca.ac.mu/programmes.htm

REFERENCES

Athukorala, P., Nasir, S. (2012), "Global production sharing and South-South trade", *Indian Growth and Development Review*, Vol. 5 No. 2, pp. 173-202.

Lu, X., Li R., (2010), "South-South cooperation: is there a foundation in trade", *Journal of Chinese Economic and Foreign Trade Studies*, Vol. 3 No. 3, pp. 221-234.

OECD (2006), "South-South trade vita for development", *OECD Observer-August*, pp. 1-7.

Soontlens, W. (2002), "Managing International trade: an analysis of South African SMEs and regional exports", *Management Decision*, Vol. 40, No. 7, pp. 710-719.

WTO (2003), "Selected features of south-south trade development in the 1990-2001 period", *World Trade Report 2003*, World Trade Organisation, Geneva, pp. 22-45.

Chapter 15

Africa's Economic Relations with the Indian Ocean Rim: A Systems of Innovation Approach

Mario Scerri

ABSTRACT

This chapter examines the conditions that will determine the engagement of the four IORA member countries in sub-Saharan Africa—Kenya, Tanzania, Mozambique and South Africa—with the other economies in the Association. These four countries are not viewed in isolation from other African economies, given the increasing importance of the regional economic agreements that link them to the rest of the continent. The theoretical lens that is used in this examination is that of an innovation systems approach to development. Using the broad perspective of this approach, the chapter analyses the historical determinants of the viability of national systems of innovation in sub-Saharan Africa and at their current development prospects. The viability prospects of most African systems of innovation tend to be poor, due to a large extent to the conditions of their formation at independence and their subsequent post-colonial history. The chapter argues that the only credible path to viability is that of an effective programme of economic and institutional integration across sub-Saharan Africa. The engagement of post-colonial African economies with the rest of the world, through trade and investment flows has in general served to reinforce resource dependency and its attendant adverse effects on economic transformation. The engagement of these four countries with the other IORA economies is still incipient and thus holds a strong potential to be directed in a manner that can aid the needed transformation of their national systems of innovation onto a development trajectory. This developing political and economic relationship can help engender a rupture in the history of post-colonial African development or alternatively serve to reinforce its current path dependent course. The chapter concludes with a brief exploration of the conditions for the two outcomes.

Keywords: systems of innovation, economic relations, Indian Ocean Rim, post-colonial African development.

Introduction

The four countries on the eastern littoral of the Africa continent that now form a part of the Indian Ocean Rim Association (IORA)—Kenya, Tanzania, Mozambique and South Africa—do not as yet have strong trade or investment relations with most of the other IORA member states, except for limited flows with India. As such, there is a possibility of forming economic relations within the IORA context which may help shift the historical positioning of peripheral dependence which marks most of Africa's economic relations with the outside world. In order to address this issue effectively, these four African economies cannot be seen in isolation from the regional economic communities (REC) that link them to other African economies. The assessment of the possible forms which economic relations formed within the IORA may take should therefore be within the overall context of economic integration initiatives in Africa. In addressing this issue, this chapter adopts the systems of innovation approach as a broad political economy framework which may serve to capture the role of history and institutions in economic dynamics, especially within a developing economy context.

In the following sections, the systems of innovation approach is briefly discussed, in its variations and in terms of its relevance to economic development. This is followed by a discussion of the state of the four members of the IORA in particular, and of African economies in general, with specific regard to their innovation profile and the prospects for their viability. The case for the necessity of effective economic integration for development and its possibilities in Africa is made in the subsequent section. The final section in the chapter ends with an exploration of the possible implications of the engagement of African economies with the IORA for their development prospects. The main question here is whether this engagement will serve to reinforce Africa's peripheral position in the global economy or provide the basis for a rupture in the evolutionary path of African economies.

National Systems of Innovation and Economic Development

A system of innovation may be defined as the web of institutions within which innovation emerges, and is diffused and deployed[1]. While this may sound reasonably unambiguous, the conceptualisation of the components of this term is liable to a wide range of interpretations. In the first place, what is considered an innovation may be restricted to technology or may be extended to capture any change in the way that economic activity is organised that is demonstrably an improvement on the current state of the art. The choice of institutions which should be considered may be narrowly confined to those directly related to the science and technology sector of the economy or enlarged to consider those which alter the context within which technology is generated and diffused. Moreover, the institutions which are considered as forming the system of innovation may cover both formal organisations and established routines and practices which tend to govern interpersonal relations. Finally, systems of institutions are normally spatially and legally defined. The most common usage refers to national systems of innovation (NSI) but systems of innovation may be identified at the sub-national (local) and the supra-national (regional, continental and global) levels. The variations in the interpretation of the various components of systems of innovation obviously open up a variety of versions of the concept, but we can differentiate between two broad categories. The narrower version of the NSI concept ties it down to the science and technology (S and T) sub-sector and its interaction with the production sub-sector. This version is more typical of mainstream economics. The broader version of the NSI is a political economy rendition which places the S and T and production sub-sectors within the broader socio-economic and global contexts[2]. Figure 1 portrays these two versions.

If the notion of innovation is sufficiently broad to incorporate all economically significant change, then the NSI may be extended to provide an alternative account of the general economy, with historical streams of innovation and accumulated knowledge providing the basis for an associated theory of value[3]. From this perspective, knowledge and the human capabilities generated by and generated from knowledge now occupy the core space of economic dynamics. The generation of human capabilities and their location within the political economy of the NSI consequently become one of the main concerns of development policy.

Figure 1. The narrow and broad versions of the national system of innovation

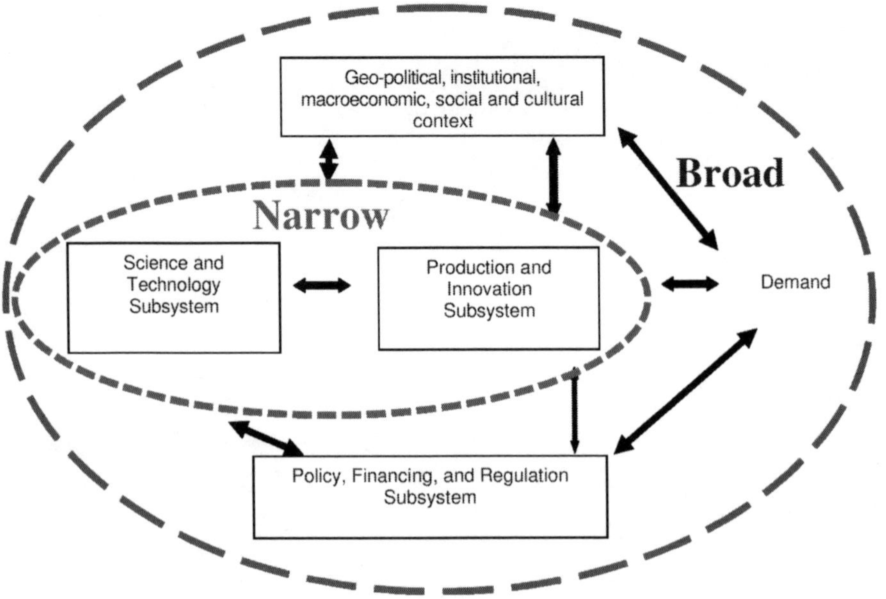

Source: Derived from Cassiolato and Lastres.

Figure 2 depicts policy spheres relevant to the narrow and broad versions of the NSI.

As may be seen in Figure 2, the standard macroeconomic tools, especially monetary and fiscal policy, are no longer at the core of economic policy but serve as the tools to manage fluctuations in the business cycle. Financial regulation and the general legal framework similarly set the stabilising conditions of the political economy. Policies affecting tertiary education, science, technology and innovation (STI), and industrial policy directly affect the direction and rate of scientific discovery and technological innovation, and their impact on industrial development rates and paths.

On the broader level, however, a wider spectrum of policies affecting various aspects of human capabilities development has to be considered and the human capabilities development pipeline is considered to start in early childhood with a broad range of socio-economic factors affecting its course. Finally, the evolution of the NSI has to be placed within a supra-national context, as is reflected by policies on integration

Figure 2. Policy spheres relative to the Narrow and Broad Perspectives of the NSI

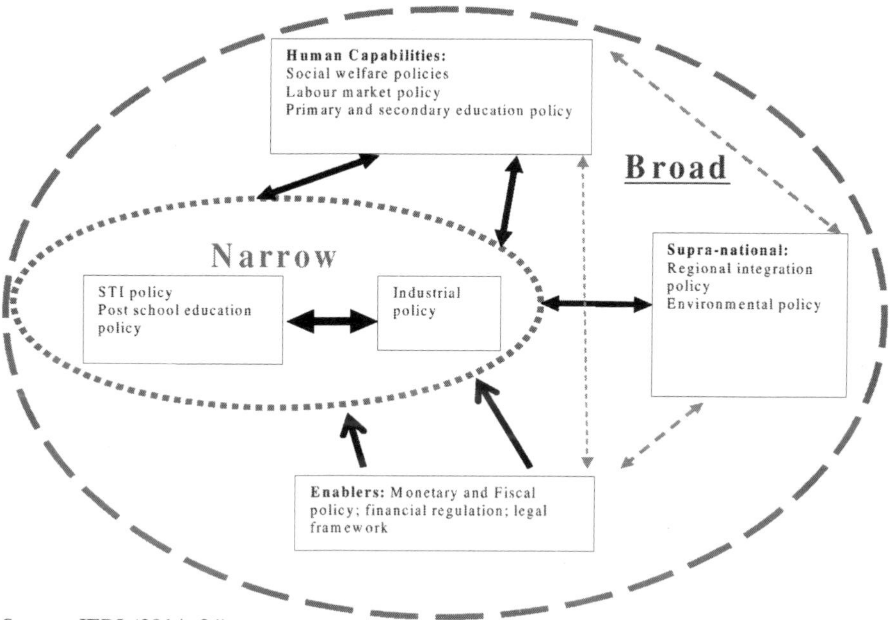

Source: IERI (2014: 34).

and various global levels of engagement. The layering of the NSI may be depicted in greater detail by taking human capabilities formation as an example. This is shown in Figure 3.

Figure 3. The layers of human capabilities provision

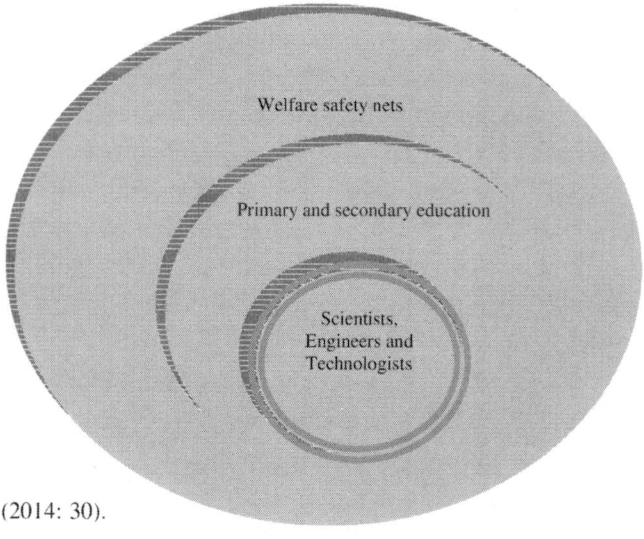

Source: IERI (2014: 30).

From a mainstream economics perspective, the analysis of the narrowly-defined NSI would normally focus on the tertiary education sector, usually with specific reference to the training of scientists and engineers. However, as depicted in Figure 3, this level of human capabilities provision is built on the broader foundation of school education. Moreover, the foundation level for the formation of human capabilities extends considerably beyond formal education. Given that the process of forming a skilled citizen is a long-term investment, extending over a couple of decades after birth, it is crucial that the integrity of the family unit which normally forms the base for the development of human capabilities should be protected in order to ensure the continuity of this particular investment. This is why the broad base in Figure 3 represents "welfare nets"—that is, the guaranteed state provision of basic needs, such as health and nutrition, housing, water and sanitation, energy and connectivity, as well as sound public education. This role is allocated to the state because the treatment of education as a private good would result in significant underinvestment.

Using a biological metaphor, the health and viability of systems of innovation may be assessed on a number of levels. At the basic level of survival, a NSI should be able to reproduce itself, in terms of having a sustainable economic base. A main indicator of this capability is the degree of dependence of the national economy on foreign funds injections, such as Overseas Development Assistance (ODA) and its indebtedness to global financial institutions such as the World Bank and the IMF. At a higher level, successful systems would grow and expand with a paradigmatic continuity. Indicators which would point to this level of viability would include per capita GDP, a deepening of the technology of the NSI base as evidenced in R and D/GDP ratios, a shift to high technology exports, as well as the reproduction and expansion of the human capabilities base. Finally, in recognition that NSIs inhabit a global political economy context, the highest level of viability depends on the national system's capacity to evolve—that is, to adapt to a changing regional or global environment through feedback effects and adjustments. There is also the possibility that a particular NSI, on the basis of its political and economic power base, may initiate systemic changes which themselves alter the global political/economic ecology. The following section examines these various indicators for the IORA member states, with a particular focus on the four African members in order to assess the positioning of African NSIs within the IORA community.

The National Systems of Innovation of the Mainland African Members of IORA

As mentioned in the previous section, a critical indicator of the basic level of the viability of a NSI is the dependence of the economy on foreign aid. Table 1 depicts this in terms of the ratio of ODA to gross national income for the members of the IORA. In three of the four African member countries, ODA constitutes a significant proportion of GNI, especially in Mozambique and Tanzania. In the case of Kenya, this proportion has increased over the six-year period under consideration. In general, apart from South Africa, the dependency of the African member states on ODA is higher than those of the other IORA members, except for the Comoros.

Table 1. Overseas Development Assistance as a percentage of Gross National Income

Country Name	*Year*							
	2005	*2006*	*2007*	*2008*	*2009*	*2010*	*2011*	*2012*
Kenya	4.1	4.2	4.9	4.5	5.8	5.1	7.4	6.5
Mozambique	20.9	25.3	23.8	21.8	21.3	21.2	16.8	14.8
South Africa	0.3	0.3	0.3	0.4	0.4	0.3	0.4	0.3
Tanzania	10.8	13.3	16.9	11.4	13.9	13.1	10.4	10.1
Australia	0	0	0	0	0	0	0	0
Bangladesh	2.1	1.9	2.1	2.4	1.3	1.3	1.2	1.7
Comoros	5.9	7.9	9.6	7.9	9.4	12.4	8.5	11.5
Indonesia	0.9	0.4	0.2	0.3	0.2	0.2	0.1	0.0
India	0.2	0.1	0.1	0.2	0.2	0.2	0.2	0.1
Iran, Islamic Rep.	0.1	0.1	0.0	0.0	0.0			
Sri Lanka	4.8	2.8	1.9	1.8	1.7	1.2	1.0	0.8
Madagascar	18.4	14.4	12.3	9.0	5.2	5.4	4.6	3.9
Mauritius	0.6	0.3	0.9	1.1	1.8	1.3	1.6	1.7
Malaysia	0.0	0.2	0.1	0.1	0.1	0.0	0.0	0.0
Oman	0.1	0.1	0.5	0.1	0.3	-0.1		
Seychelles	1.9	1.4	1.1	1.4	2.8	6.1	2.2	3.3
Singapore	0	0	0	0	0	0	0	0
Thailand	-0.1	-0.1	-0.1	-0.2	0.0	0.0	0.0	0.0
United Arab Emirates	0	0	0	0	0	0	0	0
Yemen, Rep.	2.0	1.6	1.2	1.7	2.4	2.2	1.6	2.1

Source: World Bank Indicators at http://data.worldbank.org/indicator/DT.ODA.ODAT.GN.ZS/countries, accessed 10th March 2014.

Following the discussion in the previous section, NSIs may be assessed on two levels. The first the narrow version of the NSI may be portrayed by standard research and development (R and D) indicators. A composite indicator of the health of the system of science, technology and innovation may be provided by the knowledge and knowledge economy indices. The Knowledge Economy Index (KEI) is a composite of sets of indicators reflecting (a) indicators of the incentives offered by the economic and institutional regime for the efficient use of existing and new knowledge and the flourishing of entrepreneurship; (b) the education and skills levels of the population; (c) an efficient innovation system of firms, research centres, universities, consultants and other organisations; and, (d) information and communication technology.

Table 2a. Knowledge Economy Index and Knowledge Index for IORA members—2012

Country	*Knowledge Economy Index*	*Knowledge Index*	*World Ranking (144 countries)*
Kenya	2.88	2.91	110
Mozambique	1.76	0.99	129
South Africa	5.21	5.11	67
Tanzania	1.79	1.36	127
Australia	8.88	8.98	9
Bangladesh	1.49	1.48	136
India	3.06	2.89	109
Indonesia	3.11	2.99	107
Iran	3.91	4.97	94
Madagascar	1.77	1.43	128
Malaysia	6.10	6.25	48
Mauritius	5.52	4.62	62
Oman	6.14	5.87	47
Singapore	8.26	7.79	23
Sri Lanka	3.63	3.49	101
Thailand	5.21	5.25	66
UAE	6.94	7.09	42
Yemen	1.92	1.58	121

Source: World Bank, at http://info.worldbank.org/etools/kam2/KAM_page5.asp, accessed 9th March 2014.

The Knowledge Index (KI) is a composite of indicators sets (b), (c) and (d) while the "knowledge economy index" adds on the market grounding of the knowledge system. While these indices are largely based on the perceptions of the business sector and offer an inevitably biased view of the NSI, they do offer a limited basis for comparison across different NSIs. Table 2a shows the KEI and KI indices for IORA countries and it is obvious that the values for the African members, except for South Africa, are at the lower end of the scale.

Table 2b provides a component breakdown of the indices for the African IORA members and they indicate a division between South Africa and Kenya on the one hand, whose indices show a higher value than the average for Africa as a whole, and Tanzania and Mozambique on the other hand, whose KEI and KI indices are lower than the African average. It is also worth noting that in the case of all countries, except for Kenya, the "economic incentive regime" component shows a higher value than the African average, indicating a relatively high degree of "business friendliness" in these countries. This may carry implications for the effectiveness of overly market friendly policy regimes in isolation from the institutional context of a sound NSI which can generate, adopt, adapt and absorb new knowledge.

Table 2b. Knowledge Economy Index and Knowledge Index for African IORA members—2012

Country	*KEI*	*KI*	*Economic Incentive Regime*	*Innovation*	*Education*	*ICT*
South Africa	5.21	5.11	5.49	6.89	4.87	3.58
Kenya	2.88	2.91	2.78	3.72	2.1	2.91
Tanzania	1.79	1.36	3.07	1.98	0.83	1.26
Mozambique	1.76	0.99	4.05	1.76	0.17	1.05
Africa	2.55	2.43	2.91	3.95	1.44	1.9

Source: World Bank, at http://info.worldbank.org/etools/kam2/KAM_page5.asp, accessed 9th March 2014.

Table 3 shows two sets of R and D indicators for IORA member states. In the case of two African member states there were some significant changes in the percentage share of gross expenditure on R and D (GERD) in the gross domestic product (GDP) between the years 2007 and 2010 (AIO 2014, p. 24; AIO 2011, p. 37). The percentage for South Africa declined from 1.05 to 0.76, while that for Kenya more than doubled from 0.48 to 0.98. The number of researchers per million of the population more than trebled in Kenya since 2007, while that for South Africa dropped by twelve percent over the same period (AIO 2011, p. 43). Overall, these indicators place the four African member states well within the range of values for the IORA community, but the sharp decline in South Africa's R and D intensity and the very short history of Kenya's rising indicators put up a cautionary note in interpreting the implications of this table for the technological depth of these two NSIs.

Table 3. R&D indicators for IORA member countries

Country	*Researchers per million people*	*% GERD/GDP*
Kenya	321 (2010)*	0.98 (2010)*
Mozambique	68 (2010)*	0.47 (2010)
South Africa	716 (2010)*	0.76 (2010)*
Tanzania	na	0.43 (2007)
Australia	4280.4 (2008)	2.38 (2010)
Bangladesh	na	na
Comoros	na	na
India	137.4 (2005)	0.76 (2007)
Indonesia	89.6 (2009)	0.08 (2009)
Iran, Islamic Rep.	746.9 (2008)	0.79 (2008)
Madagascar	51 (2011)	0.11 (2011)
Malaysia	1542.7 (2011)	1.07 (2011)
Mauritius	na	0.37 (2005)
Oman	159.1 (2011)	0.13 (2011)
Seychelles	149.3 (2005)	0.3 (2005)
Singapore	6306.5 (2010)	2.1 (2010)
Sri Lanka	103.1 (2010)	0.16 (2010)
Thailand	331.9 (2009)	0.25 (2009)
United Arab Emirates	na	0.47 (2011)
Yemen, Rep.	na	na

*AIO (2014), accessed 5th March 2014.

Source: World Development Indicators 2013, at http://data.worldbank.org/topic/science-and-technology, accessed 5th March 2014.

When we move to the broader version of the NSI, other aspects of the general political economy become relevant. From this perspective, the human capabilities base of the economy and the stability of the political economy assume paramount importance in the assessment of the viability of the NSI. This is one important area where the system of innovation approach, in its broad interpretation, differs significantly from mainstream economics, both analytically and in its policy implications. In the case of orthodox economics, most indicators of the general wellbeing of the population are normally viewed as the goals of economic policy, whose instruments are the standard macroeconomic tools of fiscal and monetary policy, along with a sound industrial policy, nowadays increasingly linked to the assumption of the inherent efficiency of markets liberated from state intervention. In the case of the broad version of the systems of innovation approach the argument is diametrically opposite. Within this analytical framework human capabilities are at the core of economic dynamics and the national capability to generate and retain broad-based human capabilities is possibly the core determinant of the viability of the NSI, both directly and as the proxy for the health of a considerable section of the institutional web constituting the NSI. In this case, therefore, the improvement of the quality of life of the population is both the objective and the instrument of policy. It has to be an instrument of state policy because of the public good and externalities content of human capabilities development and the inherent fragility of the human capabilities investment life cycle.

Table 4 shows the Human Development Indicators (HDI) values for the IORA member states. The values for the African member states lie at the lower end of the scale for IORA members in general and below the world average. Moreover, the HDI value for South Africa, which is the highest among the African members, shows the lowest growth rate over the period under consideration among all IORA members.

Table 5 depicts poverty levels in the IORA, measured as the percentage of the population living below $2 a day. Among the African member states, South Africa stands out as having the significantly lowest poverty levels, putting it at the upper end of the IORA scale. The other three African member states indicate very high poverty levels. High levels of poverty and low HDI values provide an indication of a poor human capabilities base in the NSI. They may also serve as proxy indicators for the level of domestic demand for national production. Domestic demand is the base on which, through some form of protection, even if it is of the non-tariff variety, allows for the development of competitiveness of the local production base which

Table 4. Human Development Indicators (HDI) for the IORA member countries

Country	*HDI*				*Average Annual HDI Growth*		
	1990	*2007*	*2010*	*2012*	*1990-2000*	*2000-2010*	*2000-2012*
Kenya	0.463	0.491	0.511	0.519	-0.33	1.34	1.24
Mozambique	0.202	0.301	0.318	0.327	2	2.57	2.37
South Africa	0.621	0.609	0.621	0.629	0.01	-0.01	0.11
Tanzania	0.353	0.408	0.466	0.476	0.43	2.36	2.15
Australia	0.88	0.931	0.935	0.938	0.37	0.23	0.22
Singapore	0.796		0.892	0.895	0.89	0.77	0.67
United Arab Emirates		0.827	0.816	0.818			
Seychelles		0.792	0.799	0.806		0.31	0.33
Malaysia	0.635	0.753	0.763	0.769	1.15	0.69	0.64
Iran	0.54	0.706	0.74	0.742	1.94	1.25	1.05
Mauritius	0.626	0.72	0.732	0.737	0.77	0.81	0.73
Oman			0.728	0.731			
Sri Lanka	0.608	0.693	0.705	0.715	0.72	0.78	0.76
Thailand	0.569	0.676	0.686	0.69	0.94	0.93	0.82
Indonesia	0.479	0.595	0.62	0.629	1.21	1.39	1.28
India	0.41	0.525	0.547	0.554	1.23	1.67	1.5
Bangladesh	0.361	0.488	0.508	0.515	1.83	1.61	1.46
Madagascar		0.478	0.484	0.483		1.24	1.02
Yemen	0.286	0.444	0.466	0.458	2.78	2.16	1.66
Comoros		0.425	0.426	0.429			
World	0.6	0.678	0.69	0.692	0.64	0.77	0.68

Source: derived from UNDP data base, at https://data.undp.org/dataset/Table-2-Human-Development-Index-trends/efc4-gjvq, accessed 15th January 2014.

normally provides the learning space for the development of a deepening knowledge base for the NSI.

A further indicator of local demand and its growth prospects may be provided by the levels of income inequality that serves as an inverse proxy indicator of the spread of purchasing power. This also serves as an indication of the potential for the development of the human capabilities base since income inequality also reflects the spread of wealth and life opportunities. Table 6 shows the GINI index values for the IORA member states. The levels of income inequality for the African member states lie at the higher end, with South Africa exhibiting the second highest level of inequality within the IORA.

Table 5. Poverty headcount ratio at $2 a day (PPP) (% of population) for the IORA

Country	*2000*	*2001*	*2002*	*2003*	*2004*	*2005*	*2006*	*2007*	*2008*	*2009*	*2010*	*2011*
Kenya						67.2						
Mozambique				90					81.8			
South Africa	18.3						12.3			10.2		
Tanzania	95.3							87.9				
United Arab Emirates				19.5*								
Australia												
Bangladesh	84.4					80.3					76.5	
Comoros					65							
Indonesia			67			53.8	63.4	56.1	54.4	52.7	46.1	43.3
India						75.6					68.8	
Iran, Islamic Rep.						1.8						
Sri Lanka			11.9					7.38			5.37	
Madagascar		88.8				89.6					92.6	
Mauritius												
Malaysia					7.81			2.93		2.27		
Oman												
Seychelles	0							1.84				
Thailand	18.1		13.4				7.63		4.98	4.58	4.05	
Yemen, Rep.						46.6						

*CIA Worldfact Book, at https://www.cia.gov/library/publications/the-world-factbook/fields/2046.html, accessed 18th January 2014

Source: World Bank data, at http://data.worldbank.org/topic/poverty, accessed 18th January 2014

Table 6. GINI Index for the IORA member states

Country	*2000*	*2001*	*2002*	*2003*	*2004*	*2005*	*2006*	*2007*	*2008*	*2009*	*2010*	*2011*
Kenya						47.7						
Mozambique				47.1					45.66			
South Africa	57.8						67.4			63.1		
Tanzania	34.6							37.6				
United Arab Emirates												
Australia									30.3*			
Bangladesh	33.5					33.2					32.1	
Comoros					64.3							
Indonesia			29.7			34			34.11		35.6	38.1
India						33.4					33.9	
Iran, Islamic Rep.						38.3						
Sri Lanka			41.1					40.3			36.4	
Madagascar		47.5				47.2					44.1	
Mauritius							39.0*					
Oman												
Seychelles	42.7							65.8				
Thailand	42.8		42				42.4		40.51	40	39.4	
Yemen, Rep.						37.7						

*CIA World Factbook, at https://www.cia.gov/library/publications/the-world-factbook/rankorder/2172rank.html, accessed 18th January 2014.

Source: http://data.worldbank.org/indicator/SI.POV.GINI, accessed 18th January 2014.

High levels of inequality not only indicate possible constraints on the "supply" and "demand" sides of the NSI but may also have implications for the political, social and economic stability of the NSI. The Failed States Index (Table 7) is a composite of a wide range of social, economic and political stability indicators. Except for South Africa, the African member states show relatively high levels of instability towards the lower middle part of the range for the IORA as a whole.

Overall, the indicators of the health of the NSIs of the African members of the IORA, crude and preliminary as they may be, draw a picture of generally ailing systems of innovation, with the possible exception of South Africa. Even South Africa, which has the most diversified NSI among the African members, shows deteriorating or stagnant indicators regarding most aspects of the narrow and broad versions of the NSI. One of the main historical determinants of the dependency *malaise* that has locked post-independent Africa, south of the Sahara, into the periphery of the global economic order, in spite of the waves of radical mutations of the global economy since the end of the Second World War, is the fragmentation of the sub-continent at independence. A meaningful erosion of the fragmented political and economic map of sub-Saharan Africa through effective regional integration strategies is one of the essential pre-requisites to altering the development path of African economies in general towards a sustainable growth trajectory. This applies to all four African members of the IORA, including the relatively well-endowed South African NSI[4].

The Economic Size and Shape of Africa in the 21st century

The McKinsey Global Institute report (MGI 2010) identifies Africa as the location of the next wave of emerging economies. The report brings in a number of gross indicators such as the continent's collective GDP, consumer spending and discretionary income, both in current volumes and in terms of projections, to support this thesis. Other indicators are quoted in support of the argument. These include the rapid rate of urbanisation and foreign capital inflows. However, some reservations should arise with the classification of African economies in the report. Only four of the African countries have diversified economies that provide the springboard towards sustainable development. Of these only

Table 7. Failed States Index (2013) for the IORA member states

Ranking (of 178 countries)	Country	Total	Demographic Pressures	Refugees and IDPs	Group Grievance	Human Flight	Uneven Development	Poverty and Economic Decline	Legitimacy of the State	Public Services	Human Rights	Security Apparatus	Factionalized Elites	External Intervention
17	Kenya	**99.6**	9.1	8.7	9.0	7.8	8.3	7.6	8.3	8.1	7.1	8.1	9.0	8.5
59	Mozambique	**82.8**	9.2	4.6	4.9	7.2	8.0	8.0	7.0	8.5	6.4	6.5	5.6	6.8
113	South Africa	**67.6**	7.8	6.5	5.7	4.3	8.0	5.9	5.3	6.3	4.2	5.1	5.6	2.9
65	Tanzania	**81.1**	8.6	6.8	6.0	6.4	6.4	6.8	6.2	8.8	6.2	5.5	5.7	7.7
169	Australia	**25.4**	3.3	2.7	3.6	1.1	3.3	2.1	1.0	1.8	2.2	1.7	1.6	1.0
29	Bangladesh	**92.5**	8.1	7.3	8.6	7.5	7.8	7.3	8.3	8.0	7.3	7.7	8.9	5.8
56	Comoros	**84.0**	7.4	4.5	5.3	7.2	6.4	8.2	7.4	7.9	6.6	7.5	7.5	8.1
79	India	**77.5**	7.5	5.2	8.2	5.4	8.1	5.4	5.2	6.7	5.9	7.8	6.8	5.2
76	Indonesia	**78.2**	7.5	6.0	7.3	6.3	6.9	5.5	6.4	6.1	6.5	6.8	7.0	5.9
37	Iran	**89.7**	5.5	7.3	8.8	6.1	6.7	6.5	8.9	5.0	9.4	8.6	9.4	7.5
61	Madagascar	**82.7**	8.1	4.3	4.9	5.5	7.9	8.2	7.2	8.6	5.9	7.0	7.5	7.7
116	Malaysia	**66.1**	5.6	4.6	6.1	4.8	5.9	4.1	6.2	4.5	7.1	6.0	6.8	4.4
148	Mauritius	**44.5**	3.8	2.2	3.5	3.6	4.8	4.1	4.1	3.8	3.5	3.3	3.2	4.6
136	Oman	**52.0**	5.0	2.0	2.7	1.8	3.6	4.5	6.1	4.4	7.5	5.3	6.6	2.4
121	Seychelles	**64.0**	5.2	3.3	4.8	4.9	6.6	5.2	6.3	3.5	5.2	6.4	5.7	6.9
158	Singapore	**34.0**	2.5	1.1	2.7	3.3	3.7	3.0	3.2	1.9	4.9	1.5	4.0	2.2
28	Sri Lanka	**92.9**	6.8	8.4	9.5	7.3	7.8	5.9	8.2	5.5	9.0	8.5	9.3	6.8
90	Thailand	**75.1**	7.9	6.4	8.1	3.5	6.4	3.5	6.2	4.6	7.3	7.8	8.8	4.6
142	United Arab Emirates	**47.3**	3.9	2.5	4.3	2.4	4.8	3.5	6.5	2.9	6.4	2.9	3.6	3.5
6	Yemen	**107.0**	9.3	9.2	9.0	7.4	8.1	9.2	9.3	8.7	8.7	9.8	9.5	8.7

Source: Fund for Peace, at http://ffp.statesindex.org/rankings-2013-sortable, accessed 15th January 2014

one, South Africa, lies south of the Sahara and two of the other three saw a collapse of their economy during the Arab Spring which started after the report was written. NSIs in sub-Saharan Africa are still mostly formed on a restricted economic resource base, either mineral deposits or agriculture, with poor and deteriorating manufacturing sectors, and service sectors which have few spillover effects to the wider economy in terms of employment generation. The capacity of most sub-Saharan NSIs to generate human capabilities at professional levels and to retain those which have been generated is low. This is to a large extent due to the rent-seeking accumulation regimes in most African economies and the blocks to moving towards more diversified accumulation regimes which would intrinsically raise the absorptive capacity for human capabilities[5]. To a large extent, the constraints on development path on the African sub-continent were set by the nature of colonialism and its aftermath in sub-Saharan Africa.

The history of colonialism in sub-Saharan Africa was late and rapidly driven by the massive resource requirements of the second industrial revolution. It culminated in the accord on the partition of Africa among the colonial powers at the Berlin conference of 1884-5. Given the rapid, mostly resource-driven, type of colonialism which emerged, the local administrative structures which were set in place were usually basic and the colonies were usually required to be self-financing. The manner in which the partition happened, mostly ignoring as it did local communities and alliances, resulted in a post-colonial map of the ersatz newly-independent states whose viability was mostly seriously compromised from inception[6]. The case of South Africa is atypical in that the post-colonial period starts with the formation of the Union of South Africa in 1910, a peculiar period with dominion status granted to an indigenous white minority (Afrikaner) government and a disenfranchised black[7] majority. The inter-war period saw a radical state-driven industrialisation process which shifted the base of the NSI somewhat from the minerals-energy-complex towards manufacturing. The apartheid era advanced the system of science and technology, largely through military R and D spending, but impoverished the broader NSI through the effects of apartheid legislation on education, the movement of labour, and ownership rights on broad-based human capabilities development (Scerri 2009).

Early in the wave of independence in Africa, from the late fifties onward, it was understood by intellectual politicians such as Kwame Nkrumah of Ghana and Julius Nyerere of Tanzania that the prospects for economic viability in Africa were strongly dependent on a programme of pan-African integration to break down the crippling constraints of post-colonial fragmentation. From the systems of innovation perspective, integration may be understood as the transition from national to regional systems, with a merging and integration of institutions at the formal level leading to the emergence of new common institutional formations. Although there are numerous regional economic communities (REC) across sub-Saharan Africa, the prospects for effective integration are poor. Normally, successful cases of economic integration have only happened where the prospective member economies had viable and diversified NISs and had established strong trade and investment links among each other prior to integration. Neither condition holds for most African economies. In most cases, and certainly for the African members of the IORA, except for South Africa, the viability of the NSI is fragile and inter-Africa trade flows have remained low at around eleven to twelve percent of total African trade for the past couple of decades (MGI 2010). There are numerous other obstacles to effective integration[8] but one of the more effective impediments is the lack of political will to relinquish the national sovereignty bestowed by the colonial powers in the wave of independence granted to the new African states after the second world war. Fanon (1962, p. 132) referred to the newly-independent African countries as "national systems of oppression", based on the rent-seeking behaviour of the new African bourgeoisieas concession holders of mineral and agricultural deposits.

The NEPAD document is clear about the main impediment to a coordinated development in the continent when it states that:

> (t)he resources, including capital, technology and human skills, that are required to launch a global war on poverty exist in abundance, and are within our reach. What is required to mobilise these resources and to use them properly, is bold and imaginative leadership.... (t)oday, the weak state remains a major constraint to sustainable development in a number of countries" (AU 2001, pp. 1-2)

The "weak state" in sub-Saharan Africa is, as I have already argued, largely a historical formation of communities which arose from the nationalism of the colonial imagination, driven by the scramble for the continent's resources. The resulting constructs of independent African countries perpetuated NSIs based on strategies of extraversion (Bayart 2000) where the prevalent accumulation regime is based on the reliance of revenue required to run governments on the export of factors of production in raw form[9]. These factors of production take the form of working capacity in the form of migration, agricultural and mineral resources, and capital which is expatriated in the form of flight capital and as debt repayment (Bayart, *op cit*, p. 231).

Trade and investment flows between African economies and the rest of the world have, since independence, mostly served to reinforce the periphery-centre relationship with Africa exporting raw materials and importing finished products often made from those very same materials. Foreign direct investment on large national and even cross-national projects has not had a significant lasting effect on the capacity of most of the recipient NSIs in sub-Saharan Africa and this syndrome seems to have continued regardless of the source of the investment. This trade exhibited the characteristics of the Prebisch-Singer (Prebisch 1950; Singer 1950) thesis on dependency and deteriorating terms of trade and the much earlier List contention that free trade between manufacturing and primary product-producing states would entrench and widen the gap in the rates of growth and development between the two (List 1841). Bayart's theory of extraversion adds a further reinforcement of underdevelopment through the introduction of local vested interests in maintaining the accumulation regimes linked with extractive economies. This therefore provides the context for our exploration of the possible forms and effects of the deepening engagement of African member states in the IORA trade and investment flows.

Africa's Economic Engagement with the IORA—Continuity or Rupture?

While, as argued earlier, the standard criteria for the formation of customs unions are not particularly promising for economic integration in Africa, they are not the only ones that are relevant. Apart from the issue of the inherent historically-determined structural obstacles to the viability of individual NSIs in Africa, a fragmented engagement in trade and investment in a global economy dominated by economic blocs and large economies significantly reduces the bargaining power of African economies. Consequently the transition from national to regional systems of innovation across the sub-continent, on the back of a successful programme of economic integration, is the essential requirement for development regardless of the conventional wisdom which sees little probability of success in such initiatives.

There are in fact some strong indications that initiatives towards integration in sub-Saharan Africa are shifting from statements of aspiration to more effective implementation. In the first place, the big wars fought on the continent as a proxy for the Cold War came to an end in the early nineties. The region is no longer polarised on the basis of allegiance to different military superpowers. Concurrently, with the end of the Cold War, the end of apartheid in South Africa marked the start of a normalisation process across regional and continental organisations across Africa. The Organisation of African Unity (OAU) transformed to the African Union (AU) with the inclusion of South Africa, and the New Partnership for Africa's Development (NEPAD) was launched as the technical planning and coordinating body of the AU. With the end of apartheid, the Southern African Development Coordination Conference, which had been formed by frontline states primarily as a bulwark against the regional depredations of the apartheid regime, was transformed into the Southern African Development Community (SADC).

In 2011, the Common Market for Eastern and Southern Africa (COMESA), the East African Community (EAC) and SADC agreed on a plan for a single Free Trade Area (FTA). The launch of this tripartite FTA initiative covering 26 African countries, representing more than half of AU membership, with a combined population of 530 million (57% of Africa's population) and a total GDP of $630 billion or 53% of Africa's total GDP (UNECA 2012b, p. 63) is planned to come into effect in 2017. Should it be implemented as planned, this would constitute a major step on the path to the creation of a continent wide African Common Market (AU 1991) by 2023. Erasmus and Hartzenburg (2012) point out the difference between this tripartite FTA and previous REC agreements, such as the SADC, as lying in provisions for integration that go beyond trade liberalisation. The three pillars of the Tripartite Alliance are 'market integration based on the Tripartite Free

Trade Area, infrastructure development to enhance connectivity and reduce costs of doing business, and industrial development to address productive capacity constraints' (Erasmus and Hartzenburg 2012, p. 3). This multi-pronged strategy offers the possibility that this regional agreement may serve as the vehicle towards a more effectual integration process than hitherto achieved.

Of the six priority areas that were identified at the 11th meeting of the Council of Ministers of the IOR-ARC in 2011 (http://mea.gov.in/Images/pdf/bengaluru-communique-infocus.pdf, accessed 12th January 2014), two are especially relevant to the evolution of African systems of innovation. These are trade and investment facilitation, and academic, science and technology cooperation. It is evident that trade and investment ties within the association are deepening within a broader framework of geopolitical, as well as economic, cooperation. The manner in which the African member states are engage in this emerging regional node, possibly as the forefront members of the Tripartite FTA, will determine whether the economic relations developed within the IORA reinforce the historic patterns of Africa's economic engagement with the rest of the world or help alter this relationship.

NOTES

1. "...a system of innovation is constituted by elements and relationships which interact in the production, diffusion and use of new, and economically useful, knowledge ... and are either located within or rooted inside the borders of a nation state" (Lundvall 2010, p. 2).
2. "The narrow definition would include organisations and institutions involved in searching and exploring. The broad definition...includes all parts and aspects of the economic structure...affecting learning as well as searching and exploring" (Lundvall 2010, p. 13).
3. "The exchange-value of commodities, material or otherwise, *is no longer determined* in the last instance by the quantity of generalised social labour they contain but mainly by their content in terms of general information, knowledge and intelligence." (Gorz 2013, pp. 34-5, emphasis added).
4. For a discussion about the necessity for economic integration in Africa against the context of the global economic order, see Scerri (2012, 2013).
5. See Scerri (2013) for an elaboration of this argument.
6. "Many African states are too small to make viable economic markets and are below the threshold of any possible industrialization. Others are so large and diverse that effective government becomes difficult. There are 14 landlocked states in Africa, more than in the rest of the world put together" (Griffiths 1986, p. 204).

7. I use "black" here in a political, not a biological, sense to represents all those population groups which were disenfranchised under segregation and apartheid.
8. "Africa has more regional organizations than any other continent, and most African countries are members of more than one. Yet, they have failed to set free the continent's development potential and ensure sustainable growth and liberalization, mainly because of institutional and economic impediments to intra-African trade. The policy and regulatory environment, the transparency and predictability of trade and business administration, and the business climate for promoting intra-African trade remain weak and complicated. Other institutional challenges include bureaucratic and physical hindrances, such as road charges, transit fees and administrative delays at borders and ports. The economic obstacles include the high dependence of most countries on exports of primary commodities, strict rules of origin emanating from trade liberalization schemes and poor infrastructure." (UNECA 2012a, p. 129).
9. "...at the heart of (the strategy of extraversion" is the creation and the capture of a rent generated by dependency and which functions as a historical matrix of inequality, political centralization and social struggle" (Bayart 2001, p. 222).

REFERENCES

AU (African Union) (1991), *Treaty Establishing the African Economic Community*, at http://www.africa-union.org/root/au/Documents/Treaties/Text/AEC_Treaty_1991.pdf, accessed 15th March 2014.

AU (African Union) (2010), *The New Partnership for Africa's Development (NEPAD)*, at http://www.nepad.org/system/files/NEPAD%20Framework%20(English).pdf, accessed 20th March 2014.

Bayart, Jean-François (2000), 'Africa in the World: A History of Extraversion', *African Affairs*, Vol. 99, pp. 217-267.

Erasmus, Gerard and Trudi Hartzenburg (2012), 'The Tripartite Free Trade Area—towards a new African Integration Paradigm?', Hartzenburg et al (eds.), *The Tripartite Free Trade Area—towards a new African Integration Paradigm?*, Stellenbosch: TRALAC (Trade Law Centre for South Africa).

Fanon, Franz (1962), *The Wretched of the Earth*, reprinted (1985) UK: Penguin.

Griffiths, Ieuan (1986), 'The Scramble for Africa: Inherited Political Boundaries', *The Geographical Journal*, Vol. 152, no. 2, pp. 204-216.

IERI (Institute for Economic Research on Innovation) (2014), *Revisiting some of the Theoretical and Policy Aspects of Innovation and Development*, IERI 10th Anniversary Working Paper (2014), at http://www.ieri.org.za/sites/default/files/outputs/IERI_Working_Paper_2014_1.pdf, accessed 26th April 2014.

Lundvall, Bengt-Åke (ed.) (2010), *National Innovation Systems: Toward a Theory of Innovation and Interactive Learning*, UK: Anthem Press.

List, Friedrich (1841), *National System of Political Economy, Vols. I-III*, reprinted 2005, USA: Cosimo.

MGI (McKinsey Global Institute) (2010), *Lions on the Move: The Progress and Potential of African Economies*.

Nkrumah, Kwame (1962), *I Speak of Freedom*, UK: Mercury Books.

Prebisch, Raul (1950), *The Economic Development of Latin America and its Principal Problems*, New York: Economic Commission for Latin America, United Nations Department of Economic Affairs.

Scerri, Mario (2009), *The Evolution of the South African System of Innovation since 1916*, UK: Cambridge Scholars Publishing.

Scerri, Mario (2013), 'Modes of Innovation and the Prospects for Economic Integration in Africa', *Africa Insight*, Vol. 43, no. 3, pp. 80-99.

Scerri, Mario (2012), 'Economic Integration in Africa—The Systems of Innovation Approach', in Osha, Olusanya, Mammo Muchie, and Matlou Matlotleng (eds.), *The Africana World: From Fragmentation to Unity and Renaissance*, Pretoria: Africa Institute of South Africa.

Singer, Hans W. (1950): 'The Distribution of Gains between Investing and Borrowing Countries', *American Economic Review, Papers & Proceedings*, Vol. 40, pp. 473-485.

UNECA (United Nations Economic Commission for Africa) (2012a), *Economic Report on Africa: Unleashing Africa's Potential as a Pole of Global Growth*, Addis Ababa: UNECA.

UNECA (United Nations Economic Commission for Africa) (2012b), *Boosting Intra-African Trade Issues Affecting Intra-African Trade, Proposed Action Plan for boosting Intra-African Trade and Framework for the fast tracking of a Continental Free Trade Area*, Addis Ababa: UNECA.

Chapter 16

Conclusion: Towards an Agenda for Stronger Africa-Indian Ocean Linkages

Dennis Rumley

The purpose of this final Chapter is to briefly summarise the main suggestions and policy recommendations that have been made in this book regarding the creation of an *Agenda for Stronger African-Indian Ocean Linkages* (ASAIL). The editor does not pretend that all relevant issues are listed below, but he hopes that they might form the basis for further discussion and analysis among IOMA peoples and states within the IORA framework.

In a real sense, the Kenya meeting could be regarded as the Inaugural ASAIL Conference. IOMA states are clearly in the process of significant change. However, several commentators have cautioned against the overall ability of regional states to meet Millennium Goals. Nonetheless, as the chapters in this book have clearly demonstrated, there exists considerable scope for enhanced interaction with other IORA member states and Dialogue Partners for greater regional prosperity and stability.

The principal and often interrelated and overlapping policy recommendations are organised below according to four headings—stability and security; trade, investment and aid; maritime security; and education and innovation.

1. Stability and Security

1. Enhance interactions with other IORA states, especially in terms of economic, political, environmental, military and maritime issues.

2. More research is required on the impacts of extra-regional investment.
3. Develop an "Afrocentric global South paradigm".
4. Development should benefit local IOMA communities.
5. Create an annual *Western Indian Ocean Dialogue* (WIOD), the Agenda of which is driven by WIO states.
6. Increased debate is needed over the actual and potential regional role of Dialogue Partners—especially China, Japan and the United States—in the geo-economic and geopolitical emergence of IOMA states.
7. There is potentially an enhanced role for increased collaboration among IORA members and Dialogue Partners in the IOMA to ensure that the development process is designed above all for the benefit of regional inhabitants.

2. Trade, Investment and Aid

1. Strengthen IOMA state trade linkages with other IORA states.
2. Preferential treatment is needed for trading goods and services for IOMA states with other IORA member countries.
3. Strengthen IOMA state institutions, improve state infrastructure—road, rail, port, air - and develop a more business-friendly environment.
4. Invest more in the regional tourism sector, improve the nature of the investor environment, deal with associated policy and governance issues, and tackle problems of risk management and weak and expensive air services.
5. Improve regional educational programmes. Education should be viewed as an investment rather than as a cost in state development.
6. Need for IORA aid donors (members plus Dialogue Partners) to be concerned with specific aid outcomes determined by IOMA recipient states.
7. IORA Dialogue Partners could take on a more coordinated and focussed role in facilitating IOMA state development, especially in terms of improving regional educational programmes and state infrastructure.
8. IOMA states with an agricultural base and that are dependent on primary commodities for exports need to diversify and require FDI in value-added commodities from other IORA states.
9. Stronger regionalism and increased South-South cooperation will facilitate development and enhance security.

3. Maritime Security

1. Indian Ocean maritime security is good for business.
2. A cooperative approach is needed to a range of maritime security problems similar to the 2003 Caribbean Agreement.
3. There is a need to expand and strengthen regional state legal capacity, including the creation of an IORA Legal Group of Experts (LEGOE) and the introduction of regional legal training programmes.
4. Regional states need to develop a uniform legal framework to deal with maritime security broadly defined.
5. All regional states need to ratify appropriate international legal conventions regarding maritime security issues.
6. There is a need to develop a coordinated regional maritime security strategy among Indian Ocean states to facilitate trade and long-term regional economic growth.
7. There is scope to enhance the capability of IORA and IONS in order to more effectively deal with maritime security challenges.
8. Greater policy cooperation is highly desirable between the two Indian Ocean pan-regional bodies in the area of maritime security.
9. Greater cooperation is needed in properly managing the marine environment and resources in the Indian Ocean as part of an integrated regional framework.
10. Create a multi-layered regional maritime security system.

4. Education and Innovation

1. Develop an Indian Ocean Rim Virtual Open University (IORVOU).
2. Strengthen the University Mobility in the Indian Ocean Region (UMIOR) scheme.
3. Reform the Indian Ocean Rim Academic Group (IORAG).
4. Education should be given a higher priority among ODA donors, especially IORA member states and Dialogue Partners.
5. National systems of innovation require enhanced regional institutional and economic linkages.

Conclusion

The above is a compilation of policy suggestions arising out of the preceding chapters. It is clear that much more discussion, debate and research are needed to fully explore the prospects for developing ASAIL and for enhancing IOMA-IORA linkages across a wide range of regional interests of common concern. It is essential that there is an ongoing programme of debate—perhaps coordinated jointly by IORA and IORG but driven by IOMA state agendas—that includes more Conferences, research and education (undertaken by the current team and others) to ensure that the preliminary policy Agenda discussed in this volume can be properly fleshed out and appropriately implemented for the benefit of all IOMA state inhabitants.

Index

ABS protocol 213
Afghanistan 80, 86, 220–21
Afghanistan-India-Pakistan trinity 86
Africa
  contested spaces in 161
  future of IORA in 133
  industrialisation of 84
  infrastructural projects 65
  in the Indian Ocean Region 1
  maritime 1, 5, 82–3, 89, 92, 94, 97, 99
    prospects 82
    states of 1
  self-enhancement 61
  vision of integration 62
Africa and China trade 52
Africa-Asia Solidarity Conference, Bandung, Indonesia 190
Africa-India relations 15, 274
Africa-Indian Ocean Linkages 302
African Capacity for Immediate Response to Crises (ACIRC) 257
African Century 2
African continent coastal states 26
African Development Bank (ADB) 63–4
African Economic Community (AEC) 84, 258
African Growth and Opportunity Act (AGOA) 82
African Indian Ocean 1–2, 17–8, 20–28, 30–32, 34–6, 38–40, 42–5
African Indian Ocean littoral and hinterland 2, 17–8, 20–23, 29–32, 35–6, 38–40, 42–5
African Indian Ocean marine resources 27
African IORA 6, 103–4, 106–7, 109–10, 112, 114, 116–8, 121–2, 125, 129–30, 135–7, 139–48, 166–7, 175, 287
African littoral 17–8, 20, 28–31, 37, 44–5, 78, 81–3, 85–6, 93, 184, 192–3, 196–8, 217
  geopolitical-economics of the 82
  significance of 20, 45, 93
African oceans policy agenda 183
African Red Sea coastal states 30
African Union (AU) 61, 63, 82–3, 191, 195, 199, 257–8, 267, 271, 278, 296, 298
African Union (AU) Summit, Addis Ababa 63, 257
African Union Commission 63
African Union Millennium Development Goals 278
Africa's new start 18
Afrocentric global South paradigm 5, 89, 303
Afr. Red Sea states 29
Agenda for Stronger African-Indian Ocean Linkages (ASAIL) 1, 16, 302, 305
Aid 1–3, 6, 8–9, 15, 79, 160–61, 163–75, 177, 179–80, 184, 189, 244, 279, 285, 302–3
  allocations 8, 160, 164, 170, 180
  Australian 8, 160–61, 173–5
  Chinese 168
  development 9, 164, 184, 189
  donors 8, 303

DAC 8, 168, 174
non-DAC 8, 168
geopolitics of 160, 168
relationships 1, 175
Albertine Basin 53
Al Qaeda 220
Al Shabab 220
Amsterdam 20
Andaman Islands 4, 162
Andaman Sea 19, 222
Anti-piracy 60, 81, 250, 253
Anti-piracy operations 60, 81, 250
Anti-piracy strategy 253
Arabian Gulf 246–7, 251
Arabian Sea 19, 251
ARC 18, 109, 114, 199, 226, 299
Armed robbery 25, 39, 253, 258
Arms race 79
ASCLME Project 26
Asia 8–9, 19, 23–4, 31, 37, 53, 59, 66, 77, 79, 82–3, 85–6, 96–8, 132, 158, 161, 170, 173, 177, 179–80, 183–4, 188, 190–91, 197, 200, 217, 226–7, 238, 245, 247–8, 260, 267
Asia-Pacific Economic Cooperation (APEC) 85, 101
Association of South East Asian Nations (ASEAN) 78, 82, 85
AusAID 169, 174–5, 177, 179
AUSMIN 97
Australia 4, 6–9, 19–20, 24, 55, 77, 86–8, 92, 94, 96–9, 101, 103–4, 109, 112, 117, 121, 135, 141–8, 158, 160, 162, 164, 169–72, 174–80, 187–8, 194, 197, 217, 223, 226–7, 245, 285–6, 288, 290–92, 294
external linkages 98
geopolitical constraint 160
investment in IORA Africa 175
Official Development Assistance Policy 169
Trade and Investment with IORA Africa 176
Australian Department of Foreign Affairs and Trade (DFAT) 169, 171–2, 174–5, 177
Australian Development Assistance Bureau (AIDAB) 170
Australian ODA
geopolitics of 169, 171
goals 170
to Africa 171
to IORA States 173–4

Bab-al-Mandab 217
Bab-el-Mandeb 24, 245
Bahrain 4, 162, 245
Baltic and International Maritime Council (BIMCO) 219
Band Lease Services (BLS) 270
Bangladesh 4, 55, 60, 68, 81, 102, 117, 141–8, 162, 222, 245, 285–6, 288, 290–92, 294
Banking 133
Barnett, Colin 178
Bay of Bengal 19, 79
Belgium 135–6
Black Lion Hospital of Addis Ababa and Nekempte Hospital, Ethiopia 268
Botswana 19, 22–3, 34–5, 43, 158
Brazil 5, 64, 76, 86, 135–6, 194
Bretton Woods Institutions 189
Brewster 80–82
Brewster, David 80
BRICS 86–7
BRICSMAR 87
Britain 57, 79, 224, 246
British Indian Ocean Territory 19–20, 245
Broadcasting 133, 214, 269, 270
unauthorised 214
Brunei 164
Burma 4, 68, 162, 222, 245, *see also* Mynmar
Burundi 19, 22, 40, 42–3, 57, 242, 256

Canada 56, 158, 166, 169–70
Cape Agulhas 23–4, 26
Cape of Good Hope 24, 151, 245–6
CapeRoute 24

Cape Sea Route 76
Capital 7, 56, 63, 79, 132, 135, 137, 186, 198, 228, 241–2, 252, 293, 296–7
  accumulated 7, 135
Caribbean Agreement 10, 207, 304
Centre for Scientific and Industrial Research (CSIR) 194
Children 12, 30–31, 222–3
  labour 12
  mortality 30
  sex trafficking 12
  soldiers 12
China 3–5, 37, 52–68, 75–82, 85, 87, 91, 93–5, 97–9, 109, 117, 161–2, 168–9, 185, 218–9, 223, 247, 251–2, 303
  aid 3, 168
  commercial infrastructural and resource development 52
  contemporary business engagements in Africa 63
  foreign policy 59
  geopolitical influence 55
  geopolitical strategy 3
  infrastructure projects 56, 65
  interest in East Africa 53
  mineral extraction 53
  national oil companies (NOCs) 61, 66
  nature of regional presence 3
  naval ships 60
  naval vessels 80
  port 52
  presence in the Indian Ocean 68
  regional influence 3–4
  SLOCS 80
  strategic vulnerability 81
China and India 56, 81
  competition 81
  relations 81
China Communications Construction Company (CCCC) 53–4, 62
China Development Bank (CDB) 61
China-Export-Import Bank (Exim Bank) 61
China Harbour Engineering Company 55
China-India-Middle East-Africa (CHIMEA) 5, 75–8, 80, 82, 84–6, 88
China Merchants Group (CMG) 64
China National Petroleum Corporation 53, 65
China National Petroleum Corporation (CNPC) 53–4, 61, 65
China Railway Engineering Corporation (CREC) 61
China Road and Bridge Company (CRBC) 54, 62
China's State Owned Enterprises (SOEs) 55, 61
Chinese National Offshore Corporation (CNOOC) 53, 61, 65
Chinese Navy 81
Chinese pearls 162
Chinese State Owned Enterprises (SOE) 53
CII Exim Bank Conclave on India Africa Project Partnership 152
Clinton, Hillary, US Secretary of State 56
Coal 53, 112
  mine 53
Cocos Islands 178
Cold War 2, 8, 18, 76, 160, 163, 165, 168, 170–71, 178, 194, 199, 246, 252, 298
Colonialism 2, 7, 18, 52, 56–7, 62, 84, 93, 151, 185, 196, 242, 295
  Africanization of 84
  British 52, 93
  German 52, 93
Coloniality 188, 190, 200
Combined Maritime Forces (CMF) 25, 251
Combined Task Force (CTF) 25, 218
Comesa-SADC-EAC 83–4
Common Market for Eastern and Southern Africa (COMESA) 36, 78, 83–5, 178, 198, 254, 298
Comoros 6, 19, 22, 26, 29, 32–4, 39, 43, 101–3, 129–31, 136, 139–40, 148–9, 162, 166–7, 174–6, 193, 245, 256, 285, 288, 290–92, 294

exports 130, 148
imports 131, 148
Competition
for influence 1, 4, 161, 169
regional process of 1
Competitors 3, 64
regional 3
Confederation of Indian Industries 151–4
Congo, Democratic Republic of 59, 167
Consumer goods 7, 79, 102, 135
Contact Group on Piracy off the Coast of Somalia (CGPCS) 219, 251
Contiguous zone 207–8, 212
Continental African Free Trade Area (CAFTA) 84
Continental Free Trade Area 63
Continuing Medical Education (CME) 272
Convention for the Suppression of unlawful Acts against the Safety of Maritime Navigation (SUA) 205–6, 212, 236
COSCO 61
Cosmopolitanism 10, 190, 196–8
decolonial 190, 196
dialogical 197
Counter-piracy cooperation 227
CPCS Transcom 64
Crimes 25
Crozet 20
Cultural heritage 6, 129

Daily Mail 56
Dar es Salaam 54, 58, 65
Dar-es-Salaam 32, 37, 253, 258, 272
Dar-es-Salam 54
Democratic Ideals and Reality 241
Denmark 157, 166–7
Development
African 9, 33, 63–4, 78, 85, 183, 192, 198, 253, 260, 279–80, 298
post-colonial 279–80
agencies 9, 185
commercial 27
concept of 185
economic 3, 7–9, 17, 30, 32, 38, 44–5, 93, 160, 164, 177, 183, 190, 197–8, 280
infrastructural 52, 129, 137, 299
international 9, 169, 179, 185, 189
policy 15, 281
resource 52, 93
rural 32
socio-economic 3, 17, 32, 44
Development Assistance Committee (DAC) 8, 160, 164–70, 173–4
Development Bank of Southern Africa (DBSA) 64
Dibb, Paul 178
Diego Garcia 4, 59, 82, 162, 245
Distance learning 266, 268, 276
Djibouti 4, 19, 22–3, 29, 33–4, 42, 54, 59, 62, 162, 219, 245, 252–3, 256, 258, 260
Djibouti Code of Conduct (DCoC) 219, 252, 260
Dlamini-Zuma, Dr Nkosazana 195
Drug 10, 11, 204, 207, 218, 221, 232, 251
Trafficking 207
Dubai's Multi-Commodities Center (DMCC) 135
Durban Resolution on Maritime Safety and Security and the Protection of Environment 195
Durban University of Technology 194

EASBRIG 256, 258
East Africa 52–4, 57–8, 62, 65–7, 84–5, 196, 217, 238, 247, 257, 260, 271
Chinese interest in 53
infrastructure in 62
East African Community (EAC) 36, 78, 83–6, 198, 254, 298
Eastern Africa 31–2, 37, 84–5, 91, 238, 241, 243–4, 247, 249, 251, 255–6
Eastern Africa Standby Force (EASF) 255–60
Eastern and Southern Africa-Indian Ocean

(ESA-IO) 254, 260
Eastern and Southern Africa-Indian Ocean (ESA-IO) Regional Strategy and Regional Plan of Action 254, 260
East Indian Ocean (EIO) 5, 56, 91, 94, 96, 99, 160, 178
Economic Community of Central African States (ECCAS) 195
Economic Community of West African States (ECOWAS) 195
Economic Cost of Somali Piracy 2012 (ECoP 2012) 224
Economic growth 2–3, 6, 9, 18, 35, 38, 43, 78, 101, 132, 191, 218, 267, 278, 304
  regional 3, 6, 304
Economic interactions 7
Economic Partnership Agreements (EPAs) 82
Economic relations 150, 280, 299
Economist, The 18, 35
Economy 9, 11–2, 15, 17, 25, 33–7, 42, 45, 52–3, 63, 75, 77, 84, 88, 101–3, 132–3, 135, 137, 157, 184–7, 194–5, 198, 212, 217, 220, 231, 234, 242, 247, 272, 279–82, 284–6, 288, 293, 295–8
  African 35, 53, 242, 279–80, 293, 295–8
  geopolitical 75
  market 52, 63
  modern 35
  political 185–6, 280–82, 284, 288
  urban 35–6
  world 25, 194, 242
Ecosystems 26, 213, 248–9
  natural 248
Education 1, 14–5, 31, 177, 180, 188, 266–73, 275–6, 278, 282, 284, 286–7, 295, 302–5
  tertiary 272, 278, 282, 284
Egypt 4, 19, 22–3, 31, 39–40, 43, 77, 83, 104, 162, 166–7, 174–6, 223, 242, 245
Employment 6, 12, 31, 129, 157, 295
Energy 3–4, 7–8, 31, 38, 56, 65–6, 76–7, 133, 135, 160–63, 169, 178, 191, 231, 237–8, 244–8, 250, 284, 295
  security 4, 66, 133, 163
Enrica Lexie case 205
Environmental degradation 13, 30, 248, 250, 260
Eritrea 19, 22, 42–3, 59, 223, 244–5, 256, 258
Ethiopia 19, 22, 31, 34–5, 40–43, 53–4, 62–4, 84, 135, 244–5, 256–8, 268
EUNAVFOR Atalanta 251
Europe 8, 13, 37, 58, 76, 98, 136, 177, 185–8, 235, 238, 241–2, 247, 250, 260
European Institute of Creative Strategies and Innovation 268
European Union (EU) 25, 36, 64, 82, 85, 166, 209, 211, 254
European Union Naval Force Somalia (EU-NAVFOR-Somalia) 25
Exclusive economic zone (EEZ) 22, 24, 27, 206–7, 209–12, 215, 218, 232, 254–5
Exports 7, 20, 25, 79, 102–4, 106, 109–10, 112–4, 116–7, 121–2, 124–5, 127, 130, 135–7, 139–48, 151, 153–7, 176–9, 247, 267, 284, 297, 303
  intra-IORA 103, 121
  markets 112, 114, 117, 121, 125
  Share of 106, 139
  Tanzania-India 7

Failed States Index 38, 42–3, 293–4
Fifth Ministerial Conference of the Forum on China-Africa Co-operation (FOCAC) 61–2
Financial Mail 84
Finland 171
Fisheries/Fishing 10, 26–7, 102, 180, 191, 193, 204, 209–11, 218, 220–21, 231–2, 250, 254–5, 277
  coastal 26
  commercial offshore 26
  illegal 27, 193, 218, 254
  illegal, unreported and unregulated (IUU) 10, 27, 204, 209–11, 232, 250, 255

importance of 10
laws 210
management 27, 277
Foreign Affairs, Trade and Development Canada (FATDEC) 170
Foreign Direct Investment (FDI) 6–8, 102, 132–5, 149, 157–8, 160, 303
inflow 132–4, 149
France 8, 19–20, 24–5, 30, 56, 61, 65, 77, 136, 158, 162, 165–7, 172, 187, 245–6
Free trade area (FTA) 36, 78, 83–4, 298–9
French island territories 17, 20, 24, 44

Geopolitics 52, 99, 160–61, 163, 168–9, 171, 179
Geo-Socio-Economic Index (GSEI) 23
Geostrategic anxieties 3
German East Africa 57–8
German East Africa Company 57–8
German rail lines 58
Germany 8, 57, 135–6, 157, 165–7, 187
GFTA 84, 86
GINI Index 292
Global Financial Crisis (GFC) 160
Globalisation 18, 185–6, 188, 196, 198
Global North 163, 185
Golden Triangle 221
Gondwanan process 89
Good day for diplomacy 174
Governance 5–7, 11, 26, 76, 83, 87–9, 91, 99, 129, 133, 163, 177–8, 180, 189, 192, 194–5, 200, 213, 218, 226, 241, 243, 268, 303
communal 243
environmental 195
global 189
issues 6, 129, 133, 303
ocean 5, 76, 87–9, 192, 194, 200
Greater Nile Oil Pipeline (GNOP) 65
Great Lakes Region 244
Gross Fixed Capital Formation (GFCF) 132
Gulf of Aden 19, 24, 39, 76, 218–9, 223–4, 228, 250–51
Gulf of Oman 19, 251
Gulf of Suez 24
Gun running 11, 218, 221–2
Gurría, Angel, OECD Secretary-General 164
Gwadar, Pakistan 4, 55, 79

Harvey, David 63
Health 31, 88, 132, 153, 177, 180, 248, 270, 284, 286, 289, 293
Hegel, Georg 187
Hermes Prize for Innovation 268
HIV/AIDS 30
Hobsbwam, Eric 60
The age of empire 60
Horn of Africa 26, 83, 223, 244, 251
Horticulture 102, 104
Hospitality 129, 133, 135
Housing 31, 284
Human development 2, 10, 15, 18, 23, 27, 31–3, 37–8, 43, 163–4, 191, 194–5, 199
Human development index (HDI) 15, 22–3, 170, 289–90

IBSAMAR 87, 88
ICAO 254
IMB Piracy reporting Centre (IMB PRC) 219
IMO 25, 192–3, 208, 236, 253–4
IMO Measures for Combating Unsafe Practices Associated with the Trafficking or Transport of Migrants by Sea 208
Imperial British East Africa Company (IBEAC) 58
Imports 7, 20, 25, 102, 104, 107–9, 111–2, 114–5, 117–8, 120–21, 123, 125–6, 128–9, 131, 135–7, 140–48, 153–7, 176–7, 247
share of 140
Independent World Commission on the Oceans 190
India 4–8, 15, 23, 24, 29–30, 37, 55–6,

64–5, 75–82, 85–8, 91–2, 94, 97–9, 101–4, 109, 112, 114, 117, 121, 123, 125, 132–3, 135–7, 141–8, 150–58, 161–2, 168, 178, 193–4, 205, 218–9, 221, 225, 227, 245–7, 251–2, 266, 268–74, 278, 280, 285–6, 288, 290–92, 294
FDI into 8
imports from 102, 117, 153, 157
National Maritime Foundation (NMF) 80
India and South Africa 6
India and Tanzania 7, 150–52, 155, 157
Agreement on Avoidance of Double Taxation and Prevention of Fiscal Evasion 152
Air Services Agreement 152
economic linkages 7
exports 7, 153–5
imports 153–4, 157
investment relations 157
relations 150
ties 151
trade 150
trade agreement 152
trade and investment 150, 152, 155
trade balance 155, 156
trade relations 152, 157
India-Brazil-South Africa (IBSA) 5, 76, 86–8, 135
India-Brazil-South Africa (IBSA) Trilateral Dialogue Forum 86
Indian Navy 225, 227
Indian nuggets 162
Indian Ocean Africa
Security and stability in 163
Indian Ocean as a Zone of Peace (IOZP) 20
Indian Ocean Commission (IOC) 26, 36, 190, 193, 199, 254
Indian Ocean community 5, 78, 84, 89, 91
Indian Ocean Dialogue (IOD) 6
Indian Ocean (IO)
African littoral 78
Chinese presence in 68
geography 245
historical context 246
importance of
geo-economic 12
littorals 11, 227–8
reconceptualization of 77
regionalism 5, 226
regional ties 5
significance of 11, 196
geo-economic 11
strategic importance 247
western 5, 76, 82, 93, 171, 177, 217, 246, 251
Indian Ocean littoral 2, 17, 19–23, 30–32, 35–6, 38–40, 42–5, 82, 84, 249
Indian Ocean locations 4, 162
Indian Ocean Maritime Africa (IOMA) 2–6, 9, 11–3, 15, 17–8, 20, 28, 30, 32–4, 37–9, 42–5, 302–3, 305
changing pattern of 6
Chinese infrastructural support and development in 3
competition for influence in 4
investment in 6
linkages of 5
sub-regional concerns of 5
Indian Ocean Region 1, 5, 11–4, 17–20, 23, 28, 30, 38, 44–5, 52, 56, 91–9, 101, 161, 178, 183–4, 190, 193, 196, 199, 226–7, 231, 235, 245, 266, 304
Africa's place in 1
Indian Ocean Research Group (IORG) 92, 99, 305
Indian Ocean Rim Academic Group (IORAG) 14, 92, 304
Indian Ocean Rim Association for Regional Cooperation (IOR-ARC) 18, 109, 114, 192–3, 199, 226, 299
non-African 114
Indian Ocean Rim Association (IORA) 1–2, 3, 5–6, 8–10, 12, 14–5, 17–9, 44, 77, 86–8, 91–2, 94–5, 99, 101–37, 139–50, 160–62, 166–7, 169, 173–6, 190, 192, 199, 203–11, 213–4, 226–8,

231, 252, 260, 276–80, 284–90, 292–4, 296–7, 299, 302–5
fisheries laws of 210
future in Africa 133
legal and regulatory framework among 10
Legal Group of Experts (LEGOE) 10, 304
Maritime Security Enforcement and Jurisdictional Issues in 203
non-African 103–4, 106–28, 130–31, 135–6, 139–48
progress of 103
Indian Ocean Rim (IOR) 1, 4, 6, 14, 17–20, 22, 24, 28, 30, 34, 44–5, 76–7, 80, 91–2, 94–6, 101, 103, 109, 114, 132–3, 135, 137, 150, 160–61, 163–4, 169, 183, 190, 192, 199, 203–4, 206, 226, 236, 245–7, 249, 252, 260, 266–7, 276, 278–80, 299, 304
locations 4, 162
maritime threats in 247
strategic value of 247, 260
Indian Ocean Rim Virtual Open University (IORVOU) 14–5, 266–7, 278, 304
Indian Ocean Tuna Commission (IOTC) 26, 210
Indira Gandhi National Open University (IGNOU) 268, 273, 275
Indonesia 4, 6, 24, 86, 88, 91, 94, 98–9, 101, 103, 109, 112, 114, 117, 125, 132, 135, 141–8, 162, 170–71, 173, 177–8, 190, 194, 197, 245, 285–6, 288, 290–92, 294
Indo-Pacific Governance Research Centre, University of Adelaide 5, 97
Indo-Pacific (I-P) 5, 91, 94–9, 161, 179
construction 97–8
security 98
Indo-Pacific Region 94, 96, 98
Inequality 15, 186, 290, 293
Infrastructure 4, 6–7, 14, 35, 52–3, 55–8, 60–62, 65, 6–8, 76, 78, 93, 102, 129, 132, 135, 137, 180, 232, 235, 237, 239, 242, 245, 259, 269–70, 299, 303
development 129, 137, 299
physical 135, 137
political 242
port 60, 132
Innovation 1, 14–5, 38, 187, 191, 194, 267–8, 279, 280–82, 284–9, 293, 296, 298–9, 302, 304
systems of 15, 279–81, 284, 289, 293, 296, 298–9, 304
Insecurity 9, 12–4, 30–31, 37–8, 43, 161, 163, 194, 236, 242, 244
economic 38, 163
human 31
Institute for Defence Studies and Analysis (IDSA) 80
Institute for Global Dialogue 194
Integration 6, 9, 14–5, 18, 35–6, 61–3, 75, 78, 82–6, 101–2, 133, 135, 179, 183, 187, 193, 196, 198–9, 242, 258, 267, 279–80, 282, 293, 296–9
African 61, 82, 296
economic 6, 15, 36, 63, 85, 198, 280, 296–8
global 35
institutional 15
interregional 75, 78
political 83
regional 9, 14–5, 35–6, 62, 101, 133, 135, 183, 193, 198–9, 267, 293
Intergovernmental Authority on Development (IGAD) 36, 198, 254–6, 258–60
Intergovernmental Authority on Drought and Development (IGADD) 258
Inter-Governmental Panel on Climate Change Report of 2007 248
International Association of Dry Cargo Ship-owners (INTERCARGO) 219
International Chamber of Shipping (ICS) 219
International Convention on Maritime Search and Rescue 253
International Hydrographic Organization (IHO) 20, 25

Internationally Recommended Transit Corridor (IRTC) 219–20
International Maritime Authority 203
International Seabed Authority 203, 215
International Ship and Port Facility Security (ISPS) Code 235
International Tribunal for the Law of the Sea 203
Internet 268, 269, 272
Inter-State Defence and Security Committee (ISDSC) 193
IO Maritime Africa 29, 33–4
IONS 12, 86–8, 227, 252, 260, 304
Iran 94, 101, 104, 112, 117, 141–8, 158, 218, 245, 285–6, 288, 290–92, 294
ISPS code 205
Israel 136
Issues 1, 3, 6, 9–10, 12–4, 23–5, 27, 31–2, 35, 37–8, 45, 88, 92, 94, 96, 102, 129, 132, 133, 161, 177, 178, 183, 203–4, 207, 212–4, 225–8, 234, 243, 258, 276, 302–4
  economic 6
  environmental 27, 32
  governance 6, 129, 133, 303
  military 10
  non-military 10
  regional 1
Italy 65, 205, 225, 253
ITLOS 210

Japan 8, 37, 55, 64, 77, 85, 91, 94, 98, 109, 117, 158, 165–7, 169, 178, 188, 218–9, 303
Jihadism 83
Juan de Nova 27

Kalam, Dr. A.P.J., Indian President 267
Kaplan, Robert 75
  Monsoon: The Indian Ocean and the Future of American Power 75
Kasuku, Silvester 64
Kenya 4, 6, 15, 19, 22–3, 25, 27, 29, 31, 33–4, 39–43, 53–5, 57, 62–4, 67, 82, 84–6, 88, 92, 101, 103–4, 109–12, 117, 129, 133, 135–6, 139–41, 149, 158, 162, 166–7, 174, 176, 222, 242, 244–5, 256–8, 279–80, 285–8, 290–92, 294, 302
  exports 104, 110, 141
  imports 111, 141
Kerguelen 20
Kibaki, Mwai, Kenyan president 63
Kiir, Salva, South Sudan's president 63
Knowledge Economy Index (KEI) 286–7
Korea, Republic of 218
Kuwait 4, 158, 162, 164, 166, 245

Labour 12, 57, 135, 137, 177, 242, 295
  child 12
LAPSETT (Lamu Port and Southern Sudan-Ethiopia Transport Corridor) 63–4
Large marine ecosystem (LME) 26
Lashkar-e-Taiba (LeT) 220–21
  maritime capability 221
Latin America 132, 183–4, 188, 191
Law of the Sea Convention 203, 205
Least Developed Countries (LDCs) 102, 132, 135
Lesotho 19, 22, 31, 43
Liberation Tigers of Tamil Eelam (LTTE) 220, 222, 249
Liberia 59
Libya 223
Libyan civil war 60
Life expectancy 31–2
Line of Credit (LoC) 151
Linkages 1–2, 5–7, 14–5, 37, 54, 82, 88, 92, 97–8, 101, 303–5
  economic 7, 304
  educational 14
Littorals 11, 20, 78, 81–3, 85–6, 217–8, 220–21, 227–8
Luxembourg 171

Mackinder 240–42, 249
Madagascar 6, 19, 22, 24–7, 29, 31–4, 42–3, 82, 85, 101–3, 121, 124–5, 129,

132, 136, 139–40, 146, 149, 162, 166–8, 174–6, 193, 245, 257, 285–6, 288, 290–92, 294
exports of 121, 125, 146
imports 125, 146
Mahan, Alford Thayer 240
The Influence of Sea Power Over History: 1793-1782 240
Malacca 19, 24, 217, 245
Malawi 19, 22, 42–3, 58
Malaysia 7, 37, 64, 101, 103, 109, 112, 114, 117, 121, 125, 133, 141–8, 158, 191, 218, 245, 285–6, 288, 290–91, 294
Maldives 4, 162, 245, 255
Mandela, Nelson 183–4, 190–91, 197, 200
Marine biodiversity 10, 212–3
conservation and management of 212
Marine environment 10, 12, 24, 26, 193, 212, 248, 304
Maritime
cargo 25
gateway 24
identity 84
power 80, 240
safety 25, 39, 45, 87–8, 192, 195
search and rescue 25
security 1, 5, 10–14, 25, 45, 76, 81, 87, 99, 193–4, 204, 208–9, 217, 219, 221, 224, 226–8, 234–8, 244, 252–5, 257–60, 302, 304
terrorism 13, 25, 220, 248–9, 260
threats 11, 217, 228
trade development of 25
trading networks 57
transport technology 57
Maritime Africa 2, 17–8, 20, 28–30, 32–4, 37–9, 42–5, 92
significance of 17
Maritime domain 9, 12, 24, 28, 44, 192–3, 195, 236, 239–40, 250
Maritime insecurity 12–4, 232, 236
elements of 13
impacts of 12
Maritime multilateralism 228
Maritime Piracy: Humanitarian Response Programme (MPHRP) 219
Maritime Rescue and Co-ordination Centres (MRCC) 253, 260
Maritime security 1, 5, 10–14, 25, 45, 76, 81, 87, 99, 193–4, 203–4, 208–9, 217, 219, 221, 224, 226–8, 231–2, 234–8, 244, 252–5, 257–60, 302, 304
challenges 10, 228, 304
conceptualization of 255, 258
legal framework for 10, 12
policies 13
private 219, 224
regional cooperation legal framework for 10
regulatory framework 10
risks on shipping 234
threats 10–13, 208
non-traditional 12
traditional 12
Maritime Space 238–9
Maritime Space Theory 238
Maritime theory 239–40
Maritime Transport Charter 195
Markets 3–4, 18, 35–7, 52, 56, 61, 63–4, 66, 68, 78, 82, 109, 112, 114, 117, 121, 125, 132–3, 135–6, 197–8, 218, 231, 267, 286–7, 289, 298
economy 52, 63
emerging 18, 35, 132
export 112, 114, 117, 121, 125
international 267
Mauritius 4, 6, 14, 19, 22–6, 29, 32–4, 43, 82, 88, 101–3, 121–3, 136, 139–40, 145, 149, 158, 162, 166–7, 174–6, 193, 245, 257, 273–5, 277, 285–6, 288, 290–92, 294
exports 121–2, 145
imports 121, 123, 145
Mayotte (France) 19–20, 22–3, 29, 32–3
Merchant Shipping Acts 235
Michel, James, President of Seychelles 195
Middle East 5, 56, 75, 77–9, 177, 197,

223, 238, 247, 260
Mignolo, Walter 186
Migration 11, 17, 163, 208, 222, 239, 297
clandestine 208
human 11, 17
illegal and forced 222
Millennium Development Goals (MDGs) 168
Millennium Ecosystem Assessment Report, 2005 248
Mine/Mining 7, 53, 57, 102, 132–3, 135, 178
Mineral 53, 77, 109, 112, 114, 117, 121, 125, 153, 295–7
extraction 53
Mission to Seafarers, Save our Seafarers, Seafarers Rights international (SRI) 219
Motivations, geoeconomic 77
Mozambique 6, 15, 19, 22, 25–7, 29, 31, 33–4, 39, 41–3, 53, 83, 101–3, 117, 120, 132, 136, 139–40, 144, 149, 162, 166–7, 169, 174–6, 193, 245, 253, 279–80, 285–8, 290–92, 294
export 117, 144
imports 117, 120, 144
Mozambique Channel 25–7, 83
MPAs 213
M V Enrica case 225
Myanmar 55, 79, 81, 221, 245

Nairobi Convention for the Protection, Management and Development of the Marine and Coastal Environment of the Eastern African Region 26
National systems of innovation (NSI) 15, 281–90, 293, 295–6
Natural gas 27
Natural resources 8, 18, 35, 53, 56, 79, 135, 137, 160, 163, 231, 241
extraction 53
extraction of 53
Naval operations 25
NAVAREA VII 25
Navigation and weather warnings 25
Neo-colonialism 2, 18, 56, 62, 185, 196
NEPAD 83, 296, 298
New Asia-Africa Strategic Partnership (NAASP) 83, 183, 199
New World 187
New Zealand 158, 178, 187–8
Nigeria 66, 84, 192, 271
Nile River Basin 83
Non-interference 59
North America 13, 185, 187, 235
North Atlantic Treaty Organization (NATO) 218, 251
North Korea 224
North-South Corridor Infrastructure Initiative 78
North-South development 184
North-South division 163
Norway 65, 157–8, 166, 169

Ocean governance 5, 89, 192, 200
Oceanic Africa 4, 162
Oceans Beyond Piracy (OBP) 39, 42, 224
OECD 2, 8, 164–5, 168–9, 267
Official Development Assistance (ODA) 8–9, 160–62, 164–7, 169–75, 177–8, 180, 284–5, 304
allocation of 8, 171
competitive process into 8
Australian 160, 169–71, 173–5, 177
neo-liberal 8, 160
state-derived 8, 160
use of 9
Ogaden Basin 27
Oil and gas 18, 25, 27, 45, 53, 55–6, 61, 63, 65–6, 77–9, 101–2, 104, 109, 112, 114, 125, 153, 192–3, 217, 231, 247
exploration and exploitation of 27, 53
reserves 78
Oil Companies International Marine Forum (OCIMF) 219
Oman 4, 19, 92, 104, 141–8, 158, 162, 197, 245, 251, 258, 285–6, 288, 290–92, 294

Operation Atlanta 25, 218
Organisation of African Unity (OAU) 298
Overseas Development Assistance 284–5

Package deal 203
Pakistan 4, 55, 79, 81, 86, 94, 158, 162, 170, 218, 220–21, 224, 245
Pan-African e-Network (PAeN) Project 15, 266–70, 272, 274, 278
Pan-African Network 273
Papua New Guinea 135, 170–71
Persian Gulf 4, 19–20, 24, 77, 79, 95, 162, 217
Pipelines 53–4, 63, 65, 282
Piracy 11–3, 24–5, 27, 39, 42, 60, 76, 81–3, 193, 204–5, 214, 218–9, 224, 226–8, 232, 234–5, 237, 239, 244, 247–55, 257–60
  attacks 218, 244
  impacts of 234
  intelligence 11
    counter 11
  legislation on 205
    domestic 205
  maritime 24–5
    Somali 24–5
  Naval deployments in 235
  prosecutions 13
  Somali 27, 39, 76, 228, 239, 250
Plan of Action on Maritime Transport 195
Plantations 102
Poaching 25
Policies 1–2, 6, 11, 13, 15–6, 32, 56, 59, 61, 75, 93, 96, 129, 160, 163–4, 169–72, 175, 177–80, 183–4, 191, 194–5, 197–8, 203–4, 219, 226, 228, 240, 243, 248–9, 281–2, 287, 289, 302–5
  development 15, 281
  education and science 15
  foreign 59, 163–4, 175
  implications 1, 289
  maritime security 13
  recommendations 16, 302
  regional 1
  responses 11, 93
Political instability 38, 43, 53, 163–4
Political ties 135
Pollution 26, 45, 192–3, 212, 248–9
  marine 212, 248–9
  sources of 26
Ports 25, 27, 37, 52–5, 57–60, 62, 64, 67–8, 78–81, 93, 132, 134, 136–7, 192, 205–6, 209–11, 217–8, 220–21, 226, 232, 235–6, 242, 246, 257, 303
  facilities 137, 232
  infrastructural 60, 81, 132
  operations 218
Poverty 8, 15, 30–32, 36–7, 165, 167, 174, 179, 186, 189, 196, 223, 289, 291, 294, 296
  reduction 36
Process of change 2
Protocol against the Smuggling of Migrants by Land, Sea and Air Supplementing the Convention against Transnational Organised Crime 208
Public-Private Partnerships (PPP) 129, 291

Qatar 4, 62, 162, 164, 245
Quarter-Sphere of Marginality 2

Racism 7, 151
Railways 53–4, 58, 67
Real estate 133
Red Sea 19–20, 22, 24, 29–30, 42, 44, 95, 223, 251
Red Sea Costal States 22
Regional African Satellite Communications Organization4 (RASCOM) 270
Regional Comprehensive Economic Partnership (RCEP) 85
Regional construction 5, 91, 95–7, 99
Regional cooperation 10, 14, 27–8, 184, 190, 192–3, 196, 198–200, 227, 266–7
Regional Economic Communities (RECs) 256, 258, 280, 296, 298

Regional economic integration 6, 36
Regional Fisheries Management Organisations (RFMOs) 210
Regional integration 9, 14–5, 35–6, 62, 101, 133, 135, 183, 193, 198–9, 267, 293
Regionalisation 97
Regionalism 5–6, 18, 61, 95, 97–9, 101–2, 135, 190, 196, 199, 226, 303
  benefits of 6, 101
  contested 98
  Indo-Pacific 97
  open 101, 102, 135
Regional Security Complex (RSC) 237, 244
Regional stability 5, 163
Regional trade arrangements (RTAs) 102
Regionness 9, 14, 183, 190–91, 196–7, 199
Resource gap 6, 132–3
Resources 3, 8, 11–3, 18, 24, 26–8, 31, 35–41, 45, 53, 56, 58, 60–62, 68, 77–9, 81–2, 92, 97–9, 101, 135, 137, 160–61, 163, 169, 178, 191, 193, 195, 207, 209, 211–3, 215, 231–2, 239–41, 244, 248, 250, 257, 260, 274, 296–7, 304
  agricultural 77
  exploration and exploitation of 27, 215, 250
  marine 12–3, 24, 27–8, 45, 193, 232, 248, 250, 260
    exploitation of 13, 248, 260
  ocean 3
  transport 53
Réunion (France) 19–20, 22–3, 25–6, 29, 32–3, 245
Rift Valley Basin 27
Risk management 6, 129, 232, 303
Rivalry 4–5, 56, 67, 75–6, 79, 80, 82, 84, 89
  Anglo-German 67
  CHIMEA vs great power 75
  great power 75–6, 84
  Indian Ocean 82
  Sino-Indian 5, 75, 80
  Soviet-American 76
    IOR 80
Roads 7, 53–4, 57–8, 62–4, 67, 137, 241, 303
Russia 251
Rwanda 19, 22, 41, 43, 57, 242, 244, 256

Sahara 59, 293, 295
Saint-Paul 20
SANParks 129
SAR Convention 253
Scattered Is (Fr) 22
Scattered Islands (France) 19–20, 27
Scott, David 56
Sea Lines of Communication (SLOC) 4, 54, 60, 80, 161, 247
Sea Tigers 220
Securitization 237–8, 242–4, 246, 252, 260
Security 1, 4–5, 9–14, 25, 27, 35, 38–9, 42, 45, 52, 54, 66–8, 75–6, 81–3, 87–8, 91, 93–9, 132–3, 161, 163–4, 170–72, 175, 178, 191–6, 198, 203–10, 214, 217–9, 221–8, 231–2, 234–9, 241, 243–6, 249–55, 257–60, 270, 294, 302–4
  Australian 97
  construction 98
  cooperation 82, 99, 193, 198, 228, 238
  energy 4, 66, 133, 163
  IMO/ILO Code of Practice on 236
  Indian 97
  legal frameworks for 235
  management 243
  maritime 1, 5, 10–14, 25, 45, 76, 81, 87, 99, 193–4, 204, 208–9, 217, 219, 221, 224, 226–8, 234–8, 244, 252–5, 257–60, 302, 304
  policy 259
  politics 243
  regional 52, 91, 94–6, 98–9, 161, 237–8, 241, 244
  tensions 246
Sex trafficking 12

Seychelles 6, 19, 22–7, 29, 32–4, 42–3, 60, 82, 101, 103, 125, 129, 136, 139–40, 147, 149, 158, 162, 166–7, 174–6, 193, 195, 245, 256, 285, 288, 290–92, 294
  imports 125, 147
Shangri-La Dialogues 88
Shared Awareness and Deconfliction (SHADE) 219
Shiprider Agreement 207
Ship/Shipping 11–2, 24–5, 28, 39, 54–5, 60–61, 133, 192–3, 205, 208, 214, 218–20, 222, 224–6, 231–2, 234–6, 239, 246–7, 250–51, 253, 258–9
  flagged 218
  industry 219, 224, 226, 232
  international 218, 220
  merchant 218
  networks 25, 28
  without nationality 214
Singapore 4, 19, 24, 37, 55, 101, 103, 109, 112, 117, 121, 125, 141–8, 162, 164, 194, 218, 245, 285–6, 288, 290, 294
Singapore Strait 19, 24
Sinopec 61
Sinoydro Corporation 55
Skills 14, 79, 178, 250, 266–7, 278, 286, 296
  educational 266
Smuggling 10–11, 25, 204, 208–9, 218, 221, 232
  arms 232
  drug 11, 218, 221
  human 218
Socialism 7, 151
Society of International Gas Tanker and Terminal Operators (SIGTTO) 219
Solemn Declaration 63
Somalia 4, 19, 22–7, 29, 31, 33–4, 39–43, 53, 60, 76, 82–3, 85, 162, 218–20, 223–4, 244, 245, 228, 232, 237, 239, 249–51, 253–6, 258, 260
Somali coast 25, 83, 218, 224, 255
Somali Piracy 224, 232, 249
South Africa 2, 5–6, 9, 15, 19, 22–6, 29, 31, 33–4, 37, 39, 41–3, 61, 76, 78–9, 81, 83–8, 101–3, 105, 109, 112–3, 115, 129, 132, 135–6, 139–40, 142, 149, 158, 162, 166–7, 174–5, 177, 184, 190–91, 193–4, 197, 227, 245, 253–4, 271, 279–80, 285–96, 298
  exports 109, 113, 142
  imports 115, 142
South-African Development 183
South African-IBSA Nexus 86
South and East China Seas 81
South Asia 82, 170, 173, 217
South Asian Association for Regional Cooperation (SAARC) 86
South Asian Free Trade Area (Safta) 86
South Atlantic Treaty Organization 76
South China Sea 55, 97–8
Southeast Asia 9, 23–4, 31, 85–6, 217
Southern Africa 31–2, 36, 64, 78, 85, 158, 178, 196, 198, 254, 260, 271, 298
Southern African Customs Union (SACU) 83
Southern African Development Community (SADC) 36, 78, 82–5, 88, 193–4, 198–9, 253–4, 260, 298
Southern African Development Coordination Conference 298
Southern and Eastern African states 32, 36
South Korea 77, 85, 109, 117, 219
South Pacific Islands 171, 178
South-South cooperation 9–10, 15, 86, 133, 183–4, 190, 197, 199, 200, 303
South Sudan 19, 22–3, 39–43, 53, 63, 65, 83, 244, 257
South Western Indian Ocean Fisheries Project (SWIOFP) 26
Southwest Indian Ocean 26, 32
Southwest Indian Ocean Fisheries Commission (SWIOFC) 26–7
Sovereignty 59
Sri Lanka 4, 55, 62, 64, 68, 81, 104, 125, 132, 141–8, 162, 220–21, 245, 249, 285–6, 288, 290–92, 294

Sri Lankan Navy 220, 222–3
Standards of living 31, 33, 37, 192–3
State Owned Enterprises (SOEs) 55, 61, 64
States
  African 8–9, 18–20, 25, 32, 36, 52–3, 61, 63, 68, 101, 103, 129, 162, 165, 167, 169, 172, 175–6, 192, 196, 198, 212, 246, 252–3, 296
  African coastal 24–5, 28, 44
  African Indian Ocean 1, 2
  African island 24, 26
  extra-regional 1, 4, 161, 245
  land-locked 19–20, 22, 30, 37, 42, 44–5, 95, 242
    African 30
  littoral 19, 56, 82, 89, 183–4, 193, 196–7, 239, 245
  regional 1, 4, 9, 11, 13, 23, 42, 76, 161, 164, 178, 194, 228, 245, 257, 302, 304
    cooperation of 1
Strait of Hormuz 217, 245
Straits of Malacca 19, 217
Strategic Action Programmes (SAP) 26
String of Pearls 3, 4, 55, 76, 80, 162
Submarines 79, 220
Sub-Saharan Africa 2, 8–9, 15, 18, 28–9, 33–5, 37, 165–6, 173–4, 279, 293, 295–8
  role of the DAC in aid to 165
Sudan 19, 22–3, 39–43, 53, 55, 59, 62–3, 65–6, 83, 104, 223, 242, 244–5, 256–8
Sudanese People's Defence Force (SPLA) 40, 244
Suez Canal 24, 245–6
Swaziland 19, 22–3, 31, 41–3

Tanganyika 57–8, 67, 151
Tanzania 6–8, 15, 19, 22, 25, 27, 29, 31, 33–4, 39, 41, 43, 53–5, 57–8, 60, 64–5, 67, 84, 101, 103, 114, 116–8, 136, 139–40, 143, 149–58, 162, 166–7, 174–7, 245, 253, 257, 279–80, 285–8, 290–92, 294, 296
  exports 114, 116, 143, 153
  FDI in 8
    from India 8
  imports 114, 117–8, 143, 153
  Indian investments in 158
Tanzania and Zambia Railways Authority (TAZARA) 54
Tanzania Electric Supply Company (Tanesco) 65
Tanzania Investment Centre (TIC) 158
TANZARA railway 58
Tea 104, 136, 153
Telecommunications 133, 137
Tele-Education (TE) 268–73
Tele-Medicine (TM) 268, 270–73
Territorial sea 23–4, 206–8, 211, 225
Terrorism 10, 13, 25, 163, 204–6, 208, 218, 220, 231, 248–9, 260
  maritime 13, 25, 220, 248–9, 260
Thailand 65, 101–3, 109, 112, 117, 121, 132, 136, 141–8, 197, 221, 245, 285–6, 288, 290–92, 294
The Political Economy of Maritime Africa in the Indian Ocean Region 92
Threats 3, 10–13, 38, 75–6, 80, 82–3, 98, 163, 198, 204, 206, 208–9, 217–9, 226–8, 237–41, 243–4, 247–51, 257, 259–60
  contemporary 250
  geopolitical 3
  jihadist terror 82
  maritime security 10–13, 208, 217, 228
    traditional 12
  sea-based 217
Tourism 6–7, 102, 129, 132–3, 135, 137, 151, 303
Trade and investment 1, 3, 6–8, 10–12, 14, 17, 20, 23–5, 35–7, 52–3, 63–4, 77–9, 82, 84–6, 88, 91, 93, 97, 101–3, 129, 132–3, 135–7, 149–52, 155–8, 160, 162, 165, 169–71, 174–80, 188–94, 198–9, 203, 217–8, 221, 231–2, 235–7, 239, 245–7, 266–7, 272, 274–

5, 277, 279–80, 284, 289, 296–9, 302–4
African 79, 103, 132, 192, 296
Afro-Asian 78
China and Africa 52
contraband 11, 221
foreign 3, 36–7
India-Tanzania 150
international 20, 23, 36, 63, 175, 198, 231, 247, 266
intra-regional 6
linkages 6, 97, 303
maritime development of 25
oil 25
private 162
regional 6, 12, 102, 176, 267
seaborne 232
state-sponsored 162
structure of 7
triangular 79
Trade architecture 6, 102
Trade balance 7, 155–7
Trade surplus 156, 175–6
Trafficking 10–12, 25, 204, 206–8, 232
drug 10, 204, 207
human 10, 11, 25, 232
sex 12
WMD 10, 204, 206
Transatlantic Trade and Investment Partnership (TTIP) 82
Trilateral Dialogue on the Indian Ocean (TDIO) 6, 178
Tshwane University of Technology 194

Uganda 19, 22, 27, 34–5, 40–43, 53, 58, 65, 84, 242, 244–5, 256–8
Unauthorised broadcasting 214
UNCOMTRADE 102, 116, 118, 130, 139–48
UN Convention on the Law of the Seas (UNCLOS) 8, 19–20, 56, 65, 77, 158, 165–7, 203–4, 206, 209, 211–4, 224, 227, 245
UNCTAD 102, 132, 133
UNDP 22, 31, 129, 290
Global Environment Facility (GEF) 129
UNEP 26
UNHCR 223
United Arab Emirates (UAE) 4, 101, 104, 109, 112, 114, 117, 122, 125, 135–6, 141–8, 158, 162, 164, 166, 168, 286
United Kingdom (UK) 19–20, 104, 136
United Nations Office on Drug and Crime (UNODC) 251
United Nations Security Council (UNSC) 171–3, 218, 249
United Nations (UN) 9, 11, 20, 22, 28–9, 31–2, 59, 79, 165, 168, 171, 189, 204–5, 209, 212–3, 218–9, 222, 227, 235, 249, 251, 258
Meeting of the Littoral and Hinterland States of the Indian Ocean 20
resolutions 11, 204, 218
United States African Command (AFRICOM) 59
United States of America (USA) 3–4, 8, 37, 53–6, 59, 61–5, 67, 77, 80–82, 85, 91, 93–9, 132, 135–6, 152, 158, 161–2, 165–7, 177, 187–8, 207, 218, 224–5, 246, 251–2, 303
military disengagement from Afghanistan 80
United States Unified Command Structure 95
University Mobility in the Indian Ocean Region (UMIOR) 14, 304
University of Adelaide 5, 92, 97
Indo-Pacific Governance Research Centre (IPGRC) 5, 97
University of Witwatersrand 194
UN Security Council 9, 171, 205, 251
Urbanisation 3, 293
Urbanization 31, 35–6, 44, 188
URT 151–2, 158
USA diamonds 162
USAFRICACOM 95
Usambara Railway 58
USAPACOM 96, 99
US-Australia security 98

US Department of Defense 4, 97, 162
US Department of Defense Base Structure Report 4, 162
U.S.E.I.A. 27
USPACOM 95

Vienna Convention against the Illicit Traffic in Narcotic Drugs and Psychotropic Substances 207
Virtual Open University 14–5, 266–7, 276, 304
Voice-Over IP (VOIP) 268
VSAT 268–70

Walker, Martin 5, 75–7, 79, 82
Wallerstein 242
  World Systems Theory 242
Wang Chaowen 62
Waste 12, 112, 117, 121, 125, 218, 232, 254
  toxic 12, 232, 254
Waters
  African Indian Ocean 24–6, 28
  Indian Ocean 237
  internal 207, 211
  territorial waters 205–9, 211–2, 218, 222, 255
West Africa 57, 79, 271
Western Indian Ocean 6, 24–6, 28, 44–5, 97, 99, 219, 241, 252–3, 255, 303
Western Indian Ocean Dialogue (WIOD) 6, 303
Western Pacific Naval Symposium (WPNS) 227
WIO-LaB project 26
WMD 10, 11, 204, 206, 223–4
  proliferation 11, 223–4
  trafficking 10, 204
  Trafficking 206
  transportation of 223
WMO 25
World Bank 22, 31–6, 129, 132, 189, 284–7, 291
World Data Bank 34
World Development Report 2009 35
World Oceans Commission 184
World order 163, 190
World War I 58, 67, 151
World War II 189, 246

Xi Jinping, Chinese President 54

Yang Yujin, Chinese Defence Spokesman 60
Yemen 4, 141–8, 158, 162, 223, 245, 285–6, 288, 290–92, 294

Zambia 19, 22, 31, 34–5, 42–3, 54
Zenawi, Meles, Ethiopian Prime Minister 63
Zimbabwe 19, 22, 31, 34–5, 41–3, 244
Zone of Peace and Cooperation in the South Atlantic (ZPCSA) 76